After the famous painting by Alberto Urdaneta. Favor of Dr. Ricardo J. Alfaro.

First view of the South Sea by Balboa, his faithful dog Leoncico close at his heels. Andrés de Vera in clerical bonnet appears in view.

Life and Letters of
Vasco Núñez de Balboa

including

The Conquest and Settlement of Darien and Panama,
The Odyssey of the Discovery of the South Sea,
A Description of the Splendid Armada
to Castilla del Oro,

and

The Execution of the Adelantado at Acla

*A history of the first years of the introduction of
Christian civilization on the continent of America.*

by
CHARLES L. G. ANDERSON, M.D.
Author of " Old Panama and Castilla Del Oro "

ILLUSTRATED

Introduction by
DR. RICARDO J. ALFARO
Ex-President of the Republic of Panama

GREENWOOD PRESS, PUBLISHERS
WESTPORT, CONNECTICUT

INTRODUCTION

I F there ever was a human life which confirms the assertion of Lord Byron that truth is stranger than fiction, it is the life of Vasco Núñez de Balboa, the gallant Spanish nobleman who discovered the Pacific Ocean. Few of the heroes of history have gone through so many vicissitudes; few have swung so much between glory and misery, between death and triumph, between success and misfortune; few can boast more incredible exploits, more far-reaching achievements; none has had a more tragic end and none among the *conquistadores* of the New World shows in his career a more honorable balance to his credit in the account of virtues and faults by which the greatness of a soul is measured.

As one of the many adventurers who came to the Indies in quest of gold and fame, Balboa leaped from obscurity and poverty to leadership and renown by the sheer force of his superior endowments. Entering the Enciso expedition as a stowaway ensconced in a cask, he ended by becoming first the saviour, then the head of the intrepid band which started the colonization of the Isthmus. He made himself loved and respected by his own men and, what is more uncommon, by the Indians whom he converted into friends and allies. He was harsh, perhaps cruel, on a few occasions, but his customary course was to be humane and loyal, to win control over the inhabitants of the lands he explored, by tactfulness, by comity, by kindness, rather than by deceit and terror. It was due to his rare combination of daring and prudence, of ability and fortitude, of diplomacy and generalship, that he was able to enlist the co-operation of the aborigines and perform with 190 Spaniards and 1000 Indians the astonishing feat of crossing the mountains of Darien, from the shores of the Caribbean to the waters of the Austral Sea, fighting nature and hostile tribes

3

without the loss of one man, and effecting a discovery which ranks in importance with those of Columbus and Magellan.

The epic of Balboa is one that can be read with the delectation and absorbing interest which are usual attributes of the great productions of the imagination. A first-class historian is required to recite the life of a first-class hero. After the four and a quarter centuries elapsed since the beheading of Balboa by the monster Pedrarias, it was necessary to have a biography free from errors and bias, palpitating with the unequaled interest of human realities.

Dr. Charles L. G. Anderson is eminently qualified to be the definitive biographer of Vasco Núñez de Balboa. Twenty-five years ago he wrote *Old Panama and Castilla del Oro*, a standard work which immediately classed him as a weighty authority on the turbulent history of the era of discoveries. He has exhausted the sources from which authentic material could be extracted to write an impartial, truthful and complete narrative of the dramatic events which culminated in the mock trial and abominable execution of Acla. Dr. Anderson could have reproduced in the first page of his book the words with which Montaigne began his famous Essays: " *Ceci est un livre de bonne foi.*" Historical good faith and the charm of a forceful, elegant prose are chief characteristics of this work. Balboa is portrayed with brilliancy and fidelity, and the background of the heroic figure is a vivid reconstruction of many of the prodigies and horrors of the superhuman enterprise of conquering the New World.

" The atrocious greed, the pitiless cruelty, were crimes of the time, not of Spain," said an eminent Spanish poet.* True it is that in the bloody days of the early sixteenth century ignorance, fanaticism and ferocity were responsible for hideous crimes everywhere. True it is that by reason of a more vast field of action, the indictment of Spain has been particularly severe and incontestably deserved. But it is also true that if a redeeming light is to be found in the somber picture of the

---

* " *La atroz codicia, la inclemente saña,*
Crimen fueron del tiempo y no de España."

conquest of America, that light is Vasco Núñez de Balboa. Against the torture of Cuauhtémoc by Cortez, against the murder of Atahualpa by Pizarro, against the wholesale massacres of Ovando in Hispaniola, there stands Balboa as the friend and ally of the Indians, as the first Spaniard who associated in an immortal achievement the efforts of the white men and the bronze men, the first to lay the foundations for the fusion of the two races called upon to share in the future the national life and the eternal destinies of Hispanic America.

RICARDO J. ALFARO.

Washington, D. C.

PREFACE

"Á fe (dijo Don Quijote) que no fué tan piadoso Eneas como Virgilio le pinta, ni tan prudente Ulises como le describe Homero. Así es, replicó Sanson; pero uno es escribir como poeta, y otro como historiador: el poeta puede contar o cantar las cosas no como fueron, sino como debían ser; y el historiador las ha de escribir no como debían ser, sino como fueron, sin añadir ni quitar á la verdad cosa alguna."

—*Don Quijote*, MIGUEL DE CERVANTES.

VASCO NÚÑEZ DE BALBOA is the most attractive and tragic figure in the Hispanic conquest of the New World. From the *cumbre,* or summit, of a mountain on the Isthmus of Panama, Balboa was the first European to view the vast Pacific Ocean. As I hold that Columbus was of Italian (Genoese) origin, Vasco Núñez appears as the first great Spanish *descubridor* in America. That the discovery of the South Sea (Pacific Ocean) occurred when and how it did, with very little fighting with the natives and no loss of Spanish lives, was due entirely to the special qualifications of Balboa for leading and caring for his soldiers, and his tact and conciliatory manner in dealing with the Indian chiefs.

Balboa the stowaway, escaping from the island Española on the ship of the *Bachiller* Enciso, leaped into importance by leading the bewildered followers of Alonso de Ojeda, starving at San Sebastián de Urabá, to the town of Cacique Cémaco, lord of the Darien Indians, where were food and gold in plenty. The absconding debtor from Salvatierra on Española, without authority or license from king or viceroy, and with only his sword and his famous dog Leoncico, deposed the clever lawyer Enciso, alcalde mayor of Ojeda, and became boss of La Antigua del Darien.

7

Balboa was the maker of his own good fortune; his evil fortune was imposed upon him by others. As a young man, Vasco Núñez sailed out of Cádiz in October 1500, with Don Rodrigo de Bastidas, who followed the northern shore of South America in the wake of Christopher Columbus and others. Bastidas sailed farther west than did Ojeda and Niño, and arrived at the Gulf of Urabá, which his chief pilot, Juan de la Cosa, entered, seeking a passage through Tierra Firme, or mainland, into the Indian Ocean. When the tide went out of the gulf, Bastidas and Juan de la Cosa found their two ships sailing through eight fathoms of fresh water. The sweet, or fresh, water came from a great river which emptied by numerous mouths into the Culata, or southern end of the gulf. Ten years later, Balboa gave a name to this river, calling it the Great River of Saint John, up which was the fabled Golden Temple of Dabaiba. Today we know this stream as the Rio Atrato or Darien River.

Bastidas coasted around the gulf, trading Spanish trifles for Indian gold. It was the knowledge of this region acquired when with Bastidas that served Vasco Núñez so well a few years later when he went there on the ship of the *Bachiller* Enciso.

The life of Balboa in Darien and Panama was intimately associated with the large expeditions of Diego de Nicuesa and Alonso de Ojeda, fostered by King Ferdinand to conquer and colonize the regions known as Urabá and Veragua on the mainland of the New World. Vasco Núñez de Balboa, uninvited member of Enciso's party going to reinforce Ojeda in Urabá, by natural ability and sheer force of character became the savior, commander and preserver of the survivors of both expeditions. It was Balboa who guided the perishing people of Ojeda to food and shelter in Darien; and it was he who cared for the starving remnant of Nicuesa's men in Nombre de Dios and carried them to safety in La Antigua.

Elected *alcalde* by his fellows, Balboa, by skill and forcefulness, ruled the turbulent bands and their discredited officials, held the colonists together, and maintained the town (*municipio*) of Antigua del Darien as the first permanent European

settlement on the continent of America. With no royal commission, and only the votes of a majority of his companions—
a license which could be recalled or overthrown at any moment
—and a strong and aggressive opposition led by the lawyer Enciso, Balboa must have possessed very exceptional
ability to dominate the colony as he did. He was the only
Spaniard in Darien with the courage to assume command
and depose the incompetent *Bachiller* Enciso on the just
ground that no official of Alonso de Ojeda, governor of Urabá,
could exercise any legal authority in the territory of Veragua
assigned to Diego de Nicuesa.

Diego Colón, governor and quasi-viceroy at Santo Domingo,
claimed jurisdiction over Darien as being part of the continent
which his father, Columbus, had discovered and named Veragua. King Ferdinand in his *asiento* with Nicuesa and Ojeda,
done at Burgos 9 June 1508, recognized that Darien was a
part of the territory of Veragua when he fixed upon the gulf of
Urabá as the eastern limit of the land of Veragua given to
Governor Nicuesa. Enciso, bachelor of law, was careful not to
remind Ferdinand of this fact when he charged Balboa with
expelling him from Darien. Naturally, Diego Colón favored
Vasco Núñez and, in a letter dated 10 September 1511, he informed the King that he had appointed him his lieutenant on
Tierra Firme. Ferdinand, on learning of the failure of his
governors Nicuesa and Ojeda, named Balboa his captain and
temporary governor (*gobernador interino*) of the province of
Darien, " acknowledging the sufficiency, ability and fidelity of
you, Vasco Núñez de Balboa."

Today it is hard to realize the prominence and importance
attained by the Darien-Urabá-Panama region when conquered and commanded by Balboa at the very beginning of the
European conquest of continental America. Santa Maria de
la Antigua del Darien—to give the town its full name—was the
first and only foothold of Spain on the mainland that gave any
promise of continuing to exist. This, too, when King Ferdinand was so eager to assert and maintain his right to new lands
discovered in the West, title to which might be disputed by

Portugal or some other country. This necessity was much en-
hanced when Balboa reported that he had found another great
ocean which, of course, must bathe the shores of Cipangu and
the Portuguese discoveries in the East. Under the provisions
of the papal Bull of Donation, Portugal was cobeneficiary with
Spain to all firm lands and islands, discovered and to be
discovered, toward India not actually heretofore possessed
by any other Christian king or prince.

Balboa was governor in fact of Darien, Panama, and western
Urabá, for a period of nearly four years, during which time his
enemies, as well as his friends, accumulated wealth in gold,
lands, and Indian slaves. Balboa possessed the ability, more
than any other person—" *más que otra ninguna persona* "—to
rule and govern the disorderly aggregation of Christians at
Antigua del Darien.

The disclosure of that " other sea " reported to exist south
of the cordillera on the Isthmus of Panama was not a chance
discovery by the captain of a roaming company of Spaniards
raiding the Indians in search of food, gold, and pearls. The
discovery of the Pacific Ocean was a carefully planned undertaking by Balboa, who made the attempt with his small command as soon as he believed that he could depend on the
friendliness and aid of Cacique Careta and Cacique Comogre,
neighboring chieftains. With the addition of a few more men
sent by Diego Colón from Española, Vasco Núñez, on his own
initiative and with an inadequate force, ventured on his daring
quest for the South Sea. Columbus' dream of a west gate to
Asia was realized by Vasco Núñez de Balboa on 25 September
1513, when he viewed the Pacific Ocean from a *raso arriba,* or
clearing, on the summit of a mountain in the province of
Quarequá.

Balboa suffered from false reports of himself made by Enciso, Colmenares, and others at the court of Spain, and much
of the time he had no knowledge of what his enemies were saying and doing. The contemporary historians Peter Martyr
and Oviedo lived in this atmosphere of defamation of Balboa
at the court, and begin their accounts of Vasco Núñez with

pronounced animus against him. Perhaps the greatest tribute to the character of Balboa is the favorable opinion of these writers as they learned more about him.

Balboa's good fortune terminated with the arrival at Darien of the Splendid Armada, with the new governor, Pedrarias Dávila. The air of the New World seemed to activate and excite the evil nature of many Spanish commanders like Roldán, Bobadilla, Pedrarias, and Pizarro. Vasco Núñez de Balboa would not have murdered a Cuauhtemoc, like Cortés, nor have assassinated Inca Atahualpa, as did Francisco Pizarro. Balboa would have dealt with them as sovereigns, which they were; and they would have become his devoted friends and vassals, paying tribute to their white conqueror. Neither deeds of daring nor glamour of romance can blind our eyes to the wanton and senseless cruelties and atrocities of many *conquistadores*. Under Governor Pedrarias, hunting, robbing, and enslaving Indians became a major sport and a lucrative business.

The judicial murder of Balboa went unpunished. The young emperor, Charles V, with little knowledge of the Spanish language and ignorant of the Indies, could not be expected to concern himself about what went on in an almost unknown corner of the New World. Charles was busily engaged in dealing with the *comuneros* in Castile, the rival schemes of Francis I and Henry VIII, and in trying to suppress the teaching of that little Saxon monk, Martin Luther, who nailed the ninety-five theses on the door of the churchyard in Wittenberg.

Balboa was with the first expedition of white men to visit the shores of Urabá and eastern Panama, the first commander to subdue and pacify the Indians of Darien and Panama, the first Spanish captain to command and preserve the first permanent colony on the mainland of the New World, the first white man to cross and recross the continent of America, and the first European to view the South Sea, build ships on its shore and navigate the Pacific Ocean on the American coast. Balboa's famous letter of 20 January 1513 is the very first document describing the Darien-Urabá-Atrato section of the continent.

Had Juan de Valdivia, carrying news of the South Sea and

golden presents to Santo Domingo, not been wrecked on the *Víboras* or rocks of Pedro Bank; had Vasco Núñez been delegated *procurador* by the settlers at Antigua to present his claims for recognition to the king; had Arbolancha returned to Spain a few months sooner than he did; had Balboa been sent in chains to Spain, as planned by Pedrarias, and had Vasco Núñez de Balboa disposed of his enemies in Darien instead of allowing them to accuse him before the court, he now would be better known and occupy a higher rank in the history of the conquest of America by Europeans.

This study of Balboa is based largely upon his letters and reports and correspondence of other officials at Antigua del Darien, all written to King Ferdinand. The king, in name at least, usually replied to these letters. During these years the king also issued many decrees and *cédulas* relating to Vasco Núñez, all of which can be consulted in the large libraries. In Washington the great source of historic material is, of course, the magnificent Library of Congress, where are gathered copies of thousands of documents preserved in the archives of Spain. The *Colección de Documentos Inéditos,* forty-two volumes, is especially rich in papers concerning Spanish discovery and conquest in the New World. Altolaguirre in Spain and Medina in America, in their histories of Balboa, have made scores of these old records conveniently available to students of early American history.

For the description of the Splendid Armada to Castilla del Oro, the author follows the writings of Manuel Serrano y Sanz. The contemporary Spanish historians, Peter Martyr, Las Casas and Oviedo, have been drawn upon and freely quoted, particularly Oviedo, who knew Balboa and lived in Darien before and after the execution of the Adelantado. Throughout this work, credit is given to the historians Gómara, Herrera, Navarrete, and others for their contributions to the record of the life of Vasco Núñez de Balboa.

In recent years the Columbus Memorial Library of the Pan-American Union has become a fertile field for research in Latin-American history. I take pleasure in expressing my thanks to the librarian, Mr. Charles E. Babcock, and his competent assistants for their courteous compliance with my frequent request for books.

For the illustrations in this book the author expresses his appreciation and thanks to the Library of Congress; Dr. Ricardo J. Alfaro; C. M. Lupfer and A. C. McIlvaine, executive department, Panama Canal; the Air Corps, U. S. Army; the Naval Institute; Major Omer E. Malsbury, consulting engineer, Panama City; Dr. S. K. Lothrop, Peabody Museum, Harvard University; Stacey C. Russell, Canal Zone; Mr. Beardsley and the Lewis Service, Panama; Major Ralph Z. Kirkpatrick; E. P. Lang, and others.

The maps were made by the author in order to indicate the location of the old sites and regions.

C. L. G. A.

University Club,
Washington, D. C.

CONTENTS

ILLUSTRATIONS

MAPS

PROLOGUE

EVERY life is determined and limited by many antecedent factors, by environment and current events and conditions, and even by stated or anticipated future events. Many factors determined and conditioned the short and illustrious career of Vasco Núñez de Balboa in Darien and Panama.

1. The discovery of a New World.
2. The donation of unknown lands by the Pope to Ferdinand and Isabella, not to Spain.
3. Balboa's urge to seek adventure and better fortune in the Indies.
4. His failure to find either on Española, and escape from the island.
5. A shipwreck in the Gulf of Urabá.
6. The claim of a viceroy to govern Tierra Firme.
7. The love of an Indian maiden in Darien.
8. The ambition and statecraft of an old king.
9. The vagaries of a crazy queen.
10. Unjust acts and cunning schemes of venal functionaries of Church and State.
11. The scorn of a young cacique for the Spaniards' thirst for gold.
12. A cannibal feast in Yucatán.
13. Jealousy, ingratitude, and lies by companions and seeming friends.
14. A boy king ignorant of the Indies.
15. Worst of all, the hatred of a vicious and covetous governor of Castilla del Oro, supported by his chief judge and other officials.

To the foregoing might be added what appears to have been the intentional procedure of the governor, Pedrarias Dávila, and his *alcalde mayor*, Gaspar de Espinosa, under guise of law, to bring about the death of Vasco Núñez. If we believe, as did Micer Codro, the Venetian astrologer, that the fate of Vasco Núñez de Balboa was foreordained in the heavens, that is still another element in his life.

Fortune exhausted all her favors to Balboa when she led him to the shores of the Pacific Ocean. During the few remaining years of his life, even the stars in their courses seemed to fight against him.

I

BALBOA

Conquistador y Descubridor

" Speak of me as I am, nothing extenuate
Nor set down aught in malice."
—*Othello,* SHAKESPEARE.

THE belief is general, and so stated in all modern histories, that Vasco Núñez de Balboa was born in Jerez de los Caballeros, about the year 1475. This belief seems to be founded upon tradition in Spain, rather than positive and undoubted historic record. Jerez de los Caballeros is a town of about 14,000 inhabitants in the province of Badajoz, which borders on the Portuguese frontier. The capital of the province is the important city of Badajoz, close to the Rio Guadiana. Jerez de los Caballeros is seventy-four kilometers south of Badajoz. The first historians of the Indies, Pedro Mártir, Oviedo, Las Casas and Gómara, write that Balboa was from Badajoz, or from Jerez de Badajoz. Felipe de la Gandara states that Vasco Núñez was of the city of Badajoz. Writing in 1677, Gandara says: " The glory of the extensive provinces of Peru is due primarily to Vasco Núñez de Balboa, originally from Galicia and native of the city of Badajoz, of the very illustrious lineage and family of the Balboas," and then the author goes on to give the genealogy of the Balboa family. Another writer declares that Balboa was descended from an ancient and noble family of the kingdom of Leon, which settled in Extremadura.

When the Arabs possessed the site of Jerez de los Caballeros, they fortified the place and called it *Xerixa*, which seems to be the origin of the word *Jerez*. After the Christians recovered the town, Fernando el Santo (Ferdinand III, A. D. 1200–1252) enlarged the population of Jerez with people from Galicia, and named it Jerez de Badajoz. This may have been the time when the ancestors of Vasco Núñez came down from northern Spain. It is obvious that the appellation Vasco, or Basco, must have originated from the Vascones, as the ancient predecessors of the Basque people were called. The surname Balboa appears to be a Portuguese name, the equivalent of Valbuena in Spanish. Vasco Núñez de Balboa usually is referred to by his country-men as Vasco Núñez, and occasionally as Núñez de Balboa. To English readers he is known simply as Balboa. The approximate date of the birth of Balboa was calculated from a statement by Las Casas that when Vasco Núñez escaped from the island of Española, in 1510, he was about thirty-five years of age. In modern times, around 1830, Washington Irving in English, and Manuel José Quintana in Spanish, wrote charm-ing accounts of the life of Balboa in the pleasing style which characterizes those authors. Both writers declare that Balboa was born in Jerez de los Caballeros. In 1913, the fourth cen-tenary of the discovery of the Pacific Ocean, the citizens of his native town collected money to erect a statue to Balboa, and named an open place the Plaza de Vasco Núñez. Practically nothing is known of the boyhood and early manhood of Balboa. In this respect he resembles his great predecessor in discovery in the New World, Christopher Columbus. While still young, Vasco Núñez entered the service of Don Pedro Puertocarrero, the deaf lord of Moguer, in the character of page. Perhaps the families were related. Pedro Mártir, then at the court of Spain, writes in Latin that Balboa was an *egregius digladiator,* meaning a master of the sword, or fencing master. On no fur-ther evidence Gómara states that he was a " ruffian or fencer " —" *rufian o esgrimidor.*" Someone wrote that Vasco Núñez at this time led a licentious and prodigal life, assertions not supported by reliable evidence. Defamatory stories about Balboa started at the Court of Spain after the arrival there of the lawyer Enciso and *procurador* Colmenares from Darien. Balboa suffered throughout the remainder of his life from the false reports spread by these two men, as well as from the unfavorable opinion of Miguel de Pasamonte.

Tierra Firme and the Pearl Coast
Bastidas—De la Cosa—Balboa

In October, 1492, Christopher Columbus discovered *Guanahani* (San Salvador) and several other islands in the Bahamas, and Cuba and Haiti of the Greater Antilles. The next year, 1493, the Spaniards made permanent settlements on Haiti, which was renamed Española. It was not until the first day of August, 1498, that Columbus, on his third voyage to the Indies, obtained his first view of the continent of America. That same year, and in the preceding year, 1497, John Cabot and his son Sebastian had reached the Atlantic coast of North America in regions visited by Norsemen about the year 1000.

Columbus discovered the continent at the northeast corner of South America, called Paria by the natives. The Admiral sailed through the turbulent waters of the *Boca del Serpiente* into the Gulf of Paria separating the large island of Trinidad from the mainland. Columbus spent two weeks about this gulf in friendly trade with the natives of Trinidad and Paria. It was here that the Admiral encountered monkeys, deer, and pearls, the first found by Spaniards in the New World. Beside pearls, the Indians wore ornaments made of an alloy of gold, called *guanin*. Failing to stem the rivers of fresh water on the western shore, Columbus made his exit from the northern end of the gulf on the rushing currents of the *Boca del Drago*, or Dragon's Mouth. Turning westward along the mainland, the Admiral continued to trade for gold and pearls as far as a large island, which he named Margarita (the Pearl). Pearls were so abundant that he called this coast *La Costa de las Perlas*.

On 16 August 1498, Columbus sailed his three small craft out of the bay of Cumaná, opposite the island Margarita, and laid his course for Santo Domingo (then called *Nueva Isabela*), the new town founded by his brother, Don Bartolomé Colón, in 1496, on the south coast of Española. Upon arriving at this new settlement at the mouth of the Ozama River, the Admiral sent to the Catholic sovereigns (Ferdinand and Isabella) a report of his voyage and with it a drawing, or *pintura*, of the new land discovered. Because of the high mountains and great rivers, Columbus believed that this land must be *tierra firme*, or mainland, the largest known to that time.

This new discovery by Christopher Columbus caused much joy in the court. The pearls and monkeys encountered seemed to prove that the Admiral had reached, finally, the main coast of Asia. King Ferdinand and Bishop Fonseca were eager to learn more of this continental mass of land and its relation to the Line of Demarcation fixed by Pope Alexander and the Treaty of Tordesillas, and to secure more pearls and gold. Alonso de Ojeda, much favored by Fonseca, was quickly authorized to equip four ships and sail, in May 1499, in the wake of Columbus, using the charts and " figure " of the coast sent back by the Admiral. Ferdinand knew, of course, that he was not keeping faith with Columbus in accordance with the *capitulaciones* signed by him at Sante Fe (Granada) in April, 1492. To save his royal conscience, the king let Fonseca sign the license to Ojeda. Ojeda took with him the skillful pilot, Juan de la Cosa, and Amerigo Vespucci, the Florentine, perhaps as cosmographer. The expedition sailed westward along the north coast of South America as far as the Gulf of Venezuela (*golfo de Venecia*), Cuquibacoa, and Cabo de la Vela. From this cape, Ojeda steered north to Española, which he reached on 5 September 1499.

When reports of these new lands became noised about Sevilla and Cádiz, many pilots and adventurers again were ready to seek their fortune in the New World. Pedro Alonso Niño, a navigator of Moguer who had been with Columbus when he discovered Paria, obtained a license to trade along the new Tierra Firme. With Cristóbal Guerra for captain and only thirty-one men, Niño embarked in a small caravel of fifty tons and set out for Paria and the Pearl Coast shortly after the de-

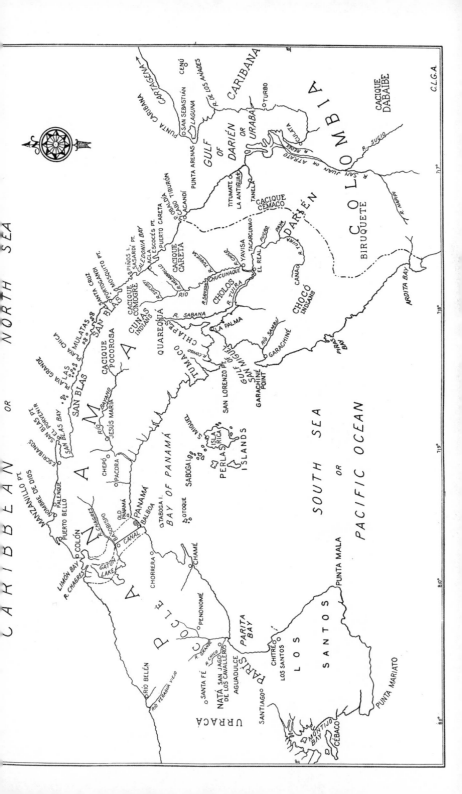

parture of Ojeda. Without proceeding to Santo Domingo, Niño returned to Bayona, in Galicia; his little vessel burdened with brazil wood and pearls as common among the sailors as chaff, as one chronicler states. This was the first voyage to the New World that was financially profitable. Because he was successful and had secured so many pearls, of which the king got his share, the Spanish officials accused Niño of concealing others, and cast him into prison. In June, 1500, two months after the return of Niño, the fleet of Ojeda came sailing into the harbor of Cádiz. By reason of his harsh methods in dealing with the Indians, Ojeda had not obtained enough gold and pearls to reward his men for their labor, so he had loaded the ship with captives, to be sold into slavery on return to Spain.

RODRIGO DE BASTIDAS

Don Rodrigo de Bastidas, a wealthy notary of Triana, the maritime suburb of Sevilla, was the next man to venture his life and savings in a trading voyage to the Pearl Coast of Tierra Firme. Bastidas (sometimes written Bastides) had no difficulty in securing a license from *Los Reyes* (Ferdinand and Isabella) to fit out two ships at his own cost and risk, to go by the Ocean Sea to discover islands and firm lands in the parts of the Indies not already discovered by the Admiral Don Cristóbal Colón, or by Niño and Guerra, or belonging to the most serene prince, the king of Portugal. The license to Bastidas, still preserved in the *Archivo de Indias,* authorized the notary to acquire gold, silver, copper, lead, tin, quicksilver, and any other metal whatever; and *aljófar,* pearls, precious stones, and jewels; and slaves, negroes, and mixed breeds; and monsters, serpents, fishes, and birds; and spices and drugs, and every other thing of whatsoever name or quality or value it might be. After deducting the cost of the vessels and other expenses, the fourth part of the remainder would belong to the sovereigns, and three-fourths to Rodrigo de Bastidas to do with as he chose, free and unencumbered.

This voyage of Bastidas is notable for the reason, as learned later, that Vasco Núñez de Balboa was a member of the expedition. The chief pilot was that able *vizcaíno*, Juan de la Cosa, who had sailed with Columbus and had just returned with Ojeda from the Pearl Coast. The expedition sailed from Cádiz in October, 1500, and steered for the Canaries. At the island Gomera they supplied themselves with " meat and water and wood and cheeses and other fresh provisions." The first land seen in the Indies was a " green island," the name of which they did not learn, for they had no speech with the Indians. After filling their casks with fresh water, the two vessels proceeded on their course to the north coast of Venezuela, a region now familiar to Juan de la Cosa.

From Cabo de la Vela, the farthermost point reached by Ojeda and Cosa in 1499, Bastidas continued on westward, exploring the coast and exchanging European trinkets for the gold and pearls of the natives. He came to Río Hacha and then to Santa Marta, where the Indians thereabouts wore crowns, which caused him to call them " *indios coronados.*" In March, 1501, Bastidas discovered the mouth of a great river, which he named Magdalena. He entered the bay where later Cartagena was founded. After this he passed to the island of Baru and the islets called Arenas, and the group called San Bernardo. At a low island named Fuerte the Indians made very fine salt, much esteemed by the Spaniards. This island lies in front of Caparoto and the mouth of the river of Cenu, now called Sinu. Farther on to the west and south appeared the little island of Tortuga, doubtless the Tortuguilla of modern maps. Continuing westward, Bastidas arrived at a place where the land turned sharply to the south, soon known as Punta Caribana. On rounding this point of land, Bastidas saw the *farellones,* or rocky islets, which are close to the opposite shore near to the site of the town of Darien. Cosa thought this body of water might be a strait leading through Tierra Firme, but when they anchored in four fathoms of water it was found to be fresh and potable. For this reason the stretch of water was named Golfo Dulce (Fresh Water Gulf), later called the

Gulf of Urabá, or Darien. From Cabo de la Vela to Punta Caribana, writes Oviedo, Bastidas had discovered 150 leagues of coast.

Balboa acquired considerable knowledge of the natives along the Caribbean shores of South America, including the fact that many of them used poison on their weapons. When coasting about the Gulf of Urabá, members of the Bastidas expedition landed on the western side of the gulf and saw, as related by Vasco Núñez, on the opposite bank of a large river, an Indian town in the midst of green and fertile fields. No doubt they traded with the Indians, for the contact was sufficient to disclose that these people of Darien did not poison their weapons.

After exploring the gulf, Bastidas sailed around Cabo Tiburon and resumed his course to the west, coasting and trading along the Caribbean shore of eastern Panama as far as Bastimentos. Thus Bastidas, De la Cosa, Balboa, and the rest of the party, were the first Europeans, in 1501, to visit the eastern half of the Isthmus of Panama.

The two ships began to leak from the borings of the sea worm called broma (*teredo navalis*), which perforates the wooden hulls of vessels, and Bastidas terminated his voyage in the region where Nombre de Dios was founded a few years later. When Christopher Columbus on his last voyage to the Indies reached this point in the following year, 1502, the natives informed him of the previous visit by white men.

Turning away from the coast, Juan de la Cosa set the course back toward Castile. The next land touched was the island of Jamaica, as yet unsettled by Europeans, where the ships took on a supply of wood and fresh water. After leaving Jamaica, Bastidas found so much water coming in through the wormholes that he stopped at an islet called Contramaestre, one league off Española, and made some repairs. He resumed the voyage, but ran into a gale, and was glad to put back to the little island for shelter. Starting out a second time, the worm-eaten vessels filled so rapidly that De la Cosa hurried into the port of Jaragua in the southwestern coast of Española (Haiti), where the two ships sank.

Like the other *descubridores,* Bastidas had captured some Indians to be sold as slaves, most of whom were in chains and so were drowned when the vessels foundered. The greater part of the gold and pearls were saved and carried ashore. Extra arms were destroyed, lest they fall into the hands of the natives. Bastidas divided his men into three bands, and each traveled by a separate route to the new town of Santo Domingo, the better to subsist off the country. Each party carried some articles of Spain to trade for food on the way.

The detestable Bobadilla, he who had sent Columbus and his brothers in chains to Spain, imprisoned Bastidas on his arrival at Santo Domingo. He was charged with trading with the Indians without license, his property was seized, and Bobadilla ordered him to Spain for trial.

At this time, 15 April 1502, the Comendador Nicolás de Ovando, with a large retinue from Spain, arrived at Santo Domingo to relieve Bobadilla as governor of Española. On 29 June, Christopher Columbus, on his fourth voyage to the New World, appeared off the mouth of the Ozama River, and requested permission from Ovando to shelter his ships in the river from an impending storm. The man who gave to Spain more kingdoms than she had provinces at home was refused refuge in the island he had discovered and settled.

The large fleet brought out by the new governor was just about to set sail to return to Spain, and Columbus sent another message to Ovando entreating him not to allow the vessels to leave the river, that the storm was imminent. The prediction of the old Admiral was derided by the pilots of the ships, and the fleet, on 30 June 1502, stood bravely out to sea on its homeward voyage. The next day when near the island Saona, off the southeastern point of Española, this fleet was struck by a typical West Indian hurricane, and more than twenty vessels were lost.

About five hundred persons perished, including a number of Indian captives. Among the latter was Guarionex, brave cacique of the Vega Real. Ex-governor Bobadilla, Francisco Roldán and other bitter enemies of Christopher Columbus were engulfed. The king's share of gold, including the largest nugget ever found on Española, and all the gold sent home by private individuals, amounting to 200,000 *castellanos*, was lost.

It is said that only one ship, the little *Aguja*, considered to be the worst vessel in the fleet, proceeded on to Spain. On board were four thousand *pesos de oro* and other property belonging to Columbus. To escape the hurricane, the Admiral found shelter in a cove of the bay of Azua. His brother, Bartolomé Colón, also a skilled navigator, in command of the ship *Bermuda*, chose to run from the land, and rode out the storm at sea. Many persons ascribed the escape of Columbus and his ships and property, as well as the destruction of his enemies, to some occult magic invoked by the Admiral. The good Bishop Las Casas regarded the hurricane as a fitting judgment sent by heaven upon the enemies of Columbus and the oppressors of the Indians.

As for Rodrigo de Bastidas, he with his gold and pearls was on one of the few ships which survived the hurricane and succeeded in returning to Santo Domingo. When Bastidas finally reached Spain, he was cleared of the charges against him, and was able to display three chests full of gold and pearls to the populace of the towns through which he passed. There is no record to show that Vasco Núñez received a share of the profits of the venture.

We have given an outline of this expedition for the reason that the voyage of Rodrigo de Bastidas also was the voyage of Vasco Núñez de Balboa. Balboa, and probably others, remained on Española. Unlike most of the immigrants arriving at the island from Spain, Balboa already had seen much of the New World and had acquired considerable experience in dealing with the natives. Governor Ovando gave Vasco Núñez some land and a *repartimiento* of Indians to work it, in Salvatierra de la Sabana, in the southwestern corner of the island. We have no accounts of the life of Balboa on Española during the next seven years. We hope that he was not called upon to engage in the bloody massacre of Indians by Ovando in the land of Queen Anacáona, widow of Caonabó. The golden jewelry and stores of gold accumulated by the natives (for the Indians, too, prized this wonderful metal) had been seized by the Spaniards before the arrival of Vasco Núñez. More gold could be obtained only in small amounts by the laborious process of mining. The indigenes, too, were fast decreasing in number under the harsh conditions of life imposed by their white masters.

Had Vasco Núñez been of the plodding, saving type of men, he could have lived the easy life of a planter and in time acquired a competence. European cattle, hogs, and horses multiplied rapidly; the near-by sea and rivers supplied aquatic food; the forest furnished native fruits; and Balboa's *naborías* could raise plenty of *maíz*, *cazabe*, melons, and peppers. Such a placid existence did not appeal to Vasco Núñez de Balboa. From subsequent statements and from the manner in which Balboa departed from the island, we know that he succeeded only in amassing debts while living on Española.

ALONSO DE OJEDA

In the year 1509, Alonso de Ojeda and Rodrigo de Nicuesa, by authority of their joint license from King Ferdinand, enlisted men on Española for their expeditions to conquer, explore, and exploit the lands east and west of the Gulf of Urabá (Darien).

Lacking any inducement to remain on the island and pining for more adventure on Tierra Firme, it was natural for the spirited young *hidalgo*, Vasco Núñez de Balboa, to seek to join one or other of these expeditions. Probably it made no difference to Balboa which party he went with, just so he got away from the dull life he was leading at Salvatierra. Under local law, a debtor was forbidden to leave Española without settling with his creditors; and Balboa was compelled to resort to strategy to escape the vigilance of the officers of Diego Colón, now viceroy of the Indies and governor of Española.

Failing to accompany either Ojeda or Nicuesa when they sailed for the mainland in November, 1509, Balboa succeeded in getting aboard the ship of the *Bachiller* Martín Fernández de Enciso, *alcalde mayor* of Ojeda, who was instructed to follow his chief with more men and supplies. One account states that Vasco Núñez ensconced himself in a large cask (*tonel*), and was carted to the shore and wheeled or rolled on board the vessel. Oviedo relates that Balboa escaped from the island by hiding himself in a ship's sail. I believe both statements are correct, as one account supplements the other. It is reasonable to believe that Vasco Núñez, with the aid of a friend, was conveyed onto the deck of the ship where, seizing on the first opportunity, he emerged from his restricted quarters and hid himself in an extra sail. Balboa had two possessions which he valued highly; his trusty sword and his dog Leoncico, both of which could easily be taken aboard by friends. The Spaniard who assisted Balboa in this escapade was Bartolomé Hurtado, who was fully rewarded for this service when Vasco Núñez came into power in Darien. On 1 September 1510, Enciso sailed from Santo Domingo in a ship and one brigantine, bearing 150 armed men, twelve mares and several stallions, hogs, and provisions, for Alonso de Ojeda, governor of Nueva Andalucía.

Balboa remained hidden until well away from the island, when, " like Aphrodite from her circling shell," he came forth from his concealment and disclosed himself to Enciso. The bachelor of law, fearing that he might be compelled to pay the debts of the absconding debtor, ranted and threatened as lawyers are wont to do, and considered marooning Balboa on some desert island. Members of the party, friends of Balboa, interceded for him, and Enciso retained him as a likely looking recruit. " God had reserved for him greater things," writes the bishop of Chiapa; for when the colonists knew not which way to turn, it was the *hombre del casco* who led them out of their perplexity, and was preferred to Enciso as their leader.

The *Bachiller* Enciso reached the shore of the continent

near the site of the present city of Cartagena, and entered the bay of Calamar, which seemed to possess some fatal charm for navigators along this coast. Ojeda had arrived here months before, and against the advice of Juan de la Cosa, who was familiar with the region, had landed a force and attacked the Indian village of Calamar (or Calamarí). The village was taken and many captives sent on the ships. Not satisfied with the slaves and gold secured, the rash and reckless Ojeda entered the country for several leagues and came upon a large town called Turbaco, which was found deserted. While the Spaniards were in disorder, looting the houses scattered among the trees, the Indians returned in force and killed nearly all of them, including Juan de la Cosa, the famous cartographer. Ojeda and one of his men managed to get back to the ships.

The governor soon departed from the port of Calamar, so deadly to Spaniards, and sailed westward to the Gulf of Urabá, the limit of his grant. On an elevation on the eastern shore of the gulf, Ojeda erected a wooden blockhouse and some small houses, surrounding the whole with a stockade. Las Casas calls this the second settlement by Spaniards on the continent of America; the first being *Nuestra Señora de Belén* in Veragua, begun in February, 1503, by Christopher Columbus.

Ojeda named his embryo capital San Sebastián in honor of the arrow-martyred saint whose protection he craved from the poisoned weapons of the natives. This attempt at settlement, in the beginning of the year 1510, lasted a few months longer than Ojeda's first effort to locate on Bahía Honda in 1502. St. Sebastián seems to have withheld his protection from the colony, for when the Spaniards issued forth for food and gold, they were fiercely assailed by Indians along the trail. Many of the colonists died from wounds, disease, and hunger. Ojeda had never been wounded in his many encounters with the natives, and always had believed that the Virgin shielded him from physical harm. He felt very despondent when the Indians led him into ambush and wounded him in the thigh. Believing that the arrow was poisoned, Ojeda ordered his surgeon to cauterize the wound with red-hot irons, and he soon recovered. It is possible that the Indians wished to take him alive, and that they did not put the deadly herb on the arrow.

Not receiving any supplies by the *Bachiller* Enciso, as expected, the situation of the weakened garrison became so desperate that Ojeda resolved to go in person to Española to secure more men and provisions. Leaving the settlement in charge of Francisco Pizarro as his lieutenant, Ojeda, in May, 1510, sailed in a vessel captained by one Talavera for Santo Domingo. The ship was stranded on the shore of the province of Xagua in Cuba, an island not yet settled by Spaniards. After various vicissitudes of fortune, Ojeda finally got back to Santo Domingo. Failing to receive further aid from Diego Colón or King Ferdinand, and broken in health, spirit, and fortune, the governor of Nueva Andalucía lost all his brag and bluster. Like many other men who have failed in their worldly ambitions, Ojeda sought solace in the Church, and, after a few years, he died in the habit of St. Francis.

Balboa Saves the Colonists

Francisco Pizarro, subsequently conqueror of Peru, had been authorized by his chief to abandon San Sebastián and return to Española, if he did not hear from Ojeda within fifty days after his departure. After the expiration of fifty hungry days and no news from Ojeda or Enciso, the people at San Sebastián deserted the unlucky post. In the first days of September, 1510, the colonists embarked in their two brigantines, the one commanded by Pizarro, the other by Valenzuela. When well outside the Gulf of Urabá, near Isla Fuerte, the boat of Valenzuela was suddenly overturned by a squall and all hands drowned. Pizarro, with about thirty-five men, in the other brigantine, continued on to the bay of Calamar (Cartagena), where he met the tardy Enciso coming from Española with the long expected supplies.

The suspicious lawyer at first doubted the story of Pizarro, thinking that they had mutinied or were fleeing from some crime they had committed. Pizarro showed his authority from Ojeda and convinced the *bachiller* that the little party was all that remained of the colony of Alonso de Ojeda, who had sailed from Española with so much bravado in November of the preceding year. The *Bachiller* Enciso, *alcalde mayor* of Ojeda, being the ranking officer present, ordered a return to San Sebastián, claiming that his agreement required him to proceed as far as Urabá. The miserable colonists offered Enciso all the gold they had collected to be allowed to proceed to Santo Domingo, or at least to seek out and join the force of Nicuesa. They were not aware that the fortune of the other expedition was no better than their own. Enciso would not accede to the request of Pizarro's men, for it meant abandoning the government of Alonso de Ojeda and the loss of his office as *alcalde mayor,* with no hope of compensating himself for the money he had put in the enterprise. A few days later, with the prospect of acquiring food and gold, the lawyer was not so reluctant to enter the territory of Diego de Nicuesa.

Both parties sailed out of the bay of Cartagena for San Sebastián. Some evil fate seemed to prevent a settlement in Urabá. As the ship of Enciso turned into the Gulf of Urabá, a blunder of the helmsman drove the vessel onto a shoal, where it soon went to pieces, losing all the stores, horses, and swine. The *bachiller* beheld the profits of years of litigation disappear in the waves. The loss of the ship deprived them not only of the animals and provisions, but also of the means of transporting the entire party back to Española or elsewhere. Aided by the brigantines, the men escaped to the shore and continued along the eastern edge of the gulf, while the two small boats kept on by sea.

Arrived at the site of San Sebastián, they found the little fort and thirty huts, which had been so laboriously erected, reduced to ashes. All these Spaniards had been in the Indies sufficiently long to know the ways of Indians, and should not have expected to find the buildings as left by Pizarro. Amid such desolation, even Enciso lost some of his arrogance and self-importance. The warlike natives, of Carib stock, renewed their attacks with an audacity and courage which filled the Spaniards with terror. The *bachiller* himself, at the head of one hundred men, attempted an *entrada* into the country for food and gold. Soon several of the Christians were wounded by the envenomed shafts of the Indians, and the party fled back to the forlorn ruins of the settlement. It was said of Enciso, as of Ojeda in the same situation, that he attempted to abandon the fatal spot and sail away with a few of his friends, leaving the rest to their fate.

For a few days the dejected colonists subsisted on the buds and tender shoots of palm trees, and the flesh of some wild pigs which they were able to kill. Said they, " Let us leave these deadly shores, where the sea, the land, the heavens and men repulse us." Where to go, and how to transport 180 men, or more, in two small brigantines was the problem of the moment. Not knowing what to do, the *bachiller* appealed to his men. None could propose any measure except flight, until it came the turn of the absconding debtor of Española to speak. Stepping forward, Vasco Núñez de Balboa addressed the assembled colonists as follows:

" I remember that in past years, coming along this coast with Rodrigo de Bastidas to discover, we entered in this gulf and disembarked on the western shore, where we found a large river and on its opposite bank we saw a town seated amid abundant fertile fields, and inhabited by people who did not put the herb on their arrows."

By herb (*yerba*), Balboa meant the juice of a poisonous plant used by the natives as an arrow poison. In this region, the accused plant was generally held to be the manzanillo.

The Spaniards hailed Vasco Núñez as another Moses pointing out a land of promise. The prospect of food and shelter only a few leagues away, with the probability of securing gold and Indians to serve them, revived the dejected spirits of the colonists. About one hundred men leaped into the two brigantines, crossed over to the western shore, and, directed by Balboa, found the river and town as he had described them. Leaving a few men on the boats, the Spaniards assembled on some elevated ground and reconnoitered the town. The river, town, and region, all bore the name of Darien. The lord of the land was called Cémaco, and when he observed the hostile approach of the white men, he prepared to defend his home and country. Sending the women and children out of the town, Cacique Cémaco formed his fighting men on a near-by hill and awaited the onslaught of the bearded white strangers.

At the sight of this martial array of five hundred warriors, the Spaniards recommended themselves to heaven. When the Spanish captains wished to do a real good job of killing Indians, they usually invoked some supernatural power or saintly character to give aid and sanctity to the undertaking. In this instance, Enciso made a vow to " Our Lady of Antigua," a venerated image in the cathedral of Sevilla, that, should she give him the victory, he would give the town the name of *Santa María de la Antigua,* as well as make a pilgrimage to her shrine and adorn it with jewels. Having propitiated the favor of the Virgin in his cause, the *bachiller* made his followers swear " that they would not turn their backs to the enemy." Over on the other hill, the Dariens solicited the support of their gods, and the *tequinas* and medicine men uttered incantations and made " medicine " to insure them the victory.

With Balboa's assurance that these Indians did not use the deadly poison, and with a courage born of hunger, the Christians attacked the Dariens with great fury, just before the dawn of day. Cacique Cémaco and his warriors received the Spaniards with great cries, and defended themselves with equal valor. But steel swords cut deeper than wooden swords, steel arrows and leaden bullets killed more often than the wooden *varas* of the Indians, hurled by throwing-sticks (*estólicas*). The white man's " medicine " was stronger than Indian " medicine," and Christian civilization prevailed over barbarian culture. The loud report, flash, and smoke of gunpowder, followed by its deadly execution, struck terror into the Dariens and they broke and fled. The historians make no mention of dogs in this fight, but they must have been there, led by Leoncico.

Photo by Mr. Beardsley.

Approach to the village of Titumate on the Gulf of Urabá.

Photo by Mr. Beardsley.

Pueblo Tanela on the Río Tanela near the ruins of La Antigua.

The Christians fared well in the battle of Darien, killing many Indians without losing one of their own men, according to the records. After the battle, the Spaniards entered the deserted village and helped themselves to the food, gold, and cotton cloth left behind by the natives. The Indians were pursued up the river valley and some stragglers captured. Best of all for the Christians, they found hidden in the canes and recesses along the river many fine coronets, plates, bracelets, anklets, and other gold pieces. The golden loot of Darien amounted to 10,000 *castellanos*, which Irving, by some refinement of calculation, valued at 53,259 dollars. The brigantines were sent back to San Sebastián to bring over the eighty Spaniards left behind, and there was feasting and joy in Cémaco's capital, now called *Nuestra Señora de la Antigua del Darien*.

It must be noted here that Martín Fernández de Enciso, chief justice of New Andalusia, the grant assigned to Ojeda, without provocation or necessity, knowingly and deliberately entered the territory of Diego de Nicuesa, then called Veragua (the Darien, Panama, and Veragua of today), attacked and killed his subjects, the Indians of Darien, and captured and held their principal town, looting it of food, gold, cloth, and other articles of value, and driving the inhabitants from the neighborhood. The chronicles of these events make no mention of any peaceful overtures by Enciso for food, shelter, or the purchase of a site for settlement.

It is true that the authority under which Ojeda and Enciso operated, the *asiento* of 9 June 1508, treats only of Indian slaves, erecting forts, and how to divide the gold; and says nothing about approaching the Indians in kindness, and by good works and example attracting them to the holy Catholic faith. But the basic grant of the New World to Spain by Pope Alexander VI made the propagation of the Christian creed an indispensable condition of conquest of the natives; and practically every other commission to conquer and settle a region contains this proviso, though generally only a legal formality.

Enciso undertook no move to negotiate with the Indians, and made a surprise attack upon them before the break of day.

Two or three years later, Enciso made many complaints of damages to himself, but he never recognized any right or interest of Governor Nicuesa in Darien. By reason of his knowledge of the districts east and west of the Gulf of Urabá, the *bachiller* was able to befuddle the minds of King Ferdinand and his councillors as to the geography of this region. Enciso, in Spain, stated that he landed with about 110 men, and that the Christians, " with great diligence," attacked the Dariens, killing many of them and taking forty-five pounds of fine gold. In the pursuit of the Indians, he secured still more gold, making in all 103 pounds, as registered by the *veedores* present. After deducting the king's fifth, Enciso claimed the balance to pay for the ships, arms, and provisions. Enciso, of course, knew that Darien was part of Nicuesa's territory, and that he had no right to invade it and no just claim to the gold. When Governor Nicuesa, at Nombre de Dios, heard of the high-handed acts of Enciso, he threatened, very properly, to demand the gold and to punish the officials at La Antigua. It was this knowledge which made Enciso oppose inviting Nicuesa, the rightful governor, to come to La Antigua.

THE SPANIARDS SETTLE IN DARIEN

The defeat of Cémaco and settlement at Darien was the first permanent step in the Hispanic conquest of Tierra Firme, and Santa Maria de la Antigua del Darien was the first seat of the Christian Church on the mainland in the spiritual domination of America, begun by killing and robbing the innocent natives.

The 180 survivors of Ojeda's expedition now possessed a habitation much better adapted to the climate than any the Spaniards themselves could erect, and surrounded by tilled fields and growing crops. La Antigua del Darien is described as situated a league, or a league and a half, up the Darien river. Seagoing craft could not pass up to the town, and they discharged their cargo at the anchorage or port at the mouth of the river. The *Bachiller* Enciso now was well satisfied with his lot. Alonso de Ojeda had gone away, never to return to Tierra Firme, and Enciso, as *alcalde mayor,* was chief of the party. Besides, the personal jewelry and ceremonial gold pieces filched from the Dariens would repay him many times for what he had expended on the expedition, and which had been swallowed up by the waves of the gulf. Elated by his high position and good luck, as he thought, the *bachiller* proceeded to make laws for the regulation of the colonists, and soon provoked opposition. Some said that it was a shame to allow themselves to be ruled by this *letrado*. Apparently, some friendly trade had developed between the white men and the Indians, and when the tactless Enciso issued an edict that no Spaniard could carry on private traffic with the natives for gold, under pain of death, the settlers resolved to remove him from the command.

The *bachiller* claimed that he was the lieutenant of Ojeda and that in the *asiento* or capitulation with his chief, the king had commanded that all persons had to declare before royal officials the gold secured by them. This was true; but the astute lawyer should have known that his own status was too precarious to precipitate a conflict. When asked to show his authority from Ojeda, he could not produce it, because it had been lost in the shipwreck. The colonists declared that Enciso was a miser who wanted all the profit for himself, and who exercised an authority which did not belong to him.

The people again turned to Vasco Núñez de Balboa—the man who had saved them from starvation and death by poisoned arrows at San Sebastián—to shield them from the arbitrary pretensions of Enciso. It is unjust to Balboa to declare, as writers have done, that he planned and schemed to overthrow Enciso. The *bachiller* was simply impossible as a leader, especially under their present environment, and Balboa was the strong man present to whom the colonists instinctively appealed for relief, and the natural course of events swept him into the command. Had Balboa been a cunning and calculating man, he never would have lost his head. Balboa was only expressing the voice of a majority of the people when he declared that the Gulf of Urabá separated the government of Alonso de Ojeda from that of Diego de Nicuesa, and now that they were in Darien, on the western side of the gulf, they owed no allegiance to Ojeda or to any of his officers. The *Bachiller* Enciso was out of his province and had no jurisdiction over them.

Under Spanish law and custom, when a party of men found themselves without a legally appointed commander, they could hold an assembly and form a town council, or municipality (*ayuntamiento*) by electing *alcaldes, regidores,* and other officers by popular vote. This the colonists at La Antigua did. Elsewhere, I have stated that this was the first town meeting of Europeans on the continent of America. (See *Old Panama and Castilla del Oro,* p. 151.)

The settlers at Antigua del Darien elected Vasco Núñez de Balboa and Martín de Zamudio to be *alcaldes* and Juan de Valdivia and others as *regidores.*. Bartolomé Hurtado, who had aided Balboa in his flight from Española, was made *alguacil mayor*.

La Antigua now was in charge of a temporary or *ad interim* government, subject to the action of Governor Nicuesa, should he ever appear; the pleasure of the king when he heard of the settlement, or the will of Viceroy Diego Colón if awarded jurisdiction on Tierra Firme. Although the colonists had elected a town government, still there was dissension in Darien. The people believed that it would be best to have only one man to rule them. The majority supported Vasco Núñez for the office; a smaller faction favored waiting to hear from Nicuesa; the *Bachiller* Enciso had a small but very active following bitterly opposed to Balboa; while *Alcalde* Zamudio had the backing of the more turbulent members of the colony.

The Spaniards had not been long at Darien—now called Santa Maria de la Antigua del Darien—when they were surprised to hear faint reports of artillery from the eastern side of the Gulf of Urabá, and they saw smoke rising from the opposite coast near the site of San Sebastián. The people at La Antigua responded with similar smoke signals, and some hours later two vessels anchored on the western shore of the gulf not far from the town. The ships were commanded by Rodrigo Enríquez de Colmenares, one of the lieutenants of Nicuesa, who had been left behind in Española to collect supplies and recruits, and now he was sailing along Tierra Firme with provisions, arms, and sixty men, searching the coast for Governor Nicuesa. Sailing south from Española, Colmenares had reached the mainland east of Calamar, near where Rodrigo de Bastidas, in 1525, founded the city of Santa Marta. A few years later, Colmenares reported in Spain that he had stopped to explore the coast in front of the Snowy Mountains—Sierra Nevada de Santa Marta—where he made the common mistake of fighting the Indians, who killed about fifty Spaniards, a fact he was careful to conceal from the king.

Colmenares arrived at La Antigua about the middle of the month of November, 1510, and his men were well pleased to find such comfortable quarters after their losses at Santa Marta and viewing the forbidding ruins of San Sebastián. There is no record that Colmenares, as the lieutenant of Nicuesa, claimed possession of La Antigua. The logic which deposed Enciso for being out of his jurisdiction also would apply to Balboa and the other officials, none of whom belonged in this territory. Perhaps Colmenares feared Balboa and the settlers, as it was not in the interest of any faction of Ojeda's expedition to turn over the town to Nicuesa or any of his officers.

Colmenares was tactful, freely issued some supplies to the needy settlers, and received considerable respect as the lieutenant of the rightful governor. After some discussion among the leaders, the town officials agreed to send a committee (*procuradores*) along with Colmenares to look for Nicuesa in the direction of Veragua, and when found, invite him to come to La Antigua, on the eastern frontier of his domain, to govern the colony. There is no evidence that Balboa objected strongly to this arrangement. According to Peter Martyr, the greatest opposition came from the *Bachiller* Enciso and his friends.

The town designated Diego del Corral, another *bachiller* of law, and Diego Albítez, both enemies of Vasco Núñez, to accompany Colmenares.   To these two delegates the historian Oviedo adds the name of Francisco de Agueros.   In one of his own ships and a brigantine belonging to the colonists, Colmenares, with the ambassadors from La Antigua, sailed out of the Gulf of Urabá, turned westward around Cabo Tiburon, and searched the bays and inlets of the Caribbean coast for Diego de Nicuesa.

But where was the governor of Veragua all this time?

DIEGO DE NICUESA,
FIRST GOVERNOR OF VERAGUA

Diego de Nicuesa had sailed from Santo Domingo eight days after the departure of Alonso de Ojeda, or on 22 November 1509, according to another record; and as the coast of Veragua then was almost unknown, his pilots steered first to the Calamar-Urabá coast to get their bearings.   Turning west from there, Nicuesa passed by the shore of Darien looking for the Veragua River, as described by Christopher Columbus.   When found, he would not listen to the pilot Ribero who had been with Columbus in 1502, but continued past the mouth of the river; and the governor came to grief among the inlets and islands about the Chiriquí Lagoon.   The fate of this expedition furnishes one of the saddest tragedies of the Spanish conquest of the New World.

At one time, Nicuesa made a great blunder in leaving his ships and proceeding by land, an action condemned by the king when he heard of it.   After the usual shipwrecks, and deaths from starvation and by the Indians, Lope de Olano, chief lieutenant of Nicuesa, finally entered the Río Belén, near the river of Veragua.   Here the Christians made another attempt at settlement on the site of *Nuestra Señora de Belén,* so disastrous to Don Bartolomé Colón in 1503.

The pilot Ribero deserves especial mention, for it was he

who stole away from Nicuesa, found Olano in the Río Belén just as he had anticipated, and then went back and brought up his commander. Nicuesa showed his ingratitude and unfitness to command by putting Olano in chains and threatening the other officers. The natives deserted their villages, and without Indians and their corn, cassava, and other food products, the Christians could not subsist. Even the lure of gold was lacking, for it required labor to mine it. These early Spaniards, though always ready to endure unheard-of hardships to secure gold, were not looking for steady jobs at hard labor.

Belén soon was abandoned, and the survivors turned back east, retracing the route they had followed. Passing the mouth of the River of Alligators (Chagres River), Gregorio of Genoa, a sailor who had been with Columbus, told Nicuesa of a fine harbor near there which the old Admiral had named Puerto Bello, and where he had left an anchor sticking in the sand near a spring of cool water at the base of a tree. When Nicuesa entered the little bay, he found the anchor, spring, and tree, just as Gregorio had foretold. The Indians around Puerto Bello had food, but they objected to the Spaniards taking it, and killed about twenty of them. This was a fine harbor, but no place for the Christians to settle. The governor of Veragua hastened to get away from there and renew his search to the eastward.

Upon arriving at the Puerto de Bastimentos of Columbus, the name suggested provisions (*bastimentos*), and the hungry, weary Nicuesa exclaimed: "*Paremos aquí en el nombre de Dios!* "—" Let us stop here in the name of God! " His weary companions, seeing a lucky augury in his utterance, named the place Nombre de Dios, even before a landing was effected. Upon a hill near the shore, called the " Hill of Nicuesa " ("*en el cerro de Nicuesa* "), the governor erected a blockhouse and some rude huts, the beginning of a town which has been occupied by white men, Indians, or Negroes to the present day. This was in the latter part of the year 1510, for on 9 November 1510, Nicuesa wrote to the king a " long account " of his misfortunes and begged for immediate aid. Nicuesa must have enlisted most of his men in Spain, for they could not adapt themselves to conditions in the tropics. They died off so fast that the enfeebled survivors wearied of burying the dead. It was observed, writes Las Casas, that none died but when the tide was ebbing.

NOMBRE DE DIOS

Rodrigo de Colmenares, with the *procuradores*, sailed sixty or seventy leagues west from La Antigua. When seeing smoke ascending on shore, he approached a small island and there met some of Nicuesa's men hunting for food. They directed Colmenares to Nombre de Dios on the mainland, where he was welcomed by Nicuesa and his party with tears of joy. When Colmenares wrote an account of this to the king, he stated that only 200 men remained alive of the 580 who had started out from Santo Domingo with Nicuesa. Another writer fixes the number of survivors at one hundred, and still another chronicle states that only sixty men survived. Colmenares, with his tendency to blame his betters, declares that the failure and losses of Nicuesa were due to the false report made by Christopher Columbus, who had told the king that Veragua was the best and richest land in the world, and that for more than one hundred leagues, this coast was so forbidding and the land so poor that the Christians could not make a settlement.

As a matter of fact, Colmenares had not sailed farther west than Nombre de Dios, and the region thereabout was not the Veragua of the old Admiral. Furthermore, the Spaniards, a few years later, deserted both La Antigua and Acla and established themselves permanently at Nombre de Dios, which became the Atlantic terminus of the Camino Real across the Isthmus of Panama, and the " Treasure-House of the World," in the language of Sir Francis Drake.

The *procuradores* presented their invitation to the governor to go to La Antigua and make that town the capital of Veragua; and Colmenares distributed his provisions among the famished

Port and town of Nombre de Dios.

colonists. After delivering their message, the *procuradores* did not fail to negotiate with Nicuesa in order to promote their personal interests. They painted a gloomy picture of affairs in La Antigua under the supremacy of Balboa and his followers. Instead of pleading for the restoration of Enciso to the command of the settlement, the lawyer Corral obtained a promise from Nicuesa that he would be appointed *alcalde,* and that Albítez would succeed Hurtado as *alguacil mayor.*

The sudden change in his fortune, and the prospect of ruling a well-situated town, with *Cabildo* and citizens busy separating the natives from their gold, seem to have turned the head of Nicuesa. With the food brought by Colmenares the governor gave a sort of banquet to the ambassadors, at which, despite his tattered finery, he presided with all the grace of the accomplished courtier that he was. Holding aloft a roasted chicken, he skillfully carved it in mid-air with his sword, a feat of his former days when chief carver at the court of Don Enríque Enríquez, uncle of the king. From the depths of despondency, Nicuesa became arrogant and garrulous, perhaps induced by some good Castilian wine from the ship of his lieutenant, and declared that he would depose all the officials elected at La Antigua, seize all the gold, and punish the settlers for unlawfully taking the gold from his subjects. The governor of Veragua had experienced so much hunger, fatigue, and stress that it is only charitable to believe that he was not his normal self when he uttered these impolitic words.

In looking about the forlorn place, the *procuradores* came upon the principal lieutenant of Nicuesa, Lope de Olano, with chains on his ankles, grinding corn on a rock like an Indian woman preparing to make tortillas. Said Olano, " I sent relief to Nicuesa and rescued him from death on a desert island. Behold my recompense. Such is the gratitude the people of Darien may expect at his hands! "

Corral and Albítez took the warning to heart and hurried back to Antigua in the brigantine, taking along the feeblest of the colonists. Before a town meeting in La Antigua they related what they heard and saw in Nombre de Dios, and finished by saying: "A blessed change we have made in inviting this Diego de Nicuesa to the command. We have called in the stork to take the rule, who will not rest satisfied until he has devoured us." Even the most conservative citizens became indignant at the prospect of losing the gold they had acquired from the Indians.

In their confusion and alarm, the people again turned to their strong and resourceful leader, *Alcalde* Balboa. "You are cast down in heart," said he, "and so you might well be, were the evil beyond all cure. But do not despair; there is an effectual relief, and you hold it in your hands. If calling Nicuesa to Darien was an error, is not receiving him a greater one?" The logic of his words was irresistible, and the solution of their trouble was simple. The people determined not to receive Diego de Nicuesa.

The Oath in the Church

We now come to what appears to be a strange and unnecessary performance, but one characteristically Spanish at that period. Probably to feel sure that they could depend on the support of the colonists, Balboa and his adherents decided to require the people solemnly to swear to keep the agreement not to admit Nicuesa to La Antigua. They put a small carpet on the ground in the church and on that a cushion, above which was placed a cross, in imitation of a custom followed in some cities of Spain on Holy Thursday and Good Friday. At this improvised altar, Balboa, Zamudio, and the *regidores*, followed by the rest of the people, made oath not to receive Nicuesa as their ruler.

To make the obligation still more binding, the proceeding in the church, then called San Sebastián, was recorded by the notary, Hernando de Argüello, a friend of Balboa. When Oviedo came to Darien, in 1514, he saw and read this strange testimony and became acquainted with most of those who participated in the act. As practically all the colonists, including the town officials, did make this solemn obligation, this document should have been sufficient to prove that responsibility for the expulsion of Nicuesa could not be confined to Vasco Núñez. When Pedrarias, and Espinosa his chief judge, ruled La Antigua, the gravest charge they could bring against Balboa was that he was guilty of the death of Diego de Nicuesa, when accounts clearly established the fact that all the people (" *todos los moradores del pueblo* ") opposed receiving the rightful governor of Darien.

Lookouts (*atalayas*) were stationed on the coast to give warning of the approach of Nicuesa, and guards were placed at the landing (*desembarcadero*) to prevent the governor coming ashore.

Meanwhile, Nicuesa was reveling in his fool's paradise. Leisurely sailing toward his ready-made capital, he sent his *veedor*, Juan de Quicedo, in advance in a small boat to announce his coming. The governor now was feeling so fine that he stopped among the islands to steal some Indians. The Spaniards were helpless without the labor of the natives, and a few husky Indian slaves would help to reimburse Nicuesa for the money he had lost in his expedition.

NICUESA REFUSED ADMISSION TO LA ANTIGUA

Upon reaching La Antigua, Quicedo confirmed the report of the envoys concerning the cruelty and ingratitude of Nicuesa. The chronicle reads that Quicedo (Caicedo) had with him his wife, the only white woman mentioned as present in this expedition, and that both had reason to dislike the governor. " What folly is it in you," said Quicedo, " being your own masters and in such free condition, to send for a tyrant, the worst man in the world, to rule over you! "

Worse still for Nicuesa, if possible, Quicedo brought with him a letter from Lope to Olano, left in chains at Nombre de Dios, addressed to *Alcalde* Zamudio, who was a relative and fellow Biscayan. Olano complained bitterly of his treatment by

Nicuesa and the danger to his life, and warned the people of the promise of the governor to depose the officials and appoint Corral and Albítez to office in Darien. Quicedo enraged the Biscayans still further when he declared that Nicuesa intended to send all the *vizcaínos* to Nombre de Dios to build a fortress at that place.

It is regrettable that we do not have a clear and unquestioned narrative of what took place in Santa Maria de la Antigua at this time, especially the part taken by Vasco Núñez de Balboa, for during the remainder of his life he was charged by officials with causing the death of Diego de Nicuesa.

When Nicuesa, governor of Veragua, arrived in the port of La Antigua he serenely viewed the crowd assembled on the shore, and complacently went forth to receive, as he believed, a royal welcome from the people. Oviedo writes that Balboa awaited him with all the settlers of the town. He allowed Nicuesa to land, accompanied by a page; and the next day the rest of the party was permitted to come ashore. Balboa then took the governor to lodge in his house. Oviedo makes the improbable statement that Vasco Núñez entertained Nicuesa for fifteen or twenty days, eating at one table and both sleeping in the same bed.

One night when talking together, one Alonso Runielo being present, Balboa asked Nicuesa what he would give him to be invested with the crown of governor. To which Nicuesa replied that he would do whatever Balboa might order.

Vasco Núñez then said, " Señor, let us go to bed, because it is late and the people may see us together and become suspicious. At daybreak, your worship will go to your brigantines and tack back and forth along the coast, while Alonso Runyelo remains here in order that I can send him to tell you what you have to do." It seems that the two commanders had agreed that Balboa should find out the will of the people by popular vote. Men in favor of accepting Nicuesa could remain in the streets of the town; those opposed to Nicuesa should stay in their houses, under pain of death. According to the imaginative Runielo, Vasco Núñez did the contrary, by ordering those willing to receive Nicuesa to remain indoors.

In the meantime, Balboa sent Runielo to inform Nicuesa that he must keep on his ships, and trust nobody, except the *regidores* Diego Albítez, the *Bachiller* Alberto, Juan Vegines, and Estéban Barrantes. Soon after this the four *regidores* arrived at the shore, finding the governor at table. Nicuesa appeared on deck and inquired whether they wished him to land, or would they come aboard and dine with him.

" Señor, as your worship commands," replied Barrantes. And as Nicuesa did not wish to put the *regidores* to any trouble, for he was a polite courtier with elegant manners, he went ashore to confer with them.

At this moment, *Alcalde* Zamudio and *Regidor* Pedro Macaz, both *vizcaínos,* appeared on the scene.

" Why have you not gone, Señor Diego de Nicuesa? " inquired Zamudio, telling him that his presence there had detained the people from making an *entrada* in which they would have obtained gold to the amount of fifty thousand pesos. Nicuesa was so astonished that for a few moments he could not reply. Then he stated that since they wished him to go away, he would finish his meal, and, meanwhile, Zamudio should send for Hernando de Argüello, the notary, to witness that the people of La Antigua del Darien sent for him and that he came there on their petition. At this, Zamudio rushed at Nicuesa and grabbed him, crying for help; at which fifty armed men sprang from concealment among the trees and surrounded the governor.

When Nicuesa was seized, Runielo rushed off to inform Balboa, whom he found in his house calmly chatting with the enemies of the governor. Upon hearing the news from Runielo, Vasco Núñez replied, " Alonso Runyelo, your governor was given very poor protection." That evening, Zamudio and his crowd took Nicuesa to the Placel, at the mouth of the creek entering the sea, where Barrantes, Bartolomé Hurtado, and many others guarded him during the night. In the morning they put the unfortunate governor in a brigantine, poorly provisioned, and compelled him to go from the land, with six companions and seven mariners.

It is probable that Oviedo gathered this story from Runielo, who must have drawn on his imagination in relating it. Much of the tale is improbable, especially the residence of Nicuesa with Balboa for fifteen or twenty days, " eating at one table and both sleeping in the same bed." Balboa and the people were fixed in their determination not to admit Nicuesa to La Antigua, and it is unlikely that they would allow him to remain in the town for nearly three weeks. More than that, the alleged agreement between Balboa and Nicuesa, as reported by Runielo, was silly and impracticable. Oviedo's account of the proceedings on the beach is substantially in accord with the narrative by Bishop Las Casas.

The history by Las Casas of this event, so important in the life of Balboa, is more reasonable and we believe more accurate. When Vasco Núñez and the colonists met Nicuesa at the landing, the *procurador* of the people, as town crier, announced to the governor that he should go back to Nombre de Dios without putting foot on shore. Nicuesa was struck speechless by this unexpected demand, so different from the warm greeting he had anticipated. The governor asked the people to let him land, and they would talk the matter over, after which they could do with him as they willed. This request met with another refusal from the angry populace. Nicuesa then begged to be put in irons and imprisoned, for he would rather die among them than of starvation and arrow wounds in Nombre de Dios. As it was getting late, and darkness comes on quickly in Darien, Nicuesa withdrew from the shore and sailed out into the gulf.

The next morning the governor again approached the shore, hoping to find the people more friendly to him. Such proved to be the case; but no sooner had he landed than the whole crowd rushed toward him in a threatening manner. Forgetting his dignity of governor, Nicuesa took to flight along the beach, and being a noted runner and not burdened with fat, he soon distanced his pursuers. It seems to be a fact that at this point Balboa restrained the mob and rescued Nicuesa from their fury.

The sad plight of this cavalier excited the support of Vasco
Núñez, and he reprehended the people for their rudeness, and
curbed the anger of his fellow *alcalde,* Martín de Zamudio,
called Juan de Zamudio by Herrera.

Nicuesa reminded the colonists that he had expended twelve
thousand *castellanos* on his expedition, and asked to be received
as a companion if not as their head.   To this, they replied that
he would come in by the sleeve and go out through the opening
for the head, referring to the proverb which says, " *Entra por
la manga, y sale por el cabezon,*" which originated in the ancient
ceremony of adoption by passing the child or person through a
wide sleeve of a shift.

Balboa, who cherished no personal enmity toward Nicuesa,
now pleaded with the crowd to let the governor remain.   When
Francisco Benítez, a loud-mouthed intimate of Zamudio, kept
urging the populace not to admit so bad a man as was Nicuesa,
Vasco Núñez commanded that he be given one hundred lashes,
a sentence immediately put into effect, thereby making a mortal
enemy of him.   This Benítez, when notary in Acla, eight years
later, arrested Luis Botello, messenger of Balboa, and helped
materially to bring about the death of the *adelantado.*   Seeing
that he could not suppress the anger of the people, Balboa hurried Nicuesa aboard his brigantine, leaving him with strict injunction not to venture on land unless he saw his face in the
crowd.

The colonists dispersed, and apparently the governor planned
to make another and more strenuous effort to remain in La
Antigua.   This account relates that Nicuesa sent a body of his
cross-bowmen to hide in a canebrake close to the landing, and
to shoot anyone opposing him when he should give the signal.
" *Sacó poco fruto desto,*" writes Herrera; he reaped little benefit
from this procedure, and it is not probable that the *ballesteros*
would have injured their friends and countrymen in Antigua.
After a time, Estévan de Barrantes, Diego de Albítez, and
Juan de Vegines appeared on the shore and represented themselves to be a delegation from the colonists.   They declared
that the people had conferred on the affair and now were sorry

for their incivility. If Nicuesa would pardon their previous resistance, the colony was ready to receive him for governor.

Disregarding the warning of Vasco Núñez, Nicuesa eagerly came ashore, where he fell into the hands of Zamudio and his adherents, who had been concealed in the thickets. They ordered him to leave at once, under pain of death, and not stop until he appeared before the king and the lords of his council in Castile. The governor protested such cruelty, and declared that the settlers in La Antigua had no right to be there without his license, which was true, according to accepted belief. Nothing he said could check the rage of the people. They put Nicuesa on the worst brigantine in the port, not the one in which he arrived at La Antigua; hurriedly added a few supplies, and on 1 March 1511, forced him to sail away. Witnesses stated afterward that they heard Nicuesa exclaim, with tears, " *Ostende faciem tuam, Domine, et salvi erimus* "—" Show Thy face, O Lord, and we shall be saved."

This chronicle states that seventeen persons, faithful to their chief, departed with Nicuesa. It never was known where the party went nor how the people perished. The crazy craft may have foundered at sea within a few days. We know that Nicuesa did not return to Nombre de Dios, where he had left the last remnant of his expedition in charge of Gonzalo de Badajoz. No doubt the governor wished to report to the king as soon as possible, and seek redress for being expelled from his territory by a band of interlopers. He may have steered direct for Española and brought up on the shores of Cuba, where the currents carried so many vessels; and there was a rumor that the unfortunate Nicuesa was killed by the natives of that island. It is possible that the helpless governor of Veragua (soon to be called *Castilla del Oro*) endeavored to go back to Belén, near which region was found, so it was reported, the following inscription carved in the bark of a tree:

" *Aquí anduvo perdido el desdichado Diego de Nicuesa.*"
(" Here wandered lost the unfortunate Diego de Nicuesa.")

There was still another story to the effect that Nicuesa had sailed to the bay of Cartagena, fatal loadstone of many early navigators, from which to lay a course to Santo Domingo. Indeed, some Indians reported that Nicuesa stopped there to seek corn and fresh water, and that the natives had killed the entire party " in satisfaction of the Indians that he had killed there when he aided Alonso de Ojeda."

The different narratives of the expulsion of Nicuesa, the essentials of which I have given, clearly show that a very large majority of the colonists at Antigua del Darien, including the deposed Enciso, *Bachiller* Corral, and Captain Francisco Pizarro, were opposed to receiving the governor. Nicuesa had boastingly declared that he would punish the intruders, oust all officials, and seize their gold; and the people needed no instigation or *maña* from Vasco Núñez de Balboa to refuse to recognize Diego de Nicuesa. Many of them, under the leadership of *Alcalde* Zamudio, were so enraged against him that they might have resorted to arms; for it seems to be established that Balboa, after a time, did favor the plea of Nicuesa to be admitted as a citizen. That Vasco Núñez became friendly to Nicuesa is proved by his punishment of Francisco Benítez for his rabid opposition to the governor, thereby making a mortal enemy of Benítez. There is no record that Colmenares, the lieutenant of Nicuesa, made any effort whatever to support his chief; nor did he offer to share his fortune when he sailed from Darien.

To receive Nicuesa was introducing another disturbing factor into the agitated settlement, and, practically speaking, the wisest thing to do for the continuance of the colony, the only one on the continent, was to send away the incompetent and impolitic governor. To exculpate themselves, the lawyers Enciso and Corral, and Colmenares, made the charge that Balboa was responsible for the death of Diego de Nicuesa. Later on, Pedrarias and his officials, all enemies of Balboa (except Bishop Quevedo) kept alive the accusation, although *Alcalde Mayor* Espinosa investigated the affair, and on 30 November 1514, wrote to King Ferdinand that everybody in La Antigua was involved in excluding Nicuesa—" *todo el pueblo es culpante.*"

That Nicuesa was forced to leave Darien in a poorly equipped brigantine was simply another example of his general ill luck. These small vessels were crudely made, usually inadequately equipped, and soon were devoured by the sea worms in those waters. The brigantine of Nicuesa was good enough to sail to Antigua and was no worse than many others used by these early Spaniards. In fact, it was not so bad as the one in which sailed Quicedo, Colmenares, and Valdivia to Santo Domingo in the following year.

Had Diego de Nicuesa been of sterner stuff, such as the successful *conquistadores* were made of, he would have returned to Nombre de Dios and kept up the struggle. No doubt he feared his own people there—Gonzalo de Badajoz, Lope de Olano, Alonso Núñez de Madrid, and others. In a long letter, dated 9 November 1510, to King Ferdinand, sent in a caravel from Nombre de Dios, Nicuesa had related his misfortunes and urgently appealed for help. It was reasonable to believe that the king would respond to this appeal, and such was the case. Ferdinand commanded the Almirante Diego Colón and other officials at Santo Domingo to aid Nicuesa, and wrote a letter to the latter that he had directed Juan de Esquivel, who had just settled on Jamaica, to compel the Indians to till many *conucos* and send all the provisions that he could to Tierra Firme.

We have been following the old records which state that Diego de Nicuesa was expelled from his own territory by the settlers at La Antigua. Just what was the right and title of Nicuesa, under his agreement with the king, to settle, exploit, and govern Darien, Panama, and Veragua " to the end of the land where lastly was the Admiral Cristóbal Colón "? Unless we admit that the king of Spain acquired a good title to the West Indies and Tierra Firme by gift from the Pope of Rome, representing the Creator, we are compelled to deny that Diego de Nicuesa possessed any right whatever to Darien and the country west of the Gulf of Urabá. Really, the only claim of Nicuesa to this region was the so-called right or title by conquest, which he had failed to establish. Nicuesa had been unable to conquer, hold, and settle any part of this large territory. On the other hand, the colonists under Balboa seized and held the town of Antigua del Darien and surrounding region by force of arms, a title still recognized in the chancelleries of the nations as the strongest claim to have and to hold specific areas of the earth's surface.

Nombre de Dios, once a famous town and port, settled by Diego de Nicuesa in 1510, nearly the same time as La Antigua, still persists as a habitation for man. In 1597, by command of Felipe II, the place was abandoned as the northern terminus of trans-Isthmian traffic, when trade and travel moved farther west to the new town of Puerto Bello, nearer the mouth of the Chagres River. Another reminder of Nicuesa is the island called Escudo de Veragua, formerly known as Escudo de Nicuesa.

Diego de Nicuesa, a nice man and polished courtier, was simply impossible as governor and captain general of an expedition to explore, conquer, and exploit a strange country peopled by hostile Indians. The basic fault goes back to the court of Spain, where so many wrongs in America originated, either from the ignorance and bigotry of Ferdinand of Aragon, or the favor or enmity of Juan de Fonseca.

One ray of light illumines this gloomy picture. Gonzalo Fernández de Oviedo y Valdés, a pious man who pretended to much knowledge of such things, declared that the expulsion and mortal exile of Diego de Nicuesa proceeded from divine clemency in part atonement of his faults, that he might go better prepared in the way of salvation.

But how about the five or six hundred men of his expedition who suffered and died by reason of Nicuesa's incompetence and unfitness to command?

II

BALBOA EXPELS ENCISO AND BECOMES
HEAD OF THE COLONY

" The first thing we do, let's kill all the lawyers "!
—*King Henry VI*, SHAKESPEARE.

WHEN Nicuesa was exiled from La Antigua, discord among the colonists did not cease. Having expelled the legal governor of the territory, why not get rid of that trouble-making lawyer Enciso, the pretender to and usurper of authority?

The *Bachiller* Enciso had sailed from Española about the month of September, 1510, with men and supplies for his chief, Alonso de Ojeda. The same month he met Francisco Pizarro in the bay of Calamar (Cartagena), fleeing from the envenomed arrows of the Indians besieging San Sebastián. The *alcalde mayor* insisted that the party of Pizarro accompany him back to the deserted settlement, much against the wishes of Pizarro and his enfeebled men.

The Gulf of Urabá was the western limit of the territory granted to Ojeda, and proceeding farther would bring Enciso to the region assigned to Diego de Nicuesa, then called Veragua in the *asiento* of 1508, where the *bachiller* would have no jurisdiction. Enciso's ship, as we know, struck upon some rocks and went to pieces; but he and his men made the eastern shore of the gulf and continued on foot to San Sebastián.

When, on advice of Balboa, the *alcalde mayor* did settle in the domain of Nicuesa, he maintained that he was the legally constituted commander of the settlers at Darien. When the Spaniards formed a town government and ignored Enciso, they said, truly, that they were in the territory belonging to Nicuesa, that Enciso did not receive his commission as *alcalde mayor* from the king, but only from Alonso de Ojeda. Even this commission had been lost in the shipwreck. Furthermore, they declared that, should Ojeda himself come to Darien, he would have no authority over them.

Those were eventful days in La Antigua del Darien. A secret inquiry (*pesquisa secreta*), probably instigated by Vasco Núñez, was made against the *Bachiller* Enciso and regular charges preferred against him as a usurper of authority and for tyrannical acts, especially in prohibiting private trade with the natives. Enciso was ordered to leave the colony, and seek redress, if he chose, from Viceroy Diego Colón at Santo Domingo, or proceed to Spain and solicit the king himself. The charges against Enciso were drawn up in due form and the *proceso* sent to Spain, doubtless with *Alcalde* Zamudio, who departed in the same boat in which Enciso was sent away. Balboa, the dominant figure in Darien, was neither shrewd nor clever in sending his chief rival and enemy to the court to defend his acts. A wicked and less scrupulous man would have brought about the death of the *alcalde mayor*.

There are different versions extant of what took place in Darien at the time. One account relates that Enciso had been imprisoned before the arrival of Nicuesa, whose acceptance by the people of Antigua would put an end to his own claims to rule the colony, he being *alcalde mayor* of Ojeda, governor of Urabá. If Nicuesa had been received, Colmenares would have been second in authority, Lope de Olano having been deposed by his chief.

The historian Oviedo says that Enciso was confined on a brigantine and sent away before the banishment of Diego de Nicuesa. Colmenares was in Darien at the time, and states that the *Bachiller* Enciso was sent away after Nicuesa was exiled from Antigua, in one of the vessels that he (Colmenares) had brought to Darien.

We learn more of what took place in La Antigua from the complaints against Balboa made by Enciso when he reached Spain. The *bachiller* charged that a *monipodio* (combine) was made against him by Vasco Núñez de Balboa, Benito Palenzuelos, Bartolomé Hurtado, a *bachiller médico,* and Barrantes, with about twenty other persons; and that the men secretly stole the *bergantines* in the port. He declared that in the absence of the said Enciso and against his will, they elected for *alcaldes* the said Vasco Núñez de Balboa and Benito Palenzuelos; and for *regidores* Juan de Valdivia, Martín de Zamudio, and Diego Albítez; and for *alguacil,* Bartolomé Hurtado; and for treasurer the *bachiller médico.*

These men seized the rods of government and issued an order to the said *alguacil* (constable) Bartolomé Hurtado that he seize the brigantines and boats with all that the said *Bachiller* Enciso possessed; as well as all the gold taken from the Indians, which was delivered to the bachelor of medicine that they had made treasurer. Enciso affirms that when he knew of the said election, he demanded that these men make no use of their offices, since they had neither power nor license for it, and, above all, not to take the gold. If they wished to divide the gold, they should lay aside the fifth part of it as the king's share, and the remainder to be divided into three parts; two parts to be given to the *Bachiller* Enciso, the one for the ships, and the other for the food and arms. The remaining third part they might dispose of in compliance with the capitulation with the said Ojeda. Enciso also made demand for the return of the ships and all that they had taken, and because he made this requisition, they seized him and put him in irons and cast him into prison, as if he were an ordinary malefactor, making his life very hard, so that he might die and they remain with all the gold they had taken.

Knowing that lawyer Enciso, upon reaching Spain, would complain to Ferdinand and his council, the *Cabildo* sent *Alcalde* Zamudio along in the same boat to act as *procurador,* or attorney, for Antigua del Darien, and to defend the action of the people in denying the authority of Enciso and setting up a municipality. In all ages and among all peoples, gold has facilitated access to ranking officials and those in power. It is stated that Zamudio carried with him some finely worked pieces of Indian jewelry with which to aid and promote the success of his mission.

Still another official departed from Darien at this time, in the same vessel with Enciso and Zamudio. On account of the failure of the crops about La Antigua, Juan de Valdivia, one of the *regidores* of the town, went as far as Santo Domingo to seek provisions and more men for the colony. Valdivia had been a neighbor to Vasco Núñez in the town of Salvatierra on Española, and was one of his reliable friends. One account states that he carried to the officials at Santo Domingo the *proceso* against the *Bachiller* Enciso. It is said that Balboa sent an especially fine present to Miguel de Pasamonte. No one in the Indies could expect favor or reward without greasing the itching palms of the king's favorite and treasurer-general of the Indies.

Regidor Valdivia, and *Alcalde* Zamudio, likewise a friend of Balboa back in Salvatierra, agents of the *Cabildo* and people at La Antigua, related their story to Viceroy Diego Colón and made known the needs of the colony in Darien. The Admiral had not heard of the loss of the ship of Enciso loaded with supplies intended for the colonists of Nicuesa. Consequently, he gave a favorable reception to the two delegates from the struggling settlement on the mainland of the Indies, which he claimed fell within his jurisdiction. Diego Colón wisely decided that the colonists of La Antigua required immediate assistance, and a strong man, like Balboa, at the head of it to establish and maintain a stable government on Tierra Firme. In support of his own claim, he appointed Balboa his representative and captain in Darien.

BALBOA NAMED ACTING GOVERNOR OF DARIEN

On 10 September 1511, Don Diego Colón wrote to Ferdinand telling him what he knew of the doings of Ojeda and Nicuesa, and informed the king that he had named Vasco Núñez to be his lieutenant on the mainland. The king not only approved of the action of Diego Colón, but on 23 December 1511, issued a royal *cédula* appointing Vasco Núñez de Balboa *gobernador interino,* or acting governor, of Darien.

This is the earliest royal commission empowering Balboa to rule in Darien, a copy of which appears elsewhere in this book. A still more imposing *cédula,* or commission, to Balboa was issued at Burgos, 31 January 1512.

In reply to the viceroy's letter from Santo Domingo, dated 10 September 1511, King Ferdinand stated that while the members of his council were determining if the government of the Firm Land belonged to Diego Colón, it would be a service to him if the viceroy extended all the favor and aid and service that he could to the persons who were or might be in the said Tierra Firme. The king informed the viceroy that he did well naming Vasco Núñez de Balboa to command in Darien until such time as he, the king, should provide a person to take charge of those people.

Viceroy Colón favored Valdivia in obtaining recruits and supplies for the settlers at Antigua, nevertheless, it was nearly six months before the *regidor* sailed in two ships for Darien. It is probable that tropical storms and hurricanes delayed his departure. So far, Valdivia and Zamudio had been successful in their negotiations at Santo Domingo with Viceroy Colón and Treasurer-General Pasamonte. Juan de Valdivia would return to La Antigua with supplies, and *Alcalde* Zamudio had to continue on to Spain to intercede with the king to favor Balboa and supply him with more men and provisions.

Ever since the discovery in 1492, the natives of Española had been melting away under the harsh rule and Christianizing efforts of the white men. The spread of " *la Santa Fe Católica,*" so much vaunted in hundreds of Spanish documents, may have saved a few souls, but it rapidly disposed of the bodies of the Indians. Of the million, more or less, natives on Española at the coming of the Europeans, the great majority had disappeared by 1512. Thousands of Indians were wantonly killed, or died off in servitude from the hard labor required of them by the Spaniards. Nearly everything brought by the white men and every requirement of their conquerors were inimical to the welfare of the Indians. The white man's diseases, especially smallpox, demanded a heavy toll in native lives. The golden jewelry and ceremonial pieces belonging to the Indians, the slow accumulation of centuries of primitive mining and fabrication, soon were appropriated by the gold-loving Spaniards. The shallow placer washings also became exhausted, and no rich deep mines were developed. All the Indians had been divided among the conquerors, and there were no more *repartimientos* to be distributed, except such as became vacant by death of the holders, or by decree of the viceroy or courts.

The growing of sugar cane was not yet a profitable industry in the West Indies. Gold still remained the lure of the Spaniards on Española. As the output of the mines lessened, more labor was required to extract the gold. To secure more slaves to work the mines and fields, the Spaniards raided the Lucayas, the Carib Islands, and coast of Tierra Firme; branded the captives and sold them in the slave market at Santo Domingo or other towns on the island. Spaniards on Española were becoming poorer, and paying less and less into the royal treasury. This is one reason why King Ferdinand promoted the expeditions of Nicuesa and Ojeda to settle and explore the continent, with the hope that they would discover rich mines and reap another harvest of gold. On express command of the king, and much against his will, Diego Colón had furnished hundreds of men from the Spaniards on Española and large quantities of supplies to both Nicuesa and Ojeda, the two leaders who had been granted vast territories on Tierra Firme. Under the terms of the *capitulación* made with his father, Christopher Columbus, the viceroy claimed that these lands should be included in his jurisdiction.

Spaniards from Española had participated in the conquest and settlement of the island of San Juan (Puerto Rico), and at this very time men were leaving Española and passing over to Cuba and Jamaica. There was a tendency to desert Española and try their luck on some other island or on Tierra Firme.

The many debtors were forbidden to leave Española until they settled with their creditors.

It is not very probable that Viceroy Diego Colón, Governor of Española and High Admiral of the Ocean Sea, shed many tears when he learned of the complete failure of the expeditions of Nicuesa and Ojeda. The remnants of their followers were now at Antigua del Darien or at Nombre de Dios, and Diego Colón had just named Vasco Núñez de Balboa, the strongest man on Tierra Firme, to be his captain and acting governor. Moreover, the king wrote that he did well in appointing Vasco Núñez to be his lieutenant on the mainland, and requested him to see that the colonists in Darien were supplied with arms and provisions.

Apparently the *Bachiller* Enciso did not receive a very cordial reception from Diego Colón, Miguel de Pasamonte, or even from the judges of appeal at Santo Domingo. He continued on to Spain to seek redress in a higher court. In the same boat with Enciso, Zamudio and Valdivia from La Antigua, went an important letter to the king, written by that Juan de Quicedo, *veedor* of Nicuesa, who preceded his chief to La Antigua and was largely instrumental in stirring up the populace against Nicuesa. From subsequent acts of Ferdinand it is reasonable to believe that Quicedo gave a truthful narrative of Nicuesa's expedition, and that it was the first complete account that the king had received of that ill-fated party. This letter accompanied Enciso and Zamudio in the next fleet sailing for Spain from Santo Domingo.

After Spain became established in the West Indies, intercommunication was carried on between the city of Sevilla, up the Guadalquivir River, and Santo Domingo, the chief city and capital of Española. Vessels were forbidden to sail from other ports. The House of Trade of the Indies (*La Casa de la Contratación de las Indias*) at both Sevilla and Santo Domingo despatched the ships and regulated the commerce back and forth. Vessels could not voyage singly, but had to sail in pairs or greater number, so that they could help each other in case of need. It was forbidden to overload the ships, and they were required to carry experienced pilots and follow prescribed courses. At times, communication between Spain and the Indies was interrupted for months by reason of the scarcity of ships, calms or storms, and an occasional shipwreck.

Soon after Enciso and Zamudio reached Santo Domingo, three vessels set out for Spain. On one of these, the ship named *Buenaventura,* went Martín de Zamudio, *alcalde* of Santa Maria la Antigua. Zamudio, usually represented as being a ruffian, must have borne a good reputation among the officials of His Highness while living in Española before going to Darien, for they trusted him to retain and carry to Spain the 1277 *pesos,* 6 *tomines* and 10 *granos* of *guanin,* or native gold, in divers pieces, which he had brought from Darien. It was the custom to turn in all the gold collected in the Indies to Treasurer-General Pasamonte, who shipped it to Spain by regular channels.

The little fleet must have reached Spain early in November, 1511. On 21 November, we find Zamudio in Sevilla, from which he departed on 3 December for the court, then at the old city of Burgos. Upon arrival of the ships from the Indies, the officials at Sevilla, on 17 November, sent to the king, by the royal courier, Collantes, the letters and reports from overseas. On 27 November, King Ferdinand wrote to the officials of the Indies House in Sevilla acknowledging receipt of the letters from the Indies, which reached him at Burgos, up in Old Castile, on 23 November 1511, at eleven o'clock in the forenoon. On that same day, 27 November, the king started Collantes back to Sevilla with the royal dispatches. On 23 December, the king wrote to the Admiral Diego Colón and officials at Santo Domingo that he saw the relation of affairs on Tierra Firme that they sent to him, and that he determined to order that they be suitably provided for; in the meantime, they should send to the people at Antigua all the supplies and other things they might require.

This same month, December, the king again wrote to the officials of the *Casa de la Contratación* in Sevilla that he saw what his officers of Española wrote about the things that had happened in Darien, that the colonists of Villa del Darien had elected for governor and *alcalde mayor* one Vasco Núñez de Balboa, a person with whom all were satisfied. The king also wrote that he noted their opinion of Balboa and thought well of it, and would command that the said Balboa be in that office until he ordered and provided another person for it. Meanwhile, they should encourage the merchants on Española to send supplies to Darien, and if any ship with merchandise left for the said province of Darien, they should send to *la Villa de Santa María de la Antigua* some arms of the kind best suited for those settlers, and in such quantity as might appear to be necessary.

ALCALDE ZAMUDIO DRIVEN FROM THE COURT

Alcalde Zamudio, delegate of the *Cabildo* and people of La Antigua, accompanied Enciso to Spain to refute the claim of the lawyer to be head of the colonists in Darien. La Antigua del Darien was in the territory granted to Diego de Nicuesa, and the Spaniards in La Antigua claimed, rightfully we believe, that the lawyer Enciso, *alcalde mayor* of Alonso de Ojeda, had no legal right to exercise his office in Darien, which fell within the jurisdiction of Governor Nicuesa, then called Veragua. Zamudio arrived at the court in Burgos and proceeded to defend the action of the colonists at La Antigua in setting up a municipality, and to plead for the appointment of Vasco Núñez for governor of Darien. Doubtless he relied much on being supported in his pleas by letters from Miguel de Pasamonte, to whom he had delivered the presents from Balboa. Perhaps he should have carried the golden ornaments to Spain and invoked their magic power nearer the court. Zamudio soon found that he was opposed by Bishop Fonseca, who for many years was omnipotent in affairs of the Indies. Juan Rodríguez de Fonseca, principal chaplain to Ferdinand, the powerful prelate of many bishoprics, died in 1524, bishop of Burgos. He never was bishop of Valencia, and did not die in 1547, as stated in one of our standard works of reference.

The *Bachiller* Martín Fernández de Enciso had received little recognition from the viceroy and officials on Española, but upon reaching Spain he found receptive soil for his charges against Balboa and his adherents. Enciso was supported by the all-powerful Fonseca, and Zamudio was given little opportunity for a hearing in order to present his side of the case. Indeed, so bitter was the feeling against him excited by Enciso that a warrant was issued by the Council of the Indies for the imprisonment of Zamudio, and he was compelled to flee from the court, and keep in hiding for a long period of time. Zamudio had been regularly appointed *procurador,* or attorney, by the town of La Antigua to present their side of the case, which he attempted to do. He deserves credit for his honesty and for not succumbing to the prevailing animosity toward Balboa, like Quicedo and Colmenares the next *procuradores* from Darien, who followed him to court.

It was not until 1516, after the decease of King Ferdinand, that Zamudio is heard from again, when he demanded pay from the citizens of Santa Maria de la Antigua as their *procurador* for more than twenty-six months, from the time that he departed from Darien to the date of the appointment of Quicedo and Colmenares who succeeded him, thereby relieving him of his commission. Zamudio charged that certain fields and a house lot in La Antigua had been delivered to Pedro de Bazozábal (probably by Pedrarias Dávila). Also, he demanded his share of the gold collected by the colony. We know of no document recording any remuneration to *Alcalde* Martín de Zamudio for his services as solicitor for the town of Antigua del Darien, or compensation for the loss of his property.

At this time, the king and his advisers in Spain regarded the then known coast of the mainland of the New World as one extensive territory, to which Enciso had been named *alcalde mayor.* The Spaniards in Darien, led by Balboa, claimed that Ojeda's grant, Urabá, lay east of the Gulf of Urabá, and Nicuesa's land was west of the gulf. Basically, it was a matter of ignorance of the true geography and cartography of those regions, and goes back to the *asiento*, or treaty, of 9 June 1508, by which two rival and ambitious courtiers were given joint grants in an ill-defined territory. This document was well calculated to initiate strife and misunderstanding between the members of the two expeditions. When Enciso went back to Spain in November 1511, he had no thought of returning to Tierra Firme, and was not particular, to say the least, about what he said of those persons in Darien who opposed him. I believe that the *bachiller* deliberately and intentionally misled the king and his officials concerning the geography and relative positions of Urabá, San Sebastián, Darien, and Santa María de la Antigua. These localities were, and still are, situated in what I have called a critical and confusing angle of the coast line of the continent—a stretch of Caribbean shore later forming a section of the Spanish Main.

The charges of Enciso as repeated in a royal *cédula*, dated 28 July 1513, are full of falsehoods. To give only one instance, he declares that at the time he arrived at " *Santa María del antygua del Darién*," he found burnt the fortress constructed in the said town of Darien—" *alló quemada la fortaleza que estaba fecha en el dicho pueblo del Darién*." Enciso was a lawyer and doubtless drew up the charges himself. He knew very well that the fortress, or blockhouse, was not in the town of Darien (Antigua), but in San Sebastián across the Gulf in Urabá, which had been burnt by Indians after the location was abandoned by Francisco Pizarro; a fact which Enciso does not mention in his accusations. Enciso would have come to grief by remaining at San Sebastián had he not followed the advice of Balboa, the *hombre del casco*, and passed over to Darien on the west shore of the gulf. In addition to his charges against Vasco Núñez and his consorts, the *bachiller* presented itemized bills for his losses in Darien and expenses incurred in his journey to Spain. Aided by the bishop of Burgos, the bills were allowed by the officials and he was compensated out of the royal treasury for all the damages he claimed to have suffered, at one time receiving 38,000 *maravedís*. Being a lawyer, and on account of his experience in the Indies, Enciso was included in a *junta* which drew up one of the many sets of " ordinances " for the treatment of the Indians, for which service he was paid 20,000 *maravedís*.

Queen Juana issued warrants or judgments in favor of the *Bachiller* Enciso against the council of the town of Santa Maria —" *la villa de Santa María delantigua del Darién* "—which were sent to Don Diego Colón, Admiral, Viceroy and Governor of the Island Española, for execution. About this time the Council of the Indies and learned jurists decided that the Darien region of Tierra Firme did not fall within the provisions of the concessions granted to Christopher Columbus in the *capitulaciones* of 17 April 1492, confirmed by subsequent acts. Accordingly, King Ferdinand, on 18 June 1513, wrote that Darien was without the jurisdiction of Diego Colón, and that the governor of Darien should execute the judgments, as if they had been directed to him—" *e no fagades ende al.*" On 13 September 1512, the king gave Enciso the office of *regidor* in Santo Domingo, provided he wait for the vacancy; and authorized him to carry five slaves to Española. Enciso may have planned to take five Guinea Negroes from Spain, or perhaps five Indians from Darien, or elsewhere. Enciso did not go to Santo Domingo, and the next we hear of this bachelor of law is when he appears as *alguacil mayor* on the staff of Pedrarias Dávila.

The departure of the weak and unfortunate Nicuesa, soon followed by the troublesome lawyer Enciso and Alcalde Zamudio, left Vasco Núñez in undisputed charge of the government of Antigua del Darien. Adherents of Nicuesa and Enciso, for the time, were suppressed.

Balboa's first care was to dispatch more provisions to the enfeebled remnant of Nicuesa's party left behind in Nombre de Dios. In his *carta*, 20 January 1513, Vasco Núñez wrote to King Ferdinand that he had sent them food on three occasions; and that a year and one-half previously he had brought those people to La Antigua, as it was obvious that they could not maintain themselves as a separate community, five or six dying daily. Upon arriving at La Antigua, these men shared in the distribution of town lots and lands for raising corn, cassava, and other foods.

Balboa sent Colmenares in two brigantines to Nombre de Dios to carry back all the Spaniards remaining alive. While returning along the coast of the province called Cueva (or Coiba), Colmenares encountered two Spaniards dressed and painted as Indians. These men (reported as three in one account) were seamen who had deserted the expedition of Nicuesa in the preceding year, when that unfortunate commander sailed westward along the Caribbean shore of the Isthmus in search of the Veragua of the old Admiral. The two white men were treated kindly and honored by Careta, chief of that district, one of the number, Juan Alonso by name, being appointed a *cabra,* or war chief. These deserters informed Colmenares that the chief possessed a goodly store of gold and was well supplied with provisions, and advised their countrymen to attack the cacique and loot the place. Careta was reported to have two thousand warriors, and Colmenares did not feel equal to raiding the village, so it was agreed that one deserter should return with Colmenares to tell Balboa all about the Indians, while Juan Alonso would remain with Careta and assist in betraying him.

The way so many Spanish commanders found interpreters on the spot when needed was simply devilish for the Indians, miraculous for the Christians, they claimed. The deserter had learned to speak the tongue of Cueva and was able to give Vasco Núñez much information of the country and of the natives. With the addition of the Spaniards from Nombre de Dios, all Europeans on the continent of America now, July, 1511, were assembled at Santa María de la Antigua del Darien under command of Vasco Núñez de Balboa. This settlement at Darien, due to Balboa, was the only result of ten years of discovery and attempts to colonize Tierra Firme. Juan de la Cosa and Diego de Nicuesa were no more, and Alonso de Ojeda wandered broken-hearted about the streets of Santo Domingo. All the gold and pearls so far filched from the Indians did not exceed in value the losses sustained by the various expeditions to the mainland of the New World. Attempts to settle at Belén in Veragua, Santa Cruz on Bahía Honda, San Sebastián in Urabá, and Nombre de Dios on the Isthmus of Panama, had ended in complete failure.

The growing population of La Antigua required more food to sustain it. Acting on the intelligence imparted by Colmenares and the deserter, Balboa set out with 130 men to pay a visit to Careta. One account states that Vasco Núñez marched overland, sending his two brigantines to the coast of Cueva to carry back the provisions he hoped to secure. Another record says that Balboa embarked his force on the boats, about October, 1511, and sailed westward twenty-five leagues to the port of Careta. Puerto Careta is inseparably connected with Balboa. It was the seat of Cacique Careta, whose proper name was Chima, loyal ally of Vasco Núñez, and the home of his beautiful daughter, whom I call Caretita, the sweetheart of Balboa. This port was the starting point and end of his memorable march to the South Sea, and the first transit of the Isthmus of Panama by Europeans. On the shore close by was an old Indian battlefield called *Acla*, because strewn with bones of men. This spot became the location of the town of Acla, rebuilt by Balboa as a base for the construction of his ships on which to explore the South Sea.

Balboa was received by Cacique Careta without resistance and courteously entertained in his village. To Balboa's demand for provisions, the chief replied that he never had denied food to Christians passing along his coast, but at that time he was without supplies because, being at war with his neighbor Ponca, his people had not been able to plant their fields. In proof of his words, Careta referred to the Spanish deserters who had been with him about eighteen months. Neither did he have any gold. The deserters told Balboa quite the contrary, and the traitor Juan Alonso advised Vasco Núñez to pretend to believe the chief and go away, but to come back by night and attack the town. Balboa acted accordingly, took cordial leave of the chieftain, and departed as if to go back to La Antigua. Returning quietly in the middle of the night, Vasco Núñez divided his force into three bands and surprised the sleeping natives, killing many of them and capturing the chief, with two of his wives and children, and many of his subjects. It is said that Juan Alonso seized his benefactor, the cacique, with his own hands—the act of a Judas Iscariot, writes the Bishop of Chiapa. Vasco Núñez made his captives bring forth their store of provisions and carry them to his brigantines. Loading all the Indians and supplies on his vessels, Balboa sailed back to La Antigua.

Cacique Careta felt his humiliation keenly and showed great respect for his conqueror. Like most of the chiefs encountered by the Spaniards, Careta was a man of much native intelligence and at once planned to obtain his release, and at the same time to benefit from association with these powerful white men who seemed determined to remain permanently in Darien. The quick-witted chieftain had not failed to note the impression made by his daughter Caretita upon the white commander. " What have I done to thee," said Careta to Vasco Núñez, " that thou shouldst treat me in this cruel manner? When thou camest to my *buhío* did I meet thee with a javelin in my hand? Set me and my people in liberty and we will remain thy friends, and cultivate the fields to supply thee with provisions. Dost thou doubt my faith? Take my daughter in pledge of friendship! "

Balboa could take the girl if he chose without any contract with her father, but the promise of Careta to furnish a constant supply of provisions appealed strongly to him. The colonists already held some Indian slaves, whom they had to guard. Instead of retaining his captives as slaves, Balboa deemed it wiser to turn them loose to be friendly neighbors producing food for the colony, and even allies in case of war with some hostile chief. This policy of making peace with the caciques, and receiving tribute in food, gold, and pearls, was the one usually followed by Balboa, and distinguishes him as superior to the majority of the *conquistadores*. Had his successor, Pedrarias, pursued the same method in dealing with the Indians, the Spanish conquest of Tierra Firme would not record so many blunders and butcheries.

It is said that Balboa entertained Careta for several days, showing him the brigantines and the arms and armor of the Spaniards. The chief was most impressed by the firing of the *falconetes*, the small ordnance of those times. While with Balboa, the cacique was given Christian baptism, being named Fernando, after the king. Before leaving La Antigua, the chief asked Balboa to aid him in a raid on Cacique Ponca. This chief, of course, possessed some provisions and gold, and would be worth a visit. Vasco Núñez promised to help his new ally, and reminded him to set his people to work raising food for the white men. On parting, Balboa delighted Careta by a gift of iron knives, hatchets, and other articles of Spanish manufacture.

Both Caretita and her father understood that she, as the daughter of a leading chief, would have the status of a wife, and not simply that of a concubine. According to Indian law and custom, a great chief like Balboa might have several wives, but they ranked as ladies (*espaves* in the language of Cueva) and possessed certain rights and dignities in the tribal organization. Whatever Vasco Núñez might have thought at the time, he became very fond of Caretita and valued her information and counsel. Caretita was wise for her years, and doubtless it was her influence which promoted the friendly relations between her people and the Spaniards at La Antigua.

Caretita remained with Vasco Núñez.

III

BALBOA HEARS OF THE SOUTH SEA AND
OF THE RICHES OF PERU

" Estrecho de tierra y no de agua."
—OVIEDO.

A BOUT this time, some affirmed that Balboa spoke of
yielding up the government of Darien to Nicuesa
should he return, while others believed it to be simply
a complimentary gesture, because his ability and valor compre-
hended greater things.

Soon after the treaty of peace and friendship with Cacique
Careta, Balboa took eighty men by sea to Coiba, where he
joined forces with Careta in invading the lands of Cacique
Ponca. The latter noted the alliance of his chronic enemy,
Careta, with the white Tiba in Darien, and fled to the mountains, leaving his houses to be sacked and destroyed. You may
be sure that the Spaniards took care of any golden objects left
behind by Ponca. Vasco Núñez then returned with Careta to
his village, where he was entertained by the chief for several
days.

Balboa, in his *carta* of 20 January 1513 to King Ferdinand,
writes that forty leagues west from Antigua del Darien, adjoining the lands of Careta, was the province of Comogre, ruled
by a chief of the same name. Cacique Comogre was lord of
over ten thousand subjects, and could muster three thousand
fighting men. He was not at war with Careta, and was advised
by a relative of the latter, called a *jura*, or wise man, then living with him, to come to terms of peace with the white invaders.
Comogre invited Balboa to visit him, and met the white commander at the boundary of his domain with much ceremony.
The chief was accompanied by seven fine sons, each begotten

72

by a separate wife, and many of his principal warriors and people. The Spaniards were conducted to the houses of the chief, and men and women assigned to serve food and wait upon them.

Comogre's dwelling, where Balboa was entertained, was surprisingly large and well constructed. The Spanish chronicles usually designate it a palace, and describe the building as one hundred and fifty steps in length and eighty in width, supported by great pillars, and the whole surrounded by a stone wall. The upper part, or attic (*zaquizamí*), was lined with beautiful fabricated wood. The edifice contained many compartments, some of which were for the storage of grain, roots, dried meat and fruits, and prepared food. In a retired part of the palace was a great hall, which served as a pantheon, wherein were preserved the dessicated cadavers of former chiefs of that province and ancestors of Comogre. The dried remains were covered with mantles of finely woven cotton, adorned with golden jewelry, pearls, and precious stones, and suspended from the ceiling with cotton ropes. The dead chieftains were held in great veneration; a species of ancestor worship.

Cacique Comogre had been informed of the love of the white men for gold, and to gain favor with them he presented Vasco Núñez with many beautiful gold pieces valued at four thousand pesos, and seven Indian slaves. The golden jewelry was weighed in the scales under the supervision of the *veedor,* the king's fifth reserved, and then came the distribution of the spoils among the soldiers. This gave rise to disputes and noisy wrangling among the Spaniards, much to the scorn of that highminded and valorous youth, Panquiaco, the eldest son of Comogre. Ashamed for having esteemed the white men as superior to such petty altercations, he expressed his disdain for their actions by striking the balance and scattering the gold pieces over the ground. Turning to the astonished Spaniards, he addressed them thus:

If you so love gold that to secure it you forsake your homes, and with
  " Christians! What means this? Why quarrel over such trifles?

so many fatigues and dangers come here to disturb the peaceful people of these lands, I will show you a province where you will be able to gratify your desire. But to do this, it is necessary that you be in greater number than you now are; for you will have to contend with great kings who will defend their lands with much courage and rigor. First you have to encounter King Tubanamá, who has abundance of this gold that you value so highly, distant from our domain of about six suns [" *que son seis días* "]."

Then pointing toward the south with his finger, the young cacique assured the white men that after crossing certain mountains, they would view another sea, on which dwelt people who navigated that sea in ships and *balsas* with sails and oars, only a little less in size than the Spanish ships. This great nation was so rich in gold that the people used large golden vessels in eating and drinking, and because Panquiaco had been informed that the swords and armor of the Spaniards were made of the metal called iron, so abundant in Vizcaya, he affirmed that those people possessed more gold than there was iron in all Biscay.

The speech of Panquiaco, eldest son of Cacique Comogre, was the first information received by the Spaniards of the existence of the Pacific Ocean, and of the location and culture of the rich empire of Peru. As writes Quintana, " These celebrated words, preserved in all the records of the time, and repeated by all the historians, were the first announcement that the Spaniards had of Peru." The famous words of that " prudent youth," Panquiaco, were interpreted by Juan Alonso and that other deserter who had lived with Careta, and it is probable that Balboa, during his frequent intercourse with the Indians, had learned considerable of the dialect of Cueva, spoken by these natives. We are told that when Diego de la Tobilla arrived at Darien in 1514, he investigated the utterance and affirmed the speech to be as given by the first historians, Peter Martyr and Las Casas. Oviedo, strange to say, does not give the speech of Panquiaco, although it was of so momentous import to the Spaniards.

The announcement of another great sea, heretofore unknown,

La Chorrera, a waterfall a short distance west of the Canal Zone.

Stacey C. Russell.

Darien Indian.

Photo by the Panama Canal.

bordered by wealthy nations, just to the south of Darien, was a crucial incident in the Spanish conquest. It determined the venture of Balboa, a few months later, to go in quest of that sea; it induced the parsimonious Ferdinand to expend large sums of money in the preparation of an armada for Castilla del Oro, and it directed exploration and conquest across this narrow " strait of land " ("*estrecho de tierra y no de agua*") to be continued up and down the Pacific shores of the new continent, leading to the conspiracy of Francisco Pizarro, Diego de Almagro, and Padre Luque to rob and overthrow the empire of the Incas.

The good news imparted by Panquiaco was received with unrestrained joy by Balboa and his companions, some even weeping for pleasure at the prospect of securing some of the wealth in gold possessed by the people living on the South Sea. The young chief added that if his words were found to be untrue, they could hang him on the nearest tree.

Vasco Núñez remained several days with Comogre, during which he made many inquiries about the new sea and the best way to reach it, and about the caciques along the route and the number of their warriors. Panquiaco told Balboa that he would need one thousand Spanish soldiers to conquer the fierce Tubanamá, and offered to act as guide and assist Vasco Núñez with all his father's fighting men.

In return for the hospitality of Comogre, the gift of gold and seventy slaves, and especially for what he learned from Panquiaco, Balboa directed the padre to baptize Cacique Comogre and his family. Panquiaco, destined to be the next chief of the tribe, was given the name of Carlos, in homage to the young prince soon to inherit the crowns of Ferdinand and of his mother, Juana Loca.

Well satisfied with the result of this *entrada* into the interior of the country, Balboa hastened back to Antigua in order to inform the admiral, Diego Colón, and the king of the wonderful news of the proximity of another sea; and of a rich and cultured people living on its shores. The colonists spoke of nothing but the South Sea, as portrayed by Don Carlos Panquiaco, and its gold and pearls, waiting to be seized by the pitiless hand of some daring robber.

BALBOA AGAIN SENDS VALDIVIA TO SANTO DOMINGO FOR SUPPLIES AND HIS SHIP IS WRECKED ON THE VÍBORAS

Balboa went back to La Antigua with the spoils of Ponca, the rich gifts of Comogre, and elated with what he had learned from Panquiaco. During his absence, the *regidor,* Juan de Valdivia, had returned from Española in a caravel loaded with provisions. Valdivia had sailed from Antigua about 4 April 1511, and had spent six months in negotiating with the officials at Santo Domingo, and perhaps had been delayed by tropical storms. Of more value even than the provisions to Vasco Núñez, was the commission from Diego Colón naming Balboa his lieutenant and captain on Tierra Firme. This gave him official endorsement and strengthened his command of the colonists.

About this time, November, 1511, the country was devastated and torn up by torrential rains and storms, which flooded the rivers and washed out the maize and other crops planted by the Indian slaves in the fields around La Antigua. The supplies brought by Valdivia would not last long, and soon famine would again menace the colony.

Valdivia had succeeded so well on his mission to Diego Colón that Balboa again sent him to Española, with letters to the Admiral informing him of the great news of another sea to the south of Darien, and of the rich and civilized nation reported by the son of Comogre. Vasco Núñez requested the viceroy to ask the king to furnish him the one thousand men considered necessary to fight a way to the South Sea. In the meantime, there was urgent need for more food on account of the loss of their growing crops. With Valdivia was forwarded the king's fifth, amounting to three hundred *marcos,* equal to 15,000 *castellanos,* which shows that Balboa had collected from the natives gold to the value of 75,000 *castellanos.* Many colonists intrusted their share of the gold to Valdivia, to be despatched from Santo Domingo to their families in Spain. As on the former mission of Valdivia, Vasco Núñez sent, *de secreto*, some choice pieces of Indian jewelry to Miguel de Pasamonte, the royal treasurer. The Licenciado Suazo at Santo Domingo wrote that Vasco Núñez had sent many Indian slaves to Pasamonte, as well as splendid gold pieces and other jewelry, which could be seen in his house.

The *regidor*, Juan de Valdivia, sailed from Antigua del Darien about 11 January 1512 (not 1511, as writes Peter Martyr), in the best caravel in port. On board the little vessel were sixteen men and two women, the latter apparently white women. The party never reached Española, and it was a long time before it was known that the voyage ended in disaster.

One account states that Valdivia was wrecked near Cabo Cruz, on the western end of Cuba, where all the Christians were killed by Indians. Months later, when the news reached the king, he wrote, on 4 July 1513, to Sancho de Matienzo, treasurer of the Indies House, to inquire into the loss of the 15,000 pesos; and to report to him whether it would be useful and profitable to erect a fort on the point of Cuba to insure the passage of those going to and coming from Tierra Firme, as well for the service of the Lord as for the increase of the royal exchequer. Bishop Las Casas, who went to Cuba with the first Spaniards invading the island, declared this report to be false, considering the kindness always shown the Spaniards by the cacique of that region, who was called *El Comendador*, or Knight Commander.

The true story of the loss of Valdivia became known in 1519, when Hernando Cortés arrived at the island of Cozumel, three leagues off the coast of Yucatán, on his way to conquer the empire of Mexico. At that island Cortés encountered Jerónimo de Aguilar, a survivor of Valdivia's party. He stated that the vessel on which they sailed from La Antigua had been wrecked on some rocks or reefs which he called the *Alacranes;* better known as the *Víboras*, or Vipers, near the south coast of Jamaica. The men and two women hurriedly escaped from the sinking caravel in the small boat (*batel*) but without oars, sail, food, or arms. They hoped the waves would land them on Jamaica or Cuba; instead of that the strong westerly currents bore them along for thirteen days, during which seven of the men died of thirst and hunger and were cast into the sea.

The nine men remaining and the women were stranded upon the shore of the province of Maya in Yucatán, where they were seized by the *Calachunis,* or chiefs of that region. We read that the women were set to work grinding maize, and soon died. The men were confined in a pen constructed of heavy logs and given plenty to eat and drink, and soon recovered their flesh and spirits. They had more and better food than if they had remained in Darien. One day the cacique and principal chiefs inspected the white strangers in the fattening pen, and selected Valdivia and four of his companions as being in prime condition to be eaten. These Spaniards were taken to their temples, and there sacrificed to the native gods by having their hearts cut out with obsidian knives. The bodies were dismembered, roasted, and given to the people to be eaten.

The remainder of the Spaniards heard the revelry of the religious *fiesta,* and knowing the fate in store for them, lost all further desire for food. At once they planned to make their escape, if possible, and trust themselves to fortune. Despair lent strength to their arms, and one night the four white men succeeded in moving the heavy logs and stealing away from the town. For some days they wandered through the woods until, forced by hunger, they approached a settlement and were again captured, fortunately by an enemy of their first master. This chief soon died and was succeeded by Cacique Taxmar, who spared the lives of his prisoners, but held them in the harshest servitude. In time, of the sixteen (or, perhaps, eighteen) men who had departed from Darien in Valdivia's caravel, only two remained. One of these was Gonzalo Guerrero, who was transferred to Nachancan, the *calachuni,* or lord of the province of Chetemal.

Guerrero was a robust mariner of Niebla, in Spain. He was able to bear the hard labor required of him and quickly adjusted himself to the life of the Maya. He made himself useful to his master, took part in his wars, and became a trusted captain. Nachancan offered him a lady of rank for a wife, and Gonzalo, being accustomed to seek a wife in every port, married the woman in native fashion, and they lived together very happily. He painted his face, bored his nose, lips, and ears, and dressed as an Indian.

MAYA INDIANS SPARE THE LIVES OF JERÓNIMO DE AGUILAR AND GONZALO GUERRERO

The other survivor of Valdivia's party was Jerónimo de Aguilar, a native of Ecija in Andalucía, a friar in minor orders. He had gone to the Indies in one of the voyages of Christopher Columbus, accompanied Nicuesa to Tierra Firme, and thus came to La Antigua with the remnant of Nicuesa's expedition. Aguilar humbly performed the hard tasks assigned to him by Taxmar. True to his vows, Aguilar closed his eyes to the charms of the pagan women. Observing that his slave paid no heed to the females, the chief took delight in subjecting him to many trials of his chastity. St. Anthony was no more sorely tempted by the Devil than was Aguilar by Cacique Taxmar. One beautiful moonlight night—and the moonlight is very alluring in Yucatán—his master ordered Aguilar to go to the seashore, so as to be ready to begin fishing at dawn. Taxmar sent along with him a pretty girl with a hammock to keep him company. Upon arriving at the edge of the sea, Aguilar suspended the *hámaca* between two trees, and withdrew to sleep on the beach. The girl threw herself in the swinging bed and bided her time. When the chill of night had cooled the sands, she called Aguilar to join her, telling him that they could sleep together. He replied that he would sleep on the sand. Again the little lady invited Aguilar to warm himself under her blanket. It was a trying situation for a man restrained by the vows of chastity. The sandy beach was cold and cheerless; the hammock warm and tempting, and the little wench solicitous. As instructed by the cacique, the buxom damsel used still further blandishments to break down the resistance of the obdurate foreigner, all of which failed to elicit any reaction from her comrade. Her pride abashed and her feelings ruffled, the girl fired a parting shot at Aguilar by telling him that he was no man, and composed herself to sleep. Aguilar acknowledged afterward that he vacillated many times, but conquered his desire and fulfilled his promise to God to have nothing to do with an infidel woman. At break of day, Aguilar began to fish, and the temptress went back to town, somewhat crestfallen at her failure to entice the stubborn white man from the path of virtue. She reported to the cacique the result of her trial, and when Aguilar returned with a string of fish, Taxmar appointed him to be in charge of his household and wives whenever he departed from the town.

Not satisfied with being the trusted *mayordomo* of Cacique Taxmar, the chaste Aguilar aspired to become a great warrior like his friend Gonzalo. He begged Taxmar to train him in the use of native weapons, and soon he became proficient in the use of bow and arrows, war club, and shield. A neighboring chief made war upon Taxmar, and Aguilar, with his European education, was able to draw him into an ambuscade and defeat him with great slaughter. This single victory made Taxmar the dominant lord in that region, and established Aguilar firmly in the good graces of his master. Despite his vows to the Church and his profession of piety, Aguilar, like many other churchmen coming to America, exhibited more activity in killing Indians than in seeking to save their souls. There is no record that Jerónimo de Aguilar, with all his knowledge of the language, life, and customs of the Maya, exerted himself to win the pagan souls to Christ by peaceful means and moral suasion, which was the specified purport of the papal license to the Spaniards to overrun the New World.

The years went by until 1517, when Aguilar heard of Christians sailing along the coast. This was the fleet of Francisco Hernández de Córdoba on a voyage of discovery from Cuba. The next year, 1518, the vessels of Juan de Grijalva stopped at the island of Cozumel, which he called Santa Cruz, a few leagues east of the mainland of Yucatán. These visits in force by white men greatly excited the natives, as there was general knowledge throughout the land of a prophecy uttered by a Maya priest named Chilam Balam that the nation would be conquered and their gods overthrown by a race of bearded white men, who would come in great ships from the region of the sunrise. Aguilar was aware that the Indians were watching him, and made no effort to escape to his brethren on the coast. The prophecy of the coming of a conquering white race was current also among the Aztecs, and accounts for the passive and vacillating policy of Montezuma in negotiating with Cortés when the latter landed on the shores of Mexico.

When Hernando Cortés, early in 1519, sailed away from Diego Velázquez, governor of Cuba, he carried instructions to be on the lookout for Christians said to be living among the Maya of Yucatán. On arriving at Cozumel, Cortés inquired of the islanders whether there were any white men in that region, and they told him there were two bearded strangers not far away on the mainland. Cortés had much need for interpreters in his daring undertaking and immediately dispatched a letter by some Indians to the white men living near Cape Catoche. Aguilar received the letter and freely showed it to his master, who looked upon it as magical and supernatural, because by it Aguilar was able to tell him all that his spies had been able to learn about the visitors in the big ships. Aguilar enlarged upon the might and power of his countrymen, and thoroughly alarmed the cacique, so that Taxmar became conciliatory and offered no objection to the departure of Aguilar, hoping that he would act as a friendly mediator with the powerful strangers.

The message of Cortés was sent on to Gonzalo Guerrero in the neighboring town of Chetemal. Gonzalo now was a great war chief, with wives and plenty of children. He was well satisfied with his lot, and declined to join Aguilar. The Spaniards explained his reluctance to leave his pagan splendor by saying that he was ashamed to appear among Christians with tattooed skin and his nose and ears pierced like an Indian. After waiting several days and Gonzalo not appearing, Aguilar, in response to the invitation of Cortés, set out with some Indians for Cozumel and reached the island just as the fleet was about to sail away.

Near Cabo Catoche, Aguilar found a stranded canoe, in which he and three Indians passed over to Cozumel. When they landed on the island, Andrés de Tapia and several other Spaniards advanced to meet them, sword in hand. The three Indians turned to flee, but Aguilar reassured them, and approaching Captain Tapia, exclaimed, " *Dios y Santa María y Sevilla.*" Falling on his knees, with tears streaming down his face, Aguilar thanked God for finding himself again among Christians. Tapia embraced the stranger, while one of the other Spaniards, named Angel Tintorero, rushed off to inform Cortés of the arrival of a Spaniard from the mainland, claiming the usual *albricias,* or reward, for bringing good news. Bernal Díaz, as our libraries card him, states that seven Indians, including Aguilar, were in the canoe which arrived at Cozumel.

Tapia conducted the party to Hernando Cortés, before whom the Indians, Aguilar included, bowed in reverence and squatted on the ground, placing their bows and arrows to the right of their bodies. Then they moistened the fingers of the right hand with saliva, touched the ground, and rubbed their chest over the region of the heart, this being the way they honored their princes. Early European writers generally called the natives of America, especially when encountered in the tropics, naked savages, and then they proceeded to describe what the Indians wore. In this instance, the Christian writers say that Aguilar was perfectly naked, and then go on to state that he was wearing a breech clout, an old sandal on one foot and the other sandal stuck in his girdle, and at his side a network bag containing some food and other small articles. This handy bag was the *chácara* of Central America, now in general use by white persons. A cotton mantle about his body completed his attire, very appropriate to his business and for the springtime in Yucatán. Aguilar's head was shorn like an Indian slave's and his skin was bronzed by the sun, so that he so much resembled an Indian that Cortés was deceived and inquired of Tapia, "Where was the Spaniard?" "I am," responded Aguilar in poorly pronounced Spanish, bowing to the Spanish commander.

Aguilar Joins Hernando Cortés on Cozumel and Shares in the Conquest of Mexico

Cortés was much pleased at the coming of Aguilar, so much needed as an interpreter, and welcomed him in rather dramatic style, perhaps to impress the Indians. He ordered that Aguilar be clothed in a Spanish shirt, doublet, breeches, hempen sandals, and a pointed cap; then removing from his own shoulders a rich yellow robe lined with crimson, he threw it over the person of Aguilar. The latter found the unaccustomed clothing insupportable; neither could he eat much of the food forced upon him by his countrymen.

In the old mantle worn by Aguilar was tied a book of *horas* (hours), its leaves much frayed and worn. One of the first questions asked by him was whether it was Wednesday? He was much relieved to be informed that it was, and that he had been reading the appropriate prayer for each day. Aguilar related the story of the shipwreck of Valdivia's party, and stated that he had been eight years among the Maya Indians. In questioning Aguilar, Cortés learned that he was related to one of his friends, the licentiate Marcos de Aguilar.

Peter Martyr tells a touching result of the effect produced upon the mind of the mother of Aguilar when rumors reached Spain that he had been cast away among cannibals and eaten. Whenever she saw meat roasting on the spit, she would cry out: "See here the most miserable mother of all women! Behold the pieces of my son!"

Jerónimo de Aguilar remained with Cortés when the expedition went on to Mexico. At Tabasco in the river of Grijalva, Cortés picked up another invaluable aid in the person of the famous slave girl, Marina, who spoke the Mexican language. From Aguilar and Marina, Cortés learned much of the life and customs of the people of Mexico, and their familiarity with the languages of the country gave Cortés a great advantage in dealing with the ambassadors of Montezuma when the expedition stopped at the site of Vera Cruz. It really looks as if the gods had foredoomed to destruction the rich and extensive empire of the Aztecs.

Aguilar served Cortés in the numerous military operations of the conquest, and after the capture of Tenochtitlan, 13 August 1521, he became a *regidor* of the new city of Mexico.

In all Hispanic-American history there is no date better verified than the year 1519, in which Hernando Cortés sailed to the conquest of Mexico, so it is somewhat startling to come upon the slip in memory made by the prolific historian José Toribio Medina, when he fixes the meeting of Cortés and Aguilar at Cozumel in the year 1522. One error leads to another. Aguilar told Cortés that he had been a prisoner among the Indians for eight years, which, according to Medina's reckoning, would make his departure from Darien fall in the year 1514. Medina easily surmounts this embarrassment of chronology by saying that Aguilar was mistaken, that in reality he was ten years among the Maya.

It is fairly well established that Valdivia and Aguilar set out from La Antigua del Darien on, or a few days before, 11 January 1512; Aguilar joined Cortés on the island Cozumel about 3 March 1519; and in 1522, Montezuma had been killed, his empire overthrown, and the Spaniards permanently settled in Mexico.

THE MONTEJOS FINALLY CONQUER YUCATÁN

Just a word more about Gonzalo Guerrero, expatriate and apostate.

Francisco de Montejo, who had been with Grijalva and Cortés, shared in the treasures of Montezuma and returned to Spain a rich man. By an *asiento* and capitulation, dated Granada, 8 December 1526, Montejo, therein described as a resident of the city of Mexico, was granted the titles of governor and *adelantado,* with authority to " discover, conquer, and settle the Islands of Yucatán and Cozumel at his own cost and *minsion."* This lengthy document, a copy of which I have before me, contains the general injunction to plant, increase, and augment the Holy Catholic Faith, and bring the natives in subjection to His Sacred Cæsarian Majesty, Carlos Quinto.

The Maya had plenty of gods and rulers of their own, who would brook no rivals in their domains. The usual years of bloody warfare followed, while the Spaniards wandered hither and yon in search of the coveted metal. The *adelantado* heard of gold mines near Chetemal, in the kingdom of the Cans; and the *contador,* Alonso Dávila, second in command, went to seek them. Dávila demanded gold and provisions of the lord of Chetemal. To the *contador's* insolent summons, the cacique replied: " Of gold I scorn to speak; of fowls you shall have all that you can take from the points of our spears, and we will send you maize in the shape of flights of arrows." It was noticed that the Can Indians fought with greater order and better strategy than their neighbors, and the Christians believed that they were trained and commanded by Gonzalo Guerrero, warrior by nature as well as by name.

Don Alonso Luxan tells us that, in 1529, the Spaniards heard from some Indians that among them was a Christian, dressed and painted as an Indian, and married to a native princess. Being greatly in need of an interpreter, the *Adelantado* Montejo immediately wrote a letter to Guerrero, believing that he still retained memory of his baptism and Christian religion, and would desire to save himself. Montejo addressed him as, " Gonzalo, brother and special friend," and prayed him not to give way to the Devil, promising him, " *como hombre hijodalgo,"* in the name of the king to favor and honor him. The next day the Indian messenger returned with the letter, on the back of which Gonzalo had written that although he was married and had children, still he was a slave and not free. Guerrero's refusal to join his countrymen caused them to declare that he was of vile lineage and worse than an Indian.

So bravely did the natives fight that, in 1535, all Spaniards were driven out of the country. But in 1537, the Montejos, father and son, returned and renewed the bloody struggle. At last, steel and gunpowder, horses and dogs prevailed over native weapons. When all resistance had been killed off, the remaining Maya accepted the forms of Christianity—and continued to adhere to their old gods. The prophecy of Chilam Balam was fulfilled: the " scum from the sea " had conquered.

Cogollundo reckoned that more Spanish lives were lost in the conquest of Yucatán, where neither gold nor silver was found, than in winning the rich empires of Mexico and Peru. Truly, it was a famous victory for God and the king.

IV

BALBOA DISCOVERS THE GREAT RIO ATRATO
AND SEEKS THE GOLDEN TEMPLE
OF DABAIBA

" Quien busca peligro, perece en el."
—*Don Quijote,* Cervantes.

"*VÁMOS al Darien,*" writes Peter Martyr. Going back to Santa Maria de la Antigua del Darien, we find that Balboa had considerable difficulty in maintaining order in the colony. As happened with nearly all the first European settlements on the shores of the New World, the chief problem for a few years was one of subsistence. To this was added the jealousy and ambition of different persons and factions to seize the government, attract the favor of the king, and, above all, secure the lion's share of the gold taken from the natives or obtained by petty traffic with the few Indians who ventured into the settlements. Only the popularity, facility to command, and physical courage of Vasco Núñez held the colony together.

To obtain sufficient provisions while the crops were growing, the Spaniards made forays on the surrounding Indian villages. These visits were led by Vasco Núñez, who usually returned with both food and gold. By tactful dealing and gifts of *chucherías,* or Spanish gewgaws, the white commander generally left the caciques disposed to be friendly toward the Christians. While a few Indians came in a friendly manner to La Antigua to trade maize, cassava, and fruit for articles of small value from Spain, the white men realized that they acted as spies to observe the doings of the white strangers, their number, and fighting strength. No doubt these native traders conferred with the Indian slaves held by the Spaniards, and reported what they learned to the caciques on returning to their villages.

Balboa realized the precarious situation of the little colony, surrounded by hostile bands of Indians governed by the sagacious barbarian, Cacique Cémaco, who might attack La Antigua both by land and water. One day Vasco Núñez ordered Captain Francisco Pizarro to take six men and make a reconnaissance in the direction of Cueva. When three leagues up the valley of the river that flowed by La Antigua, the party was attacked by Cémaco at the head of four hundred warriors. Knowing that the Dariens did not poison their weapons, and fought mainly with *varas* hurled by *estólicas,* the little body of Spaniards warded off the *varas* with their shields, and ripped up the bellies of one hundred and fifty Indians with their swords. Being hard pressed by Cémaco, the Spaniards retreated to La Antigua, leaving one of their number named Francisco Hernan wounded on the field. Vasco Núñez was angry at this desertion, and sharply commanded Pizarro, " Go instantly and bring me Francisco Hernan, and as you value your life, never again leave one of my soldiers alive upon a field of battle." Pizarro, though himself wounded, took some more men and brought back the wounded soldier in safety. Oviedo affirms that some captains took no more account of their sick and wounded soldiers than if they were stones. The marvel of this story is not that Pizarro deserted a wounded man, or that seven Spaniards were able to exenterate one hundred and fifty Indians, but rather that they found Hernan still alive and not further injured by the Indians. Balboa immediately took the field with one hundred men, hoping to encounter Cémaco; but the wily chieftain avoided a conflict.

In June, 1512, Vasco Núñez led an expedition of one hundred and sixty men, in two brigantines and divers canoes, against the famous Cacique Dabaibe, who lived far to the south of Antigua del Darien. Ever since settling in Darien, the Spaniards had been hearing of this very rich lord who lived up a great river about thirty leagues from La Antigua. It was claimed that the cacique was descended from a powerful goddess, named Dabaiba, who was the mother of the god who had created the sun and moon, and controlled the elements of nature. More likely,

Photo by Major Malsbury.

Types of the powerful, stocky Chocó Indians.
Marsh calls them Chocoi.

Photo by Major Malsbury.

Cristóbal, from the Río Chico (center) his wife
and child in front.

Dabaiba was a great and wise *cacica,* or Indian princess, who after death was revered as a supernatural being, and had a temple erected to her memory, to which the people made pilgrimages bearing offerings of gold and pearls. The Golden Temple of Dabaiba was the first *eldorado* encountered on the continent of America, an effective fiction employed by the Indians of the seacoast to induce the Christians to move inland to more barren regions up the Atrato River. This large river, bordered by immense swamps and lagoons, was subject to raging floods, in which many daring Spaniards met their end. Balboa describes his trip up the river, and in his letter of 20 January 1513, he informed the king that all the gold of that territory passed through the smelter of Cacique Dabaibe. This was a prize well worth seeking.

On St. John's Day—24 June 1512 (not 1510, as writes Oviedo)—while on the way to Dabaibe, Vasco Núñez de Balboa discovered the mouth, or mouths, of the Atrato River where it discharges its waters into the southern end of the Gulf of Urabá, about nine leagues south from La Antigua. Balboa called the river El Rio Grande de San Juan, by which name it was known for years. One historian says that the Atrato emptied by six or seven mouths, none less in size than the Guadalquivir or Tajo rivers in Spain. Oviedo states that Balboa told him that the river had ten mouths.

Balboa ordered Rodrigo de Colmenares with one-third the force in one of the brigantines to ascend the Rio Grande, while he went up another channel. On account of the fish nets in the water, Balboa named this stream the River of Nets (*Rio de las Redes*). A short distance from the mouth of this river, Vasco Núñez came upon a town recently abandoned. Nevertheless, the Spaniards were able to secure two big canoes, many bundles of bows and arrows, and seven thousand *pesos* of gold. Cémaco, the overlord of Darien, noting the approach of the white men in force, had ordered the chiefs to desert their homes and carry away all food and valuables.

Balboa then returned to the gulf, running into a great tempest, which swamped the canoes in which was the gold, and drowned the occupants. After this mishap, the commander with the brigantine and the rest of the canoes entered the Rio Grande, soon overtaking Colmenares and his party in the other brigantine. Together they continued up the great river, and about twelve leagues from its mouth discovered an island, later called Cañafístola on account of the purging *cassia* growing thereon. The Indians carried along told the Christians that the fruit of this purgative plant was good to eat, and they did eat of it, much to their surprise and discomfort.

When able to move on, the Spaniards took the route to the right of the island, and soon came to a tributary of the great river, which they named Rio Negro from the dark color of its water. Ascending this stream for five or six leagues, they came to the seat of Cacique Abenameche, a town of five hundred houses, each separate the one from another. The Indians bravely defended their homes by hurling long *varas,* and at close quarters fighting with wooden swords or clubs made of hard palm wood. Soon they were put to flight, leaving the cacique and others in the hands of the Spaniards. The chief had wounded a Spanish soldier, who now revenged himself by cutting off an arm of Abenameche near to the shoulder by one stroke of his sword. We are told that this cowardly deed much distressed Vasco Núñez. The town was sacked in the usual manner.

Leaving Colmenares there with half the men, Balboa led the other half up the Rio Negro as far as twenty leagues from the island of Cañafístola. At this point another river discharged its waters into the Rio Negro. Entering this new river, Balboa found the habitations of Cacique Abibeiba, which were built on great high trees or groves of palm trees, on account of the lagoons and swamps and because the entire region was subject to frequent inundations. Some trees were so large that seven or eight men, touching hands, were required to encircle them. The dwellings were well constructed of posts and wicker work of canes, sometimes referred to as *barbacoas,* and were divided into compartments for different family uses. Roofs of grass and large leaves covered the structures. Peter Martyr wrote that the wine cellars were under ground, meaning that the Indians kept their *chicha* and fermented fruit juices in jars on high ground, because swaying of the trees caused the liquids to become turbid. Other supplies were stored in the houses. One account states that the Indians mounted to their homes by means of ladders, each ladder being formed by splitting one very large cane in the middle. Another description says that they used vines (*bejucos*) suspended from the trees. At night and on the approach of danger, the ladders were drawn up, and the tree dwellers remained secure from men, *tigres*, and floods in the rivers. We read that the children scampered up and down these aerial stairways like monkeys. To the base of the trees were tied the canoes used for fishing, or for going to their *maizales* or *yuca* plantations on higher ground.

Cacique Abibeiba was at home in his high house when Balboa made his visit, and lost no time in pulling up his *escaleras*, or ladders. When invited to come down, the chief replied that he did not wish to do so, and he told the Spaniards to let him alone and go away, since he had done nothing to harm them. But Europeans, in their Christian zeal and thirst for gold, were not content to let the Indians live peacefully in their accustomed way. The Spaniards threatened to cut down the tree, which did not seem to alarm the chief until he saw how easily the strangers could make the chips fly with their axes. Abibeiba then descended to the ground with his wife and two sons. The first demand of the Christians was, of course, for gold, to which the cacique made answer that he possessed none, because he had no need for it, which was true, for Abibeiba was a fisherman and fish furnished a medium of exchange for trading with his neighbors. Being importuned to produce gold, the chief assured the Spaniards that he could get plenty of the coveted metal in some mountains in sight if they would let him go and fetch it. The Spaniards would agree to any proposition containing the prospect of gold, especially in this land of the Golden Temple of Dabaiba. Leaving his wife and children as hostages, the chief started off in the direction of the mountains—and that was the last seen of Cacique Abibeiba.

Vasco Núñez discovered other settlements along this river, all abandoned by the natives, wherein he found abundance of provisions, but no stores of gold. The rich Cacique Dabaibe did not live in this direction. Abibeiba not making his re-appearance within the number of days specified for his return, Balboa turned down this river, and then descended the Rio Negro (Black River) to join Colmenares, whom he had left at Abenameche on that river. Meanwhile, Colmenares, counter-manding orders, had sent out a lieutenant named Raya with nine men to raid the country. The little party attacked a town of Chief Abraiba, during which Raya and two of his men were killed, the seven others fleeing back to the town of Abenameche.

The rude soldier who severed the arm of Cacique Abena-meche with one cut of his sword did a clean operation, a guillo-tine amputation much practiced in Europe during the first years of the World War, 1914–1918. The chief did not die from hemorrhage or infection and recovered slowly under the care of his principal *tequina,* or medicine man. While the wound was healing, Abenameche planned revenge, and called on Abibaiba and Abraiba to join him in an attack upon the force left with Colmenares. More than five hundred warriors fell upon the Spaniards at the town of Abenameche, and it would have fared badly with the latter had they not been reinforced by thirty men sent forward by Vasco Núñez. The natives failed to avenge their wrongs and many were killed or taken prisoner.

The first quest of the Golden Temple was barren of treasure, nor could Balboa learn anything of the whereabouts of Cacique Dabaibe. Leaving his friend, Bartolomé Hurtado, and thirty soldiers at Abenameche to watch the natives, Vasco Núñez and Colmenares went back to La Antigua with the captives and provisions. Hurtado ranged the neighborhood for food and loot and took some prisoners. Soon the greater part of his men fell sick, and twenty-one of them started down the Rio Negro in one grand canoe to return to La Antigua, taking along twenty-four Indian prisoners to be sold into slavery. When only three leagues on the way, four canoes shot out from the bushes, con-taining one hundred warriors commanded by Cacique Cémaco.

These Indians, aided by the captives with the Spaniards, soon killed or drowned nineteen of the latter. Two Spaniards escaped by concealing themselves in the branches of a large tree drifting down the river, and managed to get back to Hurtado. Now thoroughly alarmed, Hurtado made inquiries of his friendly Indians and learned that the leading chiefs were advocating joint action to rid themselves of the arrogant white men. With his remaining soldiers, Captain Hurtado hastened to abandon the post and hurried back to Antigua with tidings of the threatened uprising. The news brought by Hurtado excited some alarm among the settlers, but no special preparation was made to repel an attack.

V

FULVIA

" Ni hay secreto tan guardado
Como el que a nadie se dice."
—Pérez de Herrera.

MANY times during the years of Hispanic discovery and conquest in America, it happened that a very unusual incident or seemingly miraculous event turned threatened disaster to the advantage of the white men. In this instance, love foiled the plan of the patriotic Cémaco, lord of Darien, to free his people.

Cherchons la femme! The Spaniards called her Fulvia, a pretty Indian girl in the household of Vasco Núñez. Between Fulvia and one of her brothers, a vassal of Cémaco, there existed a tender affection. This Indian, apparently a young chief, occasionally visited his sister at night by stealth when Balboa and most of the soldiers were away, to tell Fulvia of her family and of the doings of her absent lord. On his last visit, the young Indian warned Fulvia to hide herself on a certain night, for the town would be attacked and the foreigners destroyed. Before slipping away in the darkness, her brother admonished Fulvia thus: " Dearest sister, give ear to my words and keep most secretly that which I say to you, if you care for your own welfare and mine and that of our country and people."

Poor Fulvia was torn by strong conflicting emotions—her love and duty to her people and country, and her passion for Vasco Núñez. The last prevailed. " A woman keeps the fire better than she does a secret," said Fulvia, and then she disclosed to her white lover the story related to her by her brother of the confederation of all the Indians in the Darien-Atrato region to exterminate the Christians at La Antigua.

94

Balboa appreciated the gravity of the situation and promptly took action in a characteristic manner. He induced the girl to send for her brother, who was arrested, of course, when he stole into town. By threats and torture, Vasco Núñez compelled the Indian to tell all he knew of the efforts of the natives to get rid of the foreigners. Fulvia's brother informed Balboa that the forty Indians sent to him by Cémaco were not a peace offering, nor were they an evidence of submission to the white commander. In fact, they were given to Balboa to lull him into a sense of security from attack, and while the Indians were working in the *labranzas* or about the town, they were ordered by Cémaco to seize the first opportunity to kill the great white chief. This they had feared to attempt, partly out of respect for his well-known prowess as a soldier, and also because he always appeared among the Indian laborers mounted upon a mare and carrying a spear in his hand, as gentlemen did in Spain. The horse was a novelty in Darien and appeared a terrible animal to the wondering natives. No doubt Leoncico accompanied his master, ready to spring at the throat of any Indian who approached too near.

Failing in his plan to kill Balboa, Cémaco so stirred up the caciques about the mouth of the Rio Atrato that they determined no longer to suffer the insolence and outrages of the Spaniards. The five leading caciques were Cémaco, high chief of the Dariens; Abenameche, he of the severed arm, lord of the Rio Negro; Abibeiba, the tree dweller, who went for gold and forgot to come back; Abraiba, a chief not yet encountered by the Spaniards; and Dabaibe, the fierce guardian of the Golden Temple. All dropped their intertribal differences and swore to wipe out the white invaders. One hundred canoes, arms, and provisions had been collected at the town of Tichirí, and five thousand fighting men were ready to assault La Antigua by water and by land on the night specified.

The best defense is offense. No time could be lost if Vasco Núñez was to outwit that clever strategist, Cémaco of Darien. Without saying a word to anyone of what he had learned of the conspiracy, Balboa ordered Colmenares to proceed with seventy men in four canoes to Tichirí, using Fulvia's brother as guide. Balboa, with a like number of Spaniards, went by land to a place three leagues distant from Tichirí, where he thought to find Cémaco. That astute chieftain, learning from his spies of the approach of Balboa, did not wait to hazard battle with the white commander, but silently stole away.

Captain Colmenares found a large body of warriors at Tichirí commanded by some principal chiefs. He killed many of the Indians, captured more, and hung some of the chiefs. As a special favor, Colmenares put the " captain-general " to death by shooting him with arrows. Balboa went in pursuit of Cémaco, but failed to overtake him.

King Ferdinand decreed that if Cémaco did not obey the *requerimiento,* he could be enslaved without paying any dues to the crown. There is no record, I am glad to state, of the torture, enslavement, or killing of this famous patriotic chieftain.

This well-planned conspiracy of the five caciques failed just because a simple Indian maiden was in love with that good-looking blond *descubridor,* Vasco Núñez de Balboa. Had Fulvia been true to her people and kept the secret, Antigua would have shared the fate of Belén in Veragua and San Sebastián in Urabá. The settlement of the isthmus would have been postponed, perhaps, until after the discovery of Mexico, in 1517, which would have directed the tide of conquest wholly toward North America. The short transit of the continent at Panama and discovery of the South Sea would have remained longer unknown, and the subjugation of the Peruvians delayed so that the Spaniards might not have met with a divided people, so easy to overthrow.

After this signal victory, attained with so little effort and almost without loss, Balboa, who was a most discerning captain, ordered the erection of a blockhouse, or strong wooden fort, at Antigua del Darien for better defense in case of another conspiracy to wipe out the settlement. " Military sagacity," writes Herrera, " comprises four parts ":

1. To recognize dangers and mistakes in time, and remedy them.
2. To know how to take advantage of the occasion in order to deceive the enemy.
3. To be able to find means in unforeseen occurrences to get out of danger.
4. To know not only how to escape from danger, but to turn misfortune to advantage.

These Vasco Núñez well knew how to do, for he always fought more with judgment and good management than with arms and valor.

After suppressing the threatened uprising of the Indians about Antigua del Darien, Balboa had opportunity to devote more attention to his own fortunes. He was much perturbed in hearing nothing of *Regidor* Valdivia, who had sailed on his second voyage to Santo Domingo in the first days of January, 1512, and now the year was nearly at an end. Valdivia carried not only much gold, including the king's *quinto,* but, what was of more importance, he bore to Diego Colón and King Ferdinand the news of the existence of the South Sea, and the plea of Vasco Núñez for men and supplies necessary for its discovery. Balboa's letter of 20 January 1513 clearly proves that he had previously written of the South Sea to King Ferdinand.

The hazards of navigating the unknown waters of the New World and the terrible hurricanes encountered in the Carib Sea were well known to the settlers at Antigua, and they feared, truly, that Valdivia and his party had perished at sea or had been wrecked upon a hostile shore. Balboa, a man full of energy, could not remain inactive. As time went by, he determined to go to Spain to present his case to the king, and plead for the reinforcements needed for the march inland and over the great mountains to the south. Friends and foes alike objected strenuously to Balboa's proposal to leave Darien. His supporters did not relish the prospect of being left amid their enemies without their masterful leader. His jealous rivals feared that Vasco Núñez would dazzle Ferdinand with his tales of gold, pearls and splendor of another great ocean, and come back with enlarged power and loaded with honors. Both parties valued the presence of this one strong man to inspire fear in the natives of Darien. The people agreed that another effort should be made to inform the king of the state of affairs at La Antigua, and in place of Balboa, the *Cabildo* would endorse Alonso Núñez, who had been *alcalde* under Nicuesa, to be their delegate. A colonist recalled that he had a wife in Madrid, whose tears might keep him in Spain; so the balloting was resumed. The next selection was Juan de Quicedo (Caicedo) who was *veedor* with Nicuesa. He was a serious man of mature age, and was the only settler in Antigua accompanied by a Spanish wife. He promised to leave his wife as a pledge for his return; but, as we shall see later, Quicedo never came back to the Indies. Human life is uncertain, and the colonists did well in electing another *procurador* to act with Quicedo. This was Rodrigo Enríquez de Colmenares, a clever man, who had served in the Italian wars against the French, and then came to Darien as the lieutenant of Diego de Nicuesa, and could be counted on to return, as he had accumulated houses and lands in La Antigua. It will be noted that both these men had been officials of Nicuesa, and *ipso facto,* unfriendly to Vasco Núñez, though each had accumulated property and Indian slaves under his rule. The records show that Colmenares was not overscrupulous in not telling the whole truth, and no doubt lawyer Corral, Alonso Pérez and his crowd had been promised by Colmenares that, upon reaching the court, he would join the *Bachiller* Enciso in charges against Balboa.

These men, rivals and enemies of Vasco Núñez, knew that King Ferdinand, so far, had refused to recognize the claim of Diego Colón to any part of the mainland of the New World; consequently, any authority given to Balboa by Don Diego was only a pretense and void. As a matter of fact, Balboa maintained his position as chief of the settlement by his courage and genius for command, and because the majority of the people believed he was the best man available for the office. It seems that Balboa believed that Quicedo and Colmenares would solicit the king to make him permanent governor and captain-general on Tierra Firme. Oviedo declares that he was deceived in this election, and that when the delegates arrived at the court, they intended to oppose any recognition or honor for Vasco Núñez.

Quicedo and Colmenares were officially certified by the officials of the *Cabildo* to represent the colony and ask for special favors from the king.

The two *procuradores* sailed from Antigua del Darien on a small brigantine, " the 4th day of the calends of November in the year of grace 1512." Quicedo can be eliminated from the picture, as he died soon after reaching Spain. Zamudio was in hiding, and Enciso and Colmenares talked Darien to everybody about the court; and later to the hundreds of individuals enlisting in the armada of Pedrarias Dávila. They could utter nothing but abuse and condemnation of one Vasco Núñez de Balboa, who rose against *Alcalde Mayor* Enciso, drove Diego de Nicuesa, the royal governor, from Tierra Firme, and carried on with a high hand in Darien. None could dispute what they said, for no one else about the court had ever been in Darien.

BALBOA SUBDUES SOME MUTINEERS IN LA ANTIGUA

Vasco Núñez de Balboa, by his aptitude for leadership and command, and without royal favor or license, had risen to be head of the colony in Darien. By his valor and diplomacy, Balboa had subdued or conciliated the bands of Indians surrounding La Antigua. By his fairness in dividing the spoils acquired in the *entradas*, the thrifty colonists now possessed gold, land, and Indian slaves. Nevertheless, some opposition to, and jealousy of Balboa, existed among the settlers from the very beginning. Adherents of Enciso and Nicuesa remained, and certain individuals, like the lawyer Diego del Corral and Alonso Pérez de la Rúa, aspired to the command and the handling of the gold and slaves. The last plotted a scheme with the disaffected to depose Balboa and seize the government.

They struck first at Vasco Núñez by claiming that his friend the *alguacil mayor,* Bartolomé Hurtado, had abused his power by oppressing some of the settlers; and demanded that he be punished. Balboa paid no attention to the demand, and then Alonso Pérez made threats against Balboa. The latter acted promptly and imprisoned the ringleader. Fellow mutineers, led by Corral, gathered to free Alonso Pérez; and the friends of Balboa rallied to his support. The two armed bands faced each other in the plaza of Antigua del Darien, ready to fight, and the existence of the first foothold of Spain on the continent of America hung in the balance.

Fortunately, cooler heads intervened and negotiated the release of Alonso Pérez. The conspirators dispersed, only to plan new deviltry. The next day they came together and seized Hurtado, locking him in the *calabozo.* Again better counsel prevailed, and Hurtado was freed. The mob spirit was aroused, and Corral and Alonso Pérez directed it against Balboa, alleging that he had not made equitable division of the gold and captives.

Balboa well knew the riotous members of the colony, and he shrewdly planned to give them a chance to seize some gold not yet distributed, and divide it up among themselves. That very night Balboa, with some friends, departed from La Antigua under pretense of going to hunt game. No sooner did the conspirators learn that Vasco Núñez had left town than they seized the treasure, valued at ten thousand *castellanos;* and lawyer Corral and Pérez de la Rúa divided the gold, not failing to make liberal distributions to themselves. Nearly everyone was dissatisfied with his share, and they raised a great outcry against their leaders. Messengers were sent to beg Vasco Núñez to hurry back to town; and joining him, " with cries and oaths that they must kill them," they took the *Bachiller* Corral and Alonso Pérez and several others and put them in prison. Balboa's enemies accused him of *maña*-craft, which was not true. Had he possessed the cunning ascribed to him, Balboa would have allowed the mob to expend its blood-lust on his enemies, and he would have been rid of Diego del Corral and

Alonso Pérez. During this uprising there is no evidence that Francisco Pizarro failed to support Balboa.

The authority of Vasco Núñez remained more firmly established than before the mutiny.

Balboa Receives a Commission as Acting Governor of Darien

Shortly after this attempt to overthrow Balboa, he wrote his long letter to the king, in which he refers to the recent outbreak and complains of the *alcaldes* and *regidores*. Vasco Núñez warned Ferdinand that if they were not punished and the justice of the king not feared, no governor that he might appoint would fail to have dissensions and the king's service never would be promoted in those parts.

When the *Procuradores* Quicedo and Colmenares passed through Santo Domingo on their way to Spain, they told Diego Colón and the royal officials of the state of affairs in Darien and of the need of the colony for more men and provisions. His own interest in the riches reported to exist on the mainland, as well as the order of the king to aid the Spaniards on Tierra Firme, prompted the viceroy to encourage the merchants of Española to venture to carry foodstuffs and other supplies to La Antigua. Probably the first boat to reach the settlement was that of Sebastián de Ocampo. As elsewhere related, Balboa intrusted his letter of 20 January 1513 to him, and appointed Ocampo his solicitor to represent his interest at the court of Spain. Following Ocampo was Cristóbal Serrano, with two ships loaded with provisions and carrying two hundred persons, one hundred and fifty being fighting men to join Balboa. It seems that these men were sent by Diego Colón to support his lieutenant in Darien. I believe these were the two ships mentioned by Vasco Núñez in his letter of 20 January 1513. I can not agree with José Toribio Medina when he writes that Balboa was referring to the two vessels of Valdivia which had arrived at La Antigua more than a year prior to the coming of Serrano.

Serrano also brought what was of more value to Vasco Núñez, a commission from King Ferdinand appointing him his governor and captain in Darien until such time as he would name a permanent governor. In translating this rare and important document, as given by Angel de Altolaguirre y Duvale, I break it up into sentences and introduce punctuation and capital letters. This royal decree naming Vasco Núñez de Balboa *Gobernador interino* of Darien, reads as follows:

Zaragoza, 23 December 1511

The King—For the present, in the interim while providing a governor and justice of the province of Darien, which is on the mainland of the Indies of the Ocean Sea, it is my will and pleasure, acknowledging the sufficiency and ability and fidelity of you, Vasco Núñez de Balboa, and understanding that it is conducive to our service that you be our governor and captain of the said province of Darien, that you have for us and in our name the government and captaincy of the said island and province, and judicature of it; and by this my *cédula* I command any persons of whatever estate or condition, pre-eminence or dignity that they may be, who are or might be in the said province of Darien, that, during the said time, they have and hold and receive you as our captain and governor of it; and deal with you in all the cases and things annexed to and belonging to the said office of governor; and that in everything they treat you as our governor, and execute and obey your commands. In order to employ the said office in the form aforesaid, and for the execution and fulfilment of it, I give you full power by this my decree, with all its incidents, dependencies annexed and rights pertaining thereto. To any failing to do my will a penalty.

Done in Zaragoza, XXIII days of December, DXI years. By command of His Highness   *I the King*
    Lope Conchillos
                    Countersigned by the Bishop.

Abbreviation of the penalty clause terminating the royal orders constantly varied. In this commission to Balboa it reads: *" E los vnos ni los otros no fagades en deal."* The warrant to Pedrarias Dávila as governor and captain-general of Castilla del Oro, gives the legal formula in full—*" E los unos ni los*

*otros non fagades ni fagan ende al por alguna manera so pena
de la mi merced e de 50 mill maravedises para la mi camara e
cada uno que lo contrario hiciere."*

In this decree, Ferdinand follows the example set by Diego
Colón, who, on 10 September 1511, informed the king that he
had named Balboa his lieutenant and representative on Tierra
Firme. It is obvious that the commission to Vasco Núñez was
issued before the *Bachiller* Enciso had reached the court, and
poisoned the minds of the king and his councillors against Balboa. It is not likely that his commission was given by Miguel
de Pasamonte, as some of the old historians affirm. This recognition and authority from the king was very opportune and
pleasing to Vasco Núñez, for it put an end to any further attempt to question his status as commander of the colony in
Darien. True, the office was only temporary; but Balboa hoped
that when Ferdinand read his recent letters informing him of
the proximity of another sea, and of Balboa's plan to find that
sea and its reputed riches, it would be quite probable that the
king would be inclined to let him remain in permanent command. Besides, Vasco Núñez felt that he could rely upon
Ocampo to tell Ferdinand the truth about Darien, and how
much he had done to promote his interests on the mainland of
the New World.

Secure of his position as temporary governor, and wishing to
bring about harmony among the colonists, Balboa released
Diego del Corral, Alonso Pérez, and others from confinement.
From the day on which Balboa slipped away from Española, he
had assumed, or had forced upon him, one task after another,
and in each case he had measured up to the position. With the
king's commission in his pocket, Vasco Núñez took on new dignity and comported himself as a governor.

In a *probanza,* or proof of merits and services, made by
Pedro Sánchez, *clérigo* in the city of Santa Maria del Antigua
de Castilla del Oro, on 29 August 1514, the cleric deposed as
follows: That he departed from Spain, in 1509, in the expedi-

tion of Diego de Nicuesa, and came with that commander to
Tierra Firme, where he served well and faithfully in saying
mass, hearing confessions, and administering the sacraments;
and was especially diligent in interring the dead. He shared in
all the fatigues, dangers and hunger of the party, as well as
suffering from a leg ulcer resulting from an injury incurred in
the field. For all of which the said *clérigo* received no pay when
with Diego de Nicuesa. When Vasco Núñez brought the residuals of the Nicuesa colony at Nombre de Dios to La Antigua,
Pedro Sánchez was one of the party. He states that he saw
little opportunity to better his condition at Antigua, and
wished to return to Spain; but Balboa would not let him go,
saying there was need for him in Darien. At this time there
were three priests in Antigua del Darien, and Balboa wanted
one (Andrés de Vera) to serve as *cura* in the church, another
as *capellán*, and the third, Pedro Sánchez, to accompany him on
the *entradas*, or forays, because he was best fitted for that duty.

The *clérigo* adds that when he arrived at La Antigua from
Nombre de Dios there was paucity of provisions in the settlement, and Vasco Núñez ordered some of the colonists to the
province of Venamaque, where food was more plentiful. Despite his sore leg, Sánchez went with that party, which remained
there for seven months. From this *probanza*, we learn that
Pedro Sánchez accompanied Balboa when he discovered the
South Sea, suffering much labor and fatigue for the period of
six months (really less than five months).

Francisco Gonzalo de Guadalcanal (spelled Guadalcama by
the historian Oviedo) made oath that he was with Vasco Núñez
on the South Sea and saw Sánchez there, but did not see him
say mass, nor believe that he said it, because they had another
clérigo, the *cura* of the church at Antigua, who said mass. Another witness to this *probanza* was Lope de Olano, formerly the
lieutenant of Nicuesa, who swore that he went with Balboa on
the *entrada* to the South Sea and there saw Pedro Sánchez.
The names of Lope de Olano and Pedro Sánchez, both officers
in the Nicuesa expedition, do not appear in the lists of names
recorded by the notary Valderrábano, and preserved by Oviedo.

These two instances, as well as other names encountered in old documents, prove my assertion that when Balboa discovered the Pacific Ocean he had with him many more men than the names handed down to us by his notary. I believe that Balboa kept close to himself the men who had fought with him since first he entered Darien, and on whom he could rely as shock troops should the Indians suddenly turn on the Spaniards and give battle. No doubt Balboa had a poor opinion of members of Nicuesa's party, for they had failed so miserably to maintain themselves on Tierra Firme, though more numerous and better equipped than the Ojeda expedition. But then, they had no Vasco Núñez de Balboa!

There is no record that Bachelor-of-law Corral ever did any hard or dangerous service in the field. His followers were strong enough to keep him in office as *regidor* of Antigua, where he could keep track of what was going on and accumulate evidence to the injury of Vasco Núñez, which was sent to Spain on the first opportunity. Corral testified that Pedro Sánchez, in some *entradas*, had been given a share as a lay brother; but in the journey to the South Sea with Vasco Núñez the said *clérigo* had received neither salary, *naborías*, nor a part of the loot. Corral further deposed that the said Vasco Núñez always held ill will toward the clergy, and although Pedro Sánchez was his father confessor, the acting governor threw him in jail because he did not doff his clerical bonnet when passing his superior in the street ("*porque no le quitó el bonete*"). Quite different this from the humble demeanor of Cortés toward the clergy in Mexico.

Cristóbal Serrano brought to Darien still another communication vitally determining the life of Vasco Núñez de Balboa. Martín Zamudio, the *alcalde,* from his retreat in Spain, wrote a letter to Balboa telling him of the anger of the king and Fonseca against him, stirred up by the venomous charges of the *Bachiller* Enciso. Apparently, between the date of the royal commission to Balboa and the time that Zamudio wrote, Enciso had reached the court and poisoned the minds of Ferdinand and his councillors against Vasco Núñez. In place of commendation and reward for founding and supporting a Spanish colony on the shore of the new continent Balboa was condemned without opportunity to defend his actions. The charge that excited the greatest bitterness toward Balboa was that he had caused the death of Diego de Nicuesa. Preponderance of evidence seems to show that Enciso was more opposed to receiving Nicuesa than was Vasco Núñez, and we know that when the charge was investigated by Gaspar de Espinosa when he first arrived in Darien, he reported to the king that all the settlers were involved. It looks very much as if the lawyer was piling up charges against Balboa in order to divert attention from his own share in the affair.

Though careful to remain in hiding, *Alcalde* Zamudio had been able—probably through some Biscayan friends—to keep in touch with what was going on at the court. He informed Balboa that he was to be summoned to appear before the king to answer for his usurpation of command on Tierra Firme. That threat did not disturb Vasco Núñez, for getting to the court was the one particular thing that he sought during all his years in Darien. What did alarm Balboa was the rumor, reported by Zamudio, that the king intended to send from Spain a permanent governor to replace him.

Balboa had been hoping to receive from Española sufficient reinforcements of men and supplies with which to make an *entrada* far into the interior of the country and over the mountain ranges to look for that other sea reported to exist in the South. The coming of a new governor would mean that he would profit from the pacification of the neighboring caciques and the knowledge of Darien so laboriously acquired by Vasco Núñez. And, what was more distressing to Balboa, his successor would lead a large expedition in search of the South Sea, and if he found it, snatch from Vasco Núñez the glory of its discovery.

The bad news from Zamudio did not overwhelm Balboa. Men of daring souls and great deeds are not crushed by failure, misfortune, and defeat. Rather are they stimulated with new spirit and endowed with added courage to retrieve their good fortune and undertake new enterprises. So it was with Vasco Núñez de Balboa. If he could not obtain, or risk waiting for, the one thousand men deemed necessary by the son of Comogre to reach the Austral Sea, Balboa determined to make the attempt with such force as he had at hand. This was his one chance of wiping out the charges of usurpation of power in Darien.

The approximate number of Spaniards at Antigua del Darien at this time was about 450. They were made up of the thirty-five residuals of Ojeda's party left with Francisco Pizarro at San Sebastián, one hundred men brought by Enciso, sixty by Colmenares, forty-three to sixty from Nombre de Dios, one hundred and fifty to two hundred who came with Cristóbal Serrano, and some remaining from Ocampo's ship. A few years later, Juan de Castañeda affirmed that he carried forty men to Antigua at his own cost and *minsion,* and Diego Fernández certified that he brought certain people to Darien. Of course, allowance must be made for deaths among the Spaniards, especially during the expedition up the San Juan River (Atrato) in search of Dabaibe.

This checks with the statement of Balboa in his letter of 20 January 1513, in which he tells the king that he had three hundred men remaining from the two colonies of Alonso de Ojeda and Diego de Nicuesa, to which must be added the one hundred and fifty to two hundred men brought by Cristóbal Serrano.

From his small command, Balboa selected one hundred and ninety men best fitted for his purpose. These men, often called soldiers, were accustomed to the use of arms and to conditions in the tropics, and most of them had had experience with their commander in Indian warfare. In reviewing these men, Balboa informed them of the unusual hazards of this new venture, the greatest yet undertaken on the continent of America, which, if successful, meant wealth and glory for all; but that if they failed, none might return alive to Antigua. Vasco Núñez announced that, by reason of the great and unknown dangers they might encounter, those not caring to risk their lives might withdraw without prejudice from the undertaking. Not a man withdrew. There is no record of Diego del Corral or Alonso Pérez volunteering to accompany Balboa.

Vasco Núñez equipped his picked body of men with the best arms available, gathered supplies, and prepared to set out in quest of the great Pacific Ocean.

VI

BALBOA WRITES TO KING FERDINAND

" L'homme ici arrive où il peut et non où il veut."
—VASCO NÚÑEZ DE BALBOA.

BALBOA'S famous letter written to King Ferdinand from Darien, dated 20 January 1513, is the earliest and longest of his writings which has come to light. It never has received from English writers the attention it deserves. It is a valuable and important historical document, which merits an accurate and entire translation into English, not in the language of today, but in the form in which Balboa wrote it.

This *carta* is the very first document describing Darien, the Isthmus of Panama, and Urabá by the first commander to thoroughly discover and explore those regions. Fortunately, it is a long letter, about eight thousand words. Because his letters are difficult and tiresome to translate completely, writers belittle the literary attainments of Vasco Núñez de Balboa. Even Peter Martyr, who praises his military style, affirms that he was not a man of letters. Well, why should anyone expect Balboa to exhibit a fine literary style when other *conquistadores,* like Pizarro and Almagro, could neither read nor write?

Since the year 1500 when he sailed from Spain, Vasco Núñez had lived in contact with the natives of the New World as much as with his own people. The first Spaniards coming to America left their women folk behind them, and lived in very intimate association with the better class of Indians. Doubtless, Balboa spoke the Indian tongue of Española and of Darien, and had little occasion to write his own language prior to his elevation to the head of the colonists in Darien. Considering the scarcity of writing materials, as well as almost everything else, and the very primitive conditions under which they lived and fought, it is quite remarkable that the Spanish captains made such extensive records of what they saw and did.

Normally, the Spanish language permits great freedom in the construction of sentences. The subject or object may precede or follow the verb and both may be placed before or after the verb. Balboa took considerable license in making statements, changing mood, tense and person in the same sentence. The Spanish of 1513, nearly a century before Cervantes wrote, was still somewhat crude, and Vasco Núñez was not a product of the school at Salamanca.

The original letter contains few punctuations, then not in general use, and Balboa seldom introduced periods or capital letters. To be understood by the general reader, the translator has to divide the letter into paragraphs and form sentences. I follow the text as given by Angel de Altolaguirre y Duvale, and not the modernized version by Don Martín Fernández de Navarrete in the Spanish of 1829, the copy usually followed. Sir Clements R. Markham, the distinguished English writer on early Spanish American history, made a free translation of this letter for the readers of his day. Sir Clements did not translate the entire letter, and some of his statements are misleading, as when he makes Balboa say that he had lost three hundred of his men from hunger, whereas he declares that the three hundred men (his entire force at La Antigua) had been saved from starvation by the timely arrival of two ships from Española loaded with provisions sent by the Almirante Diego Colón. Even Navarrete changes a few words, like substituting *tanto* for *canto*, and *paños* for *Apaños*, which alters the meaning, of course.

Like other Spanish writers of his time, Vasco Núñez made frequent use of the words *gente* (people), *acá* (here) and *estas partes* (these parts); and when the meaning might not be clear to the reader, I have indicated whether the persons were Spaniards or Indians and the place in question. That convenient verb *conviene* is used in all its manifold meanings, and the same can be said of *cumple*.

Believing that it is the obligation of those who assume to write history to transmit the old records as they were written, and not as they should have been written, I have endeavored to translate the entire letter of Balboa as the great discoverer wrote it, without wandering far from the literal meaning of the words. It has been no simple task, though easy enough to skim over lightly, omitting the difficult and confusing passages.

Most Christian and Most Mighty Lord:

Some days past I wrote to Your Royal Majesty by a caravel which came to this Town making known to Your Most Royal Highness all the things that happened in these parts: likewise I wrote by a brigantine which set out from this Town for the island Española to make known to the Admiral how we were in very urgent need; and now God has supplied us with two ships loaded with provisions with which we were relieved, and it has been the cause of this land remaining settled; for we were in such great extremity that if the help had delayed much, when it might come it would not be necessary, because it would not find any one to succor on account of the famine; for by reason of the great necessity we have had, there would be lacking the three hundred men that we find here, whom I have ruled; those from Huraba of Alonso de Ojeda, and those from Veragua of Diego de Niquesa, who with much labor I have united the one to the other, as Your Royal Majesty will see in another letter that I am writing to Your Most Royal Highness making report of everything that has passed here.

Your Most Royal Highness sent me a command that I send for the persons who were in the settlement of Diego de Niquesa and bring them to this Town and do them much honor in every way possible. Your Most Royal Highness will know that after Diego de Niquesa came to this Town and from here set out to go to the island of Española, I took as much care of the people that he left in his seat [Nombre de Dios] as if they might be in my charge and I had brought them from Spain by order of Your Most Royal Highness: as soon as I knew that they were in need, I determined to send them supplies one and two and three times, until as soon as able, a year and a half ago, I brought them to this Town, seeing that in this way I executed the service of Your Most Royal Highness; for if I had not supplied them, already they would be lost, five or six dying of hunger daily, and the assaults of the Indians: all the people that Diego de Niquesa left are here in this Town with me. From the first day that they arrived at this Town [Antigua del Darien] they have been treated as good company like Your Most Royal Highness ordered me, for there has been no difference with them any more than if all came here on the same day: as soon as they came here they were given their house lots and their lands for tillage in very good locations, and at the same time with those who came with me to this Town to gain them, for the arable land and lots were not yet divided and they arrived in time to come in for a share of all the good there was.

I make known to Your Most Royal Highness that both the two Governors, as well Diego de Niquesa as Alonso de Ojeda, gave very bad account of themselves by their own fault, for they were the cause of their destruction by not knowing how to have authority, and because after they came to these parts they took on so much presumption and fancy in their thoughts that they appeared to themselves to be Lords of the land and from the bed could rule the country and govern that which is necessary, and thus they did it, and when they found themselves here they believed that there was no more to do than to give themselves to enjoyment.

And the nature of the land is such that if he who has charge of governing it sleeps, when he wishes to wake he cannot, because it is a country which requires that he who rules it pass over and around it many times; and as the land is very difficult to travel over on account of the many rivers and extensive marshes and mountains where many men die from the great toil suffered, it causes one to experience bad nights and endure fatigues, for every day it is necessary to face death a thousand times; and for this reason they like to excuse themselves with some persons who do not care much whether they do well or ill, like Diego de Niquesa has done, for which reason he was lost, as well the one as the other; and in order that Your Most Royal Highness may know by whom Diego de Niquesa was ruled and by what person he was exonerated, I am sending you an information of all that occurred, by which Your Most Royal Highness will see the affairs as they were conducted and how I was able to do that which was conducive to the said service of God and of Your Most Royal Highness: the greater part of their perdition has been due to the bad treatment of their people, for they believe that once they had them here that they were held as slaves, because even with the things that were taken to eat on the forays they were unfairly treated, as much in the govern-

ment of Alonso de Ojeda as in that of Diego de Niquesa, and never
of whatever gold that was taken nor of the other things were they
given the value of a *real;* for which reason everybody went about so
despondent that although they saw the gold alongside they did not
care to take it, knowing that they would have little share of it.

I wish to make known to Your Royal Majesty the reason why I
have obtained and know the great secrets which are in this land.
Your Most Royal Highness will know that since we came to this land
I have sought so much the service of Your Royal Highness that never
by night nor by day do I think of anything but how I shall be able
to be deserving and give good account of myself, and place in safety
myself and these few people that God cast here; and seek contriv-
ances with which we would be able to help and sustain our lives, as
Your Most Royal Highness will see by the writing, until such time
as Your Most Royal Highness provides reinforcements.   Above all,
I have striven whithersoever I have gone that the Indians of this
land be very well treated, not consenting to do them any harm, dealing with them truthfully, and giving them many articles from Spain
to attract them to our friendship.   Treating them honestly has been
the cause that I have learned very great secrets from them and things
whereby one can secure very great riches and large quantity of gold,
with which Your Most Royal Highness will be very much served.

Most powerful Lord, many times I think how it has been possible
to sustain ourselves, for the reason that we have been as poorly supplied from the island Española as if we were not Christians; but our
Lord by his infinite clemency has willed to provide us with provisions from this land, for many times we have been so near the end
that we believed ourselves lost from hunger, and at the time of the
greatest necessity our Lord showed us a way how we could help ourselves.   Your Most Royal Highness must know that since we are
here we have run over so many parts of the country on account of
the great need that we have had, that I marvel how so much fatigue
was borne, for the things that have come to pass have been by the
hand of God rather than by the hand of man.

I have managed until today never to let my men go out of this
place unless I go in advance, be the hour by night or by day, march-
ing through rivers and marshes and woods and mountains; and Your
Royal Highness should not believe that the swamps of this land are
such light affairs that we move along through them joyfully, for
many times it happens to us to go naked through swamps and water

for one and two and three leagues, with the clothing collected and placed on the shield on top of the head; and going out of some marshes we enter into others, and proceed in this manner two and three and ten days.

And if the person who holds the office of governing this land is careless with his people and remains in his house, no one of those that he sends in his place with the people can do so well as he, and who does not make many mistakes, which may cause the loss of himself and all those who go with him; because he does not care much for what concerns all, and that which they seek most to do is to give themselves to vice and excuse themselves all they can from work: and this I can well say as a person who has seen what happens, for certain times, although they have not been above three, that I have not led my men on the raids on account of being detained for sowing the fields, I have observed that the persons that I sent in my place have not acted as was right, and in conflict with the people, because the leaders gave little care to their trust.

I, my Lord, have sought constantly to make very honest division of all that has been taken to the present time of gold, *guanin*, and pearls, first putting aside what belongs to Your Most Royal Highness, as well as all the other things, like Indian cloth and things to eat: for until now we have cherished things to eat more than the gold, because we have more gold than health; for many times I was in places where I was more pleased to find a basket of corn than another of gold, accordingly, I assure Your Most Royal Highness that continually we have needed food more than the gold.

I certify to Your Most Royal Highness that if I in person had not marched at the head of my men looking for food for those who went with me and for those who remained in this Town, it would be a wonder if anyone remained in the Town or in this land, in case our Lord might not miraculously show mercy with us.

The way that I have taken in the distribution of the gold that was taken has been to give it to those who have gone to seize it, giving to each one according to his person, all remaining satisfied and contented: all come in for a share of the foodstuffs, although they may not go on the foray.

I wish to give account to Your Most Royal Highness of the things and great secrets of marvelous riches which are in this land, of which our Lord has made Your Most Royal Highness the Master, and has willed to make them known to me and permitted me to discover them before any other, for which I give Him many thanks and much praise all the days of the world; and I hold myself for the most fortunate man born in the world, and since in this manner our Lord has been pleased that by my hand rather than any other, such great beginnings have been made, I entreat Your Most Royal Highness to be pleased that I may continue such a great enterprise as this to the end: and this I am bold to beseech Your Most Royal Highness because I know that by it he must be well served, for I dare so much that, with the aid of God and my good industry, I will know how to guide it in such a way that Your Most Royal Highness be served thereby.

In order to put this in effect, Your Most Royal Majesty must command that, for the present, about five hundred men or more come from the island Española, so that with them and with those who are here with me, although no more than one hundred are fit for war, I can provide where needed and invade the interior of the country and pass to the other sea of the territory of the south; and although I may have shared some things of what I know with those who go with me, it has been with levity, and the secret and truth of everything is this which I am writing to Your Most Royal Highness.

Most puissant Lord, that which I with great industry and much labor by good fortune have discovered is this:—

In this province of Darien are found many very rich mines, there is gold in much quantity: twenty rivers have been explored, and thirty which contain gold issue from a ridge of mountains which is about two leagues from this Town, running toward the region of the south: the gold-bearing rivers flow within two leagues of this Town toward the south: this mountain turns down by this coast toward the west: from this Town to the west along this mountain no river with gold has been found: I believe that they exist.

Going up this great river of San Juan as far as thirty leagues, upon the right hand is a province which is called Abanumaqué, which has very great distribution of gold: I have very certain news that in it are rivers very rich with gold: I know it from a son of the Cacique of that province that I have here, and from other Indians here, men and women, whom I have captured from that land.

Going up this great river [Atrato] thirty leagues, on the left hand enters a very large and beautiful river, and two days journey up this river is a Cacique who is called *Davaive* [or Davaibe]: he is a very great Lord of a very large territory thickly settled with people. He has gold in great quantity in his house, and so much that for one who does not know the things of this land it will be quite dubious to believe:

I know this from sure information, that from the house of this Cacique de Vaive comes all the gold that goes out through this gulf [Urabá] and all that the Caciques of these districts possess. It is reported that they have many gold pieces of strange form, and very large. Many Indians who have seen it tell me that this Cacique de Vaive has certain baskets of gold which require a man to carry one of them on the back: this Cacique collects this gold in the way that he does, because he is distant from the mountain.

Two days' march from there is a very beautiful country in which is a very evil Carib people, they eat as many men as they can get: this people is without a Lord and they have no one to obey, they are warlike and each one lives for himself alone. These people are Lords of the mines, and these mines according to the news I have, are the richest in the world: these mines are in a province which has a mountain that appears to be the highest in the world, I believe that never has been seen another of such great height. It rises toward the Urabá side of this gulf somewhat within the land, which may be twenty leagues from the sea. This mountain goes its way running to the territory of the south; rising from the level ground it continues to increase in height until it is so high that it is covered with the clouds; two years that we are here the top of it has not been seen except two times, because continually it is hidden by the heavens. From the highest summit the mountain turns to decline until it becomes covered with woods and thickets, and from there fall some mountainous ridges without any forest, terminating in a more level country, the most beautiful in the world, close to this Cacique de Daive.

The very rich mines are in this point of this land turning toward the place of the rising sun, whose rays fall on the mines: it is two days' travel from this Cacique Davaibe to these rich mines. The method of collecting this gold is without any labor, in two ways; the one is that they wait for the streams to rise in the ravines, and when the floods pass they become dry and the gold remains exposed, washed down from the gullies in the mountain side in very large grains: the Indians indicate that they are of the size of oranges and like the fist, and according to their signs there are pieces in the form of flat plates.

The other method to gather gold is to wait until the vegetation on the mountains becomes dry and set it on fire, and after it is burnt they go and search for the gold in the most likely places on the mountain, and they collect it in great quantity and in very beautiful grains: these Indians who pick up the gold carry it in grains as they find it to this Cacique Davaibe to be melted, and they barter it with him. He gives them in exchange Indian boys and young men to eat, and Indian girls to serve their wives; these they do not eat; he gives them pigs [peccaries], of which there are many in this region, and quantities of fish and cotton clothing and salt. He gives them gold pieces worked as they wish them: only with this Cacique Davaibe do those Indians carry on this trade, because there is no place elsewhere.

This Cacique Davaibe has a large smelter for gold in his house: he keeps one hundred men continually working the gold: I know all this for a certainty, for wherever I go I never hear otherwise; I have sought to know it of many Caciques and Indians and also from the neighbors of this Cacique Davaibe, the same as from those of other parts; I find all to be true, because I have learned it in many ways and methods, giving to some torture, to others things from Spain, and from others through affection.

I have certain information that fifty leagues up the river of S. Juan there are very rich mines on the one side and the other of the river: the manner that this river has to be navigated is in canoes of the Indians, because it makes many small and narrow arms concealed with groves of trees, and one cannot enter through them except it is in canoes of about three or four palms in width. After this river is explored, boats can be built on the model of *justas,* eight palms wide, and supplied with twenty oars for rowing, because the river has a very strong current, and even with the Indian canoes one cannot navigate well. In seasons when the strong breezes blow, vessels which carry up to a dozen *botas* could navigate by sail, aiding them with the oar at some turns which the river makes; sometimes it is necessary to go three leagues out of the course, and at times detour five and even eight leagues by land.

One cannot travel by land on horseback up this river [San Juan, or Atrato], so far as we have seen, but horses can be embarked on the river sometimes through certain creeks which flow into it, for at the principal river they cannot, because it is swampy round about; the nearest place they are able to embark by the creeks is half a league.

The natives who live up this great river are bad and warlike: much cleverness is required in dealing with them: I have news of many other things which I do not certify until I know them more fully: I believe I shall know them by the help of God.

That which is down along this coast toward the west, going twenty leagues from here [La Antigua], is a province which is called Careta; there are in it certain rivers which contain gold; I know it from some Indian men and women who are in this Town. We have not gone there to test for gold in order not to excite the Indians, who are at peace, because we are few and will need more men. Going farther down the coast as far as forty leagues from this Town, and going twelve leagues inland, is a Cacique who is called *Comogre,* and another named *Pocorosa;* the one being as near the sea [Caribbean] as the other, and they carry on much war with each other. Within the land each one of them has a town, and two on the coast of this sea, from where they supply the interior with fish. The Indians assured me that in the domain of these two Caciques are rivers very rich in gold.

One day's journey from this Cacique Pocorosa are some mountains, the most beautiful that have been seen in these parts; they are very clear mountains without any thicket, save some groves along the streams which descend from the mountains. In those mountains are certain Caciques who have great quantity of gold in their houses: they say that all those Caciques keep their gold in the *barbacoas,* like corn, because they have so much gold that they do not care to hold it in baskets: they say that all the rivers of those mountains contain gold and that there are very fat grains in much quantity. The Indian manner of collecting the gold is by seizing the nuggets when they see them in the water and casting them in their baskets: they also gather it in the ravines after they are dry; and in order that Your Most Royal Highness may be more completely informed of the things of those parts, I am sending to you a branded Indian from that region who has collected it many times: Your Most Royal Highness should not take this as a laughing matter, for in truth I am well assured of it by many principal Indians and Caciques.

I, my Lord, have been quite near those mountains, within a day's journey, but I was not able to reach them on account of my want of men; for man arrives as far as he can and not as far as he wishes: along the edge of those mountains are some very level lands extending toward the south; the Indians say that the other sea is three days' journey from there: all the Caciques and Indians of the province of Comogre tell me that there is so much fabricated gold in the homes

Elasio, son of Chief Ají, proudly insisted on being photographed *solo* (alone).

(Below)
End man on right is Constantino; man in army hat and blouse is Gabriel, brother of Chief Ají, the third man. These three Indians belong to the Río Tuquesa, the others are from the Río Chico. In Panama these Indians are called Cholos, on account of their civil and social status rather than their tribal classification. In my opinion these are Chocó Indians.

of the Caciques of the other sea that it would seem to us all to be out of reason: they state that along all the rivers of the other coast there is gold in great amount and in very big grains: they say that to the house of this Cacique Comogre come Indians from the other sea in canoes by a river which approaches the house of the Cacique, and they bring much gold from the mines in very large grains to be melted: in exchange for the gold they are given cotton cloth and handsome Indians of both sexes; they do not eat them like the people near to the great river [Atrato].

They say that the Indians of the other coast are very sociable and polite: they tell me that the other sea is very good to navigate in canoes, for it is continually smooth and never rough like the sea on their side, according to what the Indians say: I believe that in that sea are many islands where are many rich pearls in abundance, and that the Caciques have baskets full of them, as well as have all the Indians, men and women, generally.

This river runs from this Cacique Comogre to the other sea, and before arriving there it forms three arms, and each one of them empties by itself into the other sea: they say that by the arm which enters toward the west come the canoes with pearls to the house of Cacique Comogre to trade: they say that through the arm that enters toward the East come the canoes with gold from all sides, which is an incredible thing and without any comparison.

Since our Lord has made you the Master of such a great land where so much treasure is, it must not be cast in oblivion, for if Your Most Royal Highness is pleased to give and send me men, I dare venture, therefore, through the goodness of our Lord, to discover very eminent things, and where one can obtain so much gold and enough riches with which to be able to conquer a large part of the world; and if Your Most Royal Majesty is pleased with this and leave me in charge of the things which are necessary to do here, I have so much confidence in the mercy of our Lord that I will know how to give it such proper skill and industry as will bring it all to a good condition and Your Most Royal Highness be well served; and in case that I should not do this, I have no better thing than my head to put in pledge.

So much I certify to Your Most Royal Highness, that I shall seek that which promotes the service of Your Most Royal Highness with more diligence than the Governors who were lost here, Alonso de Ojeda and Diego de Niquesa, for I do not stay in bed while my men go to invade and overrun the country. I must inform Your Most Royal Highness that no company has gone throughout this land, to one part or another, that I have not gone in advance as guide, and even opening the roads with my own hand for those who went with me; and if it is not so, I refer to the deeds and to the fruit that each one of those who have passed here has given.

Most powerful Lord, as a person who has seen the things of these parts and who has more knowledge of the land than anyone else hitherto has had, and because I desire that the things here which I have commenced may flourish and grow to the state that is best suited to the service of Your Most Royal Highness, I wish to make known to you what now is proper and necessary to command to be provided, and this is for the present until the land is known and it is found out what is in it.

The principal thing necessary is that one thousand men come from the island Española, for men who now might come from Spain would not be worth much until they would be habituated to the country, because they would perish and we who are here with them. Your Most Royal Highness will have to order that this colony for the present is supplied with provisions by the hand of Your Most Royal Highness, and this is fitting in order that the land will be explored and the secrets of it known, and in this will be effected two things, one, the people will make much money trading in commodities; and the other and chief thing is that the land being provided with provisions, they will be able to do and find out great things and abundant riches, as will be shown by the work, with the help of God.

At the same time there has to be continually provided here many supplies to build small vessels for the rivers [illegible in original] the pitch and nails and sails and more than enough tackle; it is necessary that some masters come who know how to build brigantines: Your Most Royal Highness ought to send two hundred cross-bows made to order, the stays well furnished and the fittings [illegible] and of very strong draw, and that they be no more than up to two pounds, and on them money will be gained, because each one of those here will be glad to have one or two cross-bows; for besides being very good arms against the Indians, they supply many birds and game to men able to possess them. Two dozen very good hand-guns of light metal are needed, because those of iron are soon damaged by the rains and moisture and they are eaten with rust: Your Most Royal Highness has to command that two dozen guns are made of metal because those of iron were lost: enough if they weigh up to twenty-five or thirty pounds, and long, so that a man can carry one of them wherever it might be needed; and very good powder.

For the present, most puissant Lord, on the coming of more men, it is necessary to construct a fortress in the province of Davaibe, the strongest that can be made, because the region is thickly settled with bad people: another fortress must be built among the mines of Tubanamá in the province of Comogre, likewise for the reason that there are many Indians in that territory; and these fortresses, most powerful Lord, at present, could not be built of lime and stone nor of mud walls, but two palisades of very stout timber have to be made, with earth between them well stopped up and very strong, and of the size that would be necessary according to the means available and ability to carry out that one might have: and around it a very good strong ditch; and he that tells Your Most Royal Highness that at the present time fortresses of lime and stone or of anything else may be built in this country, is because he who might say it has not seen the quality of the land.

This that I say, most powerful Lord, will be put in effect with the coming of reinforcements, if our Lord please; and from these two seats, the one of Dabaibe and the other of the province of Comogre, the land will be explored and the secrets of it will be known and of the other sea of the south side, and all the rest that should be necessary.

Your Most Royal Highness will have to send master mechanics to repair the cross-bows, for every day they get out of order on account of the numerous rains. In everything that I mention money will be made, and it ought not to cost Your Most Royal Highness anything more than to give orders to provide the men that are needed; for I dare, with the help of our Lord, to do everything in these parts best suited to the service of Your Most Royal Highness, most puissant Lord, for as I have said, I am here to serve and advise Your Most Royal Highness of all that might appear to me to execute your service.

And now the residents of this Town [La Antigua] send to entreat Your Most Royal Highness to do them certain favors, the greater part of which is expedient that Your Highness concede to them, for it will promote greatly his service. In that which treats of certain Indians that are in certain provinces who eat men, and others who are in the back part of this gulf of *vraba* [Urabá] and in the lowlands of the great river of San Juan, and many other extensive lands subject to overflow which are in lagoons of this river, and other marshy ground round about this gulf, which extend as far as the beginning of the flat country of the province of Davaive.

For all these Indians have no tillable lands, nor any other means of subsistence save only the fish, and with the fish they go to trade for maize: it is a people without any profit [to the Spaniards] and they do more; for when Christians pass in canoes about this great river of San Juan, they sally out with their canoes and chase them, and they have killed some of us Christians, and in the same manner they come out from the thickets where all the Indians of the neighborhood and round about congregate.

The land where the Indians eat men is very poor and unprofitable, and at no time could it be of any benefit: likewise these Indians of the Caribana have well merited death a thousand times, because they are a very wicked people and in other times have killed many Christians, and some of ours in the passage there when we lost the ship [on which was Balboa with Enciso]: I do not say to give them for slaves as being an evil race; better still to command all to be burnt, little and big, in order that no memory might remain of so vile a people: I declare this, Sire, in regard to the point of Caribana [Punta Caribana] and as far as twenty leagues inland, the one because the natives are very bad, and the other for the reason that the land is very sterile and worthless.

It is best that Your Highness give license that all these Indians may be carried to the island Española and to the other islands settled with Christians to be sold and profit from them, and with the price of them other slaves might be brought here; for in order to hold them in these parts [Darien] it is impossible to make use of them, not so much as only one day, because the land is very large where they can run away and hide; so that the Spaniards in these parts not holding Indians secure, it will not be able to do what is conducive to the service of Your Highness, nor can any gold be taken from the mines.

Likewise, the settlers are sending to beseech Your Highness to grant them the privilege to fetch Indians from the districts of Beragua [Veragua], from a gulf which is called San Bras [San Blas], which is as far as fifty leagues from this Town, down along the coast. Your Highness will be very much served in doing them this favor, because the region is very useless and rough with very large groves of trees and numerous mountains; and seen from the sea, all the land is

San Blas houses and canoes.

When a San Blas gentleman takes his family to town he dons a
derby hat—an ancient custom of this tribe of Indians.

overflowed in such a manner that it is not seen how to have any profit from the Indians of those parts of Veragua and of Caribana which are lowlands, except it is in this way, by bringing them to towns of the Christians, from whence they can be carried to the islands of Cuba and Jamaica and to other islands peopled by Christians to exchange for other *navorías* Indians, many of them wild, that they likewise have in the other islands settled by Christians, and which the Christians can not make to serve them well; and in this manner ordering the warlike Indians where they may be out of their homeland, those of these parts will work well on the islands and those from the islands here. I advise this to Your Highness for it is very suitable to your service that you give them the privilege of taking Indians from the neighboring islands to this mainland: concerning this, I inform Your Highness that in all these districts within two hundred leagues around this Town, there is no inhabited island except one in Cartagena, where for the present are plenty natives and they defend well their property.

Also in that which concerns the gold that is gathered and in possession of the Indians which is obtained through trade and in war, it is conducive to your service that you grant the Spaniards the favor, from now forward, to give one-fifth of all the gold that they should have to Your Highness; and the reason why it will benefit Your Highness is that your share now being the fourth, it makes them go forth with reluctance to explore the country and engage in war with great hardship, for in fact it is so excessive that it is a thing unbearable and they prefer rather to take out gold from the mines, for there are many good ones near here, than to go out to die; and for this reason in the event that I or the Governor who should be in the future, make the Christians go to invade and discover the land, they never will go willingly; and a thing done against one's will never can be done so well as it ought to be, and if it is done willingly, all is performed as requested and everything is found done as they wished it executed. Therefore, I certify to Your Highness that if the King's share is a fifth, the gold will be taken in much greater quantity than staying at the fourth part; and, moreover, that they will find out the country as Your Highness desires.

With respect to the cloth of the Indians and trifles in their houses, it is a matter of small account and of little value, and all the rest is taken in portion that they can not benefit from it, for in truth many

times things are left with the Indians in their houses because of
having no room to carry them; and it is expedient to the service of
Your Highness to give all these things freely to the Christians.

In regard to the arms and guns, and supplies for constructing
brigantines and skilled workmen to build them, this is expedient
above everything else, for without these one cannot do any thing well;
and although now Your Highness should order it, all would be at the
expense of the Spaniards in these parts without it costing Your Highness anything: on all that Your Highness might provide from Castile
of what I have named, much will be gained and the country will be
provided with what is needed: Your Highness may receive all this
from a most loyal servant and give faith to all of this, because in this
manner it favors the service of Your Highness.

I do not wish to build castles in the air like those set up by the
Governors [Nicuesa and Ojeda] that Your Highness sent here, who
between both together lost eight hundred men; and the Spaniards
that I have been able to rescue, of those that both left shipwrecked
and who escaped, are about fifty, and this is the truth: and Your
Highness can see what I have done and discovered, and maintained
all these Christians without any aid except that of God and with
very great industry, and who has known how to sustain and support
himself by the Indians, and it shows by what Your Highness there
will see that I will know what to tell him best suits these parts: and
if I should err in something that promotes the service of Your Highness, I entreat Your Highness that he accept my most excessive wish
and desire to serve Your Highness, and though now, most powerful
Lord, I may not comprehend everything that is needed for the future
in this land, in the meantime I certify to him that for what is suitable,
I will know how to give as good care and skill as all those commanders who until the present have come here; and in order that
Your Highness may judge it, behold what the Governors so far
appointed have discovered, found out and obtained; for all have gone
back lost, and they left here the shores well filled with graves, and
even if the many Christians who died might be interred in the ground,
the truth is that the greater part of the Christians who died were
eaten by dogs and crows: I do not want to lengthen this any more,
except to say that by the works Your Highness may see what each
one has been able to do and has done until now.

Most puissant Lord, in order that Your Highness may be better
informed of all that happened here, I am sending Sebastián de

Campo [Ocampo]; I implore Your Highness to give him complete belief, for he goes informed by me of the whole truth and of everything that can be done here in the service of Your Highness and what is necessary for the land.

Your Highness must know that in days past there were certain controversies here, because the *Alcaldes* and *Regidores* of this Town, with envy and falsehood, tried to arrest me, and since they could not do it, they made false charges against me and with false witnesses and secretly, of which I complain to Your Highness; for if they should not be punished, never any Governor of those who might come here for Your Highness would fail to have dissensions, for I being *Alcalde Mayor* for Your Highness, they entered against me a thousand iniquities, and have acted in the same manner to all those who have come to these parts; and if the justice of Your Highness is not feared, that which is best for his service never will be done.

And because the *Alcaldes* and *Regidores* transmitted an accusation against me, which I believe Your Highness will see there, I made Judges of two *Hidalgos* in order that they might make an investigation and receive information of my life and of my most loyal and great services that I have performed for Your Highness in these parts of the Indies and main land and these provinces in which now we are, which I send to Your Highness that you may see the wickedness of those people; and because I believe that Your Highness will take much pleasure in all that I have done in his service in these territories, I beg Your Highness to examine it all so that he grant me favors according to my services: I am sending also an information of what happened after they devised their evil deeds.

Most mighty Lord, one favor I want to entreat Your Highness to do me, for it conduces much to your service, and it is that Your Highness command that no Bachelor of Law nor any other thing, unless it should be of medicine, may pass to these parts of the mainland under a heavy penalty that Your Highness order to provide for it, for no *Bachiller* comes here who is not a devil, and they lead the life of devils, and not only are they bad, but they even contrive and possess methods how to bring about a thousand lawsuits and villainies: this will advance much the service of Your Highness, because the country is new.

Most potent Lord, by a brigantine that we sent from here on which went Juan de Quicedo and Rodrigo de Colmenares, I forwarded to Your Highness 500 *pesos de oro* in most beautiful grains from the mines, and for the reason that the navigation is somewhat dangerous for small vessels, I now send to Your Highness with Sebastián del Campo 370 *pesos de oro* from the mines: more would be sent if it were not because it could not be gathered while the ships were here. In everything that I have said, I beseech Your Highness to provide what most will promote his service.

May our Lord prosper the life and most Royal estate of Your Highness with increase of many more Kingdoms and Lordships to his Holy service, and which in these parts may be discovered, and all come to the hands of Your Highness as Your most Royal Highness desires, for there are more riches here than in all the world.

" *De la villa de Santa María del Antigua de la provincia del Darien en el golfo de Urava oy Jueves a 20 de Enero de 513 anos.— De Vuestra Alteza hechura i crianza que sus mui Reales manos i pies besa.*"

From the town of Santa Maria del Antigua of the province of Darien on the Gulf of Uraba today Thursday the 20th of January 1513. The creature and creation of Your Highness, who kisses your most Royal hands and feet.

Vasco Núñez de Valboa

Comments on Balboa's Letter of 20 January 1513

Balboa's letter of 20 January 1513 is the basic document describing the territories of Darién, Urabá, and Panamá. The settlement of Santa María de la Antigua del Darién was made on the advice of Vasco Núñez, and it fell to his lot to rule and maintain the colony. This Isthmian stretch of land was the first permanent conquest on the continent of America.

In the very first sentence of this letter, Balboa tells Ferdinand of two former letters which he had written to him, and of another letter addressed to the Almirante Diego Colón, governor of Española, informing him of the dire need of the colonists at La Antigua for food, to which Diego Colón responded by despatching two ships laden with provisions. This food preserved the lives of the three hundred men comprising the Colony.

Balboa then refers to the order sent to him by the king to transport the residuals of Nicuesa's party at Nombre de Dios to La Antigua; Ferdinand commanding Diego de Nicuesa, his governor and captain of the province of Veragua, to at once return to Spain. Both these orders are dated at Burgos, 31 January 1512, and would not reach Tierra Firme under three months. In the meantime, Nicuesa had come to La Antigua on the invitation of the citizens, who, learning of his threats to take away their gold and punish them, had compelled the governor to sail away on the first day of March, 1511. Knowing the sad condition of the colonists left behind at Nombre de Dios under Gonzalo de Badajoz, Balboa sent them food; and in time all were carried to La Antigua, where they shared in the distribution of lots and fields.

The failure of the two governors, Nicuesa and Ojeda, favorites of the court, was recounted by Vasco Núñez, who tells the king that they did not know how to exercise authority, mistreated their colonists, were puffed up with presumption, and gave themselves up to enjoyment.

Balboa explains that he came to know the great secrets of the land through his zeal to promote his Majesty's service, and to preserve the people who had elected him as their head. This is confirmed by his contemporaries, who represent Vasco Núñez as a man of great activity and energy.

It was true, as Balboa wrote, that he treated the Indians kindly. When they resisted or lied to him, he punished them thoroughly; but when they yielded, he treated them with great consideration and made terms of peace with them. No Spanish captain who followed him in Panama was ever so kind to the natives as was Balboa. He was not bragging when he wrote that by night and by day he marched at the head of his men. Balboa's description of the rivers and swamps of the isthmus is true to nature, and we can almost see those weary, restless gold seekers warily stepping through the streams and swamps, their clothing and arms fastened to the *tablachinas* on top of their heads. Upon returning to Antigua from these expeditions, Balboa made fair division of the spoils, first taking out the lion's share for Don Fernando of Aragon, the acting king of Castile.

Vasco Núñez was proud, and full of gratitude to the Lord that the marvelous riches of the land had been revealed to him, and entreats Ferdinand that he be allowed to complete the great enterprise by leading an expedition in search of the South Sea. With his one hundred men fit for war and five hundred men or more to be sent from Española, Balboa could enter the land and pass to the territory of the south where was the other sea—"*i pasar la otra mar de la parte de medio dia.*" This is the first mention of the South Sea in the writings of Balboa that have been preserved. From the casual way in which he alludes to the other sea, it is obvious that Balboa had written about it in his previous letters to Ferdinand, and assumed that the *Procuradores* Quicedo and Colmenares would arrive at the court long before this letter, and report their mission to the king. The districts about La Antigua were described by Balboa, either from his own experience or from what the Indians had told him. It is worthy of note that most everything related by the Indians was true. Two leagues back of La Antigua was a ridge of mountains running toward the south, from which flowed thirty streams bearing gold. Vasco Núñez had explored the lower stretches of the great river flowing into the Gulf of Urabá from the south and named it the Rio Grande de San Juan, now known as the Atrato. Captive Indians from higher up the river gave information of that region, especially of the gold and the natives.

Cacique Davaive, or Dabaibe, the great lord of that territory, had no mines in his own lands, but he had established a gold smelter and manufactured golden jewelry for neighboring chiefs. The latter brought their gold to Davaive, who gave them in exchange young men and boys to eat, and female Indians to serve their wives; not to serve as wives, as Markham translates it. Davaive also traded wild pigs, cotton clothing, salt and large quantities of fish for the gold.

Davaive stored the gold nuggets brought to him, and also the objects he fabricated, in baskets, which were heavy to carry, of course. These baskets are called bags by Markham. But why cavil at Sir Clements, the Englishman, when José Toribio Medina, the distinguished South American historian who wrote so voluminously on early Latin-American history, stumbles at the same word *cestas* (baskets) in this same sentence? Medina declares that Dabaibe possessed some large pieces of gold made in the shape of baskets—" *hechas en forma de cestas* "—which a man could scarcely carry.

Basketry is one of the oldest of arts. Baskets were in general use by the natives of America. They were made by the women from a great variety of textile plants. Some were finely made, veritable works of art, in which to keep small articles; others were large and crudely constructed for storing or transporting large objects. When Balboa reached the South Sea he found the Indians keeping their pearls in baskets, and when Valderrábano, the notary, went out to an island in the bay of Panama to secure more pearls, he brought the large pearl oyster shells back to shore in an *espuerta,* or large, coarse native basket.

Only two days' travel from the settlement of Dabaibe was a warlike cannibal tribe, who ate as many men as they could get. They were lords of the richest mines in the world, wrote Vasco Núñez. These rich mines were in a province on the Urabá side of the gulf toward the sunrise, and should be easy to locate, as within the province was a mountain covered with clouds, which appeared to be the highest in the world.

Juan de Castellanos, who sung the deeds, heroic and otherwise, of the first Spaniards in America, says in his *Elegías* that the Indians of Santa Marta, as well as of Caribana in general, were not called *Caribes,* or Cannibals, because they ate human flesh, but for the reason that they were brave fighters and defended their homes:

> " *No porque alli comiesen carne humana,*
> *Mas porque defendian bien su casa.*"

Throughout Darien and adjoining regions the Indians did not mine gold-bearing ore from shafts and tunnels, but gathered the free gold in the form of nuggets or grains. To Balboa this appeared to be without effort—"*sin ningun trabajo.*" They simply picked up the nuggets in the gullies and *barrancas* after heavy rains. In the dry season the Indians burnt the vegetation, and the gold remained exposed in very beautiful grains.

Vasco Núñez and his men never learned to handle canoes skillfully, doubtless because they generally had Indians to do the paddling; and the Spaniards usually met with defeat when attacked by natives on the water, especially up the Atrato River. Balboa advises the king that small boats could be built on the model of the *fustas,* the small sailboats used about the Mediterranean. When the strong breezes blew and the river not in flood, these boats could be propelled by sail alone, helping with the oar in narrow channels or at sharp turns in the river. The *grandes brisas* are the strong winds from the north or northeast which prevail along the coast during the dry season.

From what he had seen of the lower Atrato valley, Balboa informed Ferdinand that mounted men could not march along the river. Up to this writing, no horses had been used in the *entradas.*

Twenty leagues westward from La Antigua was the province of Careta. Balboa maintained closer relations with these Indians than with any other band on the isthmus. Caretita, the beautiful daughter of Cacique Careta, was the favorite lady friend of the white Tiba. Andagoya states that the province of Careta was thirty leagues west from Antigua, probably meaning the location of the houses of the chief, or the little port still known as Puerto Careta.

Farther to the west, about forty leagues from the Spanish settlement, was the province of Comogre, and west of that came the land of Cacique Pocorosa in the province of Cueva. Both Comogre and Pocorosa possessed two fishing villages on the Caribbean coast, though the principal town of each was twelve leagues inland. Vasco Núñez says that the river which flowed by the seat of Cacique Comogre emptied into the Southern Sea by three arms or mouths, so his capital must have been on the southern slope of the mountains, though he supplied himself with fish from the north coast.

Comogre, like the renowned Dabaibe, operated a gold smelter, or melter. For the gold brought up the river from the south coast the chief gave cotton cloth and young people of both sexes. The males were not eaten, as along the river Atrato. West of Comogre was Pocorosa, and the rivers of both regions contained gold, which was collected by the two methods previously described as practiced in Urabá, or Caribana, picking it out of dry *arroyos* and shallow streams. These two chieftains often warred with each other.

One day's journey from Pocorosa were beautiful mountains where the caciques had accumulated so much gold that they stored it in the *barbacoas*, like maize, rather than keeping it in baskets. M. Gaffarel ventures to translate the Indian word *barbacoas* as meaning sacks, which is another example of how errors get into history. See my definition of *barbacoa, barbacra, barbecue.* At this point, Navarrete inserted four words— "*Sea mas cumplidamente informado*"—to fill a void in the original; so the corrected sentence reads that, in order that the king "be more completely informed," Vasco Núñez was sending him a branded Indian ("*Yndio errado*") to demonstrate how the gold was collected.

Balboa tells Ferdinand that he had been within a day's march of those mountains, but was short of men, and could not go farther; "for man proceeds as far as he can and not as far as he wishes "—"*porque llega hombre fasta donde puede i no fasta donde quiere.*"

My copy of this letter reads, "*por el canto de aquellas Sierras,*" which I translate, "along the edge of those mountains"; changed by Navarrete, or his copyist, to "*por el tanto,*" I know not why.

Vasco Núñez then writes of the gold and pearls of "the other sea" in a manner which plainly shows that he had written extensively of the South Sea in a former communication to the king, and, of course, to Diego Colón at Santo Domingo. This new sea was only three days' travel from Comogre, and the chiefs along its shores possessed so many golden ornaments and such fine pearls that it drove the Spaniards out of their senses. Practically everything that the Indians told Balboa turned out to be true, which speaks well for their veracity. The assertions of the natives that the South Sea always was smooth and fit for canoes raised the question whether it really was a sea. Balboa depended on this information when he insisted, against the warning of Cacique Chiapes, in going out in canoes on the Gulf of San Miguel. However, it is evident that Balboa firmly believed what the Indians told him, for he writes confidently of "the other sea" and of "the other coast" long before he actually viewed the Pacific Ocean.

As Vasco Núñez enlarges on the accounts of the abundance of gold and pearls to be secured on the South Sea, he writes very much as did Fray Tomás de Berlanga, bishop of Panama, in 1535, to Charles V, grandson of King Ferdinand. The bishop told the emperor that he was lord of the great South Sea containing the treasures of Peru, which he could enter through the narrow strip of land at Panama, and hold its riches as under lock and key.

Balboa assured Ferdinand that if the king would furnish him with more men, he would obtain, with the aid of God, so much wealth that a great part of the earth could be conquered with it. In faith of which Vasco Núñez pledged his head as a forfeit. Balboa's words proved true. With the wealth of the Indies, Spain, for a time, did rule much of the earth. Ferdinand did not accept Balboa's plea to rule in Darien, but Vasco Núñez lost his head, nevertheless.

Again Balboa made the mistake of ridiculing the attempts of Ojeda and Nicuesa, favorites of both the king and of Bishop Fonseca, and he certifies to the king that he did not lie in bed while his men went forth to secure food, gold, and slaves, but that he went in advance as guide, even opening the trails with his own hands.

Vasco Núñez in his letter states truthfully that he knew more about Darien and Panama than any other person. He warned

Ferdinand that the reinforcements should come from the old settlers on Española, men acclimated and experienced in the Indies. Time proved the wisdom of his advice, for a large part of the Spaniards brought out by Pedrarias soon perished— seven hundred in one month, writes Andagoya.

The first need of the colony was to get enough food rather than gold, and Balboa stresses the necessity for the king to send a constant supply of provisions, so that he would be free to explore the country, thinking, no doubt, of those big pearls and the best way to arrive at that other sea.

Balboa exhibits foresight in asking for materials, sails, and tackle wherewith to build small sailing vessels for coasting about the Gulf of Urabá and even up the Atrato. He specifies the number and kind of cross-bows and hand-guns needed, and asks for mechanics to keep them in order.

When more men arrived, a fortress must be constructed in each of the two most populous and warlike provinces; one in the province of Dabaibe, the other among the mines of Tubanamá in the province of Comogre. These strongholds should be defended by a double row of palisades made of very strong timber, and of the size that might be necessary, according to the aptitude and ability at hand—" *Segud los Apaños que oviere de haver.*"

That word *Apaños,* begun with a capital letter, has provoked some comment. One writer thought it might be the name of a band of Indians in that region. Paul Gaffarel makes it *bagages* in French. Navarrete solves the difficulty by changing the word to *paños,* and Medina's copy is the same. This is equivalent to saying that the garment would be cut according to the cloth. I see no occasion for such subterfuge. *Apaños* is a perfectly good and appropriate word to use in this connection. One of its meanings (and many Spanish words seem to have many meanings) is aptitude or ability to do a thing—" *maña o habilidad para alguna cosa.*" Possibly Balboa wrote *Apaños,* using the plural form, to show that his vocabulary was not limited to the word *maña,* so often used by him. Or, perhaps

Balboa actually wrote, or intended to use, the word *amaños*, which means the implements or means at hand for the execution of a work.

From the two seats or fortresses in the lands of the two most formidable chiefs, Dabaibe and Tubanamá, the land could be explored, more gold secured, and the secrets of the Southern Sea discovered.

Balboa's description of the swamps and marshes, and of the *anegadizos*, or tidal lands about the mouths of the Atrato, subject to inundation, cannot be surpassed.

The cannibals about the *culata* of the gulf and over in Urabá could be caught and branded and sold into slavery on Española; or, better still, be burned, little and big. Balboa wanted permission to capture Indians along the Gulf of San Blas, then included in Veragua, and carry them to the islands settled by Christians, there to be traded for slaves taken from those localities. Bringing the latter to Darien, they would be far from their homes and not likely to run away in a strange country and hide in the mountains.

Balboa told Ferdinand that his share of the gold taken from the Indians by war or in trade should be one-fifth instead of one-quarter. Vasco Núñez here referred to the *asiento* of 9 June 1508, made with Nicuesa and Ojeda, which declared that the gold, silver, jewels, cloth, and other things obtained from the natives by trade or otherwise, must pay one-fifth to the king the first year, and one-fourth during the other three years of the duration of the agreement. The colonists now, January, 1513, under Balboa, were in the third year of their settlement in Darien. The men were reluctant to go out to take the gold held by the Indians, and so face the possibility of being killed or wounded, when under another provision of the aforesaid *asiento*, or contract, they were required during the third year to give the king only one-eighth of the gold obtained by mining. And there were very good mines near the town, wrote Vasco Núñez, the labor being performed by Indian slaves, of course.

Balboa emphasizes the necessity for arms, small vessels, and provisions, above everything else.

Vasco Núñez takes another fling at Nicuesa and Ojeda when he writes: " I do not wish to build castles in the air (*torres de viento*) like those set up by the Governors that Your Highness sent here, who between both together lost eight hundred men," leaving the beaches strewn with their bones.

Being acting governor and *alcalde mayor* by royal decree of 23 December 1511, Balboa urges that lawyer Corral, Alonso Pérez, and others should be punished for preferring false charges with the local officials against the representative of the king. To offset the charges which were forwarded to the king, Balboa appointed two *hidalgos* to be judges to inquire into his life and acts in Darien and report to Ferdinand.

It was a notorious fact that the lawyers in Española and on Tierra Firme did foment litigation. Since coming to Darien, and perhaps back in Salvatierra, Balboa had been much annoyed by lawyers, so he begs the king not to allow any *letrados*, or lawyers, to pass to Darien.

Sebastian de Ocampo had arrived at La Antigua from Española with a shipload of supplies soon after the return of Balboa from his expedition to Careta and Comogre. Ocampo was a man of some standing in the Indies and was known at the court. Balboa authorized him to act as his *procurador*, or agent to further his interest with Ferdinand.

Balboa's letter of 20 January 1513 is full of clear observations and honest reports of what he saw and heard in this new territory. He expresses great concern for the welfare of his men at La Antigua, as well as for the interests of the king. He gave Ferdinand wise counsel and told him what best to do to advance his service on Tierra Firme. The king was assured that if he gave orders as recommended by Vasco Núñez, the government of Darien would cost him nothing, all costs being at the expense of the colonists. Ferdinand would get his share of everything, and the Christians at La Antigua become rich, as many of them did under the rule of Balboa.

Ferdinand did not heed the warning of Vasco Núñez not to send men from Spain who had no experience in the Indies. Had he followed the advice of Balboa, hundreds of lives would have been spared, as well as the expense of the armada of Pedrarias and a long salary list.

When this remarkable letter finally reached Spain, Balboa had not a single friend at the court, only enemies. Enciso, the discredited *alcalde mayor* of the forlorn Ojeda, had been vitriolic in denouncing Vasco Núñez, under the guise of legality, ever since his return from Darien. Zamudio, fellow *alcalde* of Balboa, had been driven from court. Colmenares was false to the petition of the *Cabildo* and people of La Antigua. Ocampo, the latest *procurador* for Balboa, became mortally ill at Sevilla, where he died. Bishop Fonseca, the power next to the throne, seemed to hate all the honest *descubridores,* such as Columbus, Balboa, and Hernando Cortés.

Had Vasco Núñez lived much about the court of Spain, he would have been less honest and more politic in his correspondence with King Ferdinand. Columbus, Ojeda, Nicuesa, Pedrarias, and many other Spaniards coming to America possessed great advantage over Balboa in this respect. Throughout this long letter, Vasco Núñez ascribes all his success to the help of God and the Virgin. Expressing his loyalty to the king, Balboa kisses the most royal hands and feet of Ferdinand in the extravagant fashion of the period, and signs his name, *Vasco Núñez de Valboa.*

VII

BALBOA'S "OTHER SEA"

"There is more gold on the Sea of the South than there is iron in Biscay."

—Cacique Panquiaco.

THE long and informative letter, written by Balboa himself, was the most important and convincing information of Darien yet received at court. Ferdinand had counted much on Nicuesa and Ojeda, and both expeditions had been tragic failures. The king now determined to concentrate his efforts on La Antigua del Darien and proceed with the further settlement and development of Tierra Firme.

Colmenares writes that he and Quicedo were at the court of Spain, and King Ferdinand was just about to send them away, when letters arrived from Vasco Núñez, "full of lies and ravings," in order that the king might make him governor of Darien. Balboa was believed more than the *procuradores*, continues Colmenares. On account of these letters, and there were two at least, Ferdinand hastened the preparation of the armada which he had ordered on 31 May 1513, contrary to what had been agreed, says Colmenares. The *procurador* does not tell us what the king had agreed to do before he received the letter from Vasco Núñez.

If that other sea ("*la otra mar*") reported by Balboa really existed so near to La Antigua and only a few days' journey from the Sea of the Caribs, as seemed to be the case, the sooner the fact was determined the better. There were reasons of state why Spain should possess the South Sea before any other Christian nation, more particularly Portugal. By the Bull of Donation the then Pope, in May, 1493, did give, grant, and assign to King Ferdinand and Queen Isabella all the islands and firm lands, discovered and to be discovered, in the direction of India, toward the west and south of a line drawn one hundred leagues west of the Azores and Cape Verde Islands, and extending from the Pole Arctic to the Pole Antarctic. There was a proviso that none of these islands and firm lands, found and to be found, had been possessed by any Christian king or prince " prior to the day of the Nativity of our Lord Jesus Christ last past from the which beginneth this present year 1493."

Ferdinand was uncertain as to the extent of Portugal's discoveries along the coasts of Asia. If Balboa's " *otra mar* "— other sea—was found where the Indians declared it to be, it would mean that Tierra Firme was not very wide at this part, confirming the belief of Columbus in a narrow strip of land, if not of water (*estrecho*), in the neighborhood of Veragua. Although Portuguese sailors, by sailing around Africa, had reached Asia after 1493, it would be very awkward for Spain to find Portuguese ships sailing along the other side of Tierra Firme only a short distance from Antigua del Darien. Remember that the wide Pacific Ocean had not been revealed to Europeans, and that the water to the east of Cathay and about Cipangu was represented as a projection of the Indian Ocean, called by Ptolemy the *Sinus Magnus*. Without knowing of the immense Pacific Ocean, this *Sinus,* or Gulf of Ptolemy, must wash the other side of Tierra Firme. The Spice Islands, where grew cloves, nutmegs, and other spices so much valued in Europe, should be sufficiently near to Darien and Veragua to fall within Spain's share of the unknown world.

Enciso had told much of the riches of Urabá and Darien, and of the report that the Indians of Cenú set nets in the rivers to catch the big nuggets of gold as they were washed down from the hills. Tales by the *procuradores* from La Antigua supported the story, and the long letter of Vasco Núñez confirmed and augmented the reports of the golden wealth of this region. Balboa, in his letter of 20 January 1513, stated that after floods in the rivers, gold nuggets the size of oranges were found in the dry beds of the streams. He also described the gold smelter of the great Cacique Dabaibe who lived up the valley of the Atrato River; and he informed the king that the great lord kept one hundred artisans employed working the gold into diadems, breastplates, mirrors, bracelets, figures of humans and animals, necklaces, beads, and other forms. The Indians told Vasco Núñez that the great chiefs about the South Sea—" *la otra mar* "—had such stores of gold and pearls that it drove the Spaniards out of their senses.

THE DARIEN-PANAMA REGION NAMED CASTILLA DEL ORO, 4 JULY 1513

The lure of gold was just what Ferdinand needed to secure men and supplies for his armada. These glowing reports of the abundance of gold in this region of Tierra Firme (today, Urabá, Darién, and the Isthmus of Panamá) gave origin to the name of Castilla del Oro. On 4 July 1513, the king wrote to the admiral, judges and officials of Española that it was necessary to exercise great circumspection in the affairs of Tierra Firme in order to promote its population. " We have commanded to name it Castilla del Oro, even if it is not clear that it is mainland "—" *La hemos mandado nombrar Castilla del Oro y aun no consta si es tierra firme.*" Castilla del Oro might turn out to be simply another island barring the way to the East. In his decree of 23 December 1511, appointing Vasco Núñez *Gobernador interino,* the king called Darien an island. The more Ferdinand heard about the isthmian region, the bigger he decided to make his new expedition to go there—a Golden Castile on the western road to Asia. The dream of the Old Admiral was coming true at last!

It will be shown that in his order of 31 May to fit out an armada, King Ferdinand stated that he would name some prominent man in Spain—" *persona principal* "—to head the expedition, and who would relieve Vasco Núñez from command in Darien. Considering the great services that acting governor

Balboa had rendered in preserving the remnants of the expeditions of Nicuesa and Ojeda; in locating and maintaining for three years the town of Antigua del Darien, in exploring the land and pacifying numerous caciques, and in collecting gold and slaves, of which the king got his share, it would have seemed only just that Ferdinand should accede to his request and supply Vasco Núñez with a well equipped force with which to go in search of that southern sea. If successful in his quest, a permanent appointment as governor would be small recompense for so great a service.   Long before this, on 23 December 1511, Ferdinand had decided, as shown by the temporary (*interino*) commission to Balboa, to provide a regular governor for Tierra Firme.

It was due to the advice of Pasamonte and Fonseca, rather than to the damaging testimony of Enciso and Colmenares, that the king refused the request of Balboa for one thousand men and supplies with which to seek the other sea. I believe that Bishop Fonseca was much influenced by the letters of Pasamonte, who, as chief of the king's partisans on Española, opposed increasing the power of Vasco Núñez on the ground that he had been appointed by Viceroy Diego Colón to be his lieutenant on Tierra Firme, over which he claimed jurisdiction. Up to this time, the only area on the mainland allowed to Diego Colón was the region of Veragua, today in western Panama.

Had the *Regidor* Valdivia not been wrecked on the shoals known as the *Víboras*, losing the golden presents intended for Pasamonte, it is probable that the royal treasurer would have recommended Vasco Núñez for governor and captain-general of Castilla del Oro.

The *Licenciado* Suazo, judge of *residencia* on Española, writes that Pasamonte was angry with Vasco Núñez, and in order to destroy him resolved to discredit him to the Catholic king.   He advised Ferdinand to send an armada to Tierra Firme with a governor who would be over Balboa.   It was at this time that Enciso passed through Santo Domingo on his way to Spain, and Pasamonte intrusted the letter to Enciso, who was a great enemy of Balboa—"*era grande enemigo del dicho Vasco Núñez.*"

THE PROCURADORES JUAN DE QUICEDO AND RODRIGO DE COLMENARES

Juan de Quicedo and Rodrigo de Colmenares departed from La Antigua del Darien about 1 November 1512, and endured many hardships and delays before reaching the port of Santo Domingo in Española. They sailed in one of the old brigantines, which seems to have been in worse condition than the one in which Diego de Nicuesa was banished from Darien.

In his *Memorial* against Vasco Núñez, in which Colmenares speaks quite highly of himself, the *procurador* tells us that the brigantine was calked without pitch, the tackle and rigging made of vines, and the cable of twisted bark from certain trees, and that a stone served as an anchor. Food for the voyage as far as Santo Domingo, the first stop, consisted only of eight bushels of corn and twenty-five *arrobas* of drinking water. In this instance the *arroba* was the old Spanish liquid measure of thirty-two pints, and not the common dry measure. The crew was made up of eleven Christians and three Indian slaves, one of the latter a woman, all without the least experience in seamanship and navigation. The *procuradores* bore not only their credentials and presents for officials, but also letters and gold from many colonists for their families at home.

The two agents steered for Española, and, like many other vessels sailing from the Darien region, the brigantine brought up on the shores of Cuba, recently settled by Spaniards. It took some years for the regular pilots to allow for the westward drift of the equatorial currents in the Caribbean Sea, and these inexperienced sailors were very fortunate to make land where they could be succored, and from whence they proceeded to the adjoining island of Española. Four months were spent in reaching Española, where, writes Colmenares, all but one died as the result of their labors, little food and impure water, Colmenares being the survivor—"*ni hai otro vivo que este*

Colmenares." Despite the preceding lines, Colmenares goes on to state that the two *procuradores,* Quicedo and himself, arrived in Spain and presented their petition to the king. From another source we learn that they reached Spain in the middle of May, 1513, bringing along an Indian man and woman to give faith to their assertions.

In part explanation of the foregoing discrepancies, it should be remembered that the writers of these old chronicles often paid scant attention to time, subject, verb, or the sequence of events. The Spanish, like other European languages, had not reached its present stage of development. Colmenares wrote his *Memorial* about three years after his mission to Spain with Quicedo, and after he had returned a second time from Darien. Juan de Quicedo died soon after arriving in Spain, and the Indian man and woman, like many Indians carried to Spain either as slaves or exhibits, probably died within a short time. No doubt, Colmenares knew, when he wrote the *Memorial* in 1515, that some of the Spaniards who had accompanied him on the terrible voyage to Española had passed away, so he stated that he was the sole survivor.

Alcalde Zamudio had been shown no consideration at court, and was forced to go into hiding to escape imprisonment and the risk of losing his life. Enciso, on the other hand, was well received, his bills paid out of the treasury, and he was named *regidor* of Santo Domingo. The king may have received other information from the Indies, as from returning sea captains, or perhaps Enciso showed too much malice in his charges against Balboa. Distrust of the veracity of the *bachiller's* assertions induced Ferdinand to write, on 28 April 1513, to Pasamonte in Santo Domingo, telling him that he was much concerned about what had occurred in Darien and what was taking place there now. The king directed his trusted official to find out the facts " by all the ways and methods within his power," and by the first ships sailing to send to him a complete, long and true report of them, and what was fit that the king should do in the matter.

As has been stated, the two solicitors from Darien, Quicedo and Colmenares, arrived in Sevilla about the middle of May, 1513, and reported to the officials of the *Casa de la Contratación*. They told of the proximity of the South Sea to Antigua del Darien, as announced by Cacique Panciaco, eldest son of Comogre, and of that young chieftain's advice to Balboa that to reach the sea one thousand Spaniards would be needed to fight and overcome the great Tubanamá and other caciques who would bar the way. This report was confirmed by letter from Viceroy Colón, coming in the same ship, communicating what Vasco Núñez had written to him about the South Sea. On 19 May, the officials of the Indies House wrote to the king announcing the arrival of the *procuradores* from Darien and the good news they brought of the existence of a southern sea.

First Order to Prepare an Armada for Darien, 31 May 1513

This information caused great satisfaction in the court. Without waiting for Quicedo and Colmenares to reach the court, then at Valladolid, Ferdinand, on 31 May, despatched orders to the officials of the *Casa de la Contratación* to proceed at once in the preparation of an armada for Darien, " without loss of a single day "—" *por que no se pierda vn solo dia.*"

In this long dispatch, the king told the officers of the Indies House in Sevilla how much pleasure he had in their letter announcing the coming of the *procuradores* and the great news they brought from Darien. It would be a great fault on the part of the king to fail to investigate what the Lord had revealed in those parts. The officials must begin immediately to prepare the armada with care and diligence. For the land force, eight hundred to one thousand men should be enlisted, who would be commanded by a " principal person " whom the king would name. Enough supplies should be collected to last for fifteen or sixteen months, and the men be furnished with rations during the voyage, and for one month after they reached Darien, while they were becoming settled. When some of the people would enter the land in search of mines or something else ("ó otra cosa"—Did the king have the South Sea in mind?), they had to be supported largely by wine and meat. The very first thing that the officials must do was to prepare a proclamation, in conformity with a *Memorial* enclosed, to be published in the best places to secure the men for Tierra Firme. In order not to delay the post, Ferdinand would not send all the necessary instructions at that time, but soon would send them by another messenger.

As for the mariners, they had to be provided for in another manner. They should be engaged for two years and be given provisions, as voyages to supply Tierra Firme and to go to Española would be necessary. All of which was set down in the said *Memorial* signed by Juan de Fonseca, then bishop of Palencia, and Lope Conchillos, secretary to the king. The officials were authorized to spend at once 5,000,000 *maravedís* of the gold recently come from the Indies, using great care and diligence that everything might be done and provided with the greatest despatch possible. For the pieces of artillery listed in the *Memorial*, the *Casa* would have to furnish the required metal to the artillery foundry in Málaga, as they could supply only powder and saltpeter. And because there was much need of money at that time, the officials could suspend certain payments to the Church, and immediately coin that gold and send 4,500,000 *maravedís* to the king's exchequer as soon as possible.

" Tell these *procuradores* and Francisco de Tapia [who came from Española] to hasten to my court," wrote the king, who was most eager to hear details of affairs in Darien. The promptitude with which Ferdinand acted upon the advices from Darien indicates that the king and his councillors had been giving much attention to the Portuguese voyages to the coasts of Asia. By this time the majority of learned persons in Europe were ready to admit the sphericity of the earth. If a sea south of Darien existed, as seemed very likely, it must be an extension of the waters bathing the oriental shores of Asia.

Considered in connection with extensive discoveries by

Spanish and Portuguese navigators along the coasts of the mainland of America, especially the shores of Brazil, it seemed very reasonable to believe that Darien must be quite near to Asia. The wide expanse of the Pacific Ocean not being known to Europe, Darien and the Isthmus of Panama were so far west of the " Pope's Line " that it followed, as a matter of course, that Cipango, Cathay, and the Spiceries could not be far away. This South Sea report revived and confirmed the belief held by Christopher Columbus that a waterway, or strait, led through the land in the region of Veragua.

The first lands in the West Indies encountered by the Spaniards were islands, scores of them, big and little. The first settlements were made on islands. Cuba, so large that it was thought to be a projection of the continent of Asia, turned out to be an island. So, when the expeditions sailed along the coasts of South, Central, and North America, many sections at first were considered to be islands, like Paria, Darien, Panama, Yucatán, and Florida. If islands, then there must be water routes to pass around and beyond them to Asia. Every sea captain and pilot was on the lookout for a strait through this barrier of land called Tierra Firme. In the preceding year the king wrote from Logroño, 10 December 1512, to Diego Colón for news of the settlement at Antigua del Darien, and to find out if there was a strait from the Gulf of Urabá, and if gold was found in the neighboring islands.

The sea reported by young Cacique Panciaco to the south of Darien, and which he declared to Balboa to be visible from the province of Quarequá, only six suns distant, would give a shorter route to the East than the long voyage around Africa and the Cape of Good Hope taken by the Portuguese. Above all, it would put an end to the monopoly of trade with the Orient now held by Portugal.

The *Procuradores* Quicedo and Colmenares were sent without delay to the court at Valladolid, where they were presented to the Catholic king by Juan de Fonseca, then bishop of Palencia and head of the newly created Council of the Indies. Peter Martyr, always greedy for news from the new world revealing itself in the West, seized upon the two solicitors and quizzed them about what the Christians were doing in Darien. He tells us that the bodies of these men were swollen, and that they were as yellow as though they suffered from liver disorder, or the gold they sought in the Indies.

The information brought by Quicedo and Colmenares pleased the king and all the courtiers. It was the first report from Darien that Ferdinand welcomed as good news. He would not listen to Zamudio, and despite the favor bestowed upon Enciso, the king was not satisfied with his accounts. Enciso had been filling the ears of the king with evil reports of affairs in La Antigua, consisting mainly of doleful complaints of how much he had suffered from the rule of Vasco Núñez. These charges were supported by letters from Corral, another *bachiller* of law, still in Darien. Moreover, Miguel de Pasamonte, leader of the royalist party in the Indies, opposed the pretension of Diego Colón to jurisdiction over Darien, Veragua, or any other part of the continent. Naturally, Pasamonte was unfriendly toward Balboa and any other person favored by the viceroy. This was before Pasamonte had been placated by contributions from Vasco Núñez.

Had the *Regidor* Valdivia not been wrecked on his last voyage to Santo Domingo, losing letters from Balboa to the officials and a large quantity of gold, including some fine pieces of Indian jewelry intended as gifts to Pasamonte, it is probable that the latter would have espoused at this time the cause of Vasco Núñez, as he did later.

Balboa was deceived when the people of Antigua del Darien elected Quicedo and Colmenares to go to Spain to solicit men and supplies for the South Sea expedition. Apparently, the acting governor believed that they were friendly to him and would ask the king to make him the regular governor, or, at least, give him the command of the large force said to be required to make the attempt to find the other sea.

When Quicedo and Colmenares arrived at court, then in

Valladolid in Old Castile, they found Balboa in so much dis-
favor that they realized it would be to their interest to join in
the cry against the acting governor of Darien, and trimmed
their sails to the prevailing wind.   Both *procuradores* had fared
well under the rule of Vasco Núñez, as shown by the claims of
each for the loss of gold, houses, and fields in Darien; yet
neither had a good word to say for the only man strong enough
to maintain order, and under whom they were able to accumulate riches.

Colmenares found it profitable to remain three years in La
Antigua, according to his *Memorial,* serving under Balboa, instead of going back to Santo Domingo and denouncing him to
the officials, as he could have done.   Colmenares, like Enciso,
took advantage of the king's ignorance of the outlines and limits
of sections of Tierra Firme.   We are justified in believing that
Procurador Colmenares and the *Bachiller* Enciso much mag-
nified the value of their services, and misrepresented the true
state of affairs in Darien.   Falsehoods uttered with intent to
deceive are called lies, and history is full of them.   Balboa very
generously permitted Enciso, his avowed enemy, to leave La
Antigua and seek redress for the wrong he claimed to have suffered at his hands.   Both these calumniators of Vasco Núñez
acquired gold, Indian slaves, and property in La Antigua, and
they had been able to do so while Balboa was boss in Darien.

I absolve Quicedo from participation in these rabid outcries
against Balboa.   Juan de Quicedo (often written Caicedo) was
a man of mature age, who had spent many years in the Indies.
The poison of the tropics was in his blood and he did not long
survive his mission to court.   After reporting to King Ferdinand, Quicedo went back to Sevilla, where he died, " swollen
and as yellow as that gold he went to seek."   Oviedo, the historian, declares that Quicedo, who helped to excite the people
against Nicuesa, was the first victim of the wrath of God upon
those who drove Nicuesa from La Antigua.

Balboa blundered when he permitted his enemies and rivals
to depart from Antigua, to accuse him before the officials in
Santo Domingo or at the court in Spain.   Balboa was unsus-

picious and trustful, and always failed to protect himself at critical times in his career. He exercised poor judgment in selecting men to represent him, and in dealing with sharper and more unscrupulous persons. Vasco Núñez realized his disadvantage in conflicts with lawyers and begged the king, in his letter of 20 January 1513, not to permit any more bachelors of law to come to Darien.

One of the many *cédulas* signed by the king on 9 August 1513, directed that 25,000 *maravedís* be paid to each *procurador*—Quicedo and Colmenares—for their travel expenses in going to and coming from Darien. This was after both had been selected to accompany the new armada to Darien. On this same date, Quicedo was named *veedor* of the new expedition. Quicedo complained that after he arrived at La Antigua from Nombre de Dios, he did not receive a share of the gold gathered in by Balboa, although the latter had given him lands and Indians. Juan de Quicedo died between the date of his appointment as *veedor* of Castilla del Oro—9 August 1513—and the naming of Oviedo his successor, 2 November 1513.

After the death of Quicedo, his brother-in-law, Juan de Simancas, who went in the armada, was granted special favors, and allowed to take with him to Darien certain articles for the wife and children of Quicedo. The widow, Inés de Escobar, was given permission by the king to sell the fields and town lots in La Antigua and come to Spain. If she remained in La Antigua she could keep the lands, and Indians would be distributed to her just as if her husband were alive.

Colmenares, the other *procurador*, received, as has been stated, 25,000 *maravedís* for travel expenses between La Antigua and Sevilla. Ferdinand recently had named Pedrarias Dávila to be governor of Tierra Firme (Darien), which he ordered to be called Castilla del Oro—" *La tierra que antes se llamaua firme e agora mandela llamar Castilla del Oro.*" On 9 August, the king directed Pedrarias to inquire into the complaints of Colmenares and see that he receive no injury. Still another *cédula* of the same date, 9 August 1513, stated that Colmenares had come to court as *procurador* of the city of

Santa Maria del Antigua del Darien, and Pedrarias was charged to aid, favor and honor him as a faithful servant of the king.

The bragging and blustering Alonso de Ojeda, the man who had robbed, killed, and enslaved so many Indians, now was a broken and ignoble figure in the streets of Santo Domingo. His last recourse, like that of many such failures, was in religion, and he sought final refuge in the habit of St. Francis.

Diego de Nicuesa, that other incompetent governor in Tierra Firme, had disappeared completely, and to this day the exact manner of his death is unknown. Nicuesa was not the bullying swashbuckler that Ojeda was, though equally unfitted to lead such an enterprise. Both these unfortunate commanders had caused many brave men to fill untimely graves in the jungles of the new continent.

SEBASTIÁN DE OCAMPO

The *Regidor* Valdivia and the *Procuradores* Quicedo and Colmenares, when in Santo Domingo, had told much of the life in Santa Maria de la Antigua del Darien, and of the need for provisions and other supplies, which the colonists were willing to purchase with the gold filched from the natives. For several years, business had not been so profitable on Española, and some merchants were ready, with the encouragement of Viceroy Colón, to venture sending ships to La Antigua with food and merchandise.

One of the first ships loaded with supplies to anchor in the port of La Antigua belonged to Sebastián de Ocampo, sometimes called Campo, erroneously, we believe. Balboa refers to him as Campo in his famous letter of 20 January 1513. The settlers gladly exchanged their ill-gotten gold for bacon from Española and the good wine of Spain. Bartolomé de las Casas states that Ocampo was a Galician of *hidalgo* rank, a servitor of the Queen Doña Isabel, who had passed to the Indies with Christopher Columbus on his second voyage, in 1493, remaining

in Española.   Ocampo, in 1508, was commissioned by the
Commendador Ovando to sail in two brigantines and carefully
explore the coast and ports of Cuba, or Fernandina, as the
island then was called.   Ocampo spent eight months in ex-
amining all the shores of Cuba, sailing completely around it.
Upon his return to Santo Domingo, he could declare positively
that Cuba was an island, which had been doubted by many on
account of its large size and their belief that it was a peninsula
projecting from the southeast coast of Asia.   No doubt, Ocampo
made a lengthy report of his survey, which, together with the
charts of his pilots, would make very interesting reading today.

Receiving no news from Quicedo and Colmenares, or perhaps
hearing of the charges of Enciso and Colmenares against him,
as well as the failure of Zamudio, Balboa determined to try
another agent to further his interests in Spain.   As a result of
the trading visit of Ocampo to Antigua del Darien, or because
they had been friends on Española, Vasco Núñez executed a
power of attorney before a notary authorizing Ocampo to be
his *procurador* or solicitor before the Indies House, the Council
of the Indies, or the king himself.   Upon his return to Santo
Domingo, Ocampo sailed to Sevilla, where he lodged with his
cousin, Alonso de Noya, a merchant who possessed some houses
in the precinct of San Marcos.   Ocampo presented his *carta de
poder,* or proxy, to the king's secretary, Lope de Conchillos,
and bought a grey saddle mule on which to travel to the court
in Valladolid.   While in Sevilla negotiating with the Indies
House, *Procurador* Ocampo became gravely ill.   Feeling that
his end was near, Ocampo, faithful to Balboa, delegated his
power to others.

On Monday, 26 June 1514, Sebastián de Ocampo substi-
tuted for himself Alonso de Noya, and one Cobos, official to
Lope de Conchillos.   Doubtless this was that Francisco de los
Cobos who later succeeded Conchillos.   Ocampo's document
transferred his authority to Noya and Cobos, whereby they
both or separately might appear before the king or any other
persons to negotiate and solicit and do all the things and
matters suitable and appertaining to the said power from Vasco

Núñez de Balboa. And because Ocampo was sick and weak, the two witnesses, Pedro Fernández and Cristóbal Días, both notaries, signed for him. To their own names each notary annexed his peculiar flourish, or *rúbrica,* so called because often written in red ink. By another writing on the same day, the dying Ocampo made donation of his grey mule, " saddled and bridled " (" *ensyllada e enfrenada* "), to his cousin, and forty ducats of gold for his expenses in promoting the affairs of Vasco Núñez at Court. The same witnesses signed as before, and also Alonso Guerrero. Sebastián de Ocampo also left behind him a still more important paper, which was the letter to the king from Vasco Núñez de Balboa.

PEDRO DE ARBOLANCHA

We have yet to hear from another messenger from the Indies. After long months of silence and uncertainty, the king now was hearing a great deal about Darien and the new town of Santa Maria de la Antigua, dominated by Vasco Núñez de Balboa. Early in 1511, very little was known in Spain of the outcome of the two expeditions under Nicuesa and Ojeda that Ferdinand had sent to Tierra Firme, which at that time meant Urabá, Darién, and Verágua.

At this date, the affairs of Spain in the New World were not very prosperous. The first harvest of gold on Española had been garnered. The natives had been robbed of their golden ornaments and jewelry and were dying off rapidly under the harsh rule of the Christians. The yield from the placer mines was fast becoming less. Many good Spaniards, not kept on the island by debt, had gone off with Nicuesa or Ojeda, never to be heard of again. Puerto Rico was being settled slowly by Juan Ponce; and Diego Velázquez, lieutenant of Viceroy Colón, was moving over to Cuba to inflict another plague upon the Indians of that island.

Diego de Nicuesa, starving at Nombre de Dios, had sent a letter by his brigantine reciting his sufferings and losses and begging for speedy relief. Alonso de Ojeda, void of brag and bluster, had just returned to Santo Domingo a sadly broken man, yet still asking for more help from the king. Conflicting news had been received from the colonists at La Antigua, who had been saved from misfortune by Balboa guiding them to the Indian village of Darien.

No earthly power could have saved the two incompetent leaders, Nicuesa and Ojeda, from disaster. Ferdinand had expected great things from them on Tierra Firme, and when Nicuesa and Ojeda both failed, the king blamed Diego Colón, first, for lack of enthusiasm in fitting out the expeditions, and, secondly, for tardiness in sending them aid. Diego Colón separately, and in association with the other royal officials at Santo Domingo, forwarded cheerless reports to the home government. Miguel de Pasamonte also wrote privately, as was his custom, to King Ferdinand. From orders and letters previously received from the king, it was obvious that Ferdinand and his councillors needed further enlightenment which only a personal messenger could give. On Española at that time was one Pedro de Arbolancha, an old settler who had gone to the island in 1501, in the office of the *contador* Cuéllar (or Valdecuéllar). Arbolancha was a man of affairs and known about the court of Spain. Viceroy Diego Colón selected Arbolancha to accompany his dispatches in order to give the king a better understanding of affairs in the Indies.

On 9 July 1511, the officials of the Indies House at Sevilla notified Ferdinand of the arrival of two ships from Santa Domingo, and sent to him three parcels of letters from the Admiral and other officials on Española. The officials also informed the king that Pedro de Arbolancha, who came on one of the ships, found himself ill and unable to continue his journey to the court. Arbolancha, like many other Spaniards long in the Indies, fell sick upon arriving in Spain.

On 25 July, from Tordesillas, King Ferdinand directed a general reply to the Admiral Diego Colón and the officials of Española that they did well in sending a caravel to succor the people left in the settlement that Ojeda had begun in Urabá.

The news of the losses of Ojeda and Nicuesa grieved him much, and the Admiral was ordered to give them all the favor and aid necessary to support and maintain the two towns (" *asientos* ") which they had commenced. " The coming of Arbolancha has pleased me," wrote the king, though the former had not yet reached the court, " because he is a capable person who will know to give good account of things there." This letter well illustrates how the king often issued orders many months or a year after the conditions he sought to remedy had ceased to exist. On the date of this letter, 25 July 1511, San Sebastián in Urabá had been abandoned for over a year, Nicuesa had disappeared in the Carib Sea, and Balboa was carrying the few survivors of his expedition to safety in La Antigua del Darien.

A few weeks later, 9 September, Ferdinand wrote that Arbolancha was in the court at Burgos, where he added details and explanations to the reports sent by Viceroy Colón and his staff of officials at Santo Domingo.

Before Arbolancha reached the court, King Ferdinand had ordered the officials of the Indies House to see that a shipload of provisions and arms was sent as soon as possible to Tierra Firme, there to be equally distributed between Nicuesa and Ojeda. " There appears to be no other remedy at present except to support Nicuesa and Ojeda," wrote the king, " until we know if there is gold in those wildernesses which now they occupy " (" *fasta tanto que sepamos si ay oro en aquellos desiertos que agora tomaron* ").

Behold the key to the Spanish conquest of America! If such be possible, the lust for gold was greater in the king and his councillors than in the captains in the Indies. Indeed, it was the insatiable demand in Spain for more gold that often drove the *conquistadores* to rob, torture, and kill the Indians in order to secure more of the precious metal. After the first mad rush to go with Columbus to Española in 1493, it was difficult to obtain further recruits for the West Indies. After the death of Columbus in 1506, his sons, Diego and Fernando, were pointed out as children of the man who described the lands he had discovered as replete with gold, pearls, and jewels, luring many Spaniards to misery and their graves.

The reports in hand from Diego Colón and the officers at Santo Domingo informed the king of the utter collapse of the expeditions of Nicuesa and Ojeda, and made no mention whatever of the discovery of gold. Nevertheless, in order to secure more recruits to go to Tierra Firme, King Ferdinand directed the officials of the Indies House to proclaim throughout Spain the great signs of gold where Nicuesa and Ojeda had established their settlements. Writes Altolaguirre the Spanish historian:

" The king did not hesitate to resort to deception to rouse the cupidity of the Spaniards, tearing them from the bosom of their families and transporting them to those remote and inhospitable lands where, instead of the promised riches, all would encounter dangers and privations without number, and most of them death."

Such is the way of kings and rulers; the subjects are only pawns wherewith to play the game!

It was not until Pedro de Arbolancha arrived at court and talked with Ferdinand that the king realized the uselessness of attempting to do anything more for Nicuesa and Ojeda. Convinced that nothing was to be gained from them, the king immediately, on 9 September 1511, countermanded his order to send supplies to the two governors. The whereabouts of Nicuesa was unknown, but Ojeda could be dealt with at Santo Domingo. Ferdinand's change of heart was so complete that he issued at Burgos a *Real Cédula*, 6 October 1511, to the Judges of Appeal on Española to seize and prosecute Ojeda for crimes he had committed. One of the charges in the interesting document was that Ojeda had bragged that he would cut off the head of the Admiral Diego Colón, the viceroy, and carry off to Urabá the Vice-queen María de Toledo. Probably it was due to this order to bring him to trial that Alonso de Ojeda sought sanctuary in the Franciscan convent in Santo Domingo, where he died within a few years.

Ferdinand found Arbolancha so valuable that he kept him about the court to advise him further on affairs in the Indies.

We have devoted much space to reports, written and verbal, made to Ferdinand concerning La Antigua del Darien because they determined the actions of the king which shaped the fortunes of Vasco Núñez. It is time that we heard from the most important figure in the Indies in those days, the man who, without the king's favor or substantial assistance of any kind, and in the face of much bitter opposition and rivalry, had established and maintained in the midst of a strange and hostile race the only outpost of Spain on the continent of America.

VIII

THE ODYSSEY
OF
THE QUEST FOR THE SOUTH SEA

"I have set my life upon a cast,
And I will stand the hazard of the die."
—*King Richard III*, SHAKESPEARE.

DEPARTURE FROM LA ANTIGUA DEL DARIEN

ON Thursday, 1 September 1513, Vasco Núñez de Balboa set out from Santa Maria de la Antigua del Darien with one hundred ninety Spaniards and about eight hundred Indians on his quest for the South Sea. Accounts vary as to the number of Spaniards, Indians and canoes, and there are discrepancies in names and dates.

This was, in truth, a very daring venture. It was the first time that Vasco Núñez believed that he could risk going far from the settlement, now that reinforcements had arrived from Española. Balboa proposed to extend his search far from his base at Antigua, and to pass through the lands of numerous hostile Indians, many of whom were reported to be fierce fighters. According to Panquiaco, Comogre's son, one thousand Spaniards would be needed to conquer one chieftain alone, the dread Tubanamá. That Balboa could make the attempt to find the sea reported to exist beyond the *cordillera*, was due to the fact that he had demonstrated his mastery over the surrounding caciques, and then had made peace with them, so that the principal chiefs on the north, or Caribbean, coast of the Isthmus—Careta, Comogre, and others—were admiring friends of the white commander.

Balboa did not publish his real purpose among the Indians, and to conceal the true objective of his expedition he announced that he was going to make a reconnaissance and look for mines: *"So color de buscar minas y inquirir los secretos de la tierra,"* writes Ovideo.

As Vasco Núñez had selected his best men to accompany him, La Antigua would be left in charge of the more turbulent and weaker members of the colony, and it would not do for Cémaco, rightful lord of Darien, and the fighting caciques along the Rio Atrato to learn that the great white *Tiba* would be long away from the settlement.

The Indians taken along by Balboa included both slaves and *naborías* (*indios de servicio*). The Christians rarely traveled very far without the aid of the natives. On this expedition the natives supplied canoes and acted as paddlers. On the land they carried the baggage, opened trails, built small bridges or rafts to cross the streams, constructed shelters, gathered and prepared the food, and acted as guides. When Spaniards fell sick, as often happened, the Indians carried them in native hammocks (*hámacas*) made of cotton, suspended from long poles borne on the shoulders of husky warriors. In many instances the natives became zealous allies of the Europeans and materially assisted in fighting other tribes.

It was true, as Las Casas wrote, *" porque sin estos indios no saben nuestros españoles en estas Indias andar un paso."*

An effective unit of the expedition was a pack of large European dogs, trained to attack and kill Indians—" *los perros bravos amaestrados,"* as Las Casas calls them. Among these was that famous dog named Leoncico, owned by Balboa, which drew a captain's pay when on forays against the natives. The outfit included no horses, as did most of the subsequent expeditions, and which added so materially to the success of the Spaniards in the conquest of the New World.

Vasco Núñez had acquired some knowledge of an Indian trail beginning at the port of Cacique Careta on the Caribbean coast and leading southward over the mountains, and he determined to follow that route. Balboa embarked his command in a large brigantine (*galeon*, says Oviedo) and nine or ten big canoes. Passing out of the Gulf of Urabá, the little fleet rounded Punta Tiburon and turned westward along the north shore of the Isthmus of Panama.

On Sunday, September 4, the flotilla arrived at Puerto Careta, usually stated to be twenty leagues west of Antigua, on which was situated the seat of Careta, lord of Coyba. Oviedo affirms that the chief's right name was Chima, and that he had been baptized by the Christians, receiving the name of Don Fernando, after the king of Spain. It was on or near this port that Balboa, a few years later, built the town of Acla, and it was there that he lost his life.

CARETA

Cacique Careta received his quasi son-in-law in a very friendly manner and ordered his people to assist in the debarkation and furnish the necessary provisions. Doubtless, the chief's pretty daughter, whom we call Caretita, accompanied Balboa as far as her father's house and aided her white lover in planning his journey. On account of their mutual affection, it is probable that Vasco Núñez relied more on the information given by his *dulce amiga* than on what the caciques told him.

The white commander spent Sunday and Monday with Careta, selecting the Spaniards and Indians he wished to take along, accumulating supplies, making further inquiries about the sea beyond the cordillera and the best route to follow through and over the mountains. Enough white men and some Indians were left behind to guard and care for the boats, which were directed to remain at that port.

With guides furnished by Careta, Balboa, on September 6, departed from the coast and began his memorable march to the southward, the Spaniards, Indians and dogs presenting a very warlike appearance. We are told that the party traveled for two days over a very rough and mountainous country.

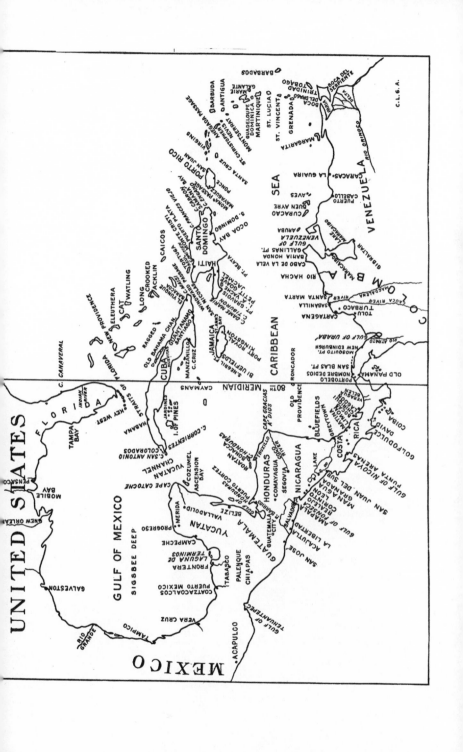

PONCA

On September 8, a Thursday, the expedition came to the lands and houses of Cacique Ponca, who, on being apprised of the approach of the white men, fled to the woods with all his people, as he had done on the former visit by Balboa. No doubt the Indians of Careta enjoyed leading the Spaniards into the territory of Ponca, with whom they carried on incessant warfare. Balboa's military genius would not allow him to leave any unfriendly Indians in his rear, between his command and his base at Careta. Pursuant to this policy, he delayed his progress while he sent out some of Careta's warriors to find Ponca and assure him that he would not be injured if he returned to his village and made peace with the white commander.

By this time it was known generally among the natives of Darien that gold was the great god of the white foreigners, and that the proper way for an Indian to approach a Christian was with a present of gold. When Ponca came back on September 13, he presented Balboa with some pieces of finely wrought gold, valued at one hundred ten pesos. He excused the small amount, saying that he had not been able to gather any more since his village had been looted by the Christians in 1511. Balboa treated Ponca with more consideration than he was accustomed to show toward a chief and gave him some shirts, hatchets, and glass beads. The latter confirmed the reports of the existence of the *pechry* or Southern Sea, as well as disclosing other secrets of the land. Assured of Ponca's good will and friendship, Vasco Núñez left twelve sick soldiers in his care to be sent back to the ship in Puerto de Careta. Careta's guides and *cargadores* were dismissed with presents and went back to the coast very well pleased with their treatment. Cacique Ponca now cheerfully furnished warriors and carriers to conduct the Spaniards to the territory of his powerful neighbor called Quarequá, with whom he was at war.

On September 20, Balboa departed from Ponca and during the following four days traveled ten leagues of the worst road encountered on the march. Many rivers which could not be waded had to be crossed on rafts, at great risk of life.

QUAREQUÁ, TORECHA, PORQUE

Here again we meet with variance in the accounts of the old chroniclers, and confusion between the name of the province, as the Spaniards called a district, and the name of the ruling cacique. At other times, the war chief (*tequina*) is featured rather than the hereditary chief.

Quarequá was a " province " of the Isthmus of Panama, like Coiba, Cueva, Natá, Escoria, etc. Both Peter Martyr and Las Casas (who follows Martyr) call the principal cacique Quarequá. When the white men, on September 23, arrived at the domain of Quarequá, they found that chieftain surrounded by his *cabras*, or fighting subchiefs, at the head of one thousand warriors, lined up to defend his land and homes and to repel the foreign invaders. Unlike the Christians, and before attacking them, the chief inquired who they were, why they came that way, and what they sought, and threatened to destroy them if they attempted to pass through his land.

The Spaniards spent no time in parley and continued to advance in spite of the warning of Quarequá. The Indians then attacked the Europeans with great impetuosity, uttering loud cries, and sounding their conch shells and war drums. The Indians were armed with lances, bows and arrows, two-handed wooden swords, and sharp rods, or javelins. The natives of Darien were not skillful archers like the people of Caribana across the Gulf of Urabá, and did not poison their weapons. The heavy wooden swords, often made of the hard *palma brava*, were called *macanas*, and could be used both as club and sword. Their principal missile was the *vara*, or small rod, made of *palma negra*, one end of which was hardened in fire and pointed, or tipped with flint. This was hurled by a throwing-stick, *tiradera*, and could traverse a naked Indian from side to side. The throwing-stick, or *atlatl*, was used by certain Indians from the Arctic circle south to Peru. In Panama it was called *estórica,* or *estólica.*

Some Indians wore plates of gold on chest and arms, and other parts of the body, which were both ornamental and protective. Many used shields made of wood or the skins of animals. The virile member was carried in a gold tube (*cañuto de oro*) or bright sea shell, secured by cords about the loins.

The Spaniards were equipped with the weapons of the time—swords, cross-bows, arquebuses, and metal helmets and corselets. This was Quarequá's first encounter with the bearded white men from overseas and his first experience with European firearms and dogs.

Primitive peoples attach magic value to strange noises, smokes, and smells. Flame and smoke seemed to issue from the mouths of the Spaniards. The use of gas at Ypres, in the World War, did not cause so much surprise as did the use of gunpowder against the Indians of Quarequá. The smoke and smell of the powder filled them with awe. The loud report of the firearms, and the flash from the clumsy muskets, as seen in the jungle shade, followed by the sudden fall and death of many warriors, led the Indians to believe that these bearded white foreigners possessed the power of controlling the thunder and lightning of the heavens. No Indian magician could make such powerful " medicine." Frightened by the unknown weapons and strange manner of fighting, and the fierce onslaught of the large dogs, the Indians soon were thrown into panic and were mercilessly cut down or dismembered by the glittering swords of the Christians. It is said that the natives were horrified to see arms and other parts of the bodies of their people strewn about the ground. Truly, the Christians must be devils, or *tuyras,* in the language of the Indians!

The victory of Balboa at Quarequá determined the supremacy of the Spaniards on the Isthmus of Panama. They seemed to possess supernatural powers and were held to be invincible by the Indians. It was not through lack of means of defense that the people of Quarequá were overcome, but from terror of the unknown. Had the Indians stood their ground like the brave Caribs east of the Gulf of Urabá, and shot their arrows and *varas* with the rapidity and accuracy of which they were capable, they could have killed off the dogs and driven back the white invaders. Had Balboa been defeated, the entire population would have risen against him, and the discovery of the Pacific Ocean would have been deferred for several years, the glory falling to some other captain.

Brave Cacique Quarequá and six hundred of his warriors were slain and many taken captive. No Spaniards were killed and only a few wounded. The houses were looted, yielding some gold and pearls; and the dead were despoiled of golden mirrors, nose-plates and other jewelry. The Spaniards feasted and rested in the village of the dead chief.

DOGS OF THE INDIANS

Spain was aided so much by European dogs, as well as horses, in the Hispanic conquest of the New World, that the reader may wonder why the Indians did not use their own dogs in resisting the Spaniards. Spanish writers describe their dogs as mastiffs and hounds. The early chronicles rarely mention the existence of dogs among the aborigines on the Isthmus of Panama. Gaspar de Espinosa makes no mention of Indian dogs in his *Relación* of his extensive foray against the caciques of the Isthmus. Oviedo tells us that the Caribs of Cartagena, then the Indian settlement of Calamar, brought very small dogs—"*unos perrillos pequeños*"—to Darien, and there bartered them for fishhooks.

These animals belonged to the breed of dumb dogs encountered on Española, San Juan, Cuba, and other lands about the Caribbean Sea. They had the face of a fox and looked like little wolves. They were shy and did not bark or howl, or cry out when beaten. These mute dogs were kept as house pets, or castrated and fattened to be eaten. Grijalva and Cortés met them on Cozumel, where at times they were sacrificed in place of children, so Gómara affirms. Alvar Núñez Cabeza de Vaca and Hernando de Soto ate native dogs in their wanderings in Apalache and Florida. Francisco Vásquez de Coronado, on his way to Quivira, in 1541, found Indian dogs large enough to fight a buffalo. He stated that these dogs could carry a burden of " *dos arrobas* "—fifty pounds. Probably a greater burden was dragged on a *travois* when the Indians changed camp in following the bison. In pre-Columbian times, northern Algonquin and Athabascan tribes, and especially the Eskimo, used half-tamed dogs for sled transportation. In tropical America, however, the little native dog was no help to the Indian, either in hunting, fighting, or moving burdens.

BLACK PEOPLE

We read that among the captives at Quarequá were some Negroes held as slaves by the Indians, who came from a district only one day's journey from there. Peter Martyr explains their presence by thinking that Negro pirates from Ethiopia were wrecked in these mountains. A few years later, Rodrigo de Colmenares, in his *Memorial* against Vasco Núñez, wrote that a captain brought news of black people located east of the Gulf of San Miguel—" *i que havia alli cerca gente negra.*"

In recent years, " white Indians " have been reported living in the old province of Quarequá by Richard O. Marsh.

The Indian prisoners included a brother of Cacique Quarequá and many principal chiefs who were dressed in cotton *naguas,* or skirts, like women, and who shared the same passion, so the interpreters informed the white men. This was sufficient evidence for the Spaniards to hold that these individuals were addicted to certain homosexual practices which were an abomination to the Christians and so merited death.

It is possible that the native interpreters, members of an enemy tribe, may have deceived the Spaniards. As Europeans played one band or tribe against another, so the Indians utilized the powerful white strangers as allies and weapons to combat or destroy hostile neighbors.

While many natives of America, as of other parts of the world, practiced abnormal sex relations, these habits were not so common in the New World as reported by Spanish priests and officials. Many early Spanish writers seemed to delight in construing a strange custom among the Indians as proof positive of some *contra natura* crime. Spanish captains and governors in the New World had powerful economic motives for accusing a group of natives of cannibalism, sodomy, and other abominations. Under authority of various royal decrees, killing, capture, and enslavement of such Indians was justified in the eyes of the laws of Church and State. I need refer only to the license by Queen Isabella, given in the City of Segovia, 30 October 1503, to one of the provisions of the *asiento* made with Diego de Nicuesa and Alonso de Ojeda, signed by King Ferdinand in Burgos, 9 June 1508, and the Laws of Burgos, promulgated December 27, 1512.

APERREAR, " TO THROW ONE TO THE DOGS TO BE TORN TO PIECES "

The Spanish language has a verb which expresses the entire action. On the accusation of the interpreters, the brother of Quarequá and nearly fifty of the principal men of the tribe (courtiers, P. Martyr calls them) were thrown to the dogs and soon torn to pieces. The dogs threw themselves upon the Indians as though they were wild boars or timid deer. When the dogs had satisfied their rage and appeased their appetite, the remains were burnt. This deed, we are told, was much acclaimed by the men and filled the females of the tribe with joy.

The American Indians suffered much injustice from the ignorance and fanaticism of their European conquerors. Anything that did not accord with the Christian teaching and practices

Valbóa Indos nefandum Sodomiæ ſcelus com- XXII.
mittentes, canibus objicit dilaniandos.

ALBOA *in iſta ad montes profectione Regulum in Eſquaragua ſuperat &*
cædit cum multis Indis: pagum deinde ingreſſus Reguli fratrem & alios
quoſdam muliebri veſtitu ornatos: valde admiratus, cauſam ſciſcitatur:
intelligit caſum Regulum & omnes eius aulicos nefando illo peccato natu-
ræ aduerſo infectos. Attonitus Valboa adeo deteſtabile ſcelus ad iſtos Bar-
baros penetraſſe, corripi omnes iubet numero forte quadraginta, & canibus quos circum-
ducebat,lacerandos objicit.

Balboa sets European dogs on Indians accused of an abominable sin.

of the time was condemned and punished. On the Isthmus of Panama, as elsewhere in the New World, native chiefs often wore skirts and other garments to indicate their rank, especially on occasions of ceremony. It was not, in any sense, conclusive evidence of sex perversion. Cacique Quarequá wore a skirt as emblematic of his rank when he advanced at the head of his warriors to confront the Spaniards. Readers of my *Old Panama and Castilla del Oro* will recall that late in 1698, when the councillors of the Darien Colony visited Chief Ambrosio, he advanced to welcome them with twenty followers, " all clothed in white loose frocks with fringes round the bottoms, and lances in their hands."

After this diversion, we will borrow a phrase frequently used by Oviedo: " Let us return to our history "—" *Tornemos a la historia.*" This historian's account differs from the foregoing. He does not mention Quarequá or the big fight in the open. Oviedo states that Vasco Núñez, guided by the men of Ponca, attacked the houses of Cacique Torecha on the night of September 24, with the usual killings and capture of Indians. Here Balboa secured some gold, pearls, and what he valued more, further assurances of his approach to the South Sea.

Whatever the name of the head chief, Quarequá, Torecha, or Porque, the tribe was so thoroughly broken and subdued that Balboa did not fear to leave here his sick and wounded. Vasco Núñez dismissed with presents the guides and bearers of Cacique Ponca, who carried back the pleasing news that their new friends, the Christians, had sent hundreds of their warlike neighbors to the happy hunting grounds.

With seventy or more Spaniards and many Indians that he had brought along, and using some of his Quarequá captives as guides, Balboa resumed his quest for the Austral Sea. One account relates that it was at this time that he arrived at the *buhíos* and seat of Cacique Porque, and found that he had fled with his people. Balboa now was too eager to prove or disprove the existence of another sea to tarry here to induce the absconding Porque to come back and pay obeisance to the Spaniards.

Vasco Núñez on the Cumbre of Quarequá

Proceeding on his way, Balboa, on the morning of September 25, was told by his Quarequá guides that from the top of a near-by mountain he could obtain a view of the Southern Sea. Balboa halted his command and began to ascend the height, to confirm or refute the tales of another sea. It is probable that Leoncico accompanied Vasco Núñez, alert to detect any danger threatening his master. Balboa knew that this was a turning point in his career. If the Austral Sea did not exist, his rule in Darien would be judged without extenuating circumstances and without mercy. Success should mean reconciliation with his king, fame, position, and riches.

It was a tense moment in the life of Vasco Núñez de Balboa and he would face his destiny alone. Arriving on the summit of the mountain, he anxiously turned his gaze to the south—and there was the sea, with a broad estuary jutting into the land toward the mountains.

Balboa dropped on his knees and with arms extended toward the new sea, he raised his eyes to heaven and gave infinite thanks to Jesus Christ and all the saints for permitting him to discover this Southern Sea, and do such signal service for God and his king. He then called his soldiers to join him, and they rushed up the mountain with cries of joy, as eager as their leader to view the object of their quest. Like the Ten Thousand Greeks retreating from the Persians, who from a hill discerned the silver gleam of the Euxine, they shouted: " The sea! the sea! " All embraced their commander and renewed their pledges to follow and obey him.

After the first outbursts of joy and felicitations, Vasco Núñez, pointing with his right hand to the new-found sea, and prouder than Hannibal showing his soldiers the inviting plains of Italy, thus addressed his men:

" There you see, friends and companions, the object of your desires and the reward of your many labors. As the notices of another sea given us by the son of Comogre have turned out to be true, so will the words of Panciaco be fulfilled concerning the great riches of the lands to the south."

Led by the devoted *clérigo*, Andrés de Vera, the entire party, on bended knees, intoned the *Te Deum Laudamus* and other airs of the Church for the good fortune which the Lord had vouchsafed to them.

Balboa then took formal possession from the *cumbre* of Quarequá of the South Sea, its islands and firm lands, discovered and to be discovered, in the name of the Catholic and most Serene Sovereigns of Castile, who then were Don Fernando, fifth of the name, and his daughter Doña Juana, mother of Don Carlos, soon to become king of Spain and emperor of Germany. In sign of possession, they cut down a tall sapling from which was made a large cross, which was set up in the *raso arriba*, or clearing on the top of the mountain from where Balboa got his first view of the sea. A tumulus of stones was piled up around the base of the cross, the letters F and J were cut in the bark of trees, branches broken, and the earth gathered in heaps. The Indians assisted in the work, much mystified by these strange rites of the white men.

The Spanish expeditions always carried a notary to make official attest of any important or unusual event. On this occasion, Vasco Núñez directed the *escribano*, Andrés de Valderrábano, to write a certificate of the discovery of the Sea of the South, with a list of the sixty-seven Europeans present. Among the names was that of Francisco Pizarro, the ignoble conqueror of Peru, who reaped the rewards of this discovery, which rightfully should have fallen to Balboa; Diego Albítez, later a rival of Balboa for leadership on the South Sea; Alonso Martín, an interesting *conquistador* of whom we shall hear more; and Nuflo de Olano " *de color negro*," perhaps an African. This important document was transcribed and preserved for posterity by Gonzalo Fernández de Oviedo y Valdés, who was appointed receiver of the papers and chattels of Balboa and Valderrábano after their execution. I reproduce this paper in my *Old Panama and Castilla del Oro*, p. 181.

John Keats, who was a better poet than historian, in 1815, wrote those beautiful lines entitled: " On First Looking into Chapman's Homer," in which he pictures stout Cortez in place of Balboa staring at the Pacific from a peak in Darien. At this time, 1513, Hernando Cortés was in Cuba and did not dream of conquering Montezuma's empire.

For many months Vasco Núñez and his friends had been making inquiries and speculating about " la mar del Sur," so that it was known as the South Sea to the Europeans at La Antigua long before it was seen by them. It needed no baptism. As the nearest water protruded into the land like an ancón or gulf, Balboa commanded that it be called the Gulf of San Miguel, because the feast of that archangel occurred four days later.

BALBOA DISCOVERS THE PACIFIC OCEAN

Preponderance of credible evidence shows that Vasco Núñez de Balboa discovered the South Sea from the cumbre of the Sierra of Quarequá at about ten o'clock in the forenoon of Sunday, September 25, 1513. For the New World, Balboa had found a new ocean.

Naturally, the greatest historical value attaches to the narrative of the great discovery written by Gonzalo Fernández de Oviedo y Valdés, first chronicler of the New World. He arrived at Santa Maria de la Antigua del Darien, as a royal official in the train of Pedrarias Dávila, a few months after the return of Balboa from the South Sea. At that time, the colonists of Darien still were talking of their strange, new experiences during the double transit of the Isthmus, and the newcomers were eager to listen and ask questions. Oviedo states, in his Historia General y Natural de las Indias, that he knew and saw and spoke many times with all the Spaniards engaged in this memorable undertaking, and after the execution of Balboa and Valderrábano, he was appointed to take charge of the papers, goods, and chattels of both of them by the young Emperor Charles.

Oviedo declares that Balboa discovered the South Sea on September 25, 1513. Strange to relate, Valderrábano's record of the discovery, at least as transcribed by Oviedo, is not dated; but the latter writes that the same *escribano* showed it to him and that he saw and read it.

Another contemporary historian of the period of the conquest, Bartolomé de las Casas, Bishop of Chiapa, who was not disposed to agree with Oviedo, gives September 25 as the date of the discovery of the South Sea. Says he: " *Llegaron a la cumbre de las mas altas Sierras a 25 dias de Setiembre del dicho año de 1513.*" Francisco Lopez de Gómara in his *Historia General de las Indias*, published in 1552, says: " *Vió Balboa la mar del Sur a los 25 de Setiembre del año de 13, antes de mediodia.*"

Antonio de Herrera y Tardesillas (*ca.* 1549–1625) was commissioned *coronista mayor*, or chief chronicler of America by Philip II. As such he had the benefit of all previous writings and free use of all official records and reports from the Indies. His great work, *Historia general de los hechos de los Castellanos en las islas y Tierra Firme del Mar Océano*, was issued in 1601. Herrera fixes upon September 25 as the date of the great discovery by Balboa.

On the other hand, Peter Martyr, a contemporary writer, declares that September 26 was the date of this notable event. Back in Spain, no Spaniard exhibited more interest and enthusiasm in the unfolding of the New World than did the Lombard scholar, Pietro Martire d'Anghiera, then employed at the court of Spain. By reason of his great concern in everything pertaining to America, Peter Martyr, as he is better known to English readers, was authorized to read all reports of important events and discoveries coming from the Indies. He was appointed historiographer and became a member of the important Council of the Indies. While he was a gossipy and entertaining letter writer rather than a careful and judicial historian, yet he wrote when the news was fresh, often from the mouth of the principal actor in the event. It is said that Martyr entertained in his house and quizzed nearly every captain or other official returning from the new lands in the West. Martyr talked with the *procuradores* from Darien, and he writes that he held in his hands and read the long letter—*la muy larga carta*—dated at La Antigua, March 4, 1514, in which Vasco Núñez reported his memorable journey of conquest and discovery to King Ferdinand. This letter now would be priceless, but like many other important papers relating to Balboa, it has disappeared, perhaps deliberately destroyed by his enemies. When Peter Martyr declares September 26 to be the date of the discovery, it is entitled to serious consideration.

The Jesuit historian, José de Acosta, passed over the Isthmus of Panama in 1570, and lived many years in Peru, and also in Mexico, returning to Spain in 1587. In his *Historia natural y Moral de las Indias,* published in 1590, Acosta agrees that September 26 was the date of the discovery.

Coming down to modern writers, we find that Alexander von Humboldt, in his *Examen Critique* (1814 *et seq.*), writes: "*Vasco Núñez de Balboa vit la Mer du Sud, le 25 September 1513, du haut de la Sierra de Quarequa.*"

Manuel José Quintana (1772–1857) includes the life of Vasco Núñez de Balboa in his biographies of famous Spaniards —*Vidas de Españoles célebres.* At the same time, 1830, appeared the story of Balboa by Washington Irving in his *Companions of Columbus.* Of these two biographies, William H. Prescott wrote: " It is rare that the life of an individual has formed the subject of two such elegant memorials, produced at nearly the same time, and in different languages, without any communication between the authors." Quintana says that the Austral Sea presented itself to the eyes of Balboa on September 25. With nearly the same historical records available, Irving writes: " The memorable event here recorded took place on the 26th of September, 1513."

Another modern writer is Dr. Wolfred Nelson, who, in his *Five Years at Panama,* published in 1889, follows Irving in stating that the Pacific was first seen by Vasco Núñez on September 26. He errs again when he declares that Balboa saw the ocean from the top of *El Cerro Gigante,* or the Big Hill, midway between the cities of Colon and Panama.

Vasco Núñez de Balboa did not discover the Pacific Ocean from any hilltop within the limits of the Canal Zone, guidebooks and news writers to the contrary notwithstanding.

And so it goes: one writer says September 25, another affirms that it was the 26th day of the month, each having good grounds upon which to support his statement.

As before mentioned, I believe that Balboa discovered the South Sea on September 25, 1513.

Agreeing with Oviedo that Vasco Núñez first viewed the new sea on the 25th day of the month, we must differ with him as to the day of the week, for he convicts himself of error when he writes that the 25th was a Tuesday—" *Y un martes, veynte e cinco de Septiembre de aquel año de mill e quinientos y trece.*" If his assertion that Balboa set out from La Antigua on Thursday the 1st day of September is correct, obviously the 25th of the same month fell on a Sunday, and not Tuesday, as Oviedo asserts. If mistaken in the latter day, then he may have erred in naming Thursday as the first day of the month, and have been wrong in both instances.

To find out if either of these dates is correct, especially the week day of the 1st of September, I addressed an inquiry to the Superintendent, U. S. Naval Observatory, Washington, D. C. A few days later, I received the following reply, for which I tender my thanks:

DEAR SIR:

In reply to your letter of 29 March, 1933, September 1, 1513 Old Style, was Thursday, and September 25, was Sunday.

Very truly yours,

(Signed) JAMES ROBERTSON.
Director Nautical Almanac.

This evidence from our highest authority proves that Oviedo

was correct in his statement that the 1st of September, 1513, was Thursday, and gives a true date from which to reckon days of the week and other dates during Balboa's quest for that other sea. In 1513, of course, all Christian nations of Europe still recorded time according to the Old Style, or Julian calendar. The calendar of Pope Gregory XIII, based on the calculations of the astronomer Clavius, was not introduced until 1582. The new calendar was accepted at once by Spain and Portugal, more slowly by Protestant nations of Europe, Great Britain making the change in 1752.

It is difficult to imagine the bewilderment in the minds of Balboa and his men in actually seeing another sea, unknown to Europeans up to that time. They thought it was the final stretch of the waterway to the East so long sought by Columbus. " It was indeed one of the most sublime discoveries that had yet been made in the New World, and must have opened a boundless field of conjecture to the wondering Spaniards. The imagination delights to picture forth the splendid confusion of their thoughts."

While the colonists in Darien had been calling this body of water, described to them by the Indians, the South Sea, as a matter of fact they did not at that time consider it to be another and new ocean of vast extent, unknown to Europe. It must be the waters about Cipango and the eastern shores of Asia, of which they had some knowledge, an offshoot of the Indian Ocean, just as the sea north of the Isthmus of Panama (the Carib Sea) was an extension of the Atlantic Ocean. Cipango and Cathay and the Moluccas, or Spice Islands, could not be far away.

To the gold-mad Spaniards this meant still more gold and pearls; and, in addition, what they had not found in the New World, silks, jewels, and spices, so highly valued in Europe. The route to the east granted to Portugal by edict of the Pope did not forbid this approach by the west. Had not Alexander Sextus, in 1493, granted to the Catholic kings clear title to " all the Firm Lands and Islands, found or to be found, discovered or to be discovered, toward the West and South of the Line of

Demarcation, not heretofore possessed by any other Christian King or Prince "?

The kingdoms of Spain would be immensely enlarged and the holy Catholic faith extended over more lands. The Old Admiral was right, after all, for he believed that there must be a passage by water through Tierra Firme into this southern sea. In 1520–21, Ferdinand Magellan did find a strait through the land and entered this new sea, and demonstrated it to be the largest body of water on earth. But Magellan's Strait was at the extreme southern tip of America and did not appreciably shorten the voyage from one ocean to the other.

The narrow Isthmus of the New World, or Middle America, with its many constrictions and indentations in the coastlines, seemed to indicate that nature had left a passage in this region. Map makers responded to the wish, and several early charts, as the Mappemonde of Waldseemüller in 1507, the John Ruysch map in 1508, Schoner's map of 1515, and the Lenox globe, depict the so-called " Straits of Panama." A few years later a waterway is shown at the isthmus of Tehuantepec in southern Mexico.

Every captain, and governor or viceroy coming to the Indies was charged to search for a strait leading into the South Sea, and each big river, bay and wide inlet along the Atlantic seaboard was carefully explored, from the broad estuary of the Rio de la Plata in the South, to the St. Lawrence River and Hudson Bay in the northern continent of America. Initiated by Spain, the quest for a strait through the Western Hemisphere was joined by the French, English, and Dutch, and the belief in its existence persisted for over a century.

Cacique Chiapes

The ceremonies on the *cumbre* completed, Balboa was eager to arrive at the shores of the great waters he had discovered. Guided by Indians of Quarequá, Vasco Núñez led his men down the southern slope of the Sierras and came to the houses of Cacique Chiapes. This powerful chieftain, like Quarequá, appeared at the head of his warriors and made a brave attempt to oppose the passage of the white men through his territory. The noise and smoke of the crude firearms (*escopetas*), more effective than the bullets, the fierce dogs, and the charge of bearded men in glittering armor, soon put the Indians to flight, leaving many of their number in the hands of the invaders.

True to his policy of making peace with the caciques, without which it was impossible fully to profit and learn the secrets of the land, Balboa treated his prisoners kindly and made them understand that he would do them no harm. He directed some of his captives, together with a few of the Quarequá guides, to hasten after Chiapes with the offer of peace and friendship of the white Tiba if he would return at once; if not, his town and fields would be destroyed. The Quarequá Indians told Chiapes how useless it was to contend against the white strangers, how much they loved gold, and what wonderful things they gave in return for a small quantity of the metal. Chiapes decided to return and place himself in the hands of Balboa. He presented the latter with some pearls and five hundred pounds of gold, as one writer asserts, doubtless meaning five hundred pesos worth of gold. Vasco Núñez received Chiapes with much friendliness, graciously accepted the gold and pearls, and, in exchange, made gifts of knives, hawks' bells and glass beads.

Balboa quartered his men in the houses of the chief, and dismissed the Quarequá guides with presents, sending back an order to the Spaniards left at Quarequá to rejoin his command at Chiapes. While resting there, Vasco Núñez sent out three patrols of twelve men each, commanded respectively by Francisco Pizarro, Juan de Ezcaray, and Alonso Martín, to search the land for the shortest way to the sea. The last was the first to reach the shore of the *ancón* or gulf, which Balboa already had named San Miguel. After searching for two days, Martín perceived two canoes lying on a sandy beach, but no water in sight. After waiting some time, he saw the great Pacific tide come hurtling in and float the canoes. Alonso Martín stepped into one of them and called his companions to witness that he was the first Christian to be borne upon the waters of the South Sea. Blas de Atienza, one of his party, jumped into the other canoe and asked all to bear witness that he was the second Spaniard to float upon these waters. The name of Atienza is not listed among the sixty-seven persons present on the mountain top when this sea was discovered, from which I judge that he, with others, had been left at the foot of the mountain to guard the baggage and Indian slaves. Indeed, Blas de Atienza does not appear on any list made by the *escribano* during this journey.

Strange to relate, Alonso Martín, the first to find and float upon the water, was not one of the witnesses when Vasco Núñez waded into the gulf of San Miguel and took formal possession of it for Spain. Martín, however, was one of the sixty-seven men on the *cumbre* on September 25, and again was with Balboa on October 29, when he executed his third possession of sea and land out on the shore of the Gulf of Panama. This same Alonso Martín de Don Benito, to give him his full name, survived the wars against the Indians of Panama and Nicaragua, and went to Peru with Francisco Pizarro and Diego de Almagro, where he shared in the rich spoils brought in by the Peruvians to ransom Inca Atahualpa.

BALBOA TAKES POSSESSION OF THE GULF OF SAN MIGUEL

Having found a road to the sea, Alonso Martín returned to Chiapes and reported to his commander. The other exploring parties came in, and the soldiers left at Quarequá rejoined the main body. On September 29, St. Michael's Day, Balboa with twenty-six Spaniards marched to the shore, accompanied by Cacique Chiapes and some of his warriors. On the afternoon of the same day the company reached an arm of the gulf at the hour of vespers, and found the tide at ebb and the beach covered with mud. Like Martín and his party, Vasco Núñez and his men seated themselves in the shade and waited for the water to return.

In due time the tide rushed in with great impetuosity, says the old chronicler, and covered the shore. Balboa waded into the water up to his knees, wearing helmet and breastplate and with buckler on arm. He carried in one hand a drawn sword and in the other a banner on which were painted the Virgin and Child in arms, and beneath them the arms of Castile and Leon. Pacing back and forth in the water, Balboa cried in a loud voice:

" Long live the high and mighty monarchs, Don Fernando and Doña Juana, sovereigns of Castile and Leon and of Aragon, in whose name and for the royal crown of Castile I take and seize, real and corporal, actual possession of these seas and lands, and coasts and ports and islands of the South, with all thereto annexed; and kingdoms and provinces belonging to them, or which may hereafter belong to them, in whatever manner and by whatever right and title acquired, now existing or which may exist, ancient and modern, in times past and present and to come, without any contradiction. And if any other prince or captain, Christian or infidel, of whatever law or sect or condition he may be, pretends any right to these lands and seas, I am ready and prepared to contradict him, and to defend them in the name of the present and future sovereigns of Castile, who are the lords paramount in these Indies, islands and mainland, northern and southern, with all their seas; as well in the artic pole as in the antartic, on either side of the equinoctial line, whether within or without the tropics of Cancer and Capricorn, according to what more completely to their Majesties and their successors belongs and is due for the whole or any part thereof; as I protest in writing shall or may be more fully specified and alleged on behalf of their royal patrimony, now and in all time while the earth revolves, and until the universal judgment of all mankind."

In this all-embracing claim, Vasco Núñez failed to recognize the title given to Portugal by the Holy Father himself to all lands found and to be found to the east of the Line of Demarcation. Balboa also braved the penalty for infringement of this grant as declared by Alexander VI in the Bull of Donation, which reads as follows:

"Let no man therefore whatsoever infringe or dare rashly to contrary this Letter of our Commendation, Exhortation, Request, Donation, Grant, Assignation, Constitution, Deputation, Decree, Commandement, Inhibition, and Determination. And if any shall presume to attempt the same, let him know that he shall thereby incurre the Indignation of Almighty God, and his holy Apostles, Peter and Paul."

No other prince or captain, Christian or infidel, appearing to dispute his claim or accept his challenge, Vasco Núñez continued his *auto* or act of possession. Drawing a dagger from his belt, Balboa cut a cross in the trunk of a tree whose roots were bathed by the water of the sea, and made crosses in two other trees, three crosses in all, in reverence of the Most Holy Trinity. His companions made crosses in other trees and cut off branches with their swords. They waded into the water and dipped it up with their hands, and tasted it to prove that it was salt like the North Sea on the northern coast of the Isthmus of Panama.

Washington Irving, who knew Hispanic-American history and was *muy simpático* with Spanish people, writes of this scene: "Such was the singular medley of chivalrous and religious ceremonial with which these Spanish adventurers took possession of the vast Pacific Ocean, and all its lands—a scene strongly characteristic of the nation and age."

At this ceremony on the Gulf of San Miguel, twenty-seven Spaniards are recorded as present. Vasco Núñez requested notary Valderrábano to make attestation of the act of possession and the witnesses present, whom he names as follows:

" *E los que allí se hallaron son los siguientes:—*

El capitán Vasco Núñez de Balboa
Andrés de Vera, *clérigo*
Francisco Pizarro
Bernardino de Morales
Diego Albítez
Rodrigo Velázquez
Fabian Pérez

Francisco de Valdenebro
Francisco González de Guardalcama
Sebastián de Grijalba
Hernando Muñoz
Hernando Hidalgo
Alvaro de Bolaños
Ortuño de Baracaldo, *vizcaíno*
Francisco de Lucena
Bernardino de Cienfuegos, *esturiano*
Martín Ruiz
Diego de Texerina
Cripstóbal Daza
Johan de Espinosa
Pascual Rubio de Malpartida
Francisco Pesado de Malpartida
Johan de Partillo
Johan Gutierrez de Toledo
Francisco Martín
Johan de Beas

"*Estos veinte e seis y el escribano Andrés de Valderrábano fueron los primeros cripstianos que los pies pusieron en la Mar del Sur, y con sus manos todos ellos probaron el agua e la metieron en sus bocas como cosa nueva, por ver si era salada, como la destotra Mar del Norte.*"

Balboa marched his men back to the houses of Chiapes, making that place a center from which to explore the seacoast. He sent out messengers and interpreters to different parts to induce neighboring chiefs to come in and make peace with the white leader, bearing the usual tribute of gold and pearls.

At this point, Oviedo abruptly announces that Cacique Chiapes was dead, and that Balboa was taken in charge by a brother of the lady (*cacica*) of the land—"*hermano de una india que era señora de aquella tierra, porque el cacique chape era muerto*"—who presented Vasco Núñez with gold and pearls and made peace with him. A little later in his chronicle, this same historian states that this chief was the brother of Chiapes. Neither Peter Martyr nor Las Casas speak of Chiapes dying, and continue to report him in attendance upon Balboa until he turned back from the South Sea, and I shall follow their narratives.

CHIEF CUQUERA

While resting with Chiapes, Vasco Núñez learned that not far from there was a chief called Cuquera (Cocura), ancient enemy of his host, possessed of pearls and gold. Chiapes cheerfully offered to furnish canoes and paddlers to carry these white warriors to subdue Cuquera.

On October 7, Balboa with fifty men embarked in eight canoes and went up a large river to the domain of Cuquera. At night they landed and marched three leagues over a very laborious route to the *buhíos* of the cacique. About two hours after midnight, when near the village, the Spaniards were perceived by the Indians, who took to flight. This Cuquera seems to have been a wise and brave chieftain. Having placed his women and children in safety, Cuquera returned at break of day to attack the invaders, believing them to be Indians. On seeing the bearded Christians, in strange clothes and arms, and presenting such determination and boldness, the Indians were smitten with fear and again fled.

Vasco Núñez pursued his usual tactics and sent some captives with men of Chiapes after the fleeing Cuquera, to tell him to return to his firesides and make peace with the strangers. Reassured by the Indians of Chiapes of the peaceful intent of the white men, the chief came back to his village and presented Balboa with 650 pesos worth of gold and a quantity of pearls. Vasco Núñez gave the chief some knives and Spanish trinkets. Asked whence came his pearls, Cuquera replied that they came from an island out in the gulf. Balboa now was more interested in pearls than in the gold he was accumulating so fast. Gold had become common and was weighty and burdensome to carry. The trail of pearls would lead to silks and spices, and all the storied wealth of the East.

Well satisfied with the gold and pearls, and the information that he had obtained from Cuquera, Balboa returned in the canoes to his headquarters with Chiapes. Vasco Núñez could not rest in idleness—"*no era amigo de gastar el tiempo en ociosidad*"—and prepared to go to that island where Cuquera said he gathered his pearls.

There are many islands, big and little, as well as mudflats (*fangos*), in the Gulf of San Miguel. I believe Cuquera's pearls came from a small island in the *boca*, or entrance of the gulf, and not from an island outside in the great Gulf of Panama, as some writers affirm. Chiapes, good friend of Balboa, tried to dissuade him from this canoe voyage at that season of the year, because the region was subject to sudden and violent storms during the months of October, November and December. Vasco Núñez replied that God and all the saints of heaven would favor his undertaking, since they could not fail to be interested in an expedition to gain great treasures with which to overthrow infidels and extend the Holy Christian faith; " and in truth this bigoted reliance on the immediate protection of heaven seems to have been in a great measure the cause of the extravagant daring of the Spaniards in their expeditions in those days, whether against Moors or Indians."

Vasco Núñez in Storm on the Gulf

On October 17, Balboa, with sixty Spaniards, embarked in nine canoes, leaving the remainder of his company at Chiapes. The cacique, of course, supplied the canoes and paddlers, and went along to look after his distinguished guest. The white commander did not seem to realize the great risk he took in dividing his force, and especially in venturing in loaded canoes with the Indians on these waters where the tidal variations are so great. The Spaniards had yet to learn by hard experience that the tides on the south side of the Isthmus of Panama are several times greater in height than those on the Caribbean coast. "*El flujo y reflujo desta mar es grande,*" writes Pedro de Cieza de Leon. The men of Chiapes were skilled canoeists and swimmers, and had their chief been unfaithful, they could have overturned their canoes and rid themselves of these grasping white men.

When well out on the gulf, the sea became rough, rain descended in sheets, and a violent tempest tossed the canoes about, so that the Spaniards did not know what to do. Even the amphibious Indians were scared and tied the canoes together in pairs, side to side, to keep them from upsetting. The pearl island was forgotten and the paddlers sought safety on a little *islote*, making fast the canoes to some small trees. During the night the tide rose and covered the island, compelling the men to stand in water up to their waists.

The old chroniclers, who were so ready to put pious and heroic phrases in the mouths of the Spanish *conquistadores*, do not tell us what Chiapes thought of the failure of the gods of the white strangers to aid them. No doubt Chiapes himself had experienced many disappointments at the hands of his own gods, which his *tequinas*, or medicine men, explained away by saying that the god was angry or perhaps had changed his mind.

The Spaniards were lucky to escape with their lives, but Chiapes' best canoes, or *culches*, were ruined.

The following morning, when the storm had passed and the waters receded, they found the canoes much broken and full of sand, and that their food and equipment had been washed away. This was not the first disaster that Balboa had suffered on the water. In fact, he was a poor waterman. We have related, already, Balboa's failure to reach the Golden Temple of Dabaiba up the Atrato River, where he was destined to meet still another defeat.

With the aid of the natives, the openings in the canoes were caulked with marine plants and the tender bark of trees. Vasco Núñez wished to proceed on his way to Cuquera's island, but the sea still was high and navigation dangerous, and as all were tired and hungry, he heeded the advice of Chiapes and steered for the nearest mainland.

Tumaco

By nightfall the canoes arrived at the main shore, described as a corner of the gulf toward the north, perhaps the cove within Punta San Lorenzo, now known as Ensenada Peña Hueca. This was the domain of Cacique Tumaco, whose seat was not far away. Leaving some men to guard the canoes, Balboa went ashore with the main body, and guided by Indians of Chiapes, he reached the village of Tumaco about midnight. One writer says that Tumaco was taken by surprise, but put up a brave defense. The Spaniards killed some Indians, took others captive, and compelled the chief and his band to seek safety in flight. A few Christians were wounded; none dangerously. As has been stated, these Indians did not poison their weapons, and the Spaniards did not hesitate to charge them, knowing they would break and run.

Another narrative of the encounter with Tumaco says that when the white men arrived at his land, the chief and his warriors came out to resist the invasion, and although the Spaniards were weak from hunger and had no weapons except their swords, they attacked the Indians with their accustomed assurance and put them to flight.

Whichever account is correct, the result was the same. Balboa made himself at home in the *buhíos* of Cacique Tumaco. The Spaniards found some gold, many large and small pearls, and *aljófar*. In the house of the chief were numerous shells of the pearl oyster kind, many as big as fans. A few fresh shells, gathered the preceding day at a small island visible from the village, contained living oysters. What Balboa's men most appreciated at the time was the abundance of food found in the houses, which they joyfully devoured.

Vasco Núñez freed some prisoners and sent them, with men of Chiapes, to find Tumaco and tell him to come back and agree to terms of peace. The chief was reluctant to return, and the Indians of Chiapes told him how cruel the Spaniards could be to their enemies, and how well they treated their friends. Making a virtue of necessity, Tumaco sent back his son, a fine young man, to act as mediator. Balboa received him kindly and presented the young barbarian with a European shirt and Spanish trifles.

When the youth reported to his father how well he had been treated, the cacique, on the third day, went back to his village and presented the white commander with finely fabricated gold worth 614 pesos, and a large quantity of pearls, of which two hundred and forty were of extraordinary size and beauty. A few months later, Balboa sent many of these pearls to Spain by Pedro de Arbolancha, as a present to King Ferdinand. That gossipy old historian, Peter Martyr, writes: " The mouths of the Spaniards fairly watered with satisfaction as they talked about this great wealth."

Cacique Tumaco told Vasco Núñez that he was lord of all that region, which he called Chitarraga. Balboa ordered that it be called the province of San Lúcas, because it was taken and gained on St. Luke's Day, October 18, " in the night." The cove in which he landed he named the Gulf of San Lúcas.

Seeing the great value attached to pearls by the white visitors, Tumaco sent out some of his pearl divers, who returned in four days with twelve marks of pearls. The Indians opened the shells by roasting them in the fire, in order to cook the oysters which were reserved for the caciques to eat, who prized the meat more than the pearls. The heat dulled the luster of the pearls, and the Christians hastened to show the Indians how to extract the pearls without the use of fire, " with greater diligence, indeed, than they exhibited in teaching the Christian doctrine, which was the condition under which Pope Alexander VI donated the Indies to Spain." In all this long journey to the South Sea and back to La Antigua there is no record of any serious effort to instruct the natives in the Christian faith. Nothing but fighting, killing, robbing, and conquest, like in all succeeding Spanish expeditions in the New World.

Conquest by the sword was Spain's only title to her American colonies.

THE PEARL ISLANDS AND NOTICE OF PERU

Chiapes and Tumaco informed Balboa that the finest pearls were found at a group of islands about five leagues to the westward. Vasco Núñez named the group *Las Islas de las Perlas*. The largest island, visible from the mainland, some Indians called Toe, and others Tarareque. Balboa named it *Isla Rica,* because there were found shells as big as fans and pearls the size of olives and beans, such as Cleopatra herself might have been proud to wear. Isla Rica appears on modern maps as Isla del Rey, or Isla de San Miguel.

These islands were ruled by a powerful chieftain who often raided the settlements on the main shores of the gulf, carrying away their women and valuables. Would not the great white *Tiba* go out and kill King Dites? This was great temptation to Balboa; not that he cared to kill Dites, for such was the chief's name, but he did hanker to possess those big pearls. The sea was very rough and it would be foolhardy to venture another hazard on the water during the season of storms. Vasco Núñez assured his friends, the caciques, that he would come again, and call upon their enemy Dites, and relieve him of any pearls he might have on hand. A few years later, Balboa did sail out to the Pearl Islands; but those master thieves, Gaspar de Morales and Francisco Pizarro, had preceded him and got all the pearls.

Balboa questioned Tumaco as to the existence of a great nation to the south, of which Panciaco had given information. The cacique replied that both land and sea extended far to the south, where lived a great people possessed of much wealth in gold. They sailed the sea in large vessels with sails, and employed certain animals to transport burdens. These animals interested the Europeans, as, so far, no large domestic quadruped had been encountered in the New World. Tumaco then moulded in clay the figure of a quadruped, which looked like a sheep with the long neck of a camel. This, of course, was the Peruvian *llama.*. Some of the Spaniards said that the cacique was lying, that there was no such animal. Others thought it

Juicio, a muscular and intellectual looking old chieftain of the Río Sambú.

Photo by Dr. Barbour, Harvard Expedition.

Scene on the Perlas Islands, Panama.

Photo by the Panama Canal.

might be a species of deer or *danta* (*tapirus americanus*); while many believed it to be the camel of the East.

" And this was the second indication that Vasco Núñez obtained of the riches and state of Peru," writes Las Casas:— " *Y éste fué el segundo indicio que Vasco Núñez alcanzó de las riquezas y estado del Perú.*"

Among those present absorbing Tumaco's story were Francisco Pizarro and Alonso Martín, who lived to reach Peru and secured a large share of its treasures.

Pearls and camels were proof positive that the Spaniards, at last, had found the back door to Asia. The South Sea would lead to Peru, as well as to Cipango, Cathay, and on into the Indian Ocean.

Third Act of Possession on Panama Bay

Not satisfied with the formalities enacted on the mountain top and in the Gulf of San Miguel, Balboa deemed it wise to execute another *acta de posesión* out in the open sea, now known as the Gulf of Panama. For this purpose, Cacique Tumaco brought forth his large canoe of state, fashioned from the trunk of a giant tree; and great was the admiration of the Spaniards on seeing that the handles of the paddles were incrusted with small pearls, and inlaid with *aljófar*, as pearls of irregular shape were called. When Vasco Núñez beheld this luxury, he directed Valderrábano, the notary, to make record of this expression of barbarian culture and of the wealth of this land which he had added to the domain of Castile and Leon. The *escribano* wrote that this scene was witnessed by Alonso Núñez de Madrid, Martín Martínez, Estéban Barrantes, Chripstóbal de Valdebuso, " and all the rest of the Christians who were assembled there."

On October 29, 1513, Balboa and his companions embarked in that great canoe, manned by Tumaco's Indians, and started for the open sea outside of the Gulf of San Miguel. They were conducted through lands subject to overflow, ponds, and tidal creeks, and came out upon the South Sea, the actual Gulf of Panama. It reads as if they reached the sea by channels through the lowlands and marshes rather than by deep water route around the point. Vasco Núñez went as far as a level beach at the point of the Gulf of San Lúcas, close to a rocky island near the mainland. The Indian name of the islet was Crucraga, and Vasco Núñez renamed it San Simón, as the preceding day was the feast day of St. Simon.

Here Balboa landed, and with buckler on arm and holding aloft the royal *pendón,* or standard of Castile, and with a drawn sword in the other hand, he entered the water to the height of his knees, repeating the ceremony observed one month previously in the Gulf of San Miguel. Balboa, in loud voice, took possession, real and corporal, for King Ferdinand and his incompetent daughter Juana, titular queen of Castile, of all these seas and lands, within and out of sight, and of the kingdoms and provinces appertaining to them, by whatever right or title acquired, in times past, present, and to come.

After this boastful and all-embracing declaration, Vasco Núñez uttered the customary challenge, and no one appearing to dispute his claim, he called upon his soldiers to bear witness to what he had done, and asked the notary to take official cognizance of the act. To add greater force to the royal right of Castile, and possibly to obtain saintly endorsement of his claim, Balboa pointed to that island of San Simón for a landmark, and named St. Simon himself as *patrón* and guardian of this *posesión* of much of the unknown world.

Despite the wear and tear of numerous tempests, it should be possible approximately to identify the site of the foregoing ceremony. I quote what Oviedo says of it: " *E salido á la mar en la costa brava, salió en tierra el gobernador, y fué hasta una playa llana a la punta del golpho de Sanct Lúcas, junto a un isleo questá allá cerca de la Tierra-Firme, al qual los indios llaman Crucraga, y Vasco Núñez le puso nombre isleo de Sanct Simon.*"

San Simón was called *isleo,* meaning an island formed by

rocks, close by the main shore, and Isla Rica of the Pearl Islands could be seen far to the westward.

At this third and last act of possession by Balboa, twenty-four Spaniards are recorded as present. Seven new names are found; among them Bartolomé Hurtado appears for the first time, heading the list. Hurtado was a friend of Vasco Núñez at Salvatierra on Española and aided him to secrete himself on the ship of Enciso when the *alcalde mayor* sailed for Urabá, the territory of Alonso de Ojeda. When Balboa rose to be chief of the colony in Darien, he made Hurtado *alguacil mayor*.

There are five occasions during this notable expedition on which certain Spaniards and a few other Europeans are recorded present by name. Four of these lists, all of which include Balboa, are attested by the notary. Three of these occasions were acts of possession, at which, in addition to Vasco Núñez and Valderrábano, were Andrés de Vera, Francisco Pizarro, Diego Albítez, Martín Ruiz, Francisco Pesado de Malpartida, Francisco de Lucena, Álvaro de Bolaños and Cristóbal Daza. Many names are listed at two acts of possession; others appear on only one occasion.

NUMBER OF EUROPEANS AT DIFFERENT TIMES

At the discovery of the South Sea and first act of possession. 67
Named with the three patrols. 4
At second act of possession on Gulf of San Miguel. 27
Witnesses to the paddles inlaid with pearls. 6
At third act of possession on Bay of Panama. 24

Many names are repeated twice, and even three times.

NUMBER OF SEPARATE AND INDIVIDUAL NAMES OF EUROPEANS

Sept. 25. At the discovery on the *cumbre*. 67
           With the three patrols. 2
Sept. 29. On the Gulf of San Miguel. 1
Oct. 20.   Witnesses to inlaid paddles. 2
Oct. 29.   At third act of possession on Panama Bay. 7
                                                              ─────
           Total number of white men named. 79

As usual where many names are listed, some confusion and uncertainty arises. On September 25, appears Johan de Beas Loro and on September 29, Johan de Beas, which I count as one and the same man. Again, on the *cumbre* on September 25, a Spaniard is noted simply as Valdenebro; on September 29, the notary writes Francisco de Valdenebro; and at the third possession appears the name of Diego de Valdenebro. I take these to be two individuals, probably related, from the town of Valdenebro in Spain.

I do not believe that many of these men signed their names or even made their marks at these " *actas*." In the year 1513, the spoken languages of Europe were still rather crude, and many of these witnesses, including Francisco Pizarro, could neither read nor write. The principal reason for requiring an *escribano* to accompany the Spanish expeditions was to have a reliable record by a competent writer and a sworn official of the crown. Neither is there any reason to believe, as some writers assume, that the notary recorded all the white men with the command when each event was noted. Indeed, on October 20, Oviedo adds to his list: " and all the rest of the Christians who were assembled there." Even on September 25, I believe there must have been more Spaniards at the base of the peak of Quarequá guarding the slaves and supplies than recorded as present on the summit with Vasco Núñez. Balboa was too able a commander to cross the mountains and approach the South Sea with only sixty-seven men, leaving the remainder of his force on the north side of the cordillera.

Balboa's command on the South Sea must have consisted of twice the number of seventy-nine Spaniards mentioned by name. He carried with him a large number of Indians from the north coast of the Isthmus; took on more slaves, male and female, during the march; and carried considerable baggage, arms, provisions, and articles from Spain for barter and gifts. When native villages were occupied, the houses had to be cleared, billets assigned, and food collected and prepared. Balboa was fast accumulating treasure of gold, pearls, and textile goods. All of which required a large part of the force constantly to guard and supervise, whether in camp or on the march.

Beside, there were the dogs, including Leoncico, Balboa's favorite war dog, leader of the pack. More valuable than gold, or even pearls, they had to be guarded and cherished.

One more observation: Of the sixty-seven white men on the *cumbre* when Balboa first saw the South Sea, sixteen were named Juan (Johan); nearly one in four. Of the twenty-four Spaniards present at the third *acta de posesión* on the Bay of Panama, not a single man was named Juan.

Pearls, now, had supplanted gold in the thoughts of the Spaniards. It would never do to leave the South Sea without making another effort to secure some of those big pearls found only about the Pearl Islands. Valderrábano, the notary, was rated a very discreet man of much ability, so Balboa ordered him and six more Christians to go with twenty Indians in a canoe to one of the islands nearest the shore.

On October 31, Valderrábano started out and went to the nearest island of the group. Arrived there, the naked divers brought up as much as three *espuertas* of the mollusks, opening which, not a single pearl was found. The Indians then said that at a large island, four leagues further from the mainland, they surely would find pearls; but the *escribano,* being a prudent man, did not feel that his commission authorized him to venture further. As it was, the party experienced much difficulty and danger, on account of the rough sea, in getting back to headquarters in the houses of Cacique Tumaco. They brought with them more than an *espuerta* of oysters in order that the governor and Christians might see them. The *espuerta* was a frail, or basket roughly woven of rushes, used in Spain for transporting raisins and figs. These receptacles held from thirty to seventy-five pounds. In this case the term was employed to indicate the quantity of pearl oysters obtained.

This trip shows two things: the large size of the sea-going canoes, and the confidence of the white men in the friendship of the natives.

Balboa was having a wonderful time with his new-found friends, Chiapes and Tumaco. His journey had been successful beyond his wildest dreams, and now it was high time to go back to his colony at La Antigua and report his discoveries to the king.

Desiring to enlarge his knowledge of the land and make further explorations, probably picking up more treasure on the way, Vasco Núñez determined to return to Darien by a different and longer route. This meant meeting new and powerful caciques and surely some more fighting, with serious losses and even defeat possible. It would have been easy to retrace his southward course, through the lands of chiefs already conquered and pacified; but Balboa was a man of restless energy— " *que no podía estar quieto* "—who had been so uniformly victorious that he had no fear of suffering defeat or losing his treasure.

BALBOA BEGINS HIS RETURN MARCH

On Thursday, November 3, 1513, Vasco Núñez began his return transit of the Isthmus. Tumaco and Chiapes supplied salted fish, maize, and other provisions; and the latter furnished canoes and paddlers to bear the Spaniards away from the Gulf of San Lúcas. Chiapes, good friend of Balboa, and a son of Tumaco accompanied the white men and acted as guides. They went up an arm of the Gulf of San Miguel, its shores lined by mangroves, and so narrow in places that branches of overhanging trees had to be cut away to allow passage of the canoes.

The flotilla then entered the mouth of a large river, usually supposed to be the Río Sabana. There are other rivers, great and small, in this section flowing from the north and emptying into the Gulf of San Miguel. Nearly every large river encountered by the first Spaniards was designated *río grande*. When truly gigantic rivers, like the Orinoco, Amazon, La Plata and Mississippi were met with, the reports were not believed at first.

Balboa ascended this river until he came to the province of Teochan, ruled by Cacique Teoca, called Thevaca by historian Oviedo. During the night the Spaniards approached close to the settlement of Teoca, located near the river, and early the next morning they took the village by a surprise attack, capturing the chief and his people. Teoca was glad to save his life and speed the parting of his unwelcome guests by giving up some very fine articles of gold weighing 160 ounces, and two hundred pearls besides.

On the morning of November 5, Vasco Núñez turned his back on the waters of the South Sea, and took leave of his friends Chiapes and the young chief of Chitarraga. Both Chiapes and Tumaco's son wept genuine tears at parting with the celestial visitants; and Teoca who had just been conquered and robbed, politely joined in the grief and added his regrets. Chiapes and the young man went back in the canoes in which they had transported the Christians. Balboa sent along ten Spaniards, probably to insure possession of the canoes wherewith to bring up the remaining white men. They bore an order from Balboa to the Spaniards left at the houses of Chiapes to join the main body at the next village, the seat of Cacique Pacra, where the governor would wait for them.

PACRA

Supplied with more provisions and carriers and guided by subjects of Teoca, commanded by his son, the expedition arrived that same day at the village of Pacra. This Pacra, or Poncra, and his band had vacated hurriedly their homes on the approach of the white men and their Indian attendants, leaving behind golden objects to the value of three thousand pesos, which the Christians dexterously appropriated.

It was public fame among his neighbors that the chief possessed gold mines in his territory, and the three thousand pesos were sufficient to bait the appetite of the Spaniards for more.

They sent messengers after Pacra, who was encouraged to return, accompanied by three of his principal chiefs. Asked where he obtained his gold, the cacique replied that his forebears had left it to him. Probably this answer was the truth, as the golden articles of utility and adornment possessed by the Indians were the slow accumulation of many generations of natives.

Torture, at which the Spaniards were adepts, was applied; but Pacra continued to deny that he had any gold mines. Surrounding chiefs, enemies of course, begged that Pacra be killed; and Vasco Núñez, as a matter of policy or irritated at his failure to extract more gold from the cacique, acceded to their request. Pacra and his three *principales* were given to the dogs to tear and eat.

In extenuation of this dastardly deed, Spanish writers say that Pacra was an ugly, misshapen creature, horrible to behold, and a cruel despot, as if deformity and ugliness justified serving the cacique and his friends as " a breakfast to the Spanish doggs," as Ogilby terms it. It is stated further that his own subjects accused the cacique of a crime against nature, which Oviedo names *extra vas debitum*. Even Quintana, writing in 1830, declares that the guilt of Pacra's death lies more with the Indians than with the Castilians.

Each splendid achievement of the *Conquistadores* was marred by similar atrocities. On Española, Nicolás de Ovando killed the queenly Anacáona; Hernando Cortés, in Mexico, hanged the noble Cuauhtemoc; down in Peru, Francisco Pizarro treacherously murdered Inca Atahualpa; and Ximenes de Quesada robbed the Zipa of the Chibchas of his gold and emeralds, and then tortured him to reveal more.

After the dogs had finished with their victims, the remains were gathered together and burnt. Balboa named this province *Todos los Santos*, because of the day on which he arrived there; but better to call it the land of All Evils, writes one historian.

The fame of Balboa was so well published throughout the land that the caciques were conquered before the Spaniards reached them. The dogs in particular were feared more than devils, says Las Casas. On learning of the harsh treatment of Pacra, his brother, Thenora, hastened to come to Vasco Núñez with presents of gold. Caciques Mahe and Tamao Othoque also paid golden tribute and brought in men and women to serve the Spaniards. Two years later, this Mahe was visited by captains of Governor Pedrarias, who appropriated three or four of his attractive daughters, after which the cacique usually was referred to as *el suegro*—the father-in-law.

Vasco Núñez spent the rest of November in Pacra's village, during which time he was joined by the Spaniards left behind with Chiapes. These soldiers, on the way, passed through the land of Cacique Bononiáma—"*la penúltima sílaba luenga,*" writes Las Casas. This chief not only gave gold to the value of 2000 crowns and entertained the strangers for two days, but insisted on escorting the Spaniards to their commander. Arrived in the presence of Balboa, he thus addressed him: " Behold, most valiant and powerful chief, I bring thee thy companions safe and well, as they entered under my roof. May he who made the thunder and lightning, and who gives us the fruits of the earth, preserve thee and thine in safety." Saying which, the chieftain raised his eyes to the sun and uttered many other words which were not understood by the Christians.

Reunited again, the expedition departed from Pacra on December 1, 1513.

The early writers now tell how the Spaniards toiled up and down steep and rugged mountains, and waded through swamps and morasses, the mud and water up to their knees. At other places on the march the springs had dried up and they suffered much from lack of water, " tantalized by sight of naked and dusty channels where water had once flowed in abundance."

There was scarcity of food as well as of water, for the region was desert, with no Indian villages to raid for supplies. As has been stated, when the Christians could not live off the stores and labor of the natives, they suffered and perished. Some of the captives died of thirst and more would have fallen by the way had not Balboa's Indians found a source of water. This, probably, was the most critical stage in the march. Had there been concerted action by the natives to desert and attack the Spaniards, they could have been destroyed. Balboa, in most of his dealings, must have been fair with the Indians to receive the friendly and loyal support accorded him during his return journey to the North Sea.

Although the Spaniards had been warned of the sterility of this part of their route, where no Indians dwelt, they had not carried as many provisions as they should have done. All their gold and pearls could not purchase a mouthful of food. With the usual exaggeration of the writers of that period, the bishop of Chiapa declares that more slaves and *cargadores* were loaded down with gold than with provisions: " *Iban todos tan cargados de oro, que más indios con cargas de oro que con bastimentos y comida ocupan.*"

Buquebuca

Four days later, on December 5, the Spaniards arrived at the small village of Bocheriboca (Buquebuca). The cacique had hidden away through shame, not possessing the riches wherewith to entertain celestial visitors. Nevertheless, his houses were searched and plundered of such food and gold as could be found. Balboa did not tarry to send for Bocheriboca, but hurried on his way.

One day, faint and footsore, the Spaniards were hailed by some Indians from the top of a hill, who stated that their lord, King Chioriso, sent them to salute the great white *Tiba* and show his love for such valiant men, at the same time presenting Balboa with thirty large plates of gold, probably mirrors, worth 1400 pesos. Cacique Chioriso had a strong motive for his homage, as he wanted the white commander to join him in attacking a powerful enemy who was reputed to possess much gold. Vasco Núñez deferred aiding Chioriso and sent him three iron hatchets, beads and other trinkets.

Pocorosa

On December 8, Balboa arrived at the abode of Pocorosa, who, like most of the other chiefs encountered, had run away with his people. This was the mountain village of Pocorosa, twelve leagues from the Caribbean Sea, as stated by Vasco Núñez in his letter of January 20, 1513. Apparently, the houses and fields were well stocked with food, as Balboa decided to stop there and recuperate his command.

On December 13, Cacique Pocorosa returned to his houses, suing for peace and offering Vasco Núñez handsome pieces of fabricated gold. The latter gave Pocorosa a few hatchets and other articles of trade.

On the following day, December 14, came two messengers from Cacique Chuyrica, of whom the Christians had no previous knowledge. Simply to show his good will to the governor, he sent him presents of gold, and declared there was nothing he wished more than to entertain the white commander beneath the roof of his palace. The name of this chief seems to identify him with the Chioriso of Peter Martyr, previously described. Another neighboring chief, named Paruraca, on December 16, appeared in person before Balboa with a peace offering of gold, receiving in return trinkets from Spain, with which he was satisfied and remained a friend of the Christians.

Tubanamá

Two days' journey from Pocorosa (where Balboa was stopping) was the seat of Tubanamá, a powerful chieftain feared by all the other chiefs on the northern side of the Isthmus of Panama. This was the renowned cacique of whom Panciaco had warned Balboa in the preceding year, that one thousand Spaniards would be required to subdue him. It would never do to pass him by, as if in fear, without making him disgorge his gold and acknowledge the supremacy of the white men. The enemies of Tubanamá assured Vasco Núñez that the cacique had declared that he did not fear the Spaniards, and bragged how he would drag them to death by the hair of their heads, or drown them in the river.

"After this, on a Sunday the 18th day of the month, two hours before daylight, Governor Vasco Núñez, with eighty men, took the *buhío* of Cacique Tubanamá, and made prisoner of the cacique and many of his people; and some gold was secured in this night attack."

It is obvious that Oviedo, in the preceding paragraph, is following a written report, probably Balboa's account to the king of his journey, or an official record by Valderrábano, the notary. Medina declares that it was a Saturday, but I believe that the old historian was correct.

A more detailed account relates that Vasco Núñez selected seventy of his men best able to hike and fight, and, guided by Pocorosa's warriors, made a forced march, covering the two days' journey in one day. The Spaniards approached the houses without being perceived, and, in the first watch of the night invaded the court of Tubanamá. The cacique was captured in his palace with eighty women and two men—with all his "*sardanapálica comitiva*," as Peter Martyr tells it.

Tubanamá's settlement was not a compact village, but his subjects lived in separate and detached houses, as was the custom of Panaman tribes. One account declares that the chief's house was two hundred and twenty paces long and fifty broad. Near by was another house of the same size, intended for a barracks to shelter his soldiers when at war.

When daylight appeared and it became known that the terrible Tubanamá was a prisoner in the hands of Balboa, the chiefs among his Indian allies hastened to make complaints against him, saying that he was worse than Pacra and should be put to death. Pretending to accede to their prayers, Vasco Núñez ordered that the cacique be bound hand and foot preparatory to giving him to the dogs, or drowning him in the river, as he said he would treat the Christians. Tubanamá, much humiliated, declared that the other chiefs were envious of his power and wealth and lied about him. Weeping grievously, he pointed to the sword of the white commander and exclaimed:

" Who can pretend to strive with one who bears this *macana*, which, with one blow, can cleave a man asunder? Ever since thy fame has spread among these mountains have I reverenced thy valor. Spare my life, I pray you, and I will give you all the gold I have and whatever I am able to acquire."

Peter Martyr's version of the speech is this: " Who then, other than a fool, would venture to raise his hand against the sword of a man like you, who can split a man open from head to navel at one stroke, and does not hesitate to do it? "

Gold necklaces, bracelets and nose-rings filched from the wives and concubines of the cacique were valued at six thousand pesos. Tubanamá was allowed to send some of his principal men to publish throughout his province that his hidden people should bring in their gold to redeem their chief and trade with the Christians. The Indians of Panama respected and obeyed their chiefs, and every day from December 18 to Christmas came Indians with pieces of gold " to buy their lord," one warrior bringing in as many as fifteen *patenas*.

" *Cada dia vinieron indios é pressentaban piecas de oro para comprar á su señor, unos con una patena, y otros á dos y á tres, otros cinco y otros ocho, y otros á doce y más e indio ovo que truxo quince patenas de oro.*"

The foregoing is quoted from Oviedo to show the abundance of gold in this district of the Isthmus. The gold obtained in this way amounted in all to thirty *marcos,* beside some pearls. These *patenas* were plates of beaten gold worn on the breast or other parts of the body as armor. When a plate of gold was polished it could be used as a mirror or ornament.

Vasco Núñez questioned Tubanamá whence came the gold and the location of the mines. The cacique denied having any on his lands, in spite of the large amount of gold furnished by his subjects, but freely told of gold mines in the territory of neighboring enemies. Not satisfied with his replies, the governor secretly sent out some experienced Spaniards to test the sand of certain rivers and *arroyos*. With no appropriate apparatus, gold was found in all the *bateas* or troughs that they washed, although in small quantity. They even found signs of gold at a place only a quarter of a league or less from the *buhío* where was Vasco Núñez with the cacique. All of which was made a matter of record by the notary. The tests by his miners led Balboa, in his report to King Ferdinand, to recommend that a settlement be planted in that region. Later on, Captain Meneses and one hundred men did establish a post in the lands of Tubanamá.

" The day of the Nativity of our Lord was given to rest." Though the Indian slaves and *naborías* bore the burdens and did the hard work, some of the Spaniards were becoming sick, and Vasco Núñez himself felt the strain of his fatigues and responsibility.

In addition to his military genius for command, Balboa possessed great aptitude for dealing with the natives. It was good policy to have a powerful ally among the Indians, who would pay a yearly tribute of gold to the conquerors. Vasco Núñez never had any intention of taking the life of Tubanamá, and soon came to terms of peace with the chief, giving him hawk bells, glass beads, knives, and other trifles, all of which were of little value in the great fair held yearly in Medina del Campo, in Castile.

After Christmas Day (which is printed as of December 21 in Oviedo's *Historia*) Balboa went back to Pocorosa, where he had left the other men of his command. Tubanamá intrusted a young son to Vasco Núñez to learn the language and religion of the white men, and act as spy for him in La Antigua. Balboa accepted the boy, that the Spaniards might wean him from the faith of his fathers, use him as an interpreter and learn more of the secrets of the Indians. Both leaders hoped to benefit from the sojourn of the princeling among the Christians.

Vasco Núñez departed from Tubanamá with his gold and slaves, male and female, not forgetting to take along those eighty select beauties from the cacique's seraglio.

BACK TO POCOROSA

Balboa returned in triumph to the houses of Pocorosa where

he had left the rest of his party. The white men were tired and exhausted from hiking and fighting, and beginning to feel the effects of the humid tropical climate. The original chroniclers seldom complain of the climate or weather, but we know that the heat and rainfall had much to do with the debility of these white foreigners. It was noticed that the last Spaniards to arrive at La Antigua were the first to succumb to sickness. The acclimated veterans of Darien were more inured to all these ills. Balboa determined to proceed to the North Sea without further delay.

The expedition reunited again, Vasco Núñez took leave of the friendly Pocorosa and departed with his slaves and captives of both sexes, gold and pearls, baggage and provisions. The cacique, relieved to be free of his guests who were consuming his food supply, furnished a large contingent of his own Indians to assist the ailing Spaniards as far as the next province.

Some of the sick Spaniards had to be carried, while those able to walk were supported by Indians placing their hands under the armpits of the exhausted men. Even Vasco Núñez, despite his robust constitution, was seized by a fever, and was carried in the native sleeping bed, called *hámaca,* suspended from a long pole borne on the shoulders of sturdy Indians. The chiefs on the Isthmus of Panama often traveled in this fashion, with relays of carriers.

When Lionel Wafer, surgeon of the buccaneers, was with Chief Lacenta, in 1681, he was carried about in a hammock among the Darien Indians, " administring both Physick and Phlebotomy to those that wanted." (*Old Panama and Castilla del Oro,* p. 458.) Our English word hammock is derived from this word *hámaca,* used by the Indians about the Carib Sea.

Don Carlos Panquiaco

By easy stages, " *poco á poco,*" the expedition proceeded to Comogre. The old chief was dead and had been succeeded by his eldest son, Panciaco, now also called Comogre (after the province); or more often Don Carlos, as he had been baptized on Balboa's former visit. He ruled his large tribe as a great lord of Cueva, and was the finest and most intelligent chief encountered by Balboa.

This Don Carlos Panquiaco, as Gómara calls him, was that wise youth who gave Vasco Núñez the first news of the South Sea and of the rich empire of Peru. He was very friendly toward the Christians—"*muy amigo de los christianos*"—and was delighted to welcome Balboa, giving him twenty pounds of gold. Vasco Núñez, who was a generous man and appreciative of the information given him by the young chieftain, bestowed upon the latter one of his own shirts, a soldier's cloak, and some hatchets.

Naturally, Balboa told his friend of his adventures beyond the mountains on the shores of the South Sea. We can picture, too, Panciaco showing Vasco Núñez the desiccated cadaver of his father—the fat and moisture roasted out of it on a *barbacoa* —suspended alongside the shriveled remains of caciques who preceded him as lord of Comogre. These gruesome relics were wrapped in cotton mantles and hung about a special hall— "*su panteón para los muertos*"—in the palace, which was said to be one hundred and fifty paces in length and eighty in breadth. *Barbacoa* is another native term from the Caribbean region which we have adopted into our language, where it becomes barbecue.

Following Oviedo, who ought to know, Balboa arrived at the town of Don Carlos (Comogre) on New Year's Day, 1514, rested there for four days, and resumed his journey on January 5.

AT PONCA AGAIN

Another account states that Balboa departed from Comogre on January 14, and passed on to the *buhío* of Cacique Ponca, where he had stopped on the southward march. Ponca received the white commander with pleasure, or appeared to do so, mak-

INDI Hiſpanis offenſi propter nimiam eorum tyrannidem & crudelita-
tem, atq́, auaritiam, quoſcumq, captebant viuos, militares praſertim duces,
reuinĉtis manibus pedibuſq, proÿciebant in terram: mox auro in os iacen-
tis infuſo, cum hac exprobratione auaritiæ, Ede, ede aurum Chriſtiane: ad
maiorem cruciatum ac probrum cultellis lapideis, alius brachium Hiſpa-
ni, alius humerum, alius crus, abſcindebant & ſubieĉtis prunis torrentes mandebant.

Pouring molten gold down the throat of a captive Spaniard. On a
barbacoa in the background, Indians are roasting the limbs of Spaniards.

ing the usual donation of golden jewelry. At Ponca's village Vasco Núñez found four young Spaniards awaiting him, with a message stating that a ship and a caravel from Española had arrived at La Antigua bringing reinforcements of men and supplies. It is probable that Cacique Careta, the father-in-law in Indian fashion of Balboa, by methods of information common among primitive peoples, had accurate knowledge of the approach of Vasco Núñez and directed the four messengers where to meet their leader.

This cheering news caused Balboa to hasten on his way, as he was anxious to learn whether there was any message from the king or letter from Zamudio in Spain. He left at Ponca the greater part of his Spaniards and six hundred Indians, with the war dogs and treasure, to follow at leisure. Vasco Núñez himself selected twenty of the strongest soldiers to act as a guard, and taking with him two hundred *naborías* of both sexes and more than 2000 *pesos de oro,* he hurried on to Puerto de Careta. On January 17, 1514, he was back at the port from which he had departed on September 6 of the preceding year on his quest for the South Sea. Needless to say, he was heartily welcomed by Cacique Careta, his Indian *suegro*. No doubt he received a warmer greeting from Caretita, and perhaps a gentle quizzing as to his behavior with the Indian girls on the other side of the mountains. Balboa did not tarry long at Puerto de Careta, and the next day, January 18, in the night, he embarked his party in the brigantine which he had left there, and with fair wind and flowing sea, sailed eastward for La Antigua.

BALBOA RETURNS IN TRIUMPH TO LA ANTIGUA

On January 19, 1514. Vasco Núñez de Balboa returned in triumph to Santa Maria de la Antigua del Darien, his seat of government. It was a great day in Cémaco's old capital. Every soul in the town turned out to greet their chief and acting governor. Amid great rejoicing, Balboa was escorted to the plaza in festive procession. He told the people of the fatigues and hardships suffered by his companions, of the victories over so many caciques, the thrilling view of the South Sea, and the wealth of gold and pearls secured on the journey.

" Conqueror of the mountains, pacifier of the isthmus, and discoverer of the Austral Sea," writes Quintana of Vasco Núñez.

Balboa sent his brigantine, and the caravel which had arrived from Española, back to Puerto Careta to bring the remainder of his party to Antigua. When all were united again, Balboa distributed the spoils of the expedition. From the large quantity of pearls, two hundred of the finest were selected for a gift to King Ferdinand. The usual fifth then was taken from the gold and pearls for the king. After providing handsomely for the shadowy claims of the king, each member of the expedition received a share according to his rank and service. Even Leoncico, son of Becerrillo of Borinquen, received more than 500 *castellanos*, because he did greater execution than an *arcabucero*. The Spaniards remaining behind were given something, and they participated in the division of the cloth, mantles, hammocks and slaves of both sexes.

The writer never has had sufficient daring to undertake to figure out the value of the gold and pearls collected by Balboa on this famous expedition. The old chroniclers write of pesos, *castellanos*, crowns, pounds, and ounces in a very confusing way. One historian estimated the value of the gold at forty thousand pesos; another at one hundred thousand. The colonists could not fail to compare their growing prosperity under the rule of Balboa, with the poverty, calamities, and deaths they suffered when governed by the king's favorites, Ojeda and Nicuesa. Harmony seems to have been established in Antigua del Darien. Even lawyer Corral could not register an objection when the *Cabildo* petitioned Ferdinand to continue Balboa as governor of Tierra Firme.

At this point I cannot do better than repeat what I wrote a quarter of a century ago:

" Despite my assertion that the passage of the Isthmus on foot in

1513 was an easier task than it is today, I hold that in performance, as well as in result, it was one of the greatest expeditions of the conquest. Aside from the discovery of the South Sea, Balboa had conciliated every cacique along the route. He could do what few other commanders could—retrace his march and be welcomed everywhere as an illustrious friend. All this had been accomplished during the rainy season on the Isthmus, and without a single reverse, or the loss of a man. I doubt that, today, a company of one hundred and ninety white men, with modern hygiene precautions, could wander over the Isthmus for four and a half months without a single fatality.

" The Spanish colonists at Antigua, by adopting the customs of the natives, had largely adapted themselves to their environment. Maize and other crops had been planted and harvested; and with plenty of food and gold, and slaves and women at their command, the rough pioneers settled down to a fairly harmonious existence. Balboa had demonstrated his ability and fitness to command; and under his practical and tactful rulership both whites and natives promised to enjoy benign and peaceful government. Spanish amusements and fiestas were revived, and Cémaco's old capital became a Spanish pueblo.

" I wish I could stop here and state, like the narrator of a fairy tale, that Vasco Núñez and his people lived happily ever afterwards; but agencies in Spain were already so shaping the future as to bring distress on the colony, annihilation to the natives, and untimely and cruel death to Vasco Núñez.

" Had Ferdinand governed the Isthmus and Castilla del Oro through his officers at Santo Domingo, much suffering and disaster would have been avoided. Indeed, each European colony established in America suffered from the control of a remote home government, until it became strong enough to successfully declare for independence."—*Old Panama and Castilla del Oro*, p. 180.

EPISTOLA CCCCCXXXVII
(EXTRACT)

" We have messengers from the New World. Marvelous things are written. Vasco Núñez de Balboa, with the
aid of his followers and against the will of authorities appointed by the King, has usurped the government in
Darien, driven out the Governor Nicuesa and thrown into
prison the Bacheller Enciso. Balboa has attempted and
accomplished a deed so great that not only has he been
pardoned for his treasonable conduct, but distinguished by
honorable titles. Partly by force, partly by conciliations
and by pacifying the native kings, he scaled the mountains
and saluted the ocean."

PETER MARTYR.

Valladolid—July 23, 1514.

The above extract from Peter Martyr's letter 537 is the
first European record of the discovery of the Pacific Ocean by
Balboa.

IX

THE LOST LETTERS OF BALBOA

" Le malheur de Balboa fut qu' Arbolancho n' arriva point en Espagne deux mois plûtot."

—CHARLEVOIX, Liv. VI, p. 433.

BALBOA wrote at least two letters to King Ferdinand narrating his march across the Isthmus of Darien and Panama, and discovery of the Pacific Ocean. The date of these letters was 12 March 1514, writes the king in his reply to them. It is just possible that Vasco Núñez wrote a third letter at this time, to which Peter Martyr assigns the date of 4 March 1514. More likely, however, this was one of the two letters mentioned by Ferdinand, and the date a misstatement by Martyr. The old historian, a famous letter writer himself, praises the long letter—"*la muy larga carta*"—of Balboa, which, he says, resembled the celebrated letter written by Tiberius to the Roman senate on Sejanus. Martyr adds that Balboa's letter, containing such signal and "new news," was written in his military style, and every leaf contained thanks to the saints and the Holy Mother of God for safely passing through so many dangers. Peter Martyr was writing to Leo X at the time, and may have forwarded Balboa's letter to Rome, and this priceless "*carta larga*" may yet emerge from the archives of the Vatican.

In preceding pages we told that Ferdinand, while equipping his armada for Castilla del Oro, feared that Vasco Núñez might not tamely surrender command on Tierra Firme to the new governor. The king hurriedly dispatched a trusted messenger, Pedro de Arbolancha, by special ship with the best pilots available to Antigua del Darien. Arbolancha had lived many years on Española and was well and favorably known to many persons at Antigua. He bore a royal *cédula* dated 11 June 1513, charging the colonists to give faith and credit to what he would say to them. Under pretense of carrying food and other supplies to the Christians on Tierra Firme, the king's commissioner was to make secret inquiries and investigation of the people as to their attitude, and especially that of their commander, Vasco Núñez, toward receiving a new governor. If Arbolancha found that the citizens were not disposed to welcome a new ruler, he was to use his diplomacy and friendship with the colonists to remove the opposition and induce them to receive the new governor without hostility.

This shows that Ferdinand and his council feared Balboa, the man who could grasp power in Darien and maintain himself for three years as head of the colony.

Pedro de Arbolancha arrived at Antigua del Darien while Vasco Núñez was away on the shores of the South Sea. Las Casas infers, erroneously I believe, that Arbolancha reached Antigua in time to accompany Balboa on his march to the sea; in which belief he is followed by Quintana and Irving. During the absence of Balboa, the king's envoy had full opportunity to learn the state of affairs in Darien, and came to be a strong partisan of the acting governor. This speaks well for the latter, as Balboa carried practically all his friends with him on the expedition; and those left behind included his enemies, like lawyer Corral and Alonso Pérez.

Arbolancha observed the welcome accorded Balboa on his return to Antigua, and the manner in which he rendered the king's share of the gold, pearls and other things; and division of the spoils among the people. He noted, too, that the same *regidores* and *alcaldes,* who formerly started an information against Balboa, praised him highly and now wrote a petition to Ferdinand asking that Vasco Núñez be retained as governor of Tierra Firme.

Arbolancha had been instructed by Ferdinand to return speedily to Spain upon completion of his mission. Balboa was eager to report his great discovery to the king as soon as possible, and entrusted his letters and the king's gold and pearls to Arbolancha. The two letters of Vasco Núñez and the petition of the *Cabildo* bear the date of 12 March. It is probable that officials in the Indies dated their letters and reports on the day the ship sailed for Spain. Then why did Arbolancha delay from 19 January to 12 March 1514 before setting out for Spain to report so great an event as the discovery of another great ocean?

Peter Martyr quotes Vasco Núñez as writing that he could not report sooner because no ship had left Antigua. We have record of two boats lying in the port during this period, the brigantine of Balboa and the caravel which brought Arbolancha to Darien. It is possible that both had been attacked by the *broma*, or sea worms, and required considerable repairs. Another reason is that it was the dry season, when strong winds—" *grandes brisas,*" wrote Balboa, blow from the north and northeast. The junklike caravels could not sail close to the wind, making it difficult to sail directly from Darien to Santo Domingo. The pilots knew that these prevailing winds, together with the westerly currents, were likely to bring them up on the south coast of Cuba and increase the hazard of shipwreck.

Whatever the reason for delaying his departure, Arbolancha sailed from La Antigua on, or directly after, 12 March 1514. Stopping at Santo Domingo, he told Diego Colón and treasurer Pasamonte of Balboa's great discovery, and of the prosperity and contentment of the colonists at La Antigua. Arbolancha showed them the two letters of Vasco Núñez and the petition of the officials in Darien, and succeeded in removing the animosity of Pasamonte against Balboa. We know that Pasamonte's opinion and favor were purchasable, which leads us to suspect that Balboa may have sent him a few of those big pearls he collected while on the South Sea. Even lawyer Corral charged the royal treasurer with accepting bribes from Vasco Núñez.

With the appointment of Pedrarias as governor of Castilla del Oro, Miguel de Pasamonte saw his power over Tierra Firme disappear. It was not likely that Pedrarias Dávila, an irascible and covetous old courtier supported by Bishop Fonseca, would need or seek any aid from Pasamonte, or be willing to pay for it if he did. The venal treasurer-general of the Indies welcomed the information brought by Arbolancha that Vasco Núñez de Balboa, with a handful of men, poorly equipped and with no expense to the royal exchequer, had accomplished what the large expedition of Pedrarias had been designed to do. Arbolancha, just from La Antigua, confirmed Balboa's account of all that he had written, and bore with him the king's share of the gold, as well as those two hundred beautiful pearls, to prove it.

Whether because of the letters and report brought by Arbolancha, or because of more presents or bribes sent by Balboa, Pasamonte now made a complete change in his attitude toward Vasco Núñez. To Pasamonte, who realized the valuable work of Vasco Núñez, it looked as if Balboa must be the coming man on the mainland of the New World. His services certainly deserved it.

Pasamonte realized the uselessness of his master, King Ferdinand, sending an expensive armada to Darien, now that Balboa, with a small body of men, had accomplished its purpose. He made copies of the important documents from Antigua, probably for the purpose of sending them to Spain in a different vessel from the one in which went Arbolancha with the originals. In case one boat was lost, the valuable reports would still reach the king. Pasamonte made another about face in his estimate of Balboa, and now wrote a letter to Ferdinand recommending that he be retained as governor on Tierra Firme.

Pedro de Arbolancha, with the original letters from La Antigua, and the copies made by Pasamonte, may have arrived at Sevilla at the same time. Perhaps Arbolancha stopped to see his wife; or he may have gone to his tailor to secure new clothes in which to appear before the king. Official papers, such as sent by Pasamonte, went to the Casa de la Contratacion or to the Consejo de las Indias, from whence the most important documents were despatched posthaste to the king, wherever he might be holding court. The copies from Pasamonte were the first to reach Ferdinand, then at Valladolid, where he had married Queen Isabella in 1469, the city where Columbus died and Cervantes lived.

The king was so pleased with the news from Darien that he immediately replied to Balboa, without waiting for the arrival of Arbolancha. Ferdinand's letter is dated 19 August 1514, from which we can calculate when the report of the discovery of the South Sea reached Spain. The king told Vasco Núñez how pleased he was to see his letters (*i. e.*, the copies sent by Pasamonte) and to learn of the things that he had discovered in the new land of the South Sea and the Gulf of San Miguel. Ferdinand thanked Balboa, and held him as a very certain and true servitor, whom he would always recognize and reward— *" yo siempre abré respeto a buestros servicios."* For years the king had been hearing of fights and atrocities committed by the Spaniards upon the Indians about the Caribbean Sea, and now he was delighted to hear of the gentle way in which Vasco Núñez treated the caciques and their people—*" ame parecido bien la manera conque en aquel camino tratastes los caziques e indios."* Ferdinand assured Balboa that he was writing to Pedrarias (who already had sailed for Darien) to favor him and treat him as a person that the king desired to honor and reward. The king ended his letter by asking Vasco Núñez to aid and counsel Pedrarias, especially in the location of forts and roads.

On this same day, Ferdinand replied to the *alcaldes, regidores,* and *homes buenos* of the town of Santa Maria del Antigua del Darien, stating that he saw their letter of 12 March 1514, and noted what they said of the great services of Vasco Núñez, and of the ability he possessed for serving in those parts, greater than any other person—*" más que otra ninguna persona."*

After years of neglect and threats of prosecution by the king, Balboa, at last, was having his day at court. The receipt of the letters from Vasco Núñez informing Ferdinand that his acting governor on Tierra Firme, without waiting for reinforcements, had led an expedition over the cordillera of the Isthmus and had found that other sea, necessitated immediate revision of the orders previously issued to Pedrarias. On this same 19 August, the king wrote a long letter of instructions to Pedrarias Dávila, telling him that he had seen his letter, dated 7 May 1514, from the port of Gomera; and was glad to know that the governor and Doña Ysabel had arrived there in safety with all the armada.

Ferdinand said that he would be much concerned until he learned that they had arrived at Castilla del Oro, especially since some letters had come from Vasco Núñez de Balboa, " who for us had charge of the *Capitanía* and government of the province of Our Lady of Darien," who wrote what he had discovered in the new land of the Sea of the South, which appeared a marvelous thing and for which he gave thanks to the Lord. The king declares exultingly that Pedrarias will have reached Darien at the best time in the world, a statement which must have irritated the old governor very much, as he had been looking forward to achieving that great honor for himself. What a big display Pedrarias would have made in conducting a large expedition across the isthmus according to the accepted rules of military campaigns of those days! The mortality and morbidity among those green Europeans would have been frightful, and think what the poor Indians would have had to put up with!

With the discoveries of Balboa and the information he could give, the governor would be able to provide all that was best and suitable for those parts. The king went on to state, doubtless following recommendations by Vasco Núñez, that it would be well to construct and supply three or four posts (*asyentos*) on the shortest and smoothest road from the town of Santa Maria del Darien to the South Sea, in order to cross over and find out the land from one part to the other. The ignorance in Spain of this region, or of any part of the continent away from the seacoast, is well shown by Ferdinand when he adds that these posts or stations should be at the most advantageous sites on the Gulf of Urabá. The settlement on the Gulf of San Miguel must be on the best port to be found, for Vasco Núñez had written that it would be very necessary to have some ships there to discover and trade about the South Sea. To be profitable, the vessels had to be made there.

If Pedrarias carried any shipwrights with him, he must order the construction of three or four caravels, two after the model of Andalucía, and the other two small *latinas* like those of Portugal, of eleven or twelve tons. Ferdinand was acting on the advice of Balboa, and attached much importance to these ships in order to extend exploration and discovery on the new sea, believing that with them he soon could get in touch with Cipango and other parts of the East. A few years later, 1518, Vasco Núñez, after great labor, completed his fleet on the South Sea; but an evil fate cheated him out of the use of them. The king informed Pedrarias that he was sending two caravels with materials for the ships to be built, and a supply of provisions.

Ferdinand then praised Balboa's method with the natives, and repeated the phrase he used in writing to Balboa: " The manner of Vasco Núñez in dealing with the caciques and Indians seemed very good to me, treating them with so much moderation and gentleness (*con tanta tenplanza y dulzura*) and leaving the caciques peaceful and friendly." The king would be well served if Pedrarias avoided all force and severity, so that the Indians would not form a bad opinion of the Christians, punishing with all vigor any person guilty of any cruelty, and watching the soldiers who had been in Italy and were addicted to evil customs and vices. The priests would have to see that the laymen treated the Indians well and not scandalize the Christians.

Pursuant to " Instructions of 4 August 1513 " to Pedrarias before sailing from Spain, to give names to lands and places, Ferdinand ordered the governor to give the name New Land (*Tierra Nueva*) to the territory beyond the mountains discovered by Vasco Núñez, extending from the crests of the mountains—" *bertientes de las syerras* "—on the coast of Veragua to the South Sea. The governor was commanded to set up landmarks and proclaim the name to the people. It must be remembered that under the grant to Diego de Nicuesa, in 1508, the eastern limit of Veragua was determined to be the mid-line of the Gulf of Urabá, that Darien was the eastern part of this extensive Veragua, and that in the commission to Pedrarias, Darien became a province of Castilla del Oro. Hazy limits were constantly changing as discoveries extended. For over four hundred years frequent changes have been made in this region by royal decrees and by treaties between nations; and in this year of grace, 1939, who can accurately define the western frontier of the Republic of Panama?

Because no one about the court could understand or comprehend the " figure " of the New Land, sent by Balboa, the king directed that the names on the drawings should conform with the relation, and the lines join points on the Caribbean coast previously known, so as to be understood by everybody —*"por los unos y por los otros."* Ferdinand ordered that none should dare to change the names on the coast of Urabá and Veragua given by the discoverers, or the first names given by Balboa to the new land of the South Sea. Pedrarias was the first to disobey this commandment. In his eagerness to obliterate the deeds of Balboa, the new governor hastened to rename many places already named by Vasco Núñez.

No one in Europe at this time knew the extent of the New World, nor understood the " lay of the land " of Darien and Panama. The confusing arrangement of land and water around and near Antigua del Darien befuddled everybody. Peter Martyr of Anghiera, the Milanese scholar, had been an official at the court of Spain ever since the first voyage of Columbus. He was delighted with Balboa's report of the discovery of another ocean. Martyr writes that the Indians declared that the land separating the two seas could be traversed in six days, and he was puzzled to understand how so great a river as the Río Grande (Atrato) could issue from mountains in the middle of this narrow stretch of land, only three days' journey from the northern sea (Caribbean). " *Yo no lo entiendo* "—" I do not understand it," he adds.

As Vasco Núñez had written of the need for provisions, Pedrarias must be careful in spending what he had taken along in the armada until, God willing, the land would supply their needs. The king was sending a copy, stamped by his secretary, of certain chapters of a letter from Balboa, which Pedrarias should note. And concerning what Vasco Núñez wrote of the Indians of Caribana and of the Culata of the Gulf of Urabá, the governor must act in harmony with counsel ("*letrados*") so that the king's conscience would be free. With the coming of Arbolancha, expected daily, Ferdinand would write what further he had to say.

The king in this letter states that Vasco Núñez wrote in one of his letters that he was about to undertake new discoveries, and Ferdinand wanted to be informed of what happened in "this second journey," and urged Pedrarias to find out the things of those parts in brief time:

Vasco Núñez, as you will have learned there, has served us greatly, as well in what he has discovered as in all the rest that he has shown there; and I hold him for a very good servitor, and have great desire to favor and reward him as is right and his services merit. Accordingly, I command and charge you that you treat him very well and favor him in all that concerns him; and, therefore, in what you should have to provide it will be well to consult him and give him part, for on account of the great experience he has there and the willingness to serve us, he cannot fail to succeed in everything, which will benefit you and do me much service and pleasure.

There is nothing in this long letter about arresting Balboa, confiscating his goods and sending him in chains to Spain for trial, as the king had directed in prior instructions to Pedrarias.

From the foregoing letters of King Ferdinand, dated 19 August 1514, we obtain a fair idea of what Balboa wrote in his two letters to the king. It is obvious that Ferdinand repeated recommendations made by Balboa in his reports; though with the usual confusion of localities and direction, as when the king orders three or four posts or settlements on the Gulf of Urabá between Santa Maria la Antigua and the South Sea.

"They praise Balboa now at court," writes Peter Martyr.

ARBOLANCHA REPORTS TO KING FERDINAND

Balboa, of course, was aware that he had traveled very roundabout ways in crossing and recrossing the Isthmus from his headquarters at Antigua del Darien. Wishing to find out a shorter and more direct route to the South Sea, he sent out Andrés de Garabito with eighty men, with orders to seek a road over the mountains back of La Antigua, and follow down the other side until he came to the sea. Garabito went up the banks of the Río de la Trepadera, near Antigua, and then ascended to the crest of the range. On modern maps these mountains appear as the *serranía* of Darien, running from Cabo Tiburon on the north, southward toward the Pacific Ocean. This ridge is seldom traversed by white men, and very little reliable information about the region is available. The old historian states that Garabito descended by another river whose waters emptied into the South Sea. The captain encountered several settlements, capturing the Caciques Chaquiná and Chacuea. Nearer the sea, Garabito came to the land of Cacique Tamahé, assaulting his village by night. To free Tamahé, his brother brought some gold, " and a girl of good appearance," saying that she was his daughter, as if that made any difference to Garabito. The captain took the maiden, without law and without benediction, says Las Casas, setting free his captives, as a pledge or dowry to his bride, in the language of the chronicle. After this exchange of courtesies, Cacique Tamahé became known as *El Suegro*—the Father-in-law. Doubtless it was this exploration by Garabito toward the South Sea that Balboa mentioned when he wrote to Ferdinand, and which the king, in his letter to Pedrarias, refers to as the " second journey " to those parts.

By this time the reader must have observed the important rôle played by Indian girls in the subjection of their race by Europeans. What happened in Darien and Panama during the Hispanic conquest took place all over the New World, and the custom was not confined alone to the Spanish conquerors.

At this time, soon after the departure of Arbolancha, Abreiba of the tree-top Indians and one-armed Abenameche, cacique of the Río Negro, denied obedience to the white men. Balboa sent his friend, Bartolomé Hurtado, once driven away by Abenameche, with forty soldiers to chastise the rebellious chieftains. Hurtado wiped out the disgrace of his flight from that section in the preceding year. What Indians he could not capture alive for slaves, he killed, so that none was left, either peaceful or warlike.

Both Garabito and Hurtado brought male and female Indians back to La Antigua, to be sold there, or shipped to the slave market at Santo Domingo.

While Pedro de Arbolancha was sailing back to Spain, bearing the petition of the colonists to King Ferdinand to make Balboa governor of Tierra Firme (now Castilla del Oro), the fine armada of Pedrarias Dávila, sailing in the opposite direction, was slowly but surely approaching Antigua del Darien. It was very soon after 19 August 1514, that Arbolancha made his tardy appearance at the Court of Spain. He was welcomed by Fonseca, now bishop of Burgos, and by Lope de Conchillos, who conducted him into the presence of the king. Ferdinand received his special messenger very graciously. Arbolancha presented the letters of Balboa, the petition from the *Cabildo* at Darien, and the royal *quinto* of gold and pearls. Beside these, he gave Ferdinand the two hundred beautiful pearls donated by the colonists and the skin of a male *tigre,* or jaguar, stuffed with straw, killed with difficulty by the settlers. He said that some of the Spaniards at Antigua ate the flesh of the beast, probably to acquire its courage, and that it was like the flesh of an ox and of good savor.

The king was much pleased with his share of the gold, amounting to twenty thousand pesos. He admired the perfection of the pearls and marveled at the size of the shells from which they were extracted. While handling the gems from the South Sea, the aging monarch hoped that Balboa's sea might enable Spain to share in the rich trade of the Orient, now monopolized by Portugal under the grant by the Pope. " Spain," wrote Peter Martyr to Leo X, " hereafter will be able to satisfy with pearls the greedy appetite of such as in wanton pleasures are like unto Cleopatra and Æsopus; Spaniards will not need to mine and dig far into the earth, nor to cut asunder mountains in quest of gold; but will find it plentifully, in a manner, on the upper crust of the earth, or in the sands of rivers dried up by the heats of summer."

Report of the discovery of another sea on which dwelt people rich in gold and jewels spread throughout Spain, and Vasco Núñez de Balboa was hailed as a discoverer second only to Christopher Columbus. No doubt those persons who failed to sail in the armada much bewailed their fate at being left behind, which turned to joy, however, when later they learned of the death of hundreds of their compatriots who had sailed for Darien.

There is no good evidence extant that Arbolancha had been named *procurador* by Balboa to negotiate his interests at court. It will be recalled that the dying Ocampo delegated his power of attorney to his cousin Alonso de Noya, and Cobos, officials of the king's secretary, Lope de Conchillos, who then held the document. Arbolancha had been sent to Darien to make secret investigations and to spy upon the actions of Vasco Núñez, and he returned to Spain to praise him. Colmenares, who had grown rich in a few years under the rule of Balboa, had nothing but defamation of Vasco Núñez when he came back from Darien. For a short time, at least, Ferdinand really seemed desirous of making amends to Balboa for the unjust and evil reports of him given by Enciso, Colmenares, Pasamonte, and Corral.

If Arbolancha had returned a few months sooner to Spain, before the departure of Pedrarias, it is very probable that Ferdinand would have stopped the sailing of the expensive armada and disbanded the force for Darien, just as he had called off the Neapolitan campaign under *El Gran Capitán*. Balboa would have received a permanent appointment as governor of Darien and Panama (now called Castilla del Oro), and he would have continued his policy of conciliation in dealing with the natives, though demanding a reasonable return in gold or labor. Vasco Núñez would have extended his discoveries on the South Sea toward the rich country he had heard of in the south, and he would have become the logical pacificator, in fact, of the Peruvians, assimilating, and not destroying the admirable Inca civilization, as did Pizarro.

Arbolancha's long narrative of what he learned at La Antigua must have been very favorable to Vasco Núñez, for we read that he recommended that Balboa be created a *caballero,* or knight, in one of the ancient orders; and otherwise rewarded in an appropriate manner. The historian Gómara states that Ferdinand revoked a sentence in the courts pronounced against Balboa. We know that within a month after the arrival of Arbolancha, the king, on 23 September 1514, commissioned Vasco Núñez de Balboa " *Adelantado* of the South Sea and of the government of the provinces of Panama and Coiba "; and then the ungrateful, suspicious, and calculating old king added the words: " *debaxo y so la governacion de Pedro Arias de Avila* "—" subordinate to and under the administration of Pedro Arias de Ávila."

X

THE SPLENDID ARMADA FOR CASTILLA DEL ORO

" Nothing gains estimation for a prince like great enterprises. Our own age has furnished a splendid example of this in Ferdinand of Aragon. Beside this, he always used religion as a cloak for undertaking great enterprises, and under pious guise practiced great cruelty."

—The Prince, MACHIAVELLI.

FERDINAND exhibited feverish activity in the preparation of his armada for Castilla del Oro, the last great effort of a king approaching his end. One wonders how, in those days, they secured enough paper on which to write the hundreds of orders, commissions, contracts, and other documents issued by the king, the Casa de la Contratación and other officials in the assembly for the equipment and provisioning of the famous armada. Very good paper it was, too, because the documents have existed for centuries, the writing still legible, tied in bundles (*legajos*) and preserved in the Archives of the Indies, now in the Casa Lonja in Sevilla, and in the old castle of Simancas. Hundreds of these packages still remain unopened, concealing much interesting information to reward the patient student of history.

Ferdinand had several objects in view in preparing this armada:

1. He feared Balboa and wished to supplant him with a governor of his own choosing; and the reports of Enciso, Colmenares, and Pasamonte caused the king to believe that Vasco Núñez might oppose by force the landing of a new governor in Darien.

2. Ferdinand also suspected the Portuguese and was pre-

paring for a possible conflict with them. There were rumors of Portuguese ships in the Caribbean Sea along Tierra Firme, and it was reported that Portugal was preparing armed vessels.

3. If the armada arrived safely at La Antigua del Darien, and there was no opposition from Balboa, the force would undertake to march over the cordillera (on the Isthmus of Panama) and search for that other sea in the direction of Cipangu.

On 11 June 1513, just before naming a new governor for Darien (soon to be called Castilla del Oro), Ferdinand wrote to the citizens, esquires, and honest men in the town of Darien and in other parts of the provinces of Urabá and Veragua, that he knew how much they had labored and suffered, and that he took pleasure in the specimens of gold which they sent him, and in their discovery of mines, and that they must continue their labors. The king announced that very shortly he would send a " principal person " to take charge of the government of that land, as their *procuradores* had supplicated him to do. In the meantime, they should work in harmony and hold themselves together until the arrival of the armada, which would be soon, God willing. Furthermore, they should give entire faith and credence to Pedro de Arbolancha, the bearer of the letter, who would speak more largely upon the matter.

Arbolancha, under the pretense of taking a few men and supplies to La Antigua, was simply a spy to view the land. He was directed to ingratiate himself with the settlers, many of whom he knew, and find out how they felt about receiving a new governor and whether they might oppose one by force of arms. Especially was he to learn the attitude of Vasco Núñez de Balboa and to what extent the people would support him.

On the same day, the king wrote to Diego Colón that he was sending Pedro de Arbolancha to Darien to visit the Christians there in order to bring back a true relation of everything in those parts. Should Arbolancha touch at Española either going or returning, the viceroy was commanded to favor him and speed his journey.

Still another letter of the same date was directed to Juan de Esquivel, head of the Spaniards on Jamaica, informing him that Arbolancha soon would arrive there and speak with him concerning provisions for Tierra Firme.

In a *cédula* of 11 June 1513, Ferdinand ordered the officials of the Indies House, who had charge of all the shipping to the West Indies, to transport Arbolancha to Darien quickly and secretly, employing only the most skillful pilots, " for it is expedient that he go and return as quickly as possible "— " *porque conuiene que vaya e buelba lo mas presto que pueda.*"

Among the documents collected by Medina is one dated 4 July 1513, in which Ferdinand directed Miguel de Pasamonte to pay no attention to the intermeddling of Viceroy Colón in the affairs of Tierra Firme, as it did not belong to him. As presently we shall see, the king, three weeks later, informed Pedrarias that his government of Castilla del Oro did not include Veragua, as it had been discovered by Christopher Columbus, the father of Diego Colón. Apparently, between 4 July 1513 and 27 July 1513, the Council decided that the region on the continent known as Veragua, the limits still undefined, fell under the rule of Diego Colón.

The reader cannot have failed to observe that fortune never favored Balboa at the Court of Don Fernando. Even after the discovery of the Pacific Ocean, when the king was compelled to recognize the great service of Balboa, the honors accorded to him were empty and valueless, as shown later.

King Ferdinand had just called off his war in Italy on account of his jealousy of the popularity of the general, Gonsalvo de Córdoba, and was not likely to turn over his fine armada to a daring and aggressive leader, such as Balboa was reputed to be. The insistent claims of Diego Colón for more power in the Indies, the new and rapidly expanding Spain in the West, was a warning not to delegate too much authority to a subject. Beside the reports of the *procuradores,* the king had received letters from Darien charging Vasco Núñez with arbitrary and dictatorial acts. These complainants were that other lawyer, Diego Corral, Luis de Mercado, Alonso Pérez de la Rúa, and Gonzalo de Badajoz, who had been lieutenant of the lost Nicuesa. The king was not aware that these men had started a cabal in La Antigua, and that Balboa had suppressed them in order to maintain and continue the colony.

I doubt that Ferdinand ever considered appointing Pedro de Arbolancha to head his expedition to Castilla del Oro, as has been affirmed. With the possibility of fighting the Portuguese on the sea and Balboa on the land, the king naturally would select a man of established reputation and military experience. Ferdinand's first choice for the command of the armada and the government of Castilla del Oro was Diego del Águila, a noble *hidalgo* of Ávila. Though urged by the king to accept, this nobleman declined the office, which was a misfortune for the natives of Darien, Panama, Veragua and Nicaragua; regions later ruled by Pedrarias Dávila. To Balboa, the refusal of Diego de Águila was a direful calamity, as he could not possibly have been as wicked as the man who did accept the position, and who brought untimely death to Vasco Núñez.

Pedrarias Dávila—" The Wrath of God "

From among the applicants for the position of Captain General of the Armada and Governor of Castilla del Oro, King Ferdinand appointed Pedro Arias de Ávila, an elderly native of Arias in Segovia. In Spain he was known as *El Justador* on account of his feats in the tournament in his youth; in America he was called *Furor Domini,* or the Wrath of God. Spanish writers speak of him as Pedro Arias, or more often as Pedrarias; while to English readers he is best known as Pedrarias Dávila. His brother, Juan Arias Dávila, became the first Count of Puñoenrostro (Fist-in-the-Face), which seems to indicate that he shoved his fist in the face of some person.

Pedrarias was a colonel of infantry who had served with honor in the war in Africa. Doubtless this was a reason why the king selected him to command the armada. Angel de Altolaguirre y Duvale, of the Spanish Academy of History, writes that Pedrarias enjoyed great influence at court on account of his aristocratic ancestry. Not so, says Manuel Serrano y Sanz, a recent historical writer on the subject. D. Manuel

Serrano declares that the grandfather of Pedrarias was a converted Jew—"*judío converso*"—who took his name and origin out of nothing—"*que sacó de la nada su nombre y su estirpe.*" It seems to be established that Pedrarias was the grandson of a Jew called Diegarias Dávila (or Diego Arias Dávila), who adopted the Christian faith and became *contador mayor,* or chief auditor, of the kingdom of Castile. His son also held this important office.

Like many other men successful in public life, Pedrarias owed much of his advancement to his wife, Doña Isabel de Bobadilla y de Peñalosa, a notable woman. Peter Martyr states that she was the grandniece on the father's side of the Marchioness de Moya, who opened the gates of Segovia to the friends of Queen Isabella when the Portuguese were invading Castile, thus enabling them to hold out; and later to take the offensive against the Portuguese and defeat them. Doña Isabel was the mother of four sons and four daughters, all of whom were left behind in Spain; but she herself insisted on accompanying the governor to Darien. When urged by Pedrarias to remain in Spain and avoid the risks of a long sea voyage, she replied in the following curious words, as given by Peter Martyr and translated by Francis A. MacNutt:

" My dear husband, we have been united from our youth, as I think, for the purpose of living together and never being separated. Wherever destiny may lead you, be it on the tempestuous ocean or be it among the hardships that await you on land, I should be your companion. There is nothing I would more fear, nor any kind of death that might threaten me, which would not be more supportable than for me to live without you and separated by such an immense distance. I would rather die and even be eaten by fish in the sea or devoured on land by cannibals, than to consume myself in perpetual mourning and in unceasing sorrow, awaiting—not my husband—but his letters. My determination is not sudden nor unconsidered; nor is it a woman's caprice that moves me to a well-weighed and merited decision. The children God has given us will not stop me for one moment. We will leave them their heritage and their marriage portions, sufficient to enable them to live in conformity with their rank; and besides these, I have no other preoccupation."

After this tender speech there was nothing for Pedrarias to do except to take the Doña Isabel with him to Darien.

Years later, in 1602, Don Francisco Arias de Ávila, Conde de Puñoenrostro, relates how his grandfather was saved by a miracle from being buried alive. Being in Torrejon de Velasco, Pedrarias apparently died and was put in a coffin, which was carried into the convent of nuns of Our Lady of the Cross, half a league from Torrejon, where he had requested to be interred. When about to lower the remains into the sepulchre, a servant of Pedrarias embraced the coffin and felt the body move. Hastily opening the coffin, Pedrarias was revived and lived many more years. On the anniversary of this event, every year thereafter, Pedrarias would enter a tomb and have the offices of the dead said to him. The count declares, when he wrote this story, that the coffin of Pedrarias was resting high on the wall of the *capilla mayor* of the convent church, on the evangel side. The grandson also tells us that Pedrarias thereafter carried a coffin with him wherever he went and kept it in his apartment.

I have encountered no record of Pedrarias taking along a coffin in his armada for Darien. Like so many other Spanish officials in the New World, he seems to have left behind him much of the piety he displayed when living under the eyes of the court in Castile.

Before the date of his official appointment, Pedrarias had been addressed by Ferdinand as our Captain and Governor in the province of Darien. On 18 June 1513, as before cited, Pedrarias was ordered to execute certain judgments in favor of Enciso against the town council of La Antigua. That shrewd and clever lawyer, Martín Fernández de Enciso, who seems to have secured everything he asked for, now obtained another favor from the king. A royal *cédula* dated 4 July 1513, directed Pedrarias Dávila, " our Captain and Governor of Tierra Firme," to assign ten men of those on salary to serve Enciso,

who was going back to Darien (now Castilla del Oro) as chief
constable. One of the ten was a woman, as shown by the following list:

- 3 musketeers
- 2 cross-bowmen
- 2 fishermen, with their nets and weights
- 2 huntsmen, one with a wife and mill
    (probably a handmill for grinding
    grain).

This looks as if that far-sighted *bachiller* of law was planning
to insure to himself a supply of fish and game, the woman to
grind the maize and do the cooking. Although returning to La
Antigua as an officer in the large force under Pedrarias, the
lawyer wanted the musketeers and bowmen to act as a bodyguard to protect him from the anticipated fury of Vasco Núñez.

The appointment of Pedrarias was not without opposition.
Quicedo and Colmenares, the *procuradores* from La Antigua,
as well as others, attempted to deprive Pedrarias of the command of the armada. It is probable that Colmenares was a
candidate. Though an enemy of Balboa, he was experienced
in matters and life in the Indies, and would have made a much
better governor for Castilla del Oro than Pedrarias Dávila.
Gómara states that if it had not been for Juan de Fonseca, the
king's confessor and president of the Council of the Indies, the
post would have been given to another, and most certainly to
Vasco Núñez de Balboa if Arbolancha had returned a little
sooner to the court. " But," writes Peter Martyr, " the first
almoner, the bishop of Burgos, whose business is to stop such
intrigues, promply spoke to the king in the following terms:
' Pedro Arias, O Most Catholic King, is a brave man, who has
often risked his life for Your Majesty, and who we know by
long experience is well adapted to command troops. He sig-
nally distinguished himself in the wars against the Moors,
where he comported himself as became a valiant soldier and a
prudent officer. In my opinion, it would be ungracious to with-

draw his appointment in response to the representations of envious persons.' "

On 27 July 1513, Pedrarias Dávila was commissioned captain-general and governor of Castilla del Oro, defined as " a very large part of land which until the present has been called Tierra Firme, and now we order it to be called *Castilla del Oro,* and in it our people have made a settlement on the Gulf of Urabá, which is in the province of Darien, that at present is called the province of New Andalusia, and the town is named Santa Maria del Antigua del Darien."

This reads very well, but illustrates the confusion in the names of provinces and their boundaries in this region of the continent. Properly speaking, Darien, always west of the Gulf of Urabá, could not be in *Nueva Andalucía,* an extensive and indefinite territory always to the east of Urabá and the Río Atrato.

The commission to Pedrarias starts out with the usual cant, that in order that our Lord be served and His holy name be known to those lands, and the natives taught and converted to the holy Catholic faith and put in the road of salvation, and not so many souls lost as have perished up to this time, the king was sending learned ecclesiastics and priests to instruct and preach to the Indians and by good example lead them to become Christians. If such was the pious motive for the expedition, why send about two thousand persons, most of them armed men; why the detailed orders how the Indians should bring in the gold; why the authorization to capture Indians on the voyage out and sell them as slaves in Española; why the branding iron carried by the esteemed historian, Oviedo; why the instructions for the distribution of Indians among the Spaniards; and, worst of all, why that terrible *requerimiento?*

As a matter of fact, King Ferdinand was sending a large military force to Darien prepared to fight and arrest Portuguese ships, if encountered; overcome resistance on the part of Balboa; go in search of the South Sea; and fight and enslave the Indians, seizing their lands, gold, pearls, and other valuables.

The king declared Pedrarias to be a person of prudence, conscience, and fidelity, who would carry on the holy work with care and zeal. In this document Ferdinand states that Castilla del Oro did not include Veragua, which here he acknowledges to belong to the government of Diego Colón, for the reason that it was discovered by the Old Admiral, his father.

Pedrarias was empowered to use the offices of civil and criminal jurisdiction, by sea as well as by land; with appeal to the Council of Castile in causes over six hundred pesos. The governor could lay out towns and give pieces of ground to the settlers according to the quality of the persons becoming citizens, and in the distribution could give to the first settlers and *descubridores,* in reward and satisfaction of their labors and dangers, more than ordinary, or what appeared just. In all parts of his government and particularly in the towns, the governor should make ordinances that the people live in peace and quiet as good Christians and desist from customary evils and vicious habits.

Particular attention had to be given to the order of taking the gold from the mines and collecting it from the banks of the rivers, and the people assigned to each place, and the work which the natives had to do in cultivating the fields, and all the other things necessary for the common good. Pedrarias or his lieutenants could investigate cases in law, and other things annexed to and pertaining to his office. Fines to be delivered to Alonso de la Puente, the treasurer. Any person or persons holding the rods of justice and of the offices of *alcaldía* and *alguacilazgo* in Darien were suspended and forbidden to use the same under dire penalty. If Pedrarias judged it to be expedient to the king's service, he could expel any nobleman and other persons from the land and command them to present themselves before the king. Here Ferdinand authorizes the new governor to do the very thing which Balboa had done when, to preserve public order, he expelled Nicuesa and Enciso from La Antigua, permitting them to appeal to the king.

One more important item remains to be noted: the salary of Pedrarias " in each one year " was fixed at 366,000 *maravedís.*

The very next day, 28 July 1513, at Valladolid, Ferdinand issued a *cédula* in the name of his deranged daughter Juana and himself, commanding Pedrarias when he reached Darien to take the rods of justice and investigate how Velasco Núñez de Balboa *alcalde mayor* of the town of Santa Maria del Antigua del Darien and the other *alcaldes* had used and exercised the offices of justice which they held. They had to make the *residencia* which the law of Toledo directs, for the period of sixty days, during which any complainants might appear against them. If found guilty, the governor was ordered to proceed against them with all rigor of justice, seizing their property and turning over the fines to the king's exchequer. The guilty ones to be arrested and at their own expense to be sent to appear before the king, together with the evidence.

In another *cédula* of the same date, Enciso scores again against Balboa. The lawyer claimed that when the Spaniards captured the Indian town of Darien, 103 pounds of gold were taken, which Balboa and his party put in charge of *Bachiller Medico,* their treasurer. Enciso charged that when they came to divide the gold only seventy-five pounds were produced. This interested Ferdinand mightily, and he ordered Pedrarias to examine and investigate how it was stolen and lost, in whose possession it had been, what they had done with it, and especially how much belonged to the king. The governor was commanded to proceed against the parties by law and judgment with the severest penalties, civil and criminal. All these charges and orders against Balboa begin by including others, but they end by fixing the guilt and punishment upon Vasco Núñez. This is a recognition of his supremacy in Darien and explains, to a great extent, why both Ferdinand and Pedrarias feared Balboa. In this case the king directed that his property be sequestered in charge of a responsible person and that Balboa be sent a prisoner to the court of Spain.

List of the officials of Castilla del Oro and yearly salaries as fixed by royal decree of 9 August 1513:

Pedrarias Dávila, captain-general and gov-
      ernor ....366,000 *maravedís*
Alonso de la Puente, treasurer...........250,000   "
Diego Márquez, *contador*...............200,000   "
Juan de Tavira, factor..................150,000   "
Gaspar de Espinosa, *alcalde mayor*.......150,000   "
Juan de Quicedo, *veedor*................ 70,000   "
The physician (*físico*)................. 50,000   "
The surgeon (*cirujano*)................. 30,000   "
The apothecary (*boticario*)............. 30,000   "

Puente, the treasurer, was authorized to carry with him twenty marks of silver plate for the service of his house; ten slaves (Negroes) provided they were Christians; and eight *toneladas* of provisions.

Contador Márquez, native of Toro, was a favorite of Fonseca.

The factor Tavira, keeper of the king's drawing-room, three years before his appointment possessed nothing but his sword and cape ("*un caballero de espada y capa*"), writes Oviedo.

Espinosa's salary at first was 100,000 *maravedís,* but on account of the good report of his person, learning and ability, the king increased the amount to 150,000.

Quicedo was named *veedor* on 9 August 1513, but died shortly thereafter. On this same date, Gonzalo Fernández de Oviedo, the chronicler of many of these events, was given power to exercise the offices of *escribano mayor,* or notary and chief clerk of mines and of criminal and judicial procedures, as lieutenant and representative of Lope Conchillos, the king's Secretary, who held this lucrative office for all the Indies. Oviedo also had charge of smelting and marking the gold, and of the branding of the Indians and slaves ("*los indios e esclavos*").

Upon the death of Juan de Quicedo, Oviedo was advanced to the office of *veedor,* or overseer, and inspector of mines and smeltings. These various offices, as well as others to which he was appointed later, brought him in contact with different phases of life in Darien and Panama, and made him the most reliable historian of events and incidents which passed under his observation during the years he was an official. By royal command, 9 August 1513, the house of Oviedo was exempt from the lodgement of strangers while he was in the Indies. Oviedo was authorized to take with him from Spain one slave and six marks of silver plate for the service of his household.

Colmenares, the surviving *procurador* from La Antigua, was not overlooked. In addition to many other gifts, King Ferdinand gave him his kingly word (*" mi palabra real "*), to give him one of the *regimientos* of the town of Darien. He could carry along six marks of silver plate, and one male and one female slave, if Christians. Still another *cédula* of 9 August 1513, gave license to Colmenares, when he returned again to Spain, to carry with him three Indian servants to be indoctrinated in things of the faith.

The *Licenciado* Barreda, a physician of some reputation, agreed to go in the armada, and provision was made for a hospital of fifty beds (*camas de ropa*) in La Antigua. The officials of the Indies House in Sevilla were ordered to purchase the necessary furnishings and medicines and conserves for the sick.

Among the many appointees on 9 August 1513, was Fernando de Sotomayor, *alcalde* of the castle of Alfaro, whom the king commanded to accompany Pedrarias and perform the office of *maestre del campo*—master of the camp—of the army. As one-fifth of all pearls and precious stones would accrue to the king, he named Ruy Díaz as *lapidario* to examine the pearls, diamonds, rubies, and any other jewels that they expected to find. Juan de Albornoz was appointed to fill the important post of *redero mayor*, or chief net-maker. Doubtless, he was supposed to make nets to catch the nuggets of gold, as well as those for ordinary fishing.

Informative items on the monthly payroll are:—

```
 5 capitanes at 4000 each.............  20,000  maravedís
15 cabos de esquadra (corporals or squad
      leaders) at three ducats each.......  16,875     "
180 hombres, or men, at two ducats each. .135,000     "
```

It was not necessary to go to the Indies in order to obtain a big share of the spoils. King Ferdinand and high officials about the court usually received a handsome rake-off when new lands were settled and the Indians distributed in *repartimientos*. Hundreds of Indians on Española and elsewhere, whether *esclavos* or *naborías*, bore the brand of the king or his favorites, and toiled in the mines and *labranzas* for the profit of their masters in Spain. Juan de Fonseca, head of the Indies House and president of the recently organized Council of the Indies, who had been promoted from one rich bishopric to another, saw to it that he was not overlooked when new favors and awards were dispensed by Ferdinand while fitting out his armada. The Catholic king solicited the Roman pontiff, then Leo X, to name Bishop Fonseca universal Patriarch of Tierra Firme, that our Lord might be served and the holy Faith augmented among the natives. The latter phrase, so often repeated in Spanish documents, was intended to keep and comply with the condition imposed in the Donation by Pope Alexander VI. In addition, King Ferdinand ordered Governor Pedrarias, when he distributed the land in Castilla Dorada, to give Fonseca two *caballerías* with house lots, which was twice the area allotted to a knight settler.

The king prevailed on Leo to create a bishopric in Castilla del Oro, whose seat would be the town of Santa Maria del Antigua, and asked that Friar Juan de Quevedo be named bishop of the new diocese. Quevedo was a Franciscan, at the time an eloquent preacher in the royal chapel. Ferdinand, on 20 August, wrote to the civil authorities of Sevilla to lodge the newly-made bishop and those with him gratuitously, and in good *posadas* which were not low public houses. Bishop Quevedo, as did most of the officials, drew one-half his yearly salary before sailing for the Indies.

Sancho de Matienzo, treasurer of the Indies House, was directed to purchase a lot of liturgical robes and church ornaments and supplies for the church of Antigua. The list included eleven bells, three of them weighing three hundred pounds each, for 24,000 *maravedís;* six altars, and one hundred pounds of wax for the altars; three hundred pounds of oil for the lamps; and a pontifical ring and pectoral cross costing 6,450 *maravedís*.

The bishop was paid more than twice as much as the governor received. In the absence of tithes (*diezmos*), the treasurer and contador of Castilla del Oro were ordered to disburse to Quevedo two thousand *pesos de oro*, a very tidy sum in those days. In Darien, the bishop, like the other officials, received slaves and *naborías*, who did all the work about his household, from raising the needful food in the fields to building a house; so that the necessaries of life and labor cost very little in La Antigua. Wine and cheese, held to be essentials by Spaniards, as well as utensils, had to come from Spain; and, at this time, bacon was purchased on Española.

The church officials appear on a separate salary list:

To the bishop, 2000 *pesos de oro*		912,000 *maravedís*	
" " dean, " in each one year "		68,400	"
" " archdeacon			
" " precentor	each 100 pesos	136,800	"
" " schoolmaster			
" " archpriest, 80 pesos		36,480	"
" " canon		18,880	"
" 3 sacristans		27,360	"

The future looked very dark for the Indians of Darien and Panama, the sale of whose bodies, or their savings and labor, would have to supply the necessary funds. The foregoing salary lists disclose that in Spain, in 1513, the *peso de oro* was equivalent to 456 *maravedís*, and the ducat to 375 *maravedís*.

Juan Pérez, *clérigo*, parish priest of Torrejon, recently back from the Indies, was named dean. The provincial of the Franciscans on Española was asked to send an Indian *fraile* to " *Castilla dorada* " to instruct and convert the natives to the true faith.

XI

MEN CLAMOR TO JOIN THE EXPEDITION TO TIERRA FIRME

" So color de religion
Van a buscar plata y oro
Del encubierto tesoro."
—*El Nuevo Mundo,* Lope de Vega.

IN Valladolid, 18 August 1513, Pedrarias Dávila made the oath of fidelity and homage before Secretary Lope Conchillos and members of the Royal Council, and swore in due form of law that he would hold and defend Castilla del Oro for Their Highnesses (King Ferdinand and his daughter Juana), and obey and comply with their commands, as a good and faithful servant and captain-general and governor; and signed it with his name. Whether due to the love of Pedrarias for ostentation, the wishes of the Lady Isabel, his wife, or because so many volunteers for the expedition had supplied themselves with finery for the war in Italy, the governor and lady were to be exempt from the *pragmática,* or royal edict, prohibiting the wearing of silk and brocade in the Indies. In a *cédula* issued on that famous date, 9 August 1513, the king states that he wished to show the natives of Castilla del Oro that he conducted his affairs with more ceremony than the Indians did theirs. Notwithstanding the *vedamiento* forbidding Spaniards to carry silver to " *Castilla aurifera,*" Pedrarias was conceded the privilege of taking with him one hundred *marcos* of plate.

Since Sevilla had profited so much from the Indies and each day lived in expectation of receiving greater benefit, Don Juan de Ribera, chief magistrate of the city, was charged to lodge Pedrarias and his people. The defeat of the Spanish and papal troops by the French at Ravenna, Italy, in the preceding year, caused Ferdinand to raise another army to protect his kingdom of Naples from the threat of the French. When it became known that Spain's great military chief, Gonzalo de Córdoba, would lead the troops, there was a grand rush to enlist in the enterprise. So great was the popularity of *El Gran Capitán* that it excited the jealousy of the king, and this is given as the reason why Ferdinand abandoned the expedition. Hundreds of cavaliers and soldiers who had expended all their funds in equipping themselves for the campaign in Italy, were set free suddenly, and turned eagerly to seek fortune as well as glory in the Indies. Neither the promise of riches made by Pedrarias nor the eloquent preachings of Bishop Quevedo were needed to induce men to join the armada for Castilla del Oro. Oviedo writes that the captains were commanded to promise rewards and wealth to the volunteers for the Golden Castile in the West.

At first, the number was limited to twelve hundred persons, later enlarged to fifteen hundred; and by the time the ships sailed there were two thousand souls aboard. The impatient Ferdinand had planned that Pedrarias should sail in August of 1513, but it was many long months before the fleet was ready to put out to sea. The attention, labor, and money expended in fitting out this expedition to Castilla del Oro were quite remarkable for those days. Despite weighty matters of state at home and the alluring distractions of his young queen, Germaine de Foix, the aging monarch devoted much time and energy in looking after every detail of preparation for the voyage; and all the resources of the kingdoms of Spain were called upon to contribute to the success of this splendid armada.

All Spain, Portugal, Naples and southern Europe were searched for supplies. Ferdinand proposed to collect twenty-five vessels—ships, caravels, and brigantines. Not securing enough in his own dominions, the king commissioned that able navigator Vincente Yánez Pinzón, who commanded the *Niña* when Columbus discovered America, and was the first European to view the wide mouth of the Amazon, to go to Portugal to acquire the necessary boats. At the same time, Ferdinand wrote a nice fatherly letter to his most dear and well beloved son, the king of Portugal. The best pilots, masters and quartermasters were encouraged to come to Sevilla and serve on the ships, including Jerónimo Vespucci, a relative of Amerigo Vespucci, now dead. Juan Diaz de Solís, who had sailed down the coast of South America with Pinzón, in 1508, then chief pilot of Spain, was consulted in the preparation of the fleet.

When men heard of the marvelous wealth of the new Golden Castile, they flocked to Sevilla from without Spain, hoping to be included in the personnel of the expedition. In some instances the prohibition against admitting foreigners to the Indies was waived. Two rich Genoese merchants and their factors were induced to go in the armada and establish themselves in Antigua del Darien for a period of six years. Like privilege was extended to Francisco Cota, a native of Milan, for the reason that he was a *buen botycario*. The children of *reconciliados*, converts to Christianity, were refused passage.

To make sure of being included in the expedition, many persons secured *cédulas* from the king commanding that they be taken along. Such a one was Diego de Bustamente, who " has been and is a good captain," whom the king ordered to be admitted among the captains. By license dated Balbuena, 24 October 1513, Ferdinand authorized Sancho Gómez of Córdoba to go to Castilla del Oro and take with him three slaves and one white female slave (" *tres esclavos e una esclava blanca* ") who had been Christians for eight years. It will be noted that a few white slaves, as well as Negroes, were carried from Spain to Darien in this armada. Ever since the discovery in 1492, Spaniards had been taking a few Negroes to the islands in the Caribbean so far settled by the whites.

Some of the men in the armada were accompanied by their wives and children, and the king agreed that they should have free passage and maintenance like the men. A few of the gentlemen, better supplied with money than most of the party, wished to take their horses to Darien; and Ferdinand gave his permission, provided they pay for the transportation and the number of horses did not exceed thirty.

SHIPS, ARMAMENT, AND SUPPLIES

The twenty-five vessels engaged for the armada consisted of:

2 ships of 100 *toneles* each, to carry the people and provisions
1 caravel of 100 *toneles*, with rigging and tackle complete
4 caravels of 70 *toneladas* each
4 Portuguese caravels
6 brigantines, 4 without decks, 2 with decks, fully rigged
8 fishing barks, each with two fishing nets

The *tonel* was an ancient measure of tonnage; 10 *toneles* equaled 12 *toneladas*.

The vessels carried supplies of pitch, oakum, rosin, tallow, tar, nails, planks and other articles for repairs. On account of the delay and postponement of date of departure, it was thought to be less expensive to buy the ships than to hire them, as first planned.

In addition to the heavy ordnance and falconets made by the gun foundry at Málaga, the arms included:

200 *espingardas*, or hand guns
 35 arquebuses
300 swords
200 daggers from Villa Real, with scabbards
400 bucklers, made of cork
200 *tablachinas de drago*, or shields of dragon wood
600 dozen arrows for the bowmen
 50 cords for the cross-bows
800 helmets
200 *vitorianos*, with their scabbards

The *tablachinas*, made from dragon wood, were taken on board at the Canary Islands, and were better than those first ordered from Naples. In addition, there were large quantities of iron, lead, tin, saltpetre and sulphur.

Among the provisions were:

15,000 *arrobas* of flour
12,000   "   " wine
12,000   "   " vinegar
11,000   "   " oil
   50   "   " honey
  100 *fanegas* of chick-peas
  100   "   " beans
3,000 *quintales* of biscuit

The last item appears to be an enormous amount of biscuit, until we learn that the *quintal* of that period did not exceed twenty pounds. Before sailing, one hundred head of cattle were put on the ships to insure fresh meat for the voyage.

The list of implements and utensils carried to Darien reads like the inventory of a hardware store:

1,000 pickaxes
  400 axes of different kinds
  300 iron shovels
  300 chisels
  200 pruning hooks
  200 spits for roasting meat
  100 frying-pans
  100 copper pans
  100 copper pots
   50 heavy hammers
   50 *quintales* of iron nails
    6 dozen saws

Large sheets of lead were taken along to cover the ships, in case no better preservative was found to protect them from the *carcoma*, or wood louse. There were numerous other articles, such as rope, dishes, and baskets; and a very large number of coarse linen bags, each holding two *fanegas* for transporting and storing maize. The iron implements came from Marquina and other places in Vizcaya famous for their iron products.

You can be sure that most of the work done with the field implements was performed by Indian slaves.

The isles of the sea, as well as Spain and southern Europe, had to contribute to the success of this famous armada. In addition to the *tablachinas* and other supplies to be taken on at the Canary Islands, the governor of those islands, Lope de Sosa (who later died at Antigua del Darien), was ordered to have ready to join the armada fifty of the best and swiftest swimmers that he could find among the islanders. Each *canario* was to carry a sleeveless blouse and a shield made of the native dragon wood, and go under command of Pedrarias to Castilla del Oro, " because it is not known in what disposition they will find the said land." This was another precautionary measure in preparation for any contest with Vasco Núñez on arriving at Darien.

Treasurer Pasamonte at Santo Domingo was directed to buy on Española four hundred cotton shirts of the kind made in Villanueva de Yaquimo; and seven hundred *bateas,* or boat-shaped vessels, to be used in washing out the gold from the sands of the rivers, and for other purposes. He must purchase one hundred mares and consign them to the factor of Castilla del Oro, where the officials would sell them to the best advantage and send the money to the Indies House in Sevilla. To these were to be added twelve mares, saddled and bridled, and a *caballo.* King Ferdinand appointed special agents to aid the governors of San Juan (Puerto Rico), Cuba and Jamaica, now settled by Spaniards, in forwarding certain supplies to the members of the expedition after reaching Darien.

It must be obvious to the reader, especially if conversant with the *asiento,* or contract, of 9 June 1508, made with Diego de Nicuesa and Alonso de Ojeda, that King Ferdinand had been endeavoring for several years to plant one or two Spanish colonies in Urabá, Darien, and Veragua. The agreement with Nicuesa and Ojeda named the entire territory Urabá and Veragua, when this part of the mainland was scarcely known to Europeans. It was Vasco Núñez de Balboa who came to the front and guided Ojeda's party to the district and Indian village he knew as Darien. The expeditions of Nicuesa and Ojeda turned out to be miserable failures, and many of the survivors of those parties owed their lives and future prosperity to the courage and resourcefulness of Balboa.

The royal commission to Pedrarias Dávila, 27 July 1513, commanded that the Darien region be called Castilla del Oro, and for many months thereafter the king's secretaries exhibited their learning by writing it *Castilla dorada, C. aurica, C. aurifera,* and in other ways.

Castilla del Oro was the first " El Dorado " on the mainland of America, where catching gold in nets—" *la pesca del oro* "— was a quick and pleasant method of accumulating a fortune to carry back to Spain. Spaniards continued to use the old name Tierra Firme, a designation which, by reason of new discoveries, soon applied to the continental coast line from Paria, opposite the island of Trinidad, around the Caribbean Sea and the Gulf of Mexico to Florida. It is well to note here that some years later the term Castilla del Oro was dropped, and the Isthmus of Panama was referred to as the kingdom or province of Tierra Firme.

Diego Colón had been named governor of the Indies in 1508, but his activities had been limited almost entirely to Española. For several years he had been engaged in litigation with the fiscal of the Crown to obtain all the rights and privileges to which he was entitled under the terms of the capitulation of the Catholic kings with his father, Christopher Columbus. The relations between Ferdinand and Diego were strained, and the former seemed to delight in drawing men and supplies from Española for other islands and the mainland. The motive, of course, was to deplete the island of Española and leave Diego Colón, governor and quasi viceroy, with a small and insignificant command. Beside, most of the Indians on Española, one million, says the bishop of Chiapa, already had perished under the hard rule of the white Christians from Europe, and the island now was sending very little gold to the home government.

Though Ferdinand had taken from Española the larger part

of the members of the expeditions of Nicuesa and Ojeda, most of whom had lost their lives, he did not refrain from calling on Diego for more men and supplies for the mainland. Balboa, during three years and more, had firmly established La Antigua and pacified the Darien caciques with scarcely any assistance. The well-equipped large armada of Pedrarias must have aid from everywhere!

Diego Colón was ordered to send to Castilla del Oro one hundred and twenty Spaniards, to be selected from those who did not hold *repartimientos* of Indians, giving them transportation and provisions for the voyage. With them should go ten Indians, male and female, who had come from Tierra Firme, who would serve as interpreters when returned to Darien. If these Indians were *naborías,* give other Indians to replace them; if they were *esclavos,* pay their owners for them. Also, fifty " *yndios de naborías* " from those who worked in the mines on Española to go to Darien to mine the gold and teach the other Indians. These Indian miners were to be selected as follows:

From those working for King Ferdinand 12
    "   "   "   " Lope Conchillos 4
    "   "   "   " Diego Colón 6
    "   "   "   " Maria de Toledo 4
    "   "   "   " Miguel de Pasamonte 2
    "   "   "   " Juan de Villoria 4
    "   "   "   " Francisco de Garay 4

The remainder to be taken from Indians distributed by Colón after the general *repartimiento* was made. Spaniards and Indians must be sent to Castilla dorada without any delay or excuse.

Each month from August, 1513, to the end of the year, Ferdinand hoped to see the armada set sail. Pedrarias did not report promptly at Sevilla and speed up the enlistments and preparations for the voyage to Darien. The king was angry at the delay, and even Fonseca could not shield his favorite.

Instead of addressing Pedrarias as " Our Captain-General and Governor of Castilla del Oro," as was his custom, the king now calls him " *mi criado*." We are indebted to Manuel Serrano for this unique letter, which reads as follows:

" El Rey.—Pedrarias de Ávila, my servant: You know, of course, that when you left here you told me that you would be in Sevilla the 27 of September past, and now I have received a dispatch from Sevilla dated the 6 of the present month, in which they write me that you have not arrived, nor do they know of you; at which I am much astonished, and I do not know what has been the cause. In the future put more diligence in my service than you have until the present, and proceed with all haste to Sevilla and engage in your departure, and report to me the cause why you were detained so long. In the meantime, put your people in order, so that they waste no time in idleness, and that they go taught and instructed in what may be needed; and you become acquainted with the members of the expedition, and they know you and the Captains. Advise me continually of all you do. Done in Valbonilla, 18 October 513 [1513].
I the King."

On this same date, 18 October, Ferdinand wrote to the officials of the Indies House commending them for the diligence and care with which they had provided supplies for the armada and for their efforts to hasten the sailing. The king ordered them to hold a consultation of all persons concerned to fix upon the best and safest time for the fleet to depart. In closing his letter, he directed them to notify him when Pedrarias arrived in Sevilla. Pedrarias finally appeared in Sevilla, one month overdue, and on 27 October reported to the king, and wrote that the sailing ought to be postponed until the following January. Ferdinand ordered Pedrarias to begin loading the ships on 20 November, to be on his guard to see that his people did no damage in the city or injury to anyone. He must keep his people occupied, treating them well and not be too strict, for they should not go away fearing that after reaching Castilla del Oro they would have to lead a more austere life than what it would be.

XII

THE ARMADA SAILS FOR DARIEN
AND PANAMA

" Nunca había surcado las aguas del Océano Atlántico una armada tan poderosa y brilliante como la que capitaneaba Pedrarias Dávila."

—D. MANUEL SERRANO Y SANZ.

SEVERAL writers of the period describe the members of the armada as the most brilliant and select company that had ever departed from Spain: *" la más lucida gente que de España ha salido,"* says the Adelantado Pascual de Andagoya, one of the party. Some one translated this as the best equipped company ever to leave Spain, and English writers carry it on. This description, of course, applies to the people and not to the equipment.

Besides the officials and ecclesiastics already mentioned, many other names have been preserved because they achieved some worthy or execrable deed in the New World. Among the notables of general interest were Hernando de Soto, who fought Indians in Panama and Nicaragua and went to Peru, where he shared in the spoils of the Inca empire. Returning rich to Spain, De Soto was appointed governor of Cuba and Florida, and died near the Mississippi River in 1542. Diego de Almagro, a better man and soldier than his tricky partner, Francisco Pizarro. He fought in Peru, Chile, and Quito, and because he was reluctant to chop off heads, he lost his own. Almagro was beheaded in 1538 by Hernando Pizarro. Sebastián de Benalcázar, *conquistador* of Quito and Popayan. Bernal Díaz del Castillo, a lovable soldier of the conquest of Mexico and Guatemala. Late in life he wrote his memoirs—*Historia verdadera de la Conquista de Nueva España*—an account we are more inclined to believe than some more elegant records. His memory failed him when he declared that he landed at Nombre de Dios, which site had been deserted before the expedition arrived at Darien, to be resettled a few years later.

Another member of the armada possessing the historical sense was Diego de la Tobilla, described as *hombre del palacio*. He wrote *La Barbarica*, an account of the barbarities committed by the captains of Pedrarias. Tobilla was a partisan of Vasco Núñez and wrote in praise of him. *La Barbarica*, like many other documents favorable to Balboa, has disappeared, only a few extracts remaining.

The personnel of the armada included many young hidalgos of good family and little fortune; and many covetous old men, affirms Peter Martyr. Juan de Ayora, brother of the *cronista*, went as lieutenant to the governor. He was no credit to his brother during his short stay in Castilla del Oro. The king commissioned six captains, who were Luis Carrillo, Gonzalo Fernández de Lago, Contreras, Francisco Vázquez Coronado, Diego de Bustamente, and Atienza.

" One of the principal endowments or preparation to attain success is this name of captain." As time went on, Pedrarias appointed many other captains, among them his cousin, Gaspar de Morales, and his nephew, Pedrarias el Mancebo (the Youth). Oviedo records these names as if all were members of the armada, whereas we know already that Francisco Pizarro, Bartolomé Hurtado, Gonzalo de Badajoz, Juan de Ezcaray, Francisco Dávila, and Diego Albítez were in Darien before the arrival of Pedrarias and served under Balboa. A most important officer was the *piloto mayor*, Juan Serrano, chief pilot of the fleet, the same who was killed with Magellan in the first circumnavigation of the earth.

On 19 January 1514, Ferdinand, his patience and energies about exhausted, wrote to Pedrarias that each hour he was hoping to receive news that the ships had gone down the river from Sevilla. This ancient city, the *Ispalis* of Roman occupation, is about fifty-four miles from the sea, on the left bank of the stream which the Moors called Guadalquivir—the Great River. The historic capital of Andalucía is still a port for smaller seagoing vessels.

When we read the long lists of arms, supplies and provisions put aboard the vessels, we wonder where they found quarters for two thousand persons, to say nothing of the one hundred head of *vacas enjarradas*. One thousand hammocks were taken along and the inference is that the better class of people used them for beds. The sailors and servants could sleep about the decks or wherever they could find room. Despite the large quantities of provisions ordered, Colmenares many times told the king, Fonseca, and Conchillos that the ships were sailing away ill supplied—" *quan mal proveida iva el armada,*" from which cause seven hundred died of hunger and disease during one month after reaching La Antigua, he writes.

Fearing that Diego Colón and his friends on Española might do something to injure the ships or detract from the success of his great armada, Ferdinand had given orders that the fleet should sail to Darien without stopping at Santo Domingo, as was the rule. This order gave much concern to all the officials in the Indies House, for in all that armada there was no pilot who had navigated from Spain to Darien without touching at Española, " as well as for other reasons." The officials, Pedrarias and Bishop Quevedo, were commanded to convene, hear the evidence of pilots and others, and decide on the course to be followed, and sign their names to the decision. If they determined to go by Española, no one was to go ashore there, except a boat to carry the king's dispatches to the Admiral Diego Colón; and no boat would be allowed to come off to the fleet, under grave penalties.

With the approach of spring, 1514, the weather became milder, and the fleet prepared to sail away. Pedrarias, who dearly loved display, held a grand review of the troops and people of the armada in the streets of Sevilla. They then embarked, and the ships passed down the river to San Lúcar de Barrameda, the port at the mouth of the Guadalquivir. On Sunday of *carnestolendas*—the Sunday before Ash Wednesday

—the ships put to sea. They had not covered more than four or five leagues before the armada was struck by a contrary storm, and turned back to seek shelter in the port. The river pilots had left the ships, and they had great difficulty in entering the mouth of the river. One account states that one or two vessels were lost and that many supplies were thrown overboard. Pedro Miguel, pilot of the ship on which was the *contador*, Diego Márquez, had foreseen the storm and remained in the Guadalquivir.

In order not to consume the provisions, the governor disembarked all the people, who spent whatever of value they had left to sustain themselves, many doing penance this Lent by eating their cloaks and coats in the inns, as Oviedo relates it. Some members of the expedition had enough of the sea, and changed their mind about securing a fortune in Castilla del Oro, perhaps preserving their lives from untimely death in Darien.

It pleased God in Holy Week to send the kind of weather the pilots were waiting for, and on Holy Tuesday, 11 April 1514, the vessels made another start, and with good weather proceeded on their course.

"Never had an armada so powerful and brilliant ploughed the waters of the Atlantic Ocean, as that headed by Pedrarias Dávila. With it went many *hidalgos* and other distinguished persons fascinated by the dazzling notices, current as undoubted truths, relative to the gold deposits of the land baptized beforehand with the pompous title of Golden Castile."

How the Gold Was to Be Melted and Divided

No nation ever made more or better regulations for the government of provinces and towns in America than did Spain, and no people, officials as well as colonists, paid less attention to them. Governor Pedrarias was given three documents which vitally affected the interests of the Spanish colonists and the lives and welfare of the Indians of the mainland. The provisions of these documents were based on the experience of Spain in governing Española, and initiated on the continent of America the Spanish methods of dealing with the natives. These three documents were entitled:

1. The Ordinances
2. The Instructions
3. The Requirement—*El Requerimiento*

The ordinances which Pedrarias and his officers had to observe and keep were issued 30 July 1513, at Valladolid. As soon as with good fortune the armada arrived at the town called Santa Maria del Antigua del Darien, the governor must change the name of the country from Tierra Firme to Castilla Dorada. In the very next sentence the term Castilla del Oro is employed. King Ferdinand ordered Pedrarias to construct a House of Trade (*Casa de Contratación*), after the manner of the country, in an apartment of which should be a council chamber, wherein the governor would convene with the treasurer, the *contador* and the factor; and do what was necessary and suitable for the good government and pacification and settlement of the land, conformable to instructions which each official carried. All the officials had to be present or suffer a fine fixed beforehand by the governor. And each and every time any affair of importance presented itself, the officials had to call in the *reverendo in Cristo padre obispo de Nuestra Señora del Antigua,* Juan de Quevedo. In this *casa* all the merchandise and supplies and provisions and other things carried in the armada would be collected and kept, as well as other supplies when brought from Sevilla, Española, San Juan (Puerto Rico), Cuba, and Jamaica, either to sell to the colonists or to trade with the Indians, care to be taken to guard the goods and see that they were not damaged.

The acquisition of gold being the chief concern of Spaniards in the New World, not excepting the oft-reiterated desire to spread the holy Catholic faith, the governor and his officials had to see that the gold brought in by the captains and others was declared before a notary and registered in the books of the *contador,* and consigned to the Indies House in Sevilla. The gold must be sent to Spain in the best ships under the most skillful pilots and captains, and be divided among several ships, so that if one was wrecked, the whole amount would not be lost. Special care had to be observed that no gold was shipped before being melted and marked, and which did not pay the duties to the monarch. The gold ships had to be well equipped and provisioned " especially those bearing the king's share."

The journal of transactions of the *junta,* or council, and the royal dispatches would be kept in a chest, usually called the chest of the three keys. The royal *cédulas* must be proclaimed by the town crier with the usual solemnities. To avoid frauds and confusions, the factor would receive all merchandise consigned to him in presence of the *contador* and treasurer, and keep a record of them. It was the obligation of the factor and treasurer to inform themselves of what merchandise was most profitable and which was necessary and desired by colonists and Indians, and communicate this to the Indies House in Sevilla. The governor and officials were obliged to visit all ships arriving at Darien to see if they brought prohibited or stolen goods. Analogous precautions had to be taken when vessels departed from the port for the Antilles or Spain.

The king directed Pedrarias, after completing the House of Trade, to immediately build a smelter (*casa de fundición*), where the gold would be melted twice yearly, and if necessary three times. The governor, *alcalde mayor,* and other officials to be present on these occasions, so there would be no unseemly disputes nor scandals. Debts due the treasury must be collected " before all things." After the king's share, generally the fifth part, was put aside and taxes paid into the treasury, the citizens should pay their debts to each other to avoid scandals. All the gold taken from the Indians or mines had to be brought to the smelter to be melted and marked. As Ferdinand wanted all the gold possible to be sent to Spain, he ordered that no one dare, under penalty of loss of life and property, to melt gold anywhere except at the royal smelter. The order of voting and signing papers in the council of officials should be first the governor, then the treasurer, and after him the *contador,* and last the factor.

INSTRUCTIONS FOR THE GOVERNMENT OF CASTILLA DEL ORO

There are variations and obvious errors in different versions of the " *Ynstrucion.*" As a rule, I follow the copy given by Angel de Altolaguirre, though Manuel de Serrano declares that both Altolaguirre and José Toribio Medina are led astray by repeating mistakes in the copy presented by Martín Fernández de Navarrete. There is no reason to believe that Navarrete himself transcribed the original. He wrote by royal command, and probably called for copies of all documents then brought to light in the archives suitable for his *Viages y Descubrimientos.* No doubt many errors creep into history by reason of faulty copies of original records made by careless or incompetent amanuenses. In the long instruction to Pedrarias Dávila, dated Valladolid, 4 August 1513, Ferdinand commanded that Tierra Firme now be called *Castilla Aurifia.*

1. The first thing that the governor had to look after was to see that the ships were not overloaded, as they frequently were, from which many had suffered diasaster, especially when the *Comendador Mayor* de Alcántara (Nicolás de Ovando) went to be governor of Española. To avoid damage and danger, the king gave orders that the ships carry no more cargo than that with which they could safely navigate, and to keep the *manguera* uncovered.

2. The fleet had to stop at the Canary Islands and take on the things provided there for the expedition.

3. Threading their course straight for the province of Darien, if not delayed too much, the armada had to stop at the islands of the cannibals, which were Fuerte, Baru, San Bernaldo, Santa Cruz, Guira, Cartagena, Caramar, and Codego, where slaves could be captured for the reason that they eat human flesh and for the evil and damage they had done the Spaniards. If these Indians did not submit to the obedience of

the Church and declare themselves vassals of Spain, the soldiers must seize all of them that they could, and send them in a ship to Española and there deliver them to Miguel de Pasamonte to be sold, the ship proceeding on to the said Castilla Aurifia. In all other parts the Spaniards were ordered to avoid injuring the Indians, so as not to offend them and excite them against the Christians; rather, to treat them well, for the news running in advance, the Indians would receive the Spaniards and come to a knowledge of the things of the holy Catholic faith, " which is principally why we send you and wish may happen."

4. In this article Ferdinand directed how the Indian slaves and other things taken, on the sea as well as on the land, had to be divided. " I have to have my usual fifth," declares the king; and besides, according to the law of the *fuero* of Oleron, they had to give him two more parts, one on account of the ships, and the other for furnishing the supplies. Indians and booty taken within the land, the ships not being used, would be equally divided among the Spaniards, first taking out the king's fifth.

5. Arrived at Darien with good fortune, the first thing that Pedrarias had to do was to give a general name to all the land, cities, towns, and places, and to establish order in the things concerning the augmentation of the holy faith, and the conversion of the Indians. For the service of God and the increase of divine worship, the king was sending Bishop Quevedo and the priests.

6. One of the most important matters that the governor had to look after was to select sites for the settlements, especially on the seacoast to shelter the ships from Spain and where they could take on water and provisions. These new settlements should be on rivers and near mines, in healthy situations not subject to overflow, where were good water, good air, and good tillable land.

7. The town sites being selected, a place must be left for the *plaza*, on which to build the church, the most principal thing. After laying out the streets, lots for the houses would be dis-

tributed according to the quality of the persons. Town officials were not to be perpetual, but elected by the people for one year and confirmed by the governor, they being persons capable to rule. Also, the inheritances (*heredamientos*) had to be assigned according to the importance of the individuals, favor to be shown to the first settlers who came with Ojeda and Nicuesa for what they had suffered.

8. Pedrarias must strive in every way and manner that he could think of to attract the Indians with good works, that they live with the Christians in love and friendship; not breaking promises made to them nor doing them any damage, and punishing severely those doing evil or injury to them without the governor's command, that the Indians come to the knowledge of God and of the holy Catholic faith, " for more is gained in converting one hundred in this manner than a hundred thousand by the other way."

All of which is as sounding brass and tinkling cymbals; for listen to what follows, and then read *El Requerimiento*.

9. In case the Indians did not wish to come to the obedience of the Christians and war had to be made upon them, the necessary requirements should be made, once, twice, thrice; the interpreters giving them to understand that they will be injured and killed, and those taken alive will be slaves, so that they cannot pretend ignorance, and the Christians can capture the Indians with a clear conscience.

The instructions declare, truly, that the foregoing is the foundation of the whole matter of treating the Indians—" *está todo el fundamento en lo susodicho.*" Ferdinand then goes on to state that the soundest opinion on this subject of the Indians will be that of the R. P. Fr. Juan de Quevedo, bishop of Darien, and of the priests, who are more without passion and with less hope of gain from them.

10. When the Indians were given as *navorías* in charge of Spaniards, the ordinances must be kept, and the Indians better treated and indoctrinated in the holy Catholic faith; and avoid forcing them when it is possible, that they live in more contentment with the Christians.

11. "It is more necessary to do this in Darien than on Española, for the Indians of Darien are less devoted to work and more accustomed to their ease, and can run away farther off in the land, which they cannot do on the island Española." For this reason it appeared doubtful whether the natives of Castilla del Oro could be put in charge (*encomendado*) of Christians in the same manner as on Española. Those Indians willing to live in peace and agreement with the Christians and in the obedience of vassals, should have their work lightened, and only a part of the people of a principal cacique be required to work a month or two, and then replaced by others. As there was so much gold in the rivers, the Indians should be set to work there, and later dig ore in the mines, when they would be habituated to labor.

12. Whether given in *encomienda* or working by agreement in *remudas,* the Indians must work and be profitable—"*e se sacara dellos el servicio e provecho que se debe sacar.*" Still a third method would be for each town according to the number of Indians in it, or for each cacique, to give so many *pesos de oro* each month or each moon, as they count; and giving the gold, they would be sure that they would not be injured nor suffer evil. They could have signs in their villages that they are under the obedience of the king, and also wear marks or tokens on their persons showing they are vassals; so no evil be done them by the Christians, they paying their tribute as agreed.

13. Item—Because one of the things that most stirred up the Indians on Española and San Juan and excited their enmity against the Christians was taking their wives and daughters and using them against their will, the governor was commanded to forbid this practice in all ways and manners that he could. A few days later, on 9 August 1513, King Ferdinand enlarged on this item and ordered Pedrarias to proclaim publicly that no Spaniard venture to use any Indian woman against her will— "*contra su voluntad*"—the Indians being at peace and coming to work. For the first conviction the offender lost his property, " and for the second time the said penalty doubled, and for

the third doubled "—punishment which the reader may ponder at his leisure. In addition, for the third offense, such Christian would be banished from Castilla del Oro.

Contra su voluntad seems to nullify the offense, for it was very easy for the white man to say that the lady gave her consent, and the word of an Indian, man or woman, could not prevail against a Christian. It will require very extended research to disclose any punishment for this offense during the years of Spanish conquest in the New World.

14. Pedrarias had to seek to make the settlements within the land at places from which to discover the other coast of the sea that the Indians said is so certain and so near this other sea, meaning the Caribbean. The governor was ordered to report with diligence if it was the truth; and if true, to determine with thought what to do.

15. The governor must prohibit by ordinance and proclaim, as many times as appeared necessary, that no one play dice or cards, or other forbidden game; nor possess or sell cards or dice, under grave penalties, so there will be no gambling in the land. If any kind of game was invented, although not declared in the ordinance or proclamation, it also was prohibited. The intention being that by suppressing gambling, scandals, enmities, curses, blasphemies and traffic in lies would cease. " Endeavor always to keep the people occupied, so that idleness will not lead them to spend the time in evil habits."

16. The governor had to forbid by public herald that any Christian swear or curse or blaspheme, or swear to God, except when ordered by the judge; and besides the usual punishment prescribed by the laws of the kingdoms of Spain, a fine of money should be added, and these fines be spent and applied to things for the profit and pleasure of all.

17. Pedrarias must announce by the crier that the *prematica* (*pragmática*), or edict, against rich vesture be kept to the letter; for experience on Española showed that when they were not ordered what to wear, the majority of the people ruined themselves by buying finery. Those knowing the Darien region can scarcely picture the need for this order. It will be

recalled that the governor and Doña Isabel were exempt from this *pragmática*.

18. There must be public notice to all citizens and merchants that the officials of justice did not have to attach the property or persons of those in debt for cloth, silk, or anything else, except for subsistence or tools for mining gold, in order that each one may observe whom he trusted, and not trust with hope that justice had to issue execution and make him pay.

19. Item—Pedrarias had to forbid any lawyer (*letrado*) from going to the said land of Castilla del Oro to plead, or any solicitor of causes; and if any should go, clerical or lay, the governor must not consent for him to plead, solicit or counsel in any lawsuit. It had been found by experience on Española that many lawsuits and disputes among the inhabitants had been incited by the activity and counsel of lawyers. In civil cases, the governor and his officials had to try to know the truth of petitions before them, supplying deficiencies, and judge the cases shortly, without superfluous or unnecessary terms. Criminal cases had to be judged according to the laws of the kingdoms of Spain, punishing with all rigor those of the abominable sin, thieves, and mutineers. In the case of thieves, the laws of Spain could be somewhat exceeded, always bearing in mind the exoneration of the royal conscience.

20. The governor had to try to carry farmers with him to test and plant the soil, and implements and things necessary for it; and order wheat and new barley and three-months wheat, and other seeds. These must be kept separate and not damaged on the sea, so that if they do not grow or yield, it would be clearly known that it was not due to any defect of the seed. The farmers should be favored in dividing the spoils, that they be satisfied and others induced to work the ground.

21. Pedrarias must decree that anyone who went to trade and barter with the Indians must have a license from him, and take along a person with power of the officials to act as inspector and see what was traded, and keep account of it to pay *el quinto* to the treasurer. If it was a pearl or precious stone of

unusual kind or size, the trader must pay one-fifth the estimated value.

22. Pedrarias was informed that all persons going with him, and those going after him, to Castilla del Oro were entirely free to write to Spain whatever they wished without hindrance from the governor, under penalty for disobedience.

23. If during the first four years that the citizens had to reside in Darien in order to acquire title to their properties, any Spaniards wished to return to Spain and enjoy their wealth, the governor had to give them license and not impede or hinder them; except it might be by chance that he had need of them to do something, and then he could not detain them longer than two months.

24. In all difficult things that concerned the good movement of the land and towns, and the common welfare of the citizens, Pedrarias must communicate and discuss them with Bishop Quevedo and the treasurer, *contador,* and factor, that action be taken with agreement of all. Besides what each official wrote separately, they had to sign together all general proceedings that concerned the entire community.

25. Accordingly, Pedrarias was commanded, conformably to the foregoing instructions, to do, comply, and keep all the things contained therein, as well by sea as on the land. If there were any other things suitable to do for the good of the voyage and the said land of Castilla del Oro, not declared and specified in the said instructions, the governor had to do and order them with the care and fidelity and good diligence that the king trusted him to do.

Had Pedrarias Dávila been a good man, even with ordinary ability as a governor, these instructions, regulations, and privileges would have promoted a flourishing and contented colony in Darien, the Indians of course doing all the work in a state of actual, though endurable, servitude.

XIII

THE REQUIREMENT—*EL REQUERIMIENTO*

" Detrás de la cruz está el diablo."
—*Don Quijote,* CERVANTES.

OVERNOR PEDRARIAS DÁVILA carried with him
in his armada the most powerful weapon ever placed
in the hands of man with which to injure and destroy
his fellow men. Its provisions applied to and affected the lives
of the millions of the natives of America.

El Requerimiento, or the Requirement, was the most damnable religio-politico legal document ever produced by the human intellect. Only Christianity as practiced in Spain, *circa* 1500, could have produced such an instrument. No other European nation, Catholic or Protestant, coming to America and exploiting the New World, ever made such preposterous demands of the Indians.

El Requerimiento was evolved by high prelates of the Church and jurisconsults in canon law. Stripped of its absurd verbiage, the Requirement amounts to this:

1. The Creator gave all the world to St. Peter for his kingdom.
2. One of the Popes, successor to St. Peter, made donation of the islands and mainland of the Ocean Sea to the King and Queen of Spain, in certain writings, which you may see if you desire—*" que podeys ver si quisiéredes."*
3. I require you to accept Christianity and acknowledge the King and Queen of Spain as your supreme overlords.
4. If you do so, you will do well, and will be received in love and charity.
5. If you do not do this, I certify to you that " with the aid of God," I will make war against you in all parts and in every manner that I can; and will subdue you to the yoke and obedience of the

Church and of their Highnesses; and I shall take you and your wives and children and make slaves of them and sell them; and I shall take your property and do you all the evil and injury in my power.

Here is Oviedo's text of the preceding paragraph which he affirms that he copied to the letter—" *a la letra* ":

" *Si no lo hiciéredes y en ello maliciosamente dilacion pussiéredes, certificoos que con el ayuda de Dios yo entraré poderosamente contra vosotros, é vos haré guerra par todas las partes é maneras que yo pudiere, é vos subjectaré al yugo é obidiencia de la Iglesia é a Sus Alteças, é tomaré vuestras personas é de vuestras mugeres é hijos, é los haré esclavos, é como tales los venderé, é disporné dellos como Sus Alteças mandaren; é vos tomaré vuestros bienes, é vos haré todos los males é daños que pudiere, como á vassallos que no obedescen ni quieren rescebir su señor, é le resisten é contradicen.*"

This was a terrible weapon and license to put in the hands of governors and captains in the Indies. Under a pretense of reading and explaining its demands, which not being acceded to promptly and absolutely, the Spanish officials could go ahead and rob and kill and enslave the Indians. We have a record that, before the death of Quicedo, the two *procuradores* from Darien receipted on 22 August 1513, in Valladolid, for a copy of the Requirement which had to be made before warring on the Indians.

The favors bestowed upon the *bachiller* Enciso can be accounted for by the legal sophistry and casuistry he furnished King Ferdinand, who usually pretended to be much concerned about his royal conscience when legislating against the Indians. It was at this time that Enciso was defending the rights of the king to capture and enslave Indians before a *junta* of the friars of Santo Domingo convened in San Pablo in Sevilla. The Laws of Burgos, promulgated 27 December 1512, prescribed how the Indians on Tierra Firme should be dealt with, and these laws were approved by the Council of the Indies.

The Dominicans, who favored the Indians more than did the

Franciscans, believed the laws to be too harsh, and opposed turning them over to Pedrarias as the rule for the treatment of the indigenes of Castilla del Oro. The clever lawyer maintained before the Dominicans that the Pope, in virtue of his apostolic authority from Christ through Saint Peter, had an incontrovertible right to dispose of the New World to the king of Spain, and that the Catholic king could require the Indians to be obedient vassals; and, if they refused, make war upon them and enslave them. So well did Enciso argue that the friars agreed on the requirements to be made of the Indians, and seven of them signed it. *El Requerimiento* was put in writing and recorded in the books of the Indies House, and a copy was given to Pedrarias.

The Bachelor of Law, Martín Fernández de Enciso, never shy about claiming something for himself, certifies that it was he who originated the idea of " requirements "; and declares that he made the first *requerimiento,* or demand on the Indians: —" *e el primer requerimiento lo hice yo,*" he writes.

Antonio de Herrera in his *Historia* says that the *Requerimiento* was already given to Alonso de Ojeda in 1508, and was read in 1510 to the Indians at Calamar (Cartagena).

El Requerimiento was the fundamental law of Spanish conquest in America. The Requirement is the key to a true understanding of Hispanic expansion in the Three Americas, which, to a large extent, was a religious crusade with the sword; an implantation of the Catholic faith, *nolens volens,* upon the people of another hemisphere. The obligation contained in the papal Donation to increase and spread the holy Catholic faith, furnished to Spaniards timely excuse and justification to seize the Indians, their lands, and their wealth in gold, pearls and emeralds.

If taken seriously, as intended, the *requerimiento* must be considered the message of European Christianity, at least the Spanish variety, to the people of America. The best that Spaniards could offer the Indians was a peremptory demand to at once accept their king and creed, or the white men would rob, kill and enslave them, " with the aid of God." The bulky encyclopedias, especially those of Spain, avoid mention of the Requirement; yet it is the key to the philosophy and religious belief of the fifteenth and sixteenth centuries among Christian nations.

El Requerimiento was based on the Bull of Donation, a title to these new lands only a few degrees removed from the Creator. In their day, both were firmly believed by bigots and ignorant persons, which included nearly everybody. Since then, the human mind has freed itself of a few of its fetters; and today both the Donation and the Requirement would be laughed out of court.

It is humiliating to what we are pleased to call our enlightened intelligence to recall that only a few centuries ago the people of western Europe took the Donation and Requirement seriously, and that when a Spanish governor received an order from the king, he first kissed the paper and then placed it on his head, declaring that he would obey it with the utmost reverence as a commandment of his king and natural lord.

The Armada Stops at the Canary Islands

In eight or nine days after sailing from San Lúcar de Barrameda, the armada reached the Canary Islands and put in at Gomera, one of the smaller islands of the group. The fleet remained here twenty days, taking on supplies of meat, fish, cheese, wood, and fresh water. No doubt the governor, Lope de Sosa, had ready the fifty swift swimmers and the dragon-wood *tablachinas* ordered by King Ferdinand. Some vessels needed repairs, especially the flagship which had lost her rudder. Peter Martyr tells us that the flagship was piloted by young Vespucci, a nephew of Amerigo Vespucci. Before leaving Spain the officials had agreed that the course to be followed from Gomera should be decided after arriving at the island. The officers and pilots now determined to touch at Dominica instead of sailing direct to Darien.

On Saturday, 3 June 1514, the armada anchored in a port

of the island of Dominica, where was a good river, from which ships took on water. The next day was Easter Sunday and mass was said. The expedition remained here three days, during which Pedrarias hanged an old servant of his, named San Martín, probably to settle some ancient grudge against him. On Monday, 12 June, the armada arrived at the port of Santa Marta, back of which rise the Snowy Mountains, and where began the government of Pedrarias Dávila. This region was inhabited by the proscribed race of *Caníbales,* or Cannibals, " who did eat human flesh," and were fit subjects for death or servitude. About thirty years after this, Girolamo Benzoni traveled along this coast and wrote that these Indians had eaten many Spaniards, and would do the same by the rest if they could. The Caribs were not the only ones to eat human flesh. In rare instances the Spanish retaliated in kind. Some years later, Captain Bascona and party on the way to Coro were reduced to such extremity for food that each day they killed one of their own Indians, male or female, cut the body in pieces and roasted them as if they were deer meat; " *abominacion extraña, y más entre cristianos,*" says the chronicle.

Indian ate Indian; white man ate Indian; white man's dog ate Indian!

Recent studies disclose that Santa Marta was the home of the Tairona Indians, now extinct, an aboriginal people of considerable culture. Rodrigo de Colmenares had been here before and lost about fifty Spaniards, a disaster he avoided mentioning to King Ferdinand in his *Memorial* against Balboa.

Pedrarias was eager to capture some Indians to be sold in Española, and sent several boat loads of soldiers to the shore, where they were confronted by painted natives with beautiful feather plumes on their heads, and armed with bows and arrows. Colmenares and a Cueva Indian of Darien who had been carried to Spain shouted some words to the Caribs, demanding that they obey the holy mother Church, the king, queen, and royal scepter of Spain. Oviedo states that the Indians understood this *requerimiento* no better than a Basque would an Arab, and responded with a flight of arrows. Later the Spaniards landed

in force, Oviedo being in charge of one of the boats. The
governor handed to Oviedo that absurd and ridiculous *requerimiento* to be read to the Indians. Pedrarias entered the land
about three leagues, killed some Indians and took a few prisoners of both sexes. Hernando de Arroyo received a slight
wound in the shin of a leg by a poisoned arrow, from which he
died delirious on the third day.

Oviedo tested the soil of a hill for gold, and Indians rolled
big stones down upon the Christians. Mounting the hill, the
Spaniards stopped in the village to rest and eat their rations.
At night they camped near a river, dining off five or six deer
which the hounds had caught. It was reported that Pedro de
Ledesma, a well-known pilot of the early voyages to America,
was wounded and had a *vómito*. Fearing that he had been
poisoned by the Indian herb, Oviedo went to see him and
found a scratch on the pilot's hip, which appeared to be more
the work of his fingernails than of the herb. Inquiry revealed
that Ledesma had imbibed too freely of some wine brought
from the ships. The next day the Spaniards entered a town
and found divers pieces of fabricated gold in baskets and hidden in the shrubbery, as well as some emeralds and what looked
like a white sapphire.

While resting in an Indian house at Santa Marta with the
governor, Espinosa, the *contador,* the factor, and others, Oviedo
thus addressed Pedrarias:

" Señor: it seems to me that these Indians do not wish to listen to
the theology of this *requerimiento,* nor have you anyone who can
make them understand it. Command, Your worship, to keep it until
we have one of these Indians in a jail, so that he can be instructed by
the lord bishop and slowly learn it."

Oviedo returned the paper to the governor, who took it with
much laughter, in which all the others joined. Dr. Palacios
Rubios is credited with being the principal author of the Requirement. When in Spain, in 1516, Oviedo encountered the
doctor, and asked him if the conscience of Christians remained

satisfied with the *requerimiento;* and the doctor replied yes, if done as the document said. Nevertheless, Palacios Rubios laughed many times when Oviedo told him how the captains in the Indies addressed the *requerimiento* to the natives.

On Corpus Christi day, 15 June, the fleet resumed the voyage, the ships and caravels following the stern light of the flagship. The next stop was at Isla Fuerte, two leagues and a half from Cenú. On the approach of the fleet, the Indians on the island fled in canoes to the mainland. Fuerte was one of the islands on which the Christians could kill and enslave the natives with approval of priest and jurist. The Spaniards found baskets filled with very fine salt, better than that produced in Spain.

On the third day, 18 June, the armada again set sail and steered for Darien, and arrived at the anchorage of that city in the Gulf of Urabá on 29 June 1514. Seagoing vessels could not enter the small river and go up to Antigua del Darien. Ships anchored at the Placel, a word meaning banks of sands or rocks in the sea. Peter Martyr writes that the flagship had been damaged in a tempest off Isla Fuerte, and did not reach Darien until four days later, " but without cargo." Perhaps most of the passengers had been transferred to other ships.

XIV

THE ARMADA OF PEDRARIAS ARRIVES
AT DARIEN

" Allá van leyes
Do quieren Reyes."
— *Don Quijote,* CERVANTES.

THE Splendid Armada of Pedrarias Dávila, as before
stated, came to anchor off the town of Antigua del
Darien on 29 June 1514. The new governor sent an aide
to the town, situated a league or more from the gulf, to announce his arrival to Vasco Núñez. The messenger from the
fleet fresh from Spain, in plumed hat, brocade, and finery, at-
tracted much curious attention from both old settlers and Indians as he went about the town inquiring for their commander.
He seemed much puzzled on seeing no evidence of the riches
he had come so far to obtain, as he was expecting to find Vasco
Núñez seated in a gilded palace, surrounded by a horde of
obsequious slaves. The messenger was astonished to find Balboa in cotton shirt and breeches, with *alpargatas,* or hempen
sandals, on his feet, directing the work of certain Indians who
were thatching the roof of a *buhío,* or house.

" Señor, Pedrarias, who comes as governor of this land, has
just arrived at the port with his fleet," said the officer from the
flota to Vasco Núñez. To which Balboa replied that the emis-
sary should say to Pedrarias " that he was much pleased at his
coming, that he would be welcomed, and that he and all the
people of the town were loyal to the king and ready to receive
and serve the new governor."

Balboa's decision peacefully to welcome Pedrarias produced
some clamour and discussion among the settlers who had gathered around him. The colonists saw an end to the careless

though hazardous life they had been leading in Darien, and resented the large influx of newcomers, including many royal officials and favorites, who would crowd them out of their houses, take their slaves, and reap the reward of their hard labor. The Indians had been subdued by Balboa, and now were peaceful and contributing to the support of the colonists. The large expedition of Pedrarias meant two thousand more people to feed and share in whatever gold and pearls were collected. It is not strange, then, that many of the " old soldiers of Darien," as Martyr calls them, advocated armed resistance to the new arrivals, most of whom wished only to accumulate gold and return rich to Spain.

La Antigua del Darien, the transformed Indian village, was situated on the banks of the Darien river (not the big Rio Darien, or Atrato river) which flowed into the western side of the Gulf of Urabá. The town was a league or a league and a half from the mouth of the river. La Antigua, at this time, from different reports, contained from one hundred to two hundred houses, constructed in the native fashion of strong wooden frames covered with straw roofs. Bishop Quevedo wrote back to the king that the town was well laid out and clean, the old settlers happy and contented. When Pedrarias arrived, the population consisted of from 450 to 515 Europeans, including at least one white woman, Inés de Escobar, the widow of *Procurador* Quicedo, who had died in Spain. There were 1500 Indians, male and female, the greater part classed as *esclavos*. Also a few Negro slaves brought in by the Spaniards.

On 30 June 1514, Pedrarias disembarked all his people and took up the march to Antigua, every man bearing arms and arrayed in his bravest raiment. Naturally suspicious, Pedrarias warned his officers to be prepared to meet with resistance by Balboa. Pedrarias loved pomp and ceremony and knew the effect it would have upon the Indians. Never before, nor since, have the jungles of Darien witnessed such a martial display. Pedrarias marched at the head of his force, holding the hand of Doña Isabel, his wife. On the other side of the governor walked Bishop Quevedo in his episcopal robes. Behind these came the royal officials, and many cavaliers and *hidalgos* in helmet and armor and with Toledo blades, forming a sort of bodyguard. The names of many of these already have been mentioned. Then came a large group of Franciscan friars, chanting the service of the Church, charged to convert the Indians to the holy Christian faith. The great mass of the members of the expedition, including some women and children, formed a long and showy retinue between Antigua and the beach. A very few of these men achieved fame and fortune in the New World; the vast majority found only hardship and early death.

Balboa and the officers of the *Cabildo,* followed by the colonists, went out unarmed to receive the new governor, all singing the *Te Deum laudamus.* The two parties met about half a league from the town. Vasco Núñez saluted Pedrarias and his staff, the two leaders exchanging the usual formal civilities. The contrast between the two groups was marked—the people of Pedrarias dressed in recent European styles of clothing, many in brocades and silks; the men of Balboa in garments made of cotton cloth filched from the Indians. Vasco Núñez was known in Spain for his daring exploits in Darien, and had been the subject of much discussion among members of the armada during the voyage. Knowing the animus of both Enciso and Colmenares toward their former boss, one can be sure that they painted the character of Balboa in the blackest colors. The young bloods of Sevilla and southern Spain were inclined to be supercilious when they saw the famous discoverer of the South Sea in simple garb, surrounded by his sallow band of veterans. The old colonists, inured to the Indies and experienced in Indian warfare, believed that, if they chose, they could overcome the men of the armada, and they looked with pity upon this mass of men, women, and children who must undergo a radical change in climate and mode of life.

Both parties proceeded together to the town, outwardly preserving a friendly appearance. The chronicles do not state how Vasco Núñez received his former associates, Enciso, and Colmenares. It would be interesting to know whether Enciso came ashore surrounded by his guard of ten men, " one of whom was a woman," as previously explained. Balboa conducted the governor and Lady Isabel to his own house on the plaza, which he turned over to them, and where he entertained them in a very genteel manner—" *con muy buena gracia* "—as wrote Bishop Quevedo.

The people of the armada were distributed among the old settlers, who housed and fed them in the best manner that they could. The new arrivals were introduced to corn bread, cassava bread, yams, squashes, native fish, game, and fruit; while the old residents were regaled with bacon, salted meat, wheat flour, oil, and wine brought from Spain.

The sudden descent of two thousand persons with no practical knowledge of life in a wild and primitive country, especially within the tropics, was a great imposition on the little town of Antigua. With twenty years of experience in sending expeditions to the Indies, Ferdinand and his officials should have known better than to hazard the lives of so many individuals by crowding them into one small native village. Never again did Antigua contain so many people nor present so gallant an appearance. Cavaliers and ladies in silks and brocades, soldiers in helmet and cuirass, the old colonists in motley garb of native cloth, merchants from Genova, Portuguese pilots and sailors from about the Mediterranean, a few Spanish children, a few African slaves, and hundreds of Indians moved about the streets of Cémaco's old capital. The advent of the people of the armada raised the population of the town to about four thousand souls, made up as follows:

Colonists under Balboa 515
Indians, *esclavos y naborías* 1500
People of the armada 2000
_____
4015

A few of the late arrivals—such as Hernando de Soto, Diego de Almagro, Francisco Vásquez Coronado, Bernal Díaz del Castillo, and Sebastián de Benalcázar—were destined to win fame or fortune in the New World; but the great majority found hardship, early death, and oblivion. Before nightfall, Cémaco, Careta, and Comogre knew that a great body of white men had joined the force at La Antigua, all well armed and accompanied by fierce dogs, and numbers of that large and terrifying animal known as the horse. The caciques wondered whether these new people loved gold as much as did the first comers.

PEDRARIAS IMMEDIATELY PROSECUTES VASCO NÚÑEZ

Balboa's evil fortune began immediately with the arrival of Pedrarias Dávila. The governor, royal officials, captains and members of his large party landed in Antigua angry and prejudiced against Vasco Núñez. The glory of conquest and discovery was past, for Balboa with his little band of followers had won the land for Spain and found the great Pacific Ocean. Pedrarias presented his commission in the *Cabildo* and took over the government of Castilla del Oro. He appointed new *regidores*, among them Corral, Alonso Pérez, and Lope de Olano, enemies of Vasco Núñez. The governor inquired if the reports of the richness of the land and discovery of a southern sea by Balboa were true. They replied that what he wrote to the king was true.

The very next day, Pedrarias called Balboa aside, and in the presence of the notary Oviedo, quizzed him concerning the land, the natives, and what he had done as acting governor. The clever old courtier, fresh from the tricks of the court, in honeyed words told Vasco Núñez how highly the king regarded him, and had commanded that he be treated well and favored, and that Pedrarias should consult him and take his opinion. The governor ordered Balboa to inform him of the condition of the country and disposition of the natives. Vasco Núñez replied that he kissed the royal feet of the king, and would furnish the information in writing. Two days later, 2 July 1514, Balboa gave Pedrarias a long report embracing all the things which he had done and planned to do, the rivers and ravines where the Christians had found gold, a narrative of his discovery of the South Sea, and the Indians that he had conquered and brought to terms of peace during the three years of his administration in Darien and Panama. The historian Oviedo read this report and writes that it contained many things well said and useful, and all that Balboa wrote was true—" *e en todo dixo verdad.*" Of the numerous Indians mentioned by Vasco Núñez, Oviedo has preserved for us the names of twenty caciques with whom Balboa had made treaties of peace. This report, called by Pedrarias " *parecer* " (opinion, advice), was of much benefit to the governor and his captains. In his letter of 1 August 1514 to the king, Pedrarias proudly told Ferdinand how he secured the valuable information from his predecessor. Ferdinand wrote back to Pedrarias that he approved of getting the *parecer*, or advice, of Vasco Núñez as he would know what best to do for the land, because he knew so much about it, " and I would like much that you send me a copy." This famous *parecer*, like many other important papers concerning Balboa, has not been found in the archives of Spain.

Having elicited from Balboa all the information he wanted, Pedrarias laid aside his unctuous mask of urbanity and friendliness, and revealed himself in his true colors, full of jealousy and hatred for Vasco Núñez. The governor proclaimed immediately—" *incontinenti* "—the *residencia* of Balboa and his officials; and Espinosa, *alcalde mayor*, was ordered to proceed with the case with all rigor of law. The *residencia* was a routine requirement on change of officials, but Pedrarias prosecuted Balboa in a needlessly harsh and offensive manner, especially in view of his great service to the State. Balboa was placed under arrest and his property seized pending the outcome of the charges against him.

The charges against Vasco Núñez were both criminal and civil—criminal for driving Nicuesa from Darien, by reason of which he perished, so it was claimed; and civil claims for damages, mainly by Enciso. It is natural to think that the young and inexperienced graduate in law sought advice in this important case of the clever old advocate Enciso, who was not only high constable, but also a claimant against Balboa. Knowing what we do of the character of Enciso, it is reasonable to believe that he advised Espinosa to continue the criminal charge against Balboa on the ground that all the people were implicated in the expulsion of Diego de Nicuesa. As for his own suit against Vasco Núñez for confiscation of his goods, Espinsoa should award him heavy damages, of course. And so decreed the young judge.

In the meantime, the suspicious governor, not satisfied with the regular conduct of the case by Espinosa, was prosecuting a secret inquiry of his own, taking testimony from the avowed enemies of Vasco Núñez. This came to the ears of Espinosa, who, jealous of his position as *alcalde mayor* of Castilla del Oro, registered an objection with Pedrarias on the ground that he was the royal official commissioned to conduct such hearings. Again, it is allowable to believe that he was advised by Enciso, who feared that further investigation might involve him in guilt as *alcalde mayor* of Alonso de Ojeda, who had opposed calling Nicuesa to Antigua. Balboa was fined several thousand *castellanos* for injury done Enciso and others. The criminal accusation for causing the death of Diego de Nicuesa was intentionally and maliciously continued and left unsettled. For years it was pendent, like a sword of Damocles, over the head of Vasco Núñez; a weapon in the hands of his enemy Pedrarias, liable to be reopened at any time; and ultimately included in the cumulative charges against Balboa in his final trial.

The trial of Spanish officials in the Indies seems to have been a very simple procedure. The accused was arrested and held to be guilty until, with much expense, labor, and frequently bribes, he was freed, if innocent. When found guilty, all his property was confiscated, and, if not executed on the spot, he was sent in chains to Spain to be sentenced by the Council of the Indies. Pedrarias was about to commit the same blunder made by Balboa when he sent Enciso, his rival and enemy, back to Spain. The governor, supported by Puente, Márquez, and Tavira, was eager to get rid of Balboa by ordering him to Spain to be punished by the king. Nothing could have been better for Vasco Núñez than to be sent home in disgrace. By the time he had traveled from Sevilla to the court at Valladolid he would have been acclaimed a popular hero, and Ferdinand would have felt compelled to grant Vasco Núñez an independent government instead of the empty honor of an *adelantamiento* under Governor Pedrarias. Balboa would have come back to Tierra Firme crowned with honors as independent governor of Panama and Coiba. He would have established his seat of government on the Pacific coast, most certainly not on the unhealthy site where Pedrarias settled Panama Vieja. His old soldiers and friends would have abandoned Pedrarias and rallied about him, and the discovery of Peru would have occurred within a few years, as a matter of course.

" *E como el obispo era sagaz,*" says the chronicle—and as the bishop was quick of apprehension and just as crafty as, and more intelligent than, Pedrarias, he saw at once that it was to his own interest to retain Balboa in Darien and play him against the governor. Quevedo despised Pedrarias and most of the other officials who came in the armada. He really liked and admired Balboa and did him many a good turn; but no greater wrong or injury ever was done Vasco Núñez than detaining him in Darien and preventing him from having a hearing at court. Bishop Quevedo did this knowingly and intentionally, urging the governor to keep Vasco Núñez under his command; for if sent to Spain, he would come back to Tierra Firme loaded with honors and governor of the best part of Castilla del Oro. Oviedo states that the bishop advised Pedrarias to dissemble and hold Balboa in continuous need with promises and lawsuits. "And the same said Espinosa." Here was a conspiracy by the three most powerful royal officials, a few days after arriving at Antigua, not only to detain Vasco Núñez in Darien, but to harass him with charges and trials, and keep him in a constant state of subjection to the government of Pedrarias. Balboa was simply a pawn in the game and never had a show among these crafty new officials, who came to the New World not to spread the Christian faith, but to enrich themselves quickly at the expense of the Indians. The historian declares that the bishop planned to become rich with the labors of Vasco Núñez de Balboa.

Balboa having been freed, for the time at least, of complicity in the death of Nicuesa, his goods were restored to him; but Pedrarias did not hesitate to take advantage of the situation to secure for himself a house belonging to Vasco Núñez. The best house in Antigua was that of Lope de Olano. Balboa had erected two houses on his *solar* facing the plaza, living in one and renting the other for three hundred pesos a year. The governor took the latter house while Balboa was making his *residencia,* giving him less money than the rental of it.

When the armada arrived at Darien, the discovery of the South Sea was still the chief subject of conversation among the old settlers. The 190 men who had participated in the great event considered themselves a favored body, and were not likely to belittle their deeds and victories. They could not tell of their labors, battles and rewards without praising the skill, ability, and good judgment of Vasco Núñez as commander of the expedition, all of which was as gall and wormwood to the new governor. The tales of gold and pearls, now much exaggerated by frequent repetition, were greedily absorbed by the newcomers. They were eager to secure gold for themselves, for that was their purpose for coming to the Indies. They asked which rivers ran with gold and where the best fishing places were. The only reply to these questions by the Darien veterans was a burst of laughter. It is a fact that many Spaniards actually believed the tales of fishing for gold spread throughout Spain before the sailing of the armada, and gave up good positions at home to go to Darien to engage in the sport of fishing for the precious metal. This delusion was not confined to the ignorant and lowly. Nobles, lawyers, and priests abandoned their familes and interests at home, secure in the belief that after a few days of fishing in Darien waters they would return independently rich to Spain. The bishop of Chiapa tells of a priest, no longer young and who appeared to be a prudent man, who gave up a benefice in Spain paying him

100,000 *maravedís* yearly, who went in the armada to fish for gold—" *a pescar el oro.*" This *clérigo* never had an opportunity to try the fishing in Darien, for during the period of hunger and *modorra* he fled from La Antigua with other persons and went to Cuba, where Las Casas talked with him. Excepting an occasional nugget picked up in the streams, fishing for gold meant placing weirs or traps in the gullies to catch the sand and silt as the soil was washed down during freshets. The sand had to be worked over and the gold laboriously collected.

XV

FAMINE AND DISEASE IN LA ANTIGUA

" El hombre pone y Dios dispone."
—Don Quijote, CERVANTES.

THE people brought by Pedrarias were much cast down in their minds on learning that some labor was required to obtain gold. Even robbing the Indians was done at some risk and Balboa's old soldiers already had harvested the golden trinkets roundabout Antigua. Soon they had to face a more serious condition. The rainy season now was well under way and a rank growth of grass, weeds, and other vegetation sprang up in the town. The streets were full of puddles of mud, the surrounding country became a marsh, and strange insects, toads, and other venomous animals seemed to come out of the ground. The people could not move about the town, and the roads to the shore of the port and to the *estero* were almost impassable. This was a serious matter, because the flour, wine, and other provisions brought on the fleet had been stored in a large building constructed for that purpose on the beach, called the *toldo*. Small quantities of supplies as needed were carried to the town and put in the House of Trade, in charge of the king's factor, or agent, Juan de Tavira.

The disappointed members of the armada, novices in the tropics, could not adjust themselves to their new environment. Nature was fast closing in on them. On 11 September 1514, the governor and his officers, including the bishop, conferred together on what to do to remedy the situation. Of the 230 laborers on salary, the governor thought he might find ten men willing to work. No one was found who cared to work by the day, " nor any other way "—" *nin en otra manera* "—says the record. Spaniards did not go to Golden Castile to work; they went to secure gold!

Pedrarias had been commanded to issue food to his people for thirty days after debarkation at Antigua. Perhaps there had been some stealing by the contractors who supplied the ships, as happened in outfitting the second fleet of Columbus, and which still occurs under similar conditions, in spite of numerous inspectors, clerks, and other officials. The Adelantado Pascual de Andagoya, a member of the expedition, writes that the provisions were distributed, probably the thirty days' rations; and the flour and other food were spoilt by the sea. It was necessary to reduce the allowance of food, and a great number died from starvation. The wine ran low, so that the bishop reserved a small cask for saying mass. The rains soon transformed the swaggering cavaliers into bedraggled figures wandering about the miry lanes of La Antigua begging for food. Some straggled away into the woods, eating strange roots and grasses, like animals. Young noblemen in brocades and scarlet silk coats, who had pledged their estates in order to come to Darien, dropped dead from hunger while crying for bread in Cémaco's old capital.

The starved and miserable colonists, fresh from Europe, fell easy victims to disease. The records say scarcely anything about the women and children, who must have been the first to succumb. Twenty to thirty persons died daily, the corpses lying about the town unburied. On one occasion the survivors dug a great hole in which they cast the dead, and then deferred closing the hole, knowing for certain that within a few hours there would be more bodies to bury. The new arrivals realized that the country had been misrepresented to them, and desired to go back to Spain. On some ships of the fleet still lying in port, many of the principal and more energetic colonists hastened to flee from the deadly spot. One party set sail for Castile, another to Española, and a boatload went to Cuba, where they found abundance of provisions.

Nearly all the first European settlers on the Atlantic shores of the Western Hemisphere suffered from famine and sickness.

We know that many Spaniards died at Isabela on Española, and at Belén, Nombre de Dios, and Antigua del Darien along the Isthmus of Panama. The numerous deaths at Jamestown in Virginia and at Plymouth in Massachusetts gave rise to a saying in England that going to America was equivalent to going to the next world. As late as 1698–1700, the Scots at New Edinburgh on Caledonia Bay, only a few miles from La Antigua, perished by hundreds from disease and lack of food. In all these instances the calamities suffered by the colonists were largely due to the ignorance and incompetence of the officials.

During this period of hunger and sickness in Antigua, there died in a short time, according to Oviedo who was present, more than five hundred men. Andagoya writes, and he, too, was in the town, that in one month seven hundred men died of hunger and of the disease of *modorra*—"*en un mes murieron 700 hombres de hambre y de enfermedad de modorra.*" This *modorra* caused drowsiness, listlessness, and sudden dissolution. Writers of the period do not mention fevers and dysenteries, commonly attacking newcomers. Oviedo declares that most of the deaths were due to want of food—"*por falta de bastimentos, puesto quel Rey los tenia sobrados.*" According to the same authority, there was plenty of flour in the king's stores. Apparently this was not issued, because the officials wished to keep the supplies for themselves. Las Casas states also that the people died "more from hunger than of diseases," although the royal armada had brought 482 *botas,* or barrels, of flour. The factor, Tavira, sent forty *botas* to the port of Santa Cruz, when Juan de Ayora and his captains set out to ravage the provinces of Comogre, Pocorosa, and Tubanamá. The officials agreed to sell the remainder for sixteen pesos for each *bota;* and one barrel might be sold on trust to four or five men conjointly to be more certain of payment. As hundreds of men either died or hurriedly departed, there was much confusion in the accounts and opportunity for fraud. Treasurer Puente complains that the factor was in no hurry to turn over funds, as the king had commanded.

Nothing like a fire or a battle to cover up a shortage in supplies! The historian Oviedo, writing in his characteristic style, declares that God, seeing that the poor colonists were not furnished with the provisions and the little service which He and the king received, permitted the *toldo*, or storehouse by the shore, to be destroyed by fire, consuming the supplies of food which might have saved many lives. This authority goes on to state that he could not desist from the suspicion, held by many, that the *mayordomo* of the factor was the firebrand which started the fire, the flames of which destroyed ten pipes of wine and flour to conceal the theft of one hundred *pipas*.

As soon as the armada arrived at Antigua, two caravels were sent to the island of Jamaica for provisions, returning to Darien in November, 1514, with hogs, bacon, *cazabe* and *maiz*. A third caravel despatched to Jamaica brought back similar supplies, which were sold to the people in Antigua, the seventy live hogs, " on foot," selling for four *pesos de oro* and four *tomines* each. It really looks as if there was food for all, if the new officials had been honest and efficient. As late as 2 May 1515, the governor and staff wrote to the king that some flour still remained from the armada. This was long after the termination of the fatalities, which I reckon ended in February, 1515. Pedrarias and officials wrote a letter to Ferdinand on 1 August 1514, announcing their safe arrival at Darien, and they say nothing of *la modorra*. On 18 October 1514, they again wrote to the king, this time reporting the many deaths. In reply to this, Ferdinand stated that he was much displeased to hear of the deaths, but was not surprised at the news, for all new settlements had a hard time in the beginning, and the mortality in Antigua appeared to be due to a pestilence— " *cosa de pestilencia.*"

" Nobody showed any charity to anyone," says Andagoya. One of the first to fall sick was the governor himself, eight days after landing in Darien, wrote the bishop to the king. Pedrarias delegated his powers to the bishop, and, on advice of the *médicos*, he went to the Rio Corabari a few leagues from town, where the air was better. This is confirmed by the minutes of a meeting of the royal officials in the Casa de la Contratacion on 14 July 1514, at which Bishop Quevedo presided by reason of the sickness of the governor. No doubt many Indian slaves took advantage of the disorder to run away. If the future existence of Antigua had depended on the sick and demoralized people of the armada, it is probable that Cacique Cémaco would have come down the river in force and recovered his village.

The historians state that Vasco Núñez now was consulted and given a voice in the government. All the first settlers in Darien must have been immune to the *modorra;* at least none of his old enemies died, more's the pity. It looks as if Balboa again saved the Spaniards in Darien. It is more than probable that the preservation and future existence of *Santa María de la Antigua del Darien* depended on the presence of Vasco Núñez supported by his faithful followers.

In the space of seven months more than half the number of persons who came in the armada had either died or hurried away from La Antigua. At the height of the famine and sickness, the royal officials, including the governor and all the newcomers, were anxious to quit and go home. They wrote to the king that the town was sickly and Darien was the worst land in the world. In a letter to Balboa, Ferdinand told him that the Spaniards remaining in Castilla del Oro, as well as those who had returned to Spain, were very dissatisfied. The officials are charged with asking license to depart. Governor Pedrarias tried to abandon the land, but the *Cabildo* of Antigua told him plainly that he could not leave without first obtaining an order from the king and making his *residencia*. This caused Pedrarias to hate the place, so that he did not rest until Antigua was depopulated. Apparently, the governor wrote to the king about forsaking Darien. There is preserved a license for Doña Isabel, wife of Pedrarias, to return to her home, of which she availed herself in time.

Years later, when Pedrarias made his *residencia,* one of the questions addressed to his witnesses by the governor reads as follows:

" 56. Item, *et cetera*, if they know that because the officials and the greater part of the people who came in the royal armada were very ill of the gravest diseases, and a great part of them died; and the said officials and the bishop and many other persons presently determined to return to Spain; and that the said Pedrarias importuned and labored with them, animating them and telling them that then men lived when they died in the service of God and of their king; and on account of this the said bishop and officials and other honorable persons changed their intention and remained in the settlement."

Pedrarias now was over in Panama on the Pacific coast, and Quevedo and most of the other persons who had come in the armada had gone away or died, and none present dared to contend with the old governor. History, however, has not rated Pedrarias Dávila a truthful and honest man.

XVI

BALBOA'S DAY IN THE COURT OF SPAIN

" Del dicho al hecho
Va mucho trecho."

WHILE Pedrarias and Espinosa were prosecuting the *residencia* and private intrigues against Balboa in Darien, Vasco Núñez also was receiving much attention in the court of Spain. King Ferdinand could not avoid recognizing the great services of Balboa. It really seemed as if the king wished properly to reward him; but who ever heard of Ferdinand V of Castile rewarding his worthy captains in the Indies in a big-hearted and generous manner? Always there was that baneful bishop of Burgos, powerful friend of Pedrarias, close to the king. Ferdinand, cautious and suspicious by nature, was ready to limit and restrict any powers and authority granted to Vasco Núñez.

Balboa never succeeded in appearing in person before the king, but there was one day—23 September 1514—when all the scribes about the court of Spain were kept busy writing commissions and letters highly praising Vasco Núñez for his work in Panama and Darien and his discovery of the South Sea.

ROYAL DECREE NAMING VASCO NÚÑEZ DE BALBOA ADELANTADO OF THE COAST OF THE SOUTH SEA AND OF THE GOVERNMENT OF THE PROVINCES OF PANAMA AND COIBA

El Rey.—Basco Núñez de Balboa, acknowledging what you have done and your desire to serve, and because with better will you may be diligent henceforth in it, we have made reward to you that you be our *adelantado* of the South Sea which you discovered and of the

277

government of the provinces of Panama and Coiba, as you will see by the titles for it that I ordered to be despatched; but, for the reason that it is my will that in those parts there be only one person and one head and no more, in order that all follow and do what he might command and order, as if I in person would command it; I directed to put in the said warrant of the government that you be under Pedrarias Dávila, lieutenant-general of that land of Castilla del Oro. For that, I command you that in all the things that you have to do and provide in the said government, as well as in the other things that might occur to you, impart them and do them with the opinion of the said Pedrarias; and as I have written to you, inform him of everything that you might know in those parts, and deal with him as you would do with my own person, for in this way you execute our service; and because I am sending to command Alonso de la Puente our treasurer of Castilla del Oro to speak with you on my part on the aforesaid, you will give him entire faith and credence.

From Valladolid, 23 September 1514

I the King

By command of His Highness—Lope de Conchillos

Still another and more lengthy commission, issued this same date, conferred upon Balboa the title of *Adelantado* of the Coast of the South Sea, with no mention of the government and administration of the provinces of Panama and Coiba. Ferdinand failed to use the name " New Land," which, on 19 August 1514, he had ordered to be applied to this region.

BALBOA MADE ADELANTADO OF THE COAST OF THE SOUTH SEA

Don Fernando, etc.—To do right and reward you, Vasco Núñez de Balboa, acknowledging the many good and loyal services which you have done to me and to the said Queen and Princess, my daughter, especially in discovering the Sea of the South, which is in Castilla del Oro, in the Indies and Firm Land of the Ocean Sea; and in all that has appertained to our service in the said Indies in the time that you have resided in it; and likewise in assuring and pacifying the Indians of those Territories, from which has ensued much benefit to us; and confiding in your sufficiency and ability; it is my will and

Statue of Balboa in Panama City facing the Pacific Ocean, unveiled
29 September 1924.

pleasure, for that which concerns me, that now and henceforth, for
the whole of your life, you be my *Adelantado* of the Coast of the
said South Sea that you have discovered, which is in the said Castilla
del Oro; and have power to use and make use of the said office in
everything relating and annexed to it, just as the rest of the
adelantados use it in these kingdoms of Castile and in the said Indies;
and with regard to the use and exercise of the said office and bearing
the rights of it, keep the laws of these our said kingdoms, and be
empowered to enjoy all the honors, favors, exemptions and liberties,
pre-eminences, prerogatives and immunities of which by reason of the
said office you can and ought to enjoy and should be reserved for
you; and observe and carry all the rights and other things annexed
and pertaining to the said office of *adelantamiento* conformable to
the said laws as enjoyed by our other *adelantados* of the said Indies;
and by this my royal ordinance I command the councils, justices,
prefects, knights, squires, officials and worthy men of all the cities
and towns and places of the said *Adelantamiento* of the Coast of the
Sea of the South, that, made by you the said Vasco Núñez de Balboa
the oath and legal formality required and accustomed to do in such a
case, they have and receive and hold you for my *Adelantado* of the
said Coast of the South Sea which you discovered, and treat with
you in the said office and in all the cases and things annexed to and
concerning it; and guard you and observe all the honors, grace, gifts,
exemptions and licenses and privileges of which by reason of the
said office you should enjoy and ought to be preserved for you; and
support and assist you with the fees and salaries which have aided
and succored our other *adelantados* of these said kingdoms and of the
said Indies, and no more nor beyond; because I, for the present,
receive and have received you for the said office, and give you power
and authority to use and exercise it in the form aforesaid; and I
command the most Illustrious Prince, my most dear and beloved
grandson and son, and the princes, prelates, dukes, marquises, counts,
noblemen, masters of the Orders, priors, commanders and sub-
commanders, wardens of the castles and fortified houses, with and
without moats; and those of our Council, presidents and associate
judges of our audiences, justices of the peace, constables, inspectors
for sheep-walks, magistrates, knights, squires, officials and honest men
of all the cities, towns and places of the said office of *Adelantamiento*
of the Coast of the said Sea of the South, they guard and execute it
for you and keep and comply absolutely, just as is contained in it;

and contrary to the tenor and form of it, do not go nor pass, nor consent to go nor pass at any time or by any manner; and I order that the language of this my decree be copied in the books of the House of the Trade of the Indies, located in the city of Sevilla, by our officials of it.

Granted in the town of Valladolid 23 September 514 [1514]—I the King

Countersigned and signed by the said [officials].

The queen and princess mentioned in this document refer to Ferdinand's unfortunate daughter Juana, who became queen of Castile in succession to her mother, Isabella the Catholic. Historians sometimes bluntly, though truthfully, allude to Juana as " Crazy Jane." Though *non compos mentis*, Juana's name appears in public documents associated with that of her father, who had been authorized to act as regent of her kingdom. Doña Juana (1479–1555) was the sister of Catherine of Aragon and of Queen Isabella of Portugal, and mother of Emperor Charles V.

Ferdinand and his ministers were careful to declare that the Coast of the South Sea, and the sea itself, were in Castilla del Oro, already assigned to Pedrarias Dávila. It is probable that Noya and Cobos, representing Balboa in Spain, supported by the latest opinion of Miguel de Pasamonte, endeavored to secure an independent government for their client. While the coast along the South Sea was the logical territory to award to Vasco Núñez, there was no good reason for making Balboa subject to Pedrarias. Indeed, all experience proved that it simply provoked enmity and strife to appoint an official to supersede another, while retaining the latter man in office. Neither was there any need to name Balboa to a region contiguous to Pedrarias, especially as the limits of both grants were so illdefined. There were hundreds of leagues of Caribbean coast now known, far from Castilla del Oro, inviting conquest and settlement. Vasco Núñez de Balboa had shown a peculiar facility in making Indians his friends, even after severely defeating them in battle. He had fully demonstrated his fitness and ability to command and govern a colony, and was more deserv-

ing of an independent command on Tierra Firme than any other
subject of the king.

A long *cédula* was issued in the name of Doña Juana, addressed to the various officials, cities, and towns in the provinces
of Panama and Coyba, in the New Land of the waters flowing
from the crest of the mountains to the South Sea. It was in the
nature of a proclamation, announcing to the people of Panama
and Coiba that the *Adelantado* Vasco Núñez de Balboa now
possessed the government and jurisdiction, civil and criminal,
of the said Coast of the South. The population was ordered to
receive Balboa as governor and justice of the said provinces
which he had discovered—meanwhile the said Vasco Núñez de
Balboa was under the government of Pedrarias Dávila. When
the foregoing was written, the only Spaniards in the South
Coast of the Isthmus of Panama were robbing, killing, and
enslaving the natives, under command of Juan de Ayora, lieutenant of Pedrarias.

Lope de Conchillos, secretary to the queen, wrote this document by command of her father, King Ferdinand, who signed
the paper.

The king sent notice to his officials at Antigua del Darien
informing them of the titles and honors he had bestowed on
Vasco Núñez. Ferdinand valued his services so highly that he
cited them as an example for others, who, seeing the honors accorded to Balboa, would be moved to labor and serve the king
as he had done. The officers were charged to advance and favor
Balboa, as a matter that appertained to the king's service.

As stated in one of his commissions, Ferdinand, on 23 September 1514, wrote to Alonso de la Puente notifying him of the
honors accorded to Balboa on account of his ability and great
skill (" *su abilidad y buena maña* ") in the affairs of those
parts. Puente was ordered to deliver to Balboa the commissions of the said offices when they arrived at Antigua, and tell
him on the part of the king of his desire to favor him, so that
he would be satisfied and contented, and in the future put in the
king's service the same diligence and care, " and better, if better
it could be " (" *y mejor, si mejor pudiese* "), which he had

exhibited to that time. Puente must favor Vasco Núñez and use him well, so that he would serve and follow Governor Pedrarias as he would the king himself. And then, as if foreseeing trouble, Ferdinand adds: " Always keep me informed of the affairs of the said Basco Núñez, especially of this item, for I would be very ill served by the contrary, and much harm might spring up again there from it."

Still another document of this same date was a *cédula* to Pedrarias, informing him that the king had made Vasco Núñez *Adelantado* of the Coast of the South Sea, that he discovered, and of the government of the provinces of Panama and Coiba; but all persons residing therein were subject to the obedience and administration of the said Pedrarias. Ferdinand wrote that he would be much pleased to see Pedrarias give good treatment to Vasco Núñez, and writes as follows:

" I command and charge you to favor and deal well with Balboa, and look upon him as a person who has served us faithfully; and since he possesses such useful ability and disposition to labor and engage in the work there, as you have seen, you must give him entire liberty in the affairs of his government."

But, it was the king's will to have only one head in Castilla del Oro, and Balboa remained in subjection to Governor Pedrarias —*" debajo de Pedrarias Dávila."*

The forementioned documents are typical of many issued from the hand of Ferdinand of Aragon. Every time he bestowed a favor he withdrew it in the next sentence.

I know of no other instance where Ferdinand lavished such profuse praise upon a *conquistador* in the Indies as he did upon Vasco Núñez de Balboa. If words mean anything, any reasonable and just tribunal would hold that the language of the foregoing decrees and *cédulas* wiped out all charges preferred against Balboa by Enciso, Colmenares, and Corral. Francisco Lopez de Gómara wrote that the king " revoked the sentence against Balboa " and made him *adelantado* and governor. While seeming to confer great honor and titles on Vasco Núñez, the whole proceeding was a pretense and hollow mockery. One cannot avoid thinking that Juan de Fonseca, bishop of Burgos, and president of the Council of the Indies, induced Ferdinand to put Balboa under the control of his friend Pedrarias.

The king had ordered Treasurer Puente to give and turn over to Vasco Núñez his commissions as *adelantado* and governor when they arrived at Antigua del Darien. They reached there in the following March, and we shall see how the command of the king was observed.

PEDRARIAS WITHHOLDS THE COMMISSIONS FOR BALBOA

On 20 March 1515,two vessels—*dos carabelas emplomadas*—arrived in the port of Antigua, loaded with flour, wine, oil, vinegar, and other provisions sent from Spain by Their Highnesses. This food was sold to the colonists at prices fixed by the factor, Juan de Tavira. By these caravels came the commissions—*provisiones*—for Vasco Núñez; but they were not delivered to him by Puente as the king had commanded.

Royal treasurers in the Indies, as a rule, were very important officials, often possessing the confidence of the monarch more than did the governors. Sometimes they were appointed to be a check and spy upon the governor, as in the case of Miguel de Pasamonte. While Pedrarias had been ordered by Ferdinand to take no important action without the concurrence of the other officials, he soon dominated them, except when the bishop chose to assert himself. Secure of the support of his great friend Fonseca, Pedrarias seems to have ignored the order to Treasurer Puente to turn over the papers to Balboa.

The sick and irascible old governor had met with nothing but disappointment since his arrival at Darien. He felt cheated of a brilliant military conquest of Tierra Firme and discovery of the South Sea; he had experienced a long rainy season, marked by famine, disease, and deaths, and had been irritated by several letters from the king commanding him to take the advice and counsel of Balboa and to favor and honor him.

We are told that every letter received and sent from Antigua passed under the inquisitorial scrutiny of Pedrarias, an act specifically prohibited in his instructions. This may account for the disappearance of important papers relating to Vasco Núñez, and to the discredit of Pedrarias Dávila. The retention of the commissions for Balboa was not so secret that it did not come to his knowledge and to the ears of Bishop Quevedo. Balboa did not remain supine, and complained of the matter, and the bishop preached from the pulpit against the tyranny under which they lived, which was contrary to the will of the king.

After withholding the commissions for one month, Pedrarias felt compelled to call the royal officers together to consider the subject, and decide whether the papers should be given to Balboa. Oviedo, as *escribano*, noted the proceedings and wrote down the vote of each official. Puente and Márquez voted no, until the king had notice of the *residencia* of Balboa, begun ten months before and still unsettled, though the usual duration was for sixty days only. The factor Tavira said he was no *letrado*, and did not know what was best to do. Espinosa the judge, who had conspired with Pedrarias to hold the *residencia* open, said it was right that the king should first know the merits of the charges of the *residencia*. Although Bishop Quevedo originally had advised keeping the *residencia* alive and retaining Balboa in Darien, he now behaved very valiantly. The bishop declared that the royal warrants discharged the conscience of the king by rewarding Vasco Núñez for his services, and that it was disobedience and disloyalty to discuss and attempt to oppose what the king had ordered. This conference had lasted nearly to midnight, but the bishop's speech so frightened the others that they hastily voted to deliver to Balboa his commissions, and the *junta* disbanded. Navarrete states that Quevedo wanted Vasco Núñez for governor of the entire country.

The following day, which was 21 or 23 April 1515, the documents were delivered to Vasco Núñez, and thereafter he was called *adelantado*, but never governor, as he had been addressed before the coming of Pedrarias. Balboa's *adelantamiento*, and the government and jurisdiction, civil and criminal, of the Coast of the South Sea, clearly entitled him to the title of governor. The offices of *adelantado* and governor might be combined in the same commission, as in the case of Francisco de Montejo, conqueror of Yucatán. A royal *cédula* declared the provinces of Panama and Coiba, assigned to Balboa, to be in the New Land, the waters of which flowed into the South Sea from the top of the mountains situated in the northern part on the coast of Veragua. The original words indicate how obscure was the knowledge of the geography of this territory at the court of Ferdinand.

There was no attempt made to name the eastern and western boundaries of these provinces. To show how the east-west trend of the Veragua-Panama-Darien Isthmus confuses writers, even the modern historian Angel de Altolaguirre says that the commissions to Balboa fixed no limits to the north or to the south of the zone of land between the mountains and the sea; whereas, the mountains on the north and South Sea in the South were the only boundaries mentioned. In other words, the grant of territory to Vasco Núñez comprised all the watershed south of the crest of the cordillera of the isthmus, with no mention of any limitation to the east or west. A few years later, in 1518, this same region was treacherously given by Pedrarias to Diego de Albítez by a certain *asiento*, or treaty, with power to found two towns, one in the north in the district of the Gulf of San Blas and Nombre de Dios, the other in the south at the seat of Cacique Chepó, with authority to discover on the land and on the South Sea. This was confirmed by Doña Juana and Don Carlos, her son (Carlos I). At this time, Balboa was toiling to complete his ships on the South Sea, and this action of Pedrarias, one of many such, leads the writer to believe that the old governor never intended that Vasco Núñez should secure any honor or profit from his labors. I believe Oviedo was correct in declaring that from the receipt of the decrees conferring titles and territory to Vasco Núñez, Pedrarias meditated the death of Balboa—" *se le trató la muerte.*"

SPANISH CAPTAINS SECURE SLAVES AND GOLD, AND SOME FAMOUS PEARLS AT THE PEARL ISLANDS

After the few years of growth and prosperity under Balboa, Darien, town and territory, began a new era when the country fell into the hands of Pedrarias Dávila. It would require a very large book to record all the robberies, vicious atrocities, wanton killings, and enslavement of thousands of Indian men, women, and children by the captains of Pedrarias. These are matters of official reports, still preserved in the archives of Spain. We are astounded to read that the greatest killing and round-up of natives (call it spreading the Christian faith, if you choose) was made by the chief judge, Gaspar de Espinosa, who took the field in person. The *alcalde mayor* ravished and roamed over the isthmus for more than a year, during which period he is credited with inventing a new terror for the Indians —tying a cacique to a tree and blowing him to smithereens with missiles fired from a piece of field artillery.

Pedrarias undid the hard pioneer work of Vasco Núñez in subduing and pacifying the natives. The governor complied with the letter of his orders from the king when he licensed the captains to raid the Indians; but he and the other royal officials received a share of the gold and slaves, and the captains went unpunished for their crimes. Often that joke of a *requerimiento* was not even whispered in Latin or Spanish to the trees when the Christians prepared to assault an Indian village by night. Sometimes the requirement was read to the Indians after they were chained (" *en cadena* ") without an interpreter, neither the reader nor the captives understanding the words. No consideration was shown the many caciques with whom Balboa had negotiated terms of peace and tribute. Bishop Quevedo, in a long letter to the king, gives the names of twenty chiefs who were at peace with Vasco Núñez when Pedrarias took over the government.

Some of the captains with Pedrarias were decent and honorable men; others were not fit to go for a pitcher of water, as the bishop mildly describes them. In the course of years, many captains were killed by Indians during the conquest of Panama, Nicaragua, and Peru, or during bitter warfare among themselves for leadership and territory. Some of these rude, cruel men, who survived the fighting and terrible hardships they experienced, were made *hidalgos* for their services to Spain. A few became frightened as they neared death, confessed remorse for their crimes, and begged the Emperor Charles to legitimize their sons by Indian women.

When Pedrarias arrived at Antigua in the last week of June, 1514, he immediately started in to discredit and belittle the work of Balboa in Darien and his discovery of the South Sea. The governor lost no time, as we have seen, in instituting investigation, and making charges against Vasco Núñez. This was in accord with law, and pursuant to the order of Ferdinand, dated 28 July 1513, to make inquiry and examination ("*pesquisa e inquisición*") of Balboa and his consorts, and to send the said Vasco Núñez a prisoner to the court. Pedrarias prosecuted the *residencia* of Balboa with excessive severity, especially in view of the changed conditions he found at La Antigua. He did not hesitate to disobey the latter part of the king's command, when, on advice of the bishop and chief judge, he realized that it was to his interest to keep Vasco Núñez under his power in Darien. To have gone back to Spain in chains, like Christopher Columbus, would have been the best fortune that could have happened at this time to Balboa.

Balboa advised Pedrarias to establish a line of posts between the North and South Seas, at places which he designated. Pedrarias was eager to minimize the services of Vasco Núñez to King Ferdinand by showing that, although Balboa viewed the South Sea, it was Pedrarias who settled and developed the new land. More than that, the governor wanted to get his hands on the gold and pearls he had heard so much about from the old settlers. Pedrarias first made Balboa and some others swear that their reports of the riches of the "New Land" were true. The governor then selected four hundred of the most healthy men of those who came in the armada, and a few of the old colonists, to make the settlements. Juan de Ayora, lieutenant to the governor, was named to lead the expedition. Although his *residencia* was still pending, as it continued to be, Balboa was the logical commander to choose for this delicate attempt to build strongholds on the lands of a strange and independent people. Though hospitable and kind to foreigners, the caciques surely would resent any permanent occupation of their territory. In Santa Maria de la Antigua del Darien, 13 July 1514, Andrés de Valderrábano and Juan de Valenzuela, who had been officials under Balboa during his government, turned over to the new treasurer, Alonso de la Puente, gold to the amount of 854 pesos, being the king's fifth of the coveted metal secured in certain *cabalgadas*.

The next day, " the very magnificent and reverend lord, don fray Juan de Quevedo, bishop of the city," met with Puente, Márquez, and Tavira in the smelting house, and decided that the 854 pesos received from the Balboa administration could not be used to succor the people who came in the armada; but part of the gold would have to be expended for careening and repairing certain vessels to carry Juan de Ayora and his party to the port of Pocorosa. From there, they would enter the land and settle the provinces of Comogre, Tubanamá, and Pocorosa, and the coast of the other Sea of the South.

In a small ship and three or four caravels, Ayora sailed west to the port of Pocorosa, where he started a town named Santa Cruz, with a garrison of eighty men, most of them sick, writes Oviedo. This same writer states that a young man of no experience, called Hurtado, was left in charge. Here one encounters the usual confusion and errors in names and dates. We believe there is stronger evidence pointing to Captain Juan de Zorita as the officer in command at Santa Cruz. Proceeding south, Ayora left Hernan Pérez de Meneses and sixty men to build a redoubt in Tubanamá, while Francisco de Ávila was ordered to continue on to the south coast and there found a town.

Hearing nothing from these captains, the bishop told the governor that it would be well to find out what God had done with Lieutenant Juan de Ayora. For this purpose, they selected Bartolomé Hurtado, formerly *alguacil mayor* of Vasco

Núñez, because he was experienced in knowledge of the land—"*plático en la tierra*." Hurtado went out with twenty men. In Tubanamá he paid Captain Meneses fifteen pesos for some provisions. When he found Ayora, he delivered the governor's letters to him, and returned to La Antigua, reporting that Ayora was sick and would be back in a few days. During his brief absence, Captain Hurtado picked up two thousand pesos of gold, and about one hundred Indians, many of them loaned as carriers by the friendly Cacique Careta. All the Indians were branded as slaves, and one-fifth of the number marked for the king as his share. Then Hurtado gave six Indians to Pedrarias; six to Bishop Quevedo; and four each to the other royal officials, Puente, Márquez, Tavira, and Espinosa.

The administration of Pedrarias Dávila at this time really was a commission form of government, although Ferdinand had just denied an independent government to Balboa on the declaration that he wanted only one head in Castilla del Oro. When the Spanish captains had to placate a swarm of officials, they were compelled to be harsher and more cruel to the Indians in order to extract more gold from them, so as to have some loot left for themselves and their men. As before asserted, much of the wrong inflicted upon the natives of America originated at the court of Castile, especially in the type of men named to high office in the New World, the multitude of conflicting laws, and failure to enforce good regulations and punish the guilty.

Juan de Ayora returned to Antigua ahead of his captains, and made the usual distribution of captive Indians to the governor and officials. On pretext of sickness, Ayora was given permission to return to Spain, and boarding a vessel about to sail to Santo Domingo, he continued on to his home in Adamuz, near Córdoba. To learn what had become of the projected settlements, the governor dispatched Antonio Téllez de Guzmán to aid those in Tubanamá and Santa Cruz. He arrived at Tubanamá, finding them sick and ready to quit. Captain Guzmán raided the surrounding Indians, and is said to have been the first Spaniard to reach the fishing hamlet called *Panamá*. He collected twenty thousand pesos of gold from three caciques in the province of Panamá, and went back to rejoin Captain Meneses at Tubanamá, after which both parties returned to Antigua, fighting hostile Indians on the way. Téllez de Guzmán did not go to Santa Cruz, claiming that he was ill. More likely he was anxious to get back to Antigua del Darien as soon as he could, for the Indians along the trail flaunted the garments of Christians, which they said belonged to the Spaniards at Santa Cruz, whom they had killed. And then they added that they would do the same to Guzmán and his men.

Enraged at Juan de Ayora for robbing and killing his people, Cacique Pocorosa watched the sick and weak garrison at Santa Cruz, and when he was certain that Ayora would not return that way, he assembled his warriors and attacked the place, leaving no one alive. Another account says that five Spaniards escaped and carried news of the disaster to Antigua. Still another report is given by Pascual de Andagoya, who writes that the chief spared the life of a Spanish woman who was there, and had her for his wife several years. His native wives, jealous that their lord preferred the white woman to themselves, killed her, telling the chief that she had been eaten by an alligator when bathing in the river.

About this time, Pedrarias sent out his cousin, Gaspar de Morales, he who committed the " Herodian cruelty " with his captives. Wishing to obscure the deeds of Vasco Núñez on the South Sea, Morales was ordered to cross over the isthmus to the south coast, go out to the Pearl Islands and secure all the pearls that he could, and take formal possession of Isla Rica and other parts. On the way he met Francisco Becerra, a captain of Francisco de Ávila, returning with booty, while Ávila followed with the sick Spaniards. When Morales, with Francisco Pizarro, reached the seacoast, Caciques Chiapes and Tumaco supplied canoes to take them out to the islands to fight their old enemy, Dites. King Dites of Tararequi, or *Isla Rica*, as Balboa had so fittingly named it, offered a brave resistance, but was conquered by the Spaniards, aided by the Indians from the mainland.

employed in warfare, especially at night, to deride the enemy. Whistling arrows and darts have been known in many parts of the world. According to Nordenskiöld,[1] they were found among the Goajiro of Venezuela, various tribes living along the Amazon and its southern affluents, the Guayaqui of Paraguay and the Eskimo of eastern Greenland. In other words, leaving the Eskimo out of consideration, whistling arrows in the New World center on the southern side of the Amazon basin and their distributional pattern is such that it seems probable that their use has as long as the pikes used in Europe. On Coiba Island they were as long and thick as the German pikes and for half a yard from the tip they were studded with the teeth of shark and other fish.

Oviedo makes the statement that the Indians of Panama did not use bows and arrows. Probably he intended to say that they did not employ them in war but used them only for hunting. Peter Martyr and Andagoya both describe bird arrows and their use among the former inhabitants of Coclé is established by a large number of tiny arrow points

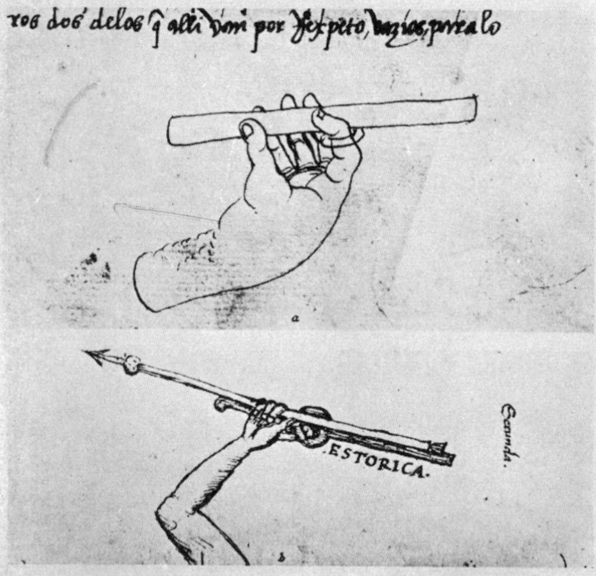

FIG. 10. Ancient spear throwers of Darien as sketched in the original manuscript of Oviedo.

spread from a single source. The Lenca of Yucuaiquin in El Salvador still perform a dance called the *baile de partesanos*, the chief feature of which is casting sixteenth century Spanish pikes high into the air and catching them as they fall. This dangerous sport is accompanied by music of whistles and drums.[2] The darts with rattles at the butt, seen by Ringrose[3] on the Atlantic coast of Panama, are not reported in Coclé.

In several parts of Panama the natives used heavy spears. Those of the Province of Parita were of black palm wood and found in the graves (fig. 64). Larger points may well have served for lances. West of Coclé, the Burica Indians used black palm wood bows about 2 meters (6½ feet) long with bowstrings of fibre.[4] The arrows were 1.8 meters (6 feet) in length and sometimes were dipped in poison. Large arrows also are reported near Bocas del Drago.[5] Early Spanish writers comment on the use of poison among the ancestors of the Choco and to the east of the Gulf of Urabá, but state that it was not employed elsewhere in Panama.

The warriors of the chief Cabo on Coiba Island to the

[1] Nordenskiöld, 1930, map 10, pp. 244–245.
[2] Lothrop, 1925, p. 20. The dance is held on October 4th.
[3] Esquemelin, 1911, p. 247.
[4] Cockburn, 1735, p. 225.
[5] Esquemelin, 1911, p. 245.

Courtesy of Dr. S. K. Lothrop, Peabody Museum, Harvard University.

Page from "Cocle"—an archaeological study of central Panama.

Seeming to realize that it was time for Indians to cease fighting among themselves, Chiapes and Tumaco urged Dites to surrender, telling him that it was hopeless to contend against these terrible white men. The chief took the advice of his old enemies, and invited the Christians to his " palace," where he gave up gold to the value of four thousand pesos and fifteen *marcos* of pearls, promising to produce a yearly tribute of one hundred marks of pearls. In return for all this wealth, Morales had his priest give Dites the baptism of the Christian Church with the name of Pedro Arias. Hoping to efface the name Isla Rica bestowed by Vasco Núñez, Captain Morales changed the name of the largest island to Flores. Neither name has survived. On modern maps the name of the largest island of the Archipelago of the Pearls appears as Isla del Rey (King's Island) or San Miguel, directly west of the entrance to the Gulf of San Miguel. The principal town on the island also bears the name of San Miguel. Morales gave the chief some Spanish *chucherías* and left the island for the main shore.

Among many fine pearls taken from Dites was a famous pear-shaped stone weighing thirty-one carats. The historian Gómara calls it the *Huérfana* or the *Sola*. Another appellation is *La Peregrina* (The Incomparable), a term also applied to other magnificent pearls. Despite frequent attacks by hostile natives, Morales got back to Antigua with his gold and pearls. From 14 to 16 August 1515, 3720 pesos of gold were put in the gold smelter from the *cabalgada* (booty) brought by Morales from the coast of the other sea and the Islands of Pearls. The big pear-shaped pearl was sold at a public auction, held at La Antigua from 19 to 21 August 1515, to a merchant named Pedro del Puerto for twelve hundred pesos. The purchaser could not sleep that night for thinking he had given so much money for one stone, and sold it the very next day to Pedrarias for what he had paid for it. It looks very much as if Pedro was simply a bidder for the governor.

When Doña Isabel de Bobadilla, wife of Pedrarias, returned to Spain, she carried this jewel with her, and sold it, together with another pearl which was " flat, like a little roll of bread," to the Empress Isabella for 900,000 *maravedís*. Soon the pearl appeared in the royal diadem, and Cervantes and Lope de Vega sang its charms.

Lord Frederic Hamilton describes a short visit he made to Panama in 1907, the year of the great earthquake at Kingston, Jamaica. He writes that from the ramparts of Panama City he obtained a distant glimpse of the Pearl Islands, which had a personal interest for him. Lord Frederic says that Balboa was the first European to set eyes on the Pacific, on 29 September 1513. Balboa crossed over to the Pearl Islands, which he found in a state of great commotion, for a slave had just found the largest pear-shaped pearl ever seen.

" Balboa, with great presence of mind, at once annexed the great pearl, and gave the slave his freedom." Having fallen out of favor with King Ferdinand, Balboa sent his sovereign some rich presents, including the great pearl, which was named *La Pelegrina* and placed amongst the crown jewels. After Ferdinand's death in 1516, the pearl descended to Charles V, and after him to his son Philip II. When Felipe Segundo married Mary Tudor, he gave her *La Pelegrina* as a wedding present. Lord Frederic states that the pearl is shown in the portrait of Queen Mary in the Prado museum at Madrid, in another picture of her at Hampton Court, and also in a small portrait in Winchester Cathedral, where Mary was married. After the death of " Bloody Mary " in 1558, *La Pelegrina* returned to the court of Spain.

In 1808, Napoleon placed his brother Joseph on the throne of Spain. The latter anticipating his enforced retirement, like a prudent man, despatched some valuable paintings toward the French frontier. These paintings, continues Lord Frederic, fell into the hands of Wellington at the battle of Victoria, and now hang on the walls of Appsley House, Piccadilly. It seems that Ferdinand VII, on his restoration to the throne, " lent " these paintings to the Duke of Wellington and to his successors. When driven from Spain, Joseph Bonaparte thoughtfully placed in his pockets some of the crown jewels, among them *La Pele-*

grina. Upon the death of Joseph, the great pearl came into possession of his nephew, Prince Louis Napoleon, afterward Napoleon III.

Prince Louis, while in exile in England, being in need of money, sold the famous jewel to the father of Lord Frederic, who gave it to his wife. *La Pelegrina* was a source of unceasing anxiety to the lady, who lost it three times while attending social or official functions, as the pearl had never been bored and was constantly falling from its setting. When *La Pelegrina* came into possession of the brother of Lord Frederic, he had the pearl bored so that it could be worn with greater security.

The foregoing is a summary of Lord Frederic's very interesting account of *La Peregrina,* and is a good example of confusion of actualities committed by many writers. Instead of *La Pelegrina,* it is better to say *La Peregrina (peregrinar*—to travel in foreign countries). We know that Balboa did not visit the Pearl Islands at the time he discovered the Pacific Ocean, though eager to do so. The great pear-shaped pearl was taken from King Dites of Isla Rica by Captain Gaspar de Morales, cousin of Pedrarias, and sold at auction in La Antigua. Moreover, Balboa states in his letter of 16 October 1515, quoted later in this book, that the famous gem had already been bored by a native lapidary. The *adelantado* sent a *figura,* or drawing, of the pearl to the king, which was seen by Navarrete when he wrote of Balboa.

Kunz and Stevenson give a different version of the *Peregrina,* or Philip II pearl. According to the Inca Garcilaso de la Vega, who says he saw it at Sevilla in 1597, this pearl was found at Panama in 1560 by a Negro, who was rewarded with his liberty, and his owner with the office of *alcalde* of Panama. The weight is given as 134 grains, which equals a little more than thirty-one carats, leading one to surmise that this might be a variant of the history of the pear-shaped pearl. This account states that *La Peregrina* was lost with other jewels in 1734, when the royal palace was destroyed by fire.

We must not confuse the famous Isla Rica pearl with another pear-shaped pearl found at Isla Margarita (Pearl Island) on the coast of Venezuela. It weighed fifty-five carats (220 grains), probably the largest pearl ever secured in American waters. It passed from the Occident to the Orient, supposed to be the home of pearls, when Tavernier, the great jewel merchant, sold it to Shaista Khan, uncle of the Grand Mogul.

A few years later, a pearl from Tararequi weighing twenty-six carats was bought by Oviedo for 650 times its weight in fine gold. The historian describes it as " the greatest, fairest, and roundest " ever seen in Panama. Oviedo took the pearl to Spain, where he sold it to the chamberlain of Emperor Charles.

Pearl fishery at the Pearl Islands flourished for many years. When the Indians were killed off, African slaves were used as divers. A party of Scots thought to improve upon this method of bringing up the pearls, and transported a diving bell, air pump, and other apparatus to Panama for that purpose. The Isthmus of Panama has never been overkind to the Scotch; as witness the tragedies at Caledonia Bay. Within a few weeks, two-thirds of the thirty pearl hunters died from yellow fever, and the rest hastily fled the deadly place, leaving their machinery in Panama.

Pedro Mártir, often quoted by the writer, who never liked to appear ignorant of anything, relates some strange tales about pearls. The true histories of valuable jewels are difficult to trace, because they change hands so easily, often by theft. Pearls and other precious stones lend themselves to quaint, curious, and fascinating stories, some of which are true, and others well invented. Various methods of breeding pearls are found in the literature. In Borneo and adjacent islands many pearl fishermen reserve every ninth pearl, regardless of its size, for breeding purposes. These are placed in a bottle with twice as many grains of rice in order to grow more pearls. To be successful, the bottle must be corked with a dead man's finger, and neighboring cemeteries are constantly desecrated in search of " corks."

Indian Slavery in the Indies

Tearing ourselves away from the pleasing and alluring subject of pearls, we resume the ghastly tales of Spanish conquest on the Isthmus of Panama. Excepting the brilliant deeds of Vasco Núñez in ruling and preserving a turbulent Spanish colony, pacifying numerous caciques, and discovering the South Sea, there is very little that is admirable or romantic connected with these *conquistadores*. Bishop Quevedo left Antigua in 1518 for Spain, on the way stopping with Governor Diego Velázquez in Cuba. No doubt the bishop knew that Oviedo and others had entered charges against Pedrarias, and himself intended to complain of him when he reached the court. The matter was discussed with Velázquez, and the latter, says Las Casas, wishing to be governor of Tierra Firme, " greased the hands " of the bishop. Quevedo appeared before the young King Charles, then holding his court in Zaragoza, and engaged in disputes with Bartolomé de las Casas on the liberty of the Indians. In this famous polemical tournament—at which Admiral Diego Colón, M. de Chièvres, the bishop of Badajoz, the Grand Chancellor and others were present—Bishop Quevedo declared that during his four or five years in Darien, those who went in the armada and survived the famine had " done nothing but rob and kill and eat." Later, when the court went to Barcelona, Quevedo wrote to Oviedo to meet him there; but the bishop sickened and died within a few days, near that city, 24 December 1519, surviving his young friend Vasco Núñez de Balboa.

Ayora and the other captains who returned to La Antigua ahead of Morales had stirred up the Indians to such fury that they harassed every outfit as it moved along the trails. Morales, the last to come back from the South Sea, was so fiercely assailed by the natives that he resorted to the " Herodian cruelty " of killing his captives and sticking their heads up on stakes at intervals along the road, hoping the frightful spectacles would delay their relatives who crowded in pursuit. The

Indians were fastened to chains or *hicos* (ropes) by the neck, and cutting through the neck released the body, so that very little time was lost by the fleeing Christians. So experienced and hardened an Indian killer as Francisco Pizarro blushed at his own ignorance and compassion when he saw this tenderfoot captain, fresh from Spain, behead the captives one by one as they hurried back to La Antigua. Morales lost the slaves by his murderous act, but clung to the gold and pearls, including *La Peregrina*.

The mortality among the Spaniards at Antigua was high, but the famine and *modorra* left larger shares of gold, pearls, and slaves for the survivors. The council complained that the people would not cut the weeds nor fill up the mudholes in the streets, but always they were ready to go out and rob the natives and bring a lot back to enslave and to sell on Española.

From the beginning of the Spanish conquest in America, the Crown made a distinction between Indians held as slaves (*esclavos*) and those held as laborers (*naborías*). This difference was emphasized in numerous and various documents. In practice, as all impartial students must acknowledge, Indians given in *encomienda*, as well as those declared to be cannibals or captured in war, were slaves, branded, beaten, sold, or killed at the will of their masters. As the years went on, hundreds of decrees and orders by kings and viceroys endeavored to ameliorate the condition of the American Indian, yet his status ever was that of a conquered and enslaved race. Many of these prolix documents were written to ease the royal conscience, rather than actually to protect the Indian. Although the aged Ferdinand now had another queen, and a young one at that, he may have dreaded facing the dead Isabella when he himself entered into glory for the concessions he had made to his officials in the New World.

The conquest and subjugation of the natives of America by European nations is a big subject, and requires volumes accurately and fully to describe. The degree of servitude varied at different times and at different places in North, Central, and South America, according to the zeal and ferocity displayed by the white men in forcing their religions, laws, and customs on the subject people. This observation goes for Spanish, French, English, Dutch, and Portuguese conquest and domination.

The dwindling number of Indians on Española, and the demand there and elsewhere for more slaves, promoted the traffic in Indian slaves at Antigua del Darien.

On 4 October 1514, Pedrarias, the lord bishop, Puente, Márquez, Tavira, and Espinosa met together and discussed the privileges granted by King Ferdinand to the settlers in Castilla del Oro, those who were there before under Balboa, as well as those who came in the armada. Considering the great expenses and diseases they had, and that they could not work the mines because the Indians ran away, it would be of much benefit to the colonists and a great service to the king, from which he would collect his fifths, to sell their slaves in Spain, Española, and other islands. The officials agreed to license all the white inhabitants of Castilla del Oro, and traders coming and going, to carry Indian slaves to Spain, Española, Jamaica, Cuba, and San Juan (Puerto Rico). All persons having slaves or *naborías* brought in by Juan de Ayora were directed to have them branded on the thigh as the king commanded, by the *veedor,* Gonzalo Hernández de Oviedo, who had charge of it for the lord secretary, Lope Conchillos. In branding the *naborías* ("*indios de servicio*"), the iron must be put transverse on the thigh, " and this is the difference." Very often, indeed, a difference in brand was the only distinction between the two classes of slaves. The town crier was directed to proclaim to the people of Antigua that any citizen could secure a license to sell an Indian slave conformable to the privilege granted by the sovereigns (Ferdinand and Juana) for the trifling sum of a *real* and a half, the *real* for the notary and the half for the judge.

" A good-looking Indian girl never saw her home again."
" *La India que parescía bien, nunca volvía a su tierra.*"

"*Oíd! Oíd! Oíd!* "—"Hear ye! Hear ye! Hear ye! "—cried the public *pregonero,* Diego Cabello, to the people assembled by sound of trumpets in the principal plaza of Santa Maria del Antigua in the kingdoms of Castilla del Oro, on Sunday, 10 December 1514:

" Know all persons that it is the will of the most high and mighty Catholic Prince, King Don Fernando the Fifth, King of Aragon and of the Two Sicilys, of Jerusalem, etc.; and the will of the most high and potent and most Christian and Catholic Princess and Queen, Doña Juana, Queen of Castile and of Leon, of Granada, of Toledo, of Galicia, and of the Indies and Islands and Firm Land of the Ocean Sea, etc., our lords, that all the lands which have been discovered from the source of waters flowing from the mountains on the coast of Veragua toward the Sea of the South, forever [*para siempre jamas*] from the date of this proclamation be called and named New Land of the South Sea; and the other sea, the South Sea. The other ports and places to retain the names given by the persons who discovered them. And because notice is given and none can pretend ignorance, it is commanded that all persons, Indians, and natives of their kingdoms and dominions, as well as foreigners of any other nation, of whatever state, condition and pre-eminence they may be, henceforth call the said parts *New Land,* and the other sea, the *South Sea.*"

Among the witnesses present who saw and heard the said proclamation were the *Bachiller* Corral, Alonso Pérez de la Rúa, Francisco de Vallejo, and Lope de Olano, all described as *regidores* of the city. This shows that Pedrarias, soon after reaching Darien, had appointed these men, all enemies of Vasco Núñez, to be members of the municipal council.

Not a reference in this long proclamation to Balboa, who had pacified the caciques of New Land and discovered the South Sea. A few weeks later, Morales, by order of Pedrarias, changed names on the south coast bestowed by Balboa, among them that of Isla Rica to Isla de Flores. Another witness to the proclamation was Pedro del Puerto, the merchant who bought the pear-shaped pearl from Isla Rica for the governor.

EXTRACTS FROM OTHER LETTERS OF BALBOA

Santa Maria de la Antigua del Darien, on the western shore of the Gulf of Urabá, was a letter-writing community during the years 1514, 1515, 1516. Many of these letters or extracts from them have been preserved, and enable us to reconstruct life in Darien during that period. Considering the time and place, the number of letters written to Ferdinand from Antigua is quite remarkable. Probably this was due to the cautious and distrustful policy of the Crown in dealing with officials in the Indies. The king had instructed Pedrarias that, in all important matters, he must consult and treat with the other royal officers, and that all the inhabitants of Castilla del Oro were perfectly free to write anything they wished to Spain. Knowing the selfish and unscrupulous character of the old governor, it is probable that many letters derogatory of him left Antigua without his knowledge, by means of mariners, traders, and persons returning to Spain.

Some letters to Ferdinand were signed by all the officials. At other times, an official would write individually, excusing or lauding his own actions, and accusing or blaming another official for the way he conducted his office. Usually there were replies to these letters, signed by the king, though it is questionable whether he saw all the letters from Darien or dictated the answers. All the letters from Pedrarias and his co-officers condemned Balboa, except those from Bishop Quevedo. Colmenares, constant enemy of Vasco Núñez, returned to Castile early in 1515, as *procurador* for the city of Antigua. At court, Colmenares opposed Vasco Núñez, and laid plans to build ships on the South Sea and sail to the Spice Islands; while in Darien, Diego Albítez, supported by Pedrarias, schemed to supplant the *adelantado* in the provinces of Panama and Coiba, build ships on the South Sea, and go on voyages of discovery, doubtless in search of Peru. Balboa always had enemies both at court and around him in Darien, all striving to defraud him of his just rewards.

Vasco Núñez de Balboa, on 13 December 1514, wrote to King Ferdinand that on the first day of that month he had received the king's letter, and kissed the feet and hands of His Highness for the honors bestowed upon him. Balboa states herein that he aided and advised Pedrarias as the king had commanded, and that sometimes the governor took his counsel and at other times it was refused. Balboa being an honest man and devoid of the cunning (*maña*) charged against him by his enemies, believed that he should respond truthfully to the order of his king to write fully his opinion of affairs in Darien. He bluntly told Ferdinand that he had sent " grand confusion " with Pedrarias when he commanded that the governor could do nothing without the advice and agreement of the officials. Too many opinions were an obstacle in managing the things of that land, and if His Highness did not correct it, much damage would be done the country. This advice, favoring his enemy Pedrarias, was adopted later by the officials in Spain. Fernández de Oviedo, who went back to Spain the following May, urged the same upon the Indies Council, and on the young Charles when he succeeded his grandfather, Ferdinand. Instead of appreciating the honest reply of Vasco Núñez, the king wrote back that he had seen his letters and wondered at his boldness in continuing to write such doubtful things to the king. For this, as well as for the things and offenses that he committed at the time he usurped the government of Darien, the king commanded his lieutenant-general to do what he would learn from him. Apparently, this reply was written after Ferdinand's laudatory letter written from Aranda, 2 August 1515, in which the king refused Balboa's request to appear at court, telling him that his services were too valuable for him to leave Darien. As pointed out by Altolaguirre, the harsh reply by Ferdinand probably was instigated by Balboa's chronic enemy, Rodrigo de Colmenares, who had just returned to Castile from Antigua. As previously stressed, Balboa always had enemies at the court, as well as in Darien.

Resuming the letter of 13 December, Vasco Núñez informed the king that in all the *entradas* sent out by Pedrarias, Indians seized from peaceful caciques, as well as those taken in war, had been branded as slaves and many of them carried to Española. This traffic in slaves would make many persons rich, but in four years the country would be depopulated and the secrets of the land remain undisclosed. "All those who went in the armada did not go with '*intincion*' to settle the land, but to grab what they could and return to Spain."

Balboa writes that Pedrarias showed him a letter wherein the king ordered the governor to treat him and the old colonists very well, and that until the present he had not done it. He took all the best houses and grounds in La Antigua and gave them to the officials who came in the armada, as well as part of the lands. Pedrarias seized upon the town lot of Vasco Núñez, for it was situated on the principal plaza and had some houses on it, giving him only four hundred pesos, although they were worth seven hundred *pesos de oro*. Vasco Núñez implored His Highness to decree that he and his friends receive no injury.

No captain in the Indies took better care of his men in the field than did Vasco Núñez de Balboa. He also tried to promote their interests at the court. A few days later, on 21 December 1514, Balboa wrote to Ferdinand in favor of Andrés de Valderrábano, who had filled municipal offices in Darien for four years without receiving any salary. Valderrábano had been appointed notary by Balboa, and to him we are indebted for recording the acts of possession of the South Sea made by Balboa in the preceding year. Valderrábano was a firm supporter of Vasco Núñez and died with him on the block in Acla.

In this same letter, Balboa also asks the king to befriend Rogel de Loria, who had served His Highness for three or four years without pay. Both these men now were ruined and in debt and should be paid for their services.

In a letter to King Ferdinand, dated 1 January 1515, Balboa states that when the captains went out to raid the Indians, he spoke to Pedrarias and told him that he should not consent to enslaving the natives, especially if they were to be sold elsewhere, for it would not be a service to His Highness, as the land would soon be depopulated. Doubtless Vasco Núñez believed that, beside the Indians carried away, the remainder would flee to other parts. At this time the Spaniards had no knowledge of the interior of the countries which now we know as Colombia, Costa Rica, Nicaragua, and regions to the north. To the protest of Balboa, the governor replied that for the present it was well to consent to the forays, for it would benefit the people. Balboa said that taking slaves would well repay the Spaniards then at Antigua, but the land would be deserted by the Indians.

Under pretense of the *requerimiento* that His Highness ordered them to make, " each captain does what he pleases wherever he goes "—" *hace cada capitán lo que se le antoja por cada parte que va."* Although the caciques come out to meet the captains and give them gold and slaves and food and textiles, all that counts for nothing; for no captain goes out without bringing back as many slaves as he can.

In order to be informed of all the *entradas,* of the gold, food and other things taken, and of the chiefs and Indians sold, His Highness should order a man of character to come from the Island Española to investigate matters and report to him. Formerly the *alcaldes* and *regidores* of the city had written things in his favor to the king, but he believed that now there would be an " *inovacion,"* or change, because they would say the contrary to please and gratify the governor. Since the arrival of the letter of His Highness praising and commending Vasco Núñez, the officials at La Antigua showed him no good will, and he entreated the king to send a fit person in order to learn the truth of everything.

On 30 April 1515, Balboa writes that he had been very badly treated in his *residencia,* and condemned to pay heavy fines, doing him much injury, mainly because he was not allowed to have a lawyer to answer for him; and what concerned him most, the *residencia* was not concluded.

As the caravel was about to sail from Antigua, Vasco Núñez wrote that as Pedrarias would not let him take any men from the city to go and settle the provinces of Panama and Coiba, as His Highness commanded, he had decided to accept the governor's permission to go and discover the mines of Davaive; and he believed, God willing, that great riches would be found.

Balboa told the king that he sent a bar of gold, melted and marked and the duties paid, to the Island Española for certain things, believing that he would be able to go to Spain to kiss the hands of His Highness; and they had seized and confiscated it for the king's treasury, because it was not registered before the notary; he begged that it be restored to him, as that was little or nothing in comparison with what was lost there. As usual, Vasco Núñez entreats the king not to allow the old settlers, who sustained that land with so much labor and hunger, to be maltreated nor insulted.

In the matter of the *requerimiento,* many offenses were committed, writes Balboa. He says that the governor took his houses, living in one and renting another for three hundred pesos yearly. His ground and houses were estimated to be worth more than three thousand pesos; and Balboa asked return of his property since he had done nothing for which they should be taken from him.

In another *carta* of this same date, 30 April 1515, Vasco Núñez reports the arrival at Antigua on 20 March 1515, of two caravels from Spain, bringing the titles of the high offices awarded to him, for which he kissed the royal hands; and since His Highness was pleased to give them, Balboa asked the king to conserve him in them, giving the favor and help that henceforth he would need.

By this time, Balboa had sufficient experience with Pedrarias and his officials to know that he would have a very hard time in asserting his rights as governor of the provinces of Panama and Coiba and *adelantado* of the South Sea, from whence the captains now were bringing back to La Antigua such quantities of gold and pearls.

Vasco Núñez wrote that his commissions arrived at a good time, for a captain had just returned from a raid beyond the territory of Cacique Tubanamá, and in only twenty leagues he took twenty thousand pesos of gold from three chiefs. The effect of this was that all the Spaniards at La Antigua became so avaricious that all wanted to go out and overrun that region, and without being able to hinder it, one hundred and fifty men had gone there, and he believed that they would not do much for the pacification of those natives.

Balboa states that he presented his commissions to Pedrarias in the presence of a notary, and the governor replied that he obeyed them; but with regard to the fulfilment, the *provisiones* did not mention him nor command him to let Balboa have any men; but, although His Highness did not order him, seeing the will of the king to settle those parts, he would give him the most he could. In the meantime, the *adelantado* could have one hundred of the thousand men in the city, and go out to discover those regions, pacify the caciques, and see where to locate the towns. Vasco Núñez says that Pedrarias could have given him the one hundred men he sent to Panama and Coiba, the territory given to Balboa, after the commissions for the latter were received, and one hundred and fifty men more to the said provinces along the South Sea, which led him to judge that the governor and officials had very little desire to give him a command. He entreated the king to authorize him to select one hundred and fifty men from those who were with him before the coming of the armada, and that they could take along their *naborías,* and asked that he be not detained on account of fines imposed in his *residencia.* Balboa also asked Ferdinand to give him license to enlist two hundred men on Española who would be glad to join him, as many Spaniards there were now without Indians on account of enforcing the *requerimiento.*

All of which would be without any cost whatever to the royal treasury, unlike the expense of the armada, which seemed to him to be too much. Balboa again advises Ferdinand to send someone from Española to inquire into and report upon all the injuries, robberies, and death of caciques and Indians, inflicted without reason. Also to take account of those officers in charge of the exchequer of the king.

XVII

GOVERNOR PEDRARIAS AND OFFICIALS WRITE TO FERDINAND

" Cada uno es como Dios le hizo, y aun peor muchas veces."
—Don Quijote, CERVANTES.

T HE administration of Pedrarias Dávila in Castilla del Oro began as a commission form of government, and King Ferdinand had directed the governor and officials at Antigua to write jointly of affairs in Darien. Bishop Quevedo declares that he never was able to achieve it with the others, so wrote alone. The bishop writes that he saw a letter in which the king commanded Pedrarias and Vasco Núñez to send him an outline of the island (meaning Darien) and as the governor always was sick and the bishop in good health, they agreed that Balboa should send the drawing, in which His Highness would see what caciques were at peace when the armada reached Darien, and now all were at war with the whites and the country destroyed. Already more than half the newcomers were dead, and a large number had gone back to Spain.

Of seventeen priests who came in the armada, only five remained; for some went away and others died of hunger. Quevedo told Ferdinand that the richest province after Dabaybe was Comogre, though the captains found there only a little gold. At date of writing, the bishop said the hope for gold was in Dabaybe, but with the long sickness of Pedrarias and contrary weather, no one had gone to discover that province. The governor wanted to send Vasco Núñez, for none could do it better; but his rivals raised so many objections that Pedrarias desisted in order not to offend them.

On 11 April 1515, the bishop writes that the *residencia* of Vasco Núñez never was finished, nor did he believe it would be finished, which was perplexing (*" está embarazado "*); and although Balboa had prayed that with the *proceso*, such as it was, they send him to His Highness, prisoner or free, there is no way to liberate him. The bishop then adds: " And the *alcalde mayor* says that he has no guilt "—" *Y dice el Alcalde Mayor que no tiene culpa ninguna.*"

Bishop Quevedo told the king that it was doubtful if Pedrarias would give the *adelantado* any people to settle his *adelantamiento* and government, for only three hundred men remained of those who went in the armada. The caciques of Tubanamá and Panamá, who formerly were as gentle as lambs and would not throw a stone, seeing their people killed and destroyed, became so brave that they killed all the Christians at Santa Cruz and those found scattered through the land. Caciques who before were enemies, now confederated and chased Tello de Guzmán for six days across the isthmus until he reached Puerto de Careta, where were some *ballesteros*, or cross-bowmen, who saved the party. The bishop makes the statement that Captain Guzmán returned with 90,000 pesos of gold and others had brought 390,000 pesos, without counting the slaves, who were many.

King Ferdinand, on 10 July 1515, gave La Antigua del Darien a coat of arms. The field of the shield was red, within which was a golden castle with the figure of the sun above. To the right of the castle was depicted a *tigre*, or jaguar, on the left side an alligator. The whole was surrounded by a border containing this device—*La Imagen de Nuestra Señora del Antigua.*

The cunning *Bachiller* Enciso lost no time in persuading Pedrarias to let him lead an expedition to the rich Cenú. The old governor, equally cunning, thought that if Cenú was as rich as rumored, he would put his nephew, Pedro de Avila, in command to insure securing the lion's share of the gold for his family. Captain Pedrarias and Enciso, with two hundred men (four hundred men, wrote the governor) in several vessels, sailed a day and a night until they came to the port of Cenú, and the following day they saw at the head of the bay a town of sixty *buhíos*, called Catarapa. This was in Caribana territory, and the warriors gathered on the shore and even came out in twenty canoes to repel the Christians. The Spaniards succeeded in taking the town, first reading the *requerimiento*. Then they set out for another place, when Pedrarias and others fell sick. In some houses they captured the cacique of Catarapa, who told them that Cenú was a very large town on the bank of a great river passing near Catarapa, which emptied by three mouths into the bay. Indians brought salt in canoes by the bay and up the river to Cenú, where they traded the salt for

large gold pieces. The famous mines of Turufi and Mocri were up the river above Cenú, where the natives caught the gold in nets. At Cenú the gold was melted and made into jewelry and other pieces. " The port of Catarapa is the best in the world," wrote Enciso. On account of sickness, the party went back to La Antigua, leaving undiscovered the rich sepulchres of Cenú for another band of robbers to loot.

Bishop Quevedo informed the king that Captain Pedrarias

was away three months, without daring to go more than six leagues within the land. In this district, writes the bishop, the Indians killed fifteen Spaniards, and thirty died of disease. They returned with one hundred and fifty sick, most of whom died. Pedrarias brought Cacique Catarapa to Antigua, where he soon died of harsh treatment and rage.

On 28 November 1514, Treasurer Puente wrote to Ferdinand, complaining of the great expenses of the administration of Governor Pedrarias. The best ships of the armada sailed back to Spain, or to Santo Domingo to be sold. There is no record that any brasil wood was loaded on the vessels for Castile.

Puente states that the Spaniards did not gather gold from the rivers, as did the natives. Each Christian in Antigua secured four or five pesos of gold from each foray, and three or four slaves to sell on Española; with this they were able to sustain themselves, and would plant for food until a force came to work the mines. Since there were no more peaceful Indians to work the mines, Puente advised the king to send all persons condemned to death or loss of limb to Darien to perform the work of that land.

Soon after arriving at Antigua del Darien, the governor had sent Luis Carrillo with sixty men to found a town on the banks of a river called Río de los Ánades by Vasco Núñez. Carrillo was a young captain, brother of Doña María Niño, wife of Lope Conchillos, secretary of the king and queen. Pedrarias was careful to accord him special consideration. The new location was only five leagues from Antigua and well situated. The Spaniards cleared some ground and sowed seed. Near-by streams and gullies showed signs of gold, but because they did not find the gold in heaps, Carrillo and his party abandoned the place; " and no one wondered at it," wrote the bishop.

Gaspar de Espinosa, the chief judge, on 30 November 1514, wrote to the king that it seemed well to him and to the governor to suspend legal proceedings in the Enciso affair until they consulted His Highness. As almost all the old colonists were involved, nearly all the people of Antigua were guilty—" la mayor *parte de aquel pueblo son culpantes* "—and if all were punished, it would be a great damage, for all their hope was in the men of Balboa; because the Christians who went in the armada, though very good people, had been so badly affected by the country that more than three hundred were dead, and they expected as many more to die; and the most of those remaining were sick and had sores or wounds, except those from Haiti (Española) and from the Canary Islands; and they believed that the trouble or failure that they had in the *entradas* was more in the people than in the land.

In all the town there were not one thousand *pesos de oro,* for counting those who went away and the sickness and want of provisions, all had spent whatever they had; and the most anyone had was a house and a patch of land and a dozen *naborías*.

For refusing to receive Diego de Nicuesa, Espinosa told the king that he had made the *protesta* and would send it to the Council of the Indies; and because all the people (the settlers under Balboa) were guilty—" *y porque todo el pueblo es culpante* "—since they called him, the *alcalde mayor* would do nothing more in the matter until commanded by His Highness.

From the foregoing extracts of a letter by Espinosa it is seen that the chief judge, under an administration hostile to Vasco Núñez, here declares that for deposing the *Bachiller* Enciso, and for refusing to receive Nicuesa as their governor, all the first settlers of Antigua del Darien were guilty; and you cannot impeach a people.

Moreover, from previous records we know that the lawyer Enciso, and Colmenares, lieutenant of Nicuesa, strongly opposed accepting Nicuesa to rule them.

One year later, 20 November 1515, the *Licenciado* Espinosa informed the king that he had taken the *residencia* of Vasco Núñez de Balboa and of his officials, a relation of which, with the secret inquiry, was sent to Spain in a ship that left Antigua four months previously. Four *procesos,* or judicial records, then unfinished, now were forwarded. By reason of the necessities and fatigues they had to endure immediately after disembarking from the armada, Espinosa agreed with Governor

Pedrarias to conceal under a false appearance and suspend some criminal lawsuits, for if they were prosecuted, it would be an endless proceeding, because all the citizens will engage in lawsuits, which were the ruin of the land. Espinosa told Ferdinand that always he ought to favor Antigua and the first settlers, for they had served much and were poor. " He believed that land would be the best in the world."

In this letter the *alcalde mayor* states that he was going to accompany the governor, who was about to set out to pacify and settle the provinces of Comogre and Pocorosa, and punish the Indians who had killed the Christians in the town of Santa Cruz, and that the governor had the desire to use mercy with them. The first Indian caught by Pedrarias in Puerto de Careta was an old blind man who had advised his people to drive out the Christians. Pedrarias killed him.

The good Cacique Careta, great friend of Balboa, now was dead, leaving two sons, the one thirteen and the other seven years of age. The two boys, brothers of Caretita, were placed in charge of the vicar of San Francisco to be instructed in matters of the faith. The vicar of St. Francis and Dean Juan Pérez went with Espinosa on his big raid through the provinces, leaving Pedrarias in the port of Acla sick with fevers and " *dolor de yjada* " [pain under the floating ribs].

Espinosa writes that he could not support himself on his salary and begs the king to increase it, so that he could serve him as he desired.

Fray Diego de Torres of the Franciscan monastery in La Antigua, on 31 December 1514, wrote a long letter to Ferdinand, advising him to order the governor and officials to be more diligent in keeping the instructions of His Highness. Although Pedrarias had been sick and was weak, and the people had suffered the pangs of death, it was necessary to hold them well in hand, " for they more desire a slave than all the rest of the world." He asked that children of caciques brought to Antigua be turned over to the friars to be raised and informed of things of the faith.

The *Licenciado* Rodrigo Barreda, physician of the king and queen in Castilla del Oro, on 1 January 1515, made a deposition that Treasurer Puente had been very ill three times since the armada arrived at the city of Darien, the last time so dangerously sick that he was obliged to receive the sacraments of the Church. The doctor declared that Puente's bodily constitution (*complisión*) was very choleric, and continually he would be sick in that land, all the time suffering from fever, compelling him to live moderately, otherwise he would be in constant danger.

Puente, like the other officials, was eager to return to Spain, and sent the doctor's affidavit to the Council of the Indies.

Lawyer Diego del Corral, rabid enemy of Balboa, on 2 May 1515, wrote to Ferdinand that when *regidor* of Darien under Balboa and wishing to rectify some things disloyal to His Highness done by Vasco Núñez, he was badly treated by the latter, and it cost him two years' imprisonment and other " torments." This is a sample of the lies about Balboa sent to the court by Enciso, Corral, Colmenares, and Alonso Pérez. Vasco Núñez never jailed Corral or anyone else for more than a few days, and then foolishly let them go free. The blunder made by Balboa when supreme in Darien was in permitting Enciso to go to Spain to plead his side of the case before the king, and in retaining Corral and Alonso Pérez alive in Antigua, instead of disposing of them when they defied him with arms. Our cities and parks are filled with statues of fierce-looking men on horseback, successful revolutionists and military leaders who were not squeamish about sacrificing the lives of their enemies.

Corral told the king that he and others were expecting to receive the royal justice after the armada arrived there, and that *Alcalde Mayor* Espinosa had not done justice to satisfy anyone; but sought ways and evasions to free Vasco Núñez, and it was notorious that he and others had taken bribes from Balboa. Corral also accused Treasurer Pasamonte at Santo Domingo of accepting presents and bribes in order to favor Vasco Núñez. Corral begged the king not to divide the government of that land, for reasons which Colmenares would explain. Property left by the many dead at Antigua should be better guarded; perhaps he was wishing to be named *receptor,* or receiver.

The *Bachiller* Corral had to acknowledge that Vasco Núñez was a vigorous commander in the field and very careful of his men; but wanted all the interest for himself, and did not care for counsel or advice from anybody. We have recorded so many mean actions by Corral that it is a pleasure to read that, in 1529, he prevailed on the queen to legitimize Ana Corral, his daughter by an Indian woman, and in case of his death, " a very natural thing," to give his Indians to Ana in *encomienda.*

The very next day, 3 May 1515, Rodrigo de Colmenares, with the historian Fernández de Oviedo and Fray Diego de Torres, sailed from Darien in the caravel *Santa María de la Consolación,* of which the famous pilot Andrés Niño was master, each eager to reach the ear of the king. Padre Torres died in the bay of Cádiz, " without putting foot on land." Ferdinand escaped listening to the tales of Colmenares and Oviedo by passing on to glory, 23 January 1516.

Governor Pedrarias, like the other officials, wrote separately to King Ferdinand by every ship departing from Antigua del Darien, vessels for Spain sailing first to Santo Domingo. The irritable old governor was very mad when he realized the great extent of the territory conceded to Balboa, with consequent reduction of his own jurisdiction. He wrote a testy letter to the sovereigns, asking them to interpret and explain their grants to Vasco Núñez, and to define the limits and bounds of the provinces of Panama and Coiba discovered by him. The word *panamá* meant fisherman in the Indian tongue, and Panama indicated some fishing sites on the coast of the South Sea.

As for Coiba, there was no such province in that land. When the Old Admiral (Columbus, in November, 1502) arrived at Puerto Bello and Nombre de Dios, he inquired of the natives whence came their gold, and they replied *coiba,* meaning far land, or far road. Columbus believed the word was the name of a district, which came to be called " Coyba la Rica "—" the Rich Coiba."

There was the same mistake about Panama. There was no gold in that province, but the present cacique, whose name was Coti, and all his ancestors were great smelters of gold and masters in working it. All the chiefs around his districts brought their gold to him to be made into cunning pieces, and when asked where they got the gold, they replied that it came from Panama. " All the fame is of Panama."

At this point in his letter Pedrarias declares that Vasco Núñez never had seen nor had been in those parts, one of the many falsehoods sent to Spain by the enemies of Balboa. The governor told the truth when he declared that at court they had knowledge only of Veragua and Urabá. The mountains ran from the Gulf of Urabá west and north to Cape Gracias á Dios, and in Darien they understood Veragua to begin 120 leagues from Urabá; and the province of Veragua was the district possessed by the cacique of Veragua, which amounted to only ten or twelve leagues along the Caribbean coast.

If the provision of the *adelantamiento* of Vasco Núñez was as announced, " great is the deception of Their Highnesses, for it would make Balboa lord of all the coast of the South Sea, with all its treasures and riches of gold, pearls, *aljófar,* and precious stones." If Their Highnesses (meaning Ferdinand and Juana, who made the grants) chose to create Vasco Núñez de Balboa *adelantado* on the coast of the South Sea, which he says he discovered and saw, it should be only what he discovered and saw, and no more; and ten persons who were with Balboa when he saw the sea should go from Darien and point out what he viewed.

Pedrarias wrote that every time he sent out people to discover and pacify the land along the South Sea, Vasco Núñez had entered protests, attracting to himself all the people on pretext of asking justice, in order to embarrass the governor. And then Pedrarias told how much his captains had discovered with so much labor and loss of men and property, refraining from explaining that his captains had robbed and killed Indians with whom Balboa had negotiated terms of peace in the name of the king.

Pedrarias exhausts the rich resources of the Spanish language in offensive epithets in defaming the character of Vasco Núñez:

He did not know how to tell the truth, nor did he feel affronted when told something that might do harm; he had no desire nor love for anything good; he boasted of conversing and conferring with persons of low extraction; he was very covetous, having great envy of any benefit that another might have; being very cruel and ungrateful, never pardoning anyone; he did not submit to any counsel, nor possess the reason nor power to use it in order to resist some vicious appetite; being very concerned, holding no obedience or reverence to the Church or its ministers; a person of very evil conscience, being based on deceiving the one conversing with him; when asked for advice, he always gave the contrary. Balboa was a person very much engaged in striving, justly or unjustly, to be superior whithersoever he might be, seeking to obtain it with leagues and combines, and by all ways that he could find, although against all fealty and service owed to God and to Their Highnesses. All this and many other things the secret investigation and *residencia* sent to the court will verify, together with the secret reports, one carried by Captain Pedrarias, and the other on the *entrada* of Davaive borne by Arriaga.

Pedrarias was very anxious that Ferdinand should demand of the *procurador fiscal,* or royal prosecutor, if these charges against Vasco Núñez, and the lawsuits of Diego de Nicuesa and the *Bachiller* Enciso, had been presented in council; and what was done about them. Apparently, the secret reports carried by Pedrarias and Arriaga were unknown to the *alcalde mayor,* Gaspar de Espinosa. Though the governor accused Balboa of so many faults and crimes, he said nothing about sending him in chains to Spain to be tried and punished. Just a short time previously, Pedrarias had informed Ferdinand that Vasco Núñez was too valuable in Darien to be spared. It looks as if Pedrarias was piling up charges against Balboa at court, in order to justify the execution of the latter that he was planning to accomplish in Darien. So far, the chief judge, supported by the bishop, had dealt justly with Vasco Núñez, protecting him from the malice of Pedrarias, Puente, Enciso, Corral, and others. Soon after this, the attitude of Espinosa toward Balboa underwent a change, probably when the *adelantado* had no more gold to give to him.

The long and bloody foray, lasting from December 1515 to April 1517, conducted by the chief judge, seems to have called forth the evil tendencies latent in his nature. During this *entrada*, so-called, the Franciscan friar, Francisco San Roman, reported that he had seen 40,000 Indians put to the sword or thrown to the dogs—"*que había visto acuchillar y echar á perros en el viage de Espinosa sobre 40,000 almas.*" On this expedition the *alcalde mayor* learned much of the riches of the provinces decreed to Vasco Núñez and of the possibilities of discovery on the South Sea toward the north, as well as southward to Peru.

Pedrarias wrote Ferdinand that Vasco Núñez was not qualified to hold the grant made him of the administration of Coiba and Panama and of *adelantado* of the South Sea, for the reward is so great that it appertains to a person of greater quality and who has served more loyally. Their Highnesses must take example of the grant that was made to the Old Admiral (Christopher Columbus) and how much it cost to get rid of it. This was a tender subject with Ferdinand the Catholic, not because his conscience troubled him for repudiating the capitulation and agreement he made with Columbus, but for the reason that he was simple enough to give a New World to an humble and impecunious mariner wandering about the courts of Europe. The governor was ready with a loophole for this second blunder by Ferdinand, and writes: " According as I am informed, he who discovered the Sea of the South and spent his money and fortune in it, they say was Diego de Nicuesa." There is not the slightest evidence that Nicuesa or any of his captains ever saw more of the Isthmus of Panama than the fringe of swamp land along the Caribbean shore, between Nombre de Dios and the Chiriquí Lagoon.

A clever old rascal was Pedrarias Dávila!

The officials at Antigua del Darien wrote so many individual letters to Ferdinand that he ordered them: " That from now henceforth they write together of particular things, in order not to require so much labor here, nor so many times make report of a single event by so many persons."

On 18 October 1515, Bishop Quevedo wrote to the king that he repeated his request that a person be sent there to learn the truth of things. A few months later, 28 January 1516, Treasurer Puente wrote that he had learned by experience that only one person should be at the head of the government, and that the other officials should attend to their own business. Meanwhile His Highness should send to Darien a person of conscience and letters to inquire into everything, and remedy and punish and reform them; and arouse the officials to execute the commandments of the king, so that they would not pursue their own interests and passions, as now they do. Puente then suggests to Ferdinand that he send one of the *oidores*, or judges, from Española to correct conditions in Darien.

The bishop and treasurer corroborate the request of Balboa that the king send a person of quality to punish faults and rectify conditions in Darien.

The officials (meaning Puente, Márquez, and Tavira) on 20 October 1515, wrote that Bishop Quevedo had not exalted the Church nor performed the duties required in the conversion of the Indians, nor other things a prelate is obliged to do; and in order to favor Vasco Núñez he had treated badly some of the people. Apparently without knowledge of the governor, these officials sent a letter by the ship of the *contador,* Juan López, telling the king how Pedrarias by reason of his diseases, as well as other things, was not fit for the office he held—" *no es para el cargo que tiene.*" The governor and the bishop did not agree; the bishop wanted Pedrarias to quit his office and the governorship to be given to Vasco Núñez. Neither was fit for the command in the opinion of these writers.

Vasco Núñez had just returned from his second attempt to reach the Golden Temple and the mines of Cacique Dabaibe, foolishly undertaken at the request of Pedrarias. The venture was a failure and Balboa's reputation as a leader of troops suffered greatly.

A month later, 20 November 1515, these same officials again wrote to the king, declaring " that neither the bishop nor Pedrarias nor Vasco Núñez were suitable for the offices they held "—"*que ni el Obispo ny Pedrarias ny Vasco Núñez son para los cargos que tienen.*"

All communication between Antigua del Darien and Sevilla in Spain was by way of Santo Domingo. For many years the city of Santo Domingo was a sort of clearing house and transfer station for the Indies, enabling the officials there to keep informed of the condition of affairs on Tierra Firme (Darien).

In a letter to Ferdinand, written 20 February 1516 by Miguel de Pasamonte, the king's confidential adviser at Santo Domingo, he states that Castilla del Oro was entirely ruined for want of good government and the cupidity of all who went there. He knew that Pedrarias had bought a pearl worth more than ten thousand *pesos de oro*, which should have been reserved for His Highness, for twelve hundred pesos; and he believed the officials at Antigua were no less guilty in consenting for the governor to secure the pearl.

Pasamonte reported that eight days before the date of his letter, a Captain Atienza had arrived at Santo Domingo from Darien, who confirmed reports of the bad treatment of the Indians on the mainland. Atienza said that it would be best for the service of His Highness and for the good of the land to have no governor, or bishop, or officials; because they make great expense without any profit. The king could avoid the drain on his treasury by commanding those persons to return to Spain, leaving there Vasco Núñez de Balboa as he was before the coming of the armada.

LETTER OF VASCO NÚÑEZ DE BALBOA TO THE KING, 16 OCTOBER 1515, DENOUNCING THE ABUSES COMMITTED UNDER PEDRARIAS DÁVILA AND THE CAUSES OF THE PRECARIOUS STATE OF THE COLONY

" Most Christian and most powerful prince, King our Lord:

" In the month of April of five hundred and fifteen [1515] I wrote to Your Majesty a letter, and two other times before, making known to Your Royal Highness the things which have happened here since the governor Pedrarias de Avila arrived here with the armada; and likewise entreating Your Majesty to command that a person should come here in order to take information of everything which has happened here until now, for the land is in such condition that it much conduces to the service of Your Royal Highness to put an end to it before all is lost; because things now are in such a state that it behooves him who should have to restore them to the condition they were accustomed to be, not to lay himself down to sleep nor be careless; for where the caciques and Indians were as sheep, they have become as fierce lions, and who in other times were wont to go out to the roads with presents for the Christians, have taken on so much boldness that now they sally forth stoutly to assault and kill them: and this has been on account of the evil treatment that the captains who have gone out on the *entradas* have done them, and the killing of many caciques and Indians without having cause or reason for it; and also the robberies which they have committed; for it was not enough to take their wealth, but also the women and children, little and big, by which God our Lord and Your Highness have been much dishonored; and beside the disloyalty, Your Royal Highness has lost a large amount of revenue, which formerly was arranged in such a manner that from now henceforth it would yield much profit; for there is wealth in the land, thanks to God."

Balboa then informed Ferdinand of the atrocities committed by the various captains sent out by Pedrarias, especially the " Herodian cruelty " inflicted upon his captives by the governor's cousin, Gaspar de Morales, " a cruelty greater than ever was done between Arabs and Christians or any other race." The *adelantado* then writes: " All these things and others most serious are passed over without punishment, for which reason there is no cacique or Indian at peace in all the land, unless it is the cacique of Careta, who has to dissemble because he is so near Antigua."

Vasco Núñez continues to beg the king to send some person to investigate the conduct of the new government in Darien, " for if things persisted as they go now for only one year, the country will be left so devastated that it will not be possible to restore it, although Your Highness should expend another forty thousand *pesos de oro* which the armada cost, and which could well have been avoided, judging from the little profit since the armada came to Antigua."

Balboa estimated the salaries and other expenses of the Pedrarias government to amount to sixty thousand pesos annually, and to collect that much money in taxes and duties each year, it was needed to have better condition and care than now given to it. " Your Royal Highness can be very sure that they will send him but little gold from these parts while the land is governed in the present manner, for Your Majesty has to know that there are many governors here, and each official seeks to protect his friends, and things go which way they please—" *vayan las cosas por do fueren* " (italicized in my copy of this letter).

In his usual tactless fashion, Vasco Núñez again reminded Ferdinand that he had spent too much money on his armada to Castilla del Oro, from which he was receiving no benefit. The historian Gómara computed the cost of the armada to be fifty-four thousand *pesos de oro*. Balboa wrote that the confusion in affairs at Antigua del Darien was due to the many voices in the government, " especially being different." Each official pursued his own interests, and the damages would be greater were it not for the bishop, who continually sought what was best for the service of His Highness, even counseling and reprehending them from the pulpit. There was very little constancy among the officials of the government, for they all spoke evil of each other—" *porque los vnos dizen mal de los otros y los otros de los otros* "—and if His Highness knew everything that went on there he would be astounded.

In this letter the *adelantado* describes the famous pearl taken from Cacique Dites on Isla Rica. " It weighed ten *tomines,* very perfect, without flaw or blemish, and of very pretty color, luster and form; in truth, a jewel which might well belong to Your Majesty. The shape and size of the pearl is this," writes Balboa, making a pear-shaped drawing showing a hole bored in the top of the stem or narrow part of it. Navarrete says that this *figura,* or drawing, by Balboa was one inch high and nine lines in width at its lower part.

"All hope was in Dabaibe," wrote Bishop Quevedo in one of his letters. While a few captains had brought in much gold and many Indians for slaves, the new colonists had suffered much from hunger, disease, and attacks by the natives; and the survivors were not inclined to slowly accumulate wealth by the laborious process of working the placer mines.

The Golden Temple of Dabaiba still exercised its fatal lure on the minds of the colonists, new as well as old. Even Balboa, who had means of securing reliable information from the natives, continued to have faith in the gold smelter and jewelry factory of Cacique Dabaibe. The legend of Dabaiba the Golden Goddess seems to have been fixed in the minds of the Indians, which they repeated to the white men. Perhaps this and similar stories of golden cities were told to the Europeans to induce them to travel inland, far from any aid their country-men could render them in case of conflict with the natives.

Pedrarias would not license Vasco Núñez to go and develop his own " New Land " on the South Sea, but he did authorize him to head an expedition to Dabaibe, fearing to trust the undertaking to one of his own captains. He assigned the young Carrillo, brother-in-law of Conchillos, to go along as second in command, and appointed Martín Martínez to be treasurer to guard the gold. It is apparent that the governor reasoned that if the venture failed, he could blame the popular hero, Balboa; if it succeeded, he would give the credit to his favorite, Carrillo.

The *adelantado* reminded the king that in the month of June of this same year, 1515, he had informed him that he was going to the province of Dabaibe which contained the greater part of the riches of that land.

Balboa and his command sailed out on the Gulf of Urabá in a brig and two caravels, accompanied by eight canoes. Another account says they sailed away in five *barcos.* In his *carta* of 16 October 1515, Balboa writes:

" I set out from Antigua del Darien with 190 men, and went to the province of Dabaibe, where we struck the town of a principal chief. Perceiving our approach, the people fled, and we took only a few persons. From there we proceeded by land to the large town of Cacique Dabaibe, who also hid away; and from the few Indians captured we had information of the mines in the country and how Dabaibe obtained the gold; and they say for certain that large mines exist about ten days' journey from there, further in the land, and that all the caciques collect it. I could not make Cacique Dabaibe come to talk with me, although I remained there ten days and sent for him several times."

The *adelantado* told the king that his failure to reach the mines was due to the want of food in the land of Dabaibe and along that coast, because the locusts had destroyed the crops. He could not march inland without leaving sixty or seventy men to guard the ships, and they would have nothing to eat, which forced him to return to Darien. On account of injuries done to Cuquiri, a cacique, two days' journey from Dabaibe, the Indians now feared the Spaniards and raised very little food.

" We departed from there [the *carta* continues] to go up the Great River [Atrato] to search for food, to where we might leave the ships and enter the country. Going up the river we agreed that the greater part of the men should go to a province called Ybebeyva, and I would proceed up the river to take a town of fishermen which was two days journey from there. Going our way up the river, Luis Carrillo in one canoe and I in another, and two other canoes, about fifty men in all, it was our fortune to have seven or eight canoes full of warriors come out against us, and as the Christians handled the canoes badly, especially those recently come from Spain, the Indians maneuvered in such a manner as to assail us with their fighting rods [*armas varas*], which wounded thirty men before we could defend ourselves. Many men received four and five wounds, and they wounded me in the head so badly that I was in great danger; now I am well, thank God. We were forced to leave my canoe, the others reaching land where they could defend themselves. It was the will of Our Lord that Luis Carillo be struck in the breast by a *vara*, from which he died after we returned to Antigua. Two other men also died."

Balboa's expedition to Dabaibe lasted thirty days, when he returned to La Antigua with a few captive Indians and a little gold. On 30 August 1515, the gold was placed in the smelter to be melted. Balboa continues:

" Most powerful Lord:

" In order that Your Majesty be not deceived, I, as a very loyal and true servant, and a person who is vowed to your most royal service all the days of my life, . . . kiss your most royal feet and hands and make known to you the things of this land, as well as the person and affairs of Governor Pedrarias Dávila.

" As to the person of the governor, although he is honored, Your Highness must know that he is very old for these parts, and is very sick of a grave disease and has not had a well day since he came here. He is a very quick and violent man; he is a man who does not grieve much, although half the people are lost in the *entradas*. He never has punished the wrongs and murders committed in the raids on the Indians, or the theft of gold and pearls openly taken by the captains. If some men who have gone out with the captains complain, they are frightened into silence so that others do not dare to murmur. In truth, everything moves along in a senseless way and without any order.

" The governor is a person who is much pleased to see discord among the people, and if there is none, he brings it about by speaking evil to some persons of others; he is a man so engaged in his profits and cupidity that he fails to remember that he is governor.

" In the affairs of the government and in populating the land it is needful that he should have better counsel than he has; and if one gives it, he believes that it is to deceive him. Many times he has shown himself very hateful and severe against the *regidores* because they told him some things that would benefit the service of Your Highness and the common good of the republic.

" In matters of the finances of Your Majesty, certainly he takes very little care nor gives much thought to them. Pedrarias is a man in whom reigns all the envy and greed in the world. It grieves him greatly if he observes friendship among honest men; it pleases him to see and hear complaints and angry words among the people; he is a man who very hastily gives credit to evil rather than to good things, not to those that would benefit him: he is a person without any administrative ability and with no skill or genius for the affairs of government; he is a man that clearly seems to have put behind him and in oblivion all service of Your Highness and things of his own honor for only one *peso de oro,* which he pursues with interest. Not to be more prolix, I leave off making known to Your Royal Highness an infinite number of other things comprised in his evil nature, and which have no place in a person who holds so great an office and has so many and such honorable people to rule and take care of.

" Your Royal Highness can be certain and believe without any doubt that the governor and officials have been unfaithful to him to such a degree and in such a large way that, though they were foreigners to the kingdoms of Spain, they could not do worse, although they might want to do it on purpose. So that, Most Mighty Lord, although they should collect much revenue, it would not be enough to pay for what they robbed and ruined; for truly, they have destroyed for Your Highness the best nation of caciques and Indians and the most sociable and domestic yet found on Española and the other islands, or on the mainland of the Indies, and in the best region that has been seen in these parts: and because I believe that I know something of the quality of the land, I certify truly to Your Majesty that the New Land of the South Sea is the most beautiful, pleasing, and healthful ever encountered in the New World.

" As already I have supplicated Your Majesty, I entreat that he will command the Indies House of Trade at Sevilla to make extensive inquiry of all persons going from here, in order to remove any doubt.

" Our Lord prosper with increase of many more kingdoms and dominions the life and most Royal state of Your Majesty. From Santa Maria de la Antigua, today Tuesday, 16 October 1515 [XVI *de Otubre de* DXV *años*].

" I kiss the Royal feet and hands of Your Majesty.
Vasco Núñez de Valboa—*Adelantado.*"

EXTRACTS FROM INSTRUCCIONES GIVEN BY JUAN DE QUEVEDO, BISHOP OF DARIEN, TO THE SCHOOLMASTER TORIBIO CINTADO CONCERNING WHAT TO INFORM THE KING OF EVENTS AND HAPPENINGS IN CASTILLA DEL ORO

As long as he remained in La Antigua, Bishop Quevedo was paramount among the royal officials. Like the other officers intrusted with the government of Castilla del Oro, Quevedo wrote separate or conjoint letters to King Ferdinand. When Maestrescuela Toribio Cintado sailed from Darien in the latter part of the year 1515, the bishop gave him long instructions of what to tell Ferdinand when he reached Spain: "You will tell the King that all the armada arrived here safe and sound on 27 June 1514, and how Vasco Núñez received and lodged us with very good grace, and supplied the governor, me, and others with plenty of food; and immediately after two days they got busy with the *residencia* of Balboa, and even today it is not finished."

It seems clear that Vasco Núñez did not want so large an armada, and he desired that men should come from Española who would be inured to the climate. They knew in Spain who gave advice to send so many people in the armada, which was not necessary and has caused all the damage—"*que este fué el que ha hecho el daño.*" The artillery and powder were corrupted by the climate. When the armada arrived, they found Antigua a well-built town of two hundred houses, the colonists happy and contented, with plenty of corn, cassava, and hogs to eat. Balboa had made terms of peace with eighteen caciques, whom the bishop names.

"You will tell the king," wrote Quevedo, "that now the town is ruined, everybody sad, and the fields destroyed. The captains have so stirred up the Indians by their evil treatment that the Christians have to move around as if among the Moors of Granada"—"*como entre los Moros de Granada.*" Captain Juan de Ayora set the dogs on the brother of Cacique Careta and they killed him. Panquiaco, Cacique of Comogre, was chased into the territory of an enemy chief, whose Indians took his life.

"It was not a lie what Balboa wrote of the gold in this land, but the people are not disposed to dig and mine it," wrote the bishop. The officials agreed to build a town five leagues from Antigua, where were beautiful rivers and signs of much gold, with Luis Carrillo for captain and *corregidor.* The settlers started to build houses and plant the fields, when they soon deserted the place because the gold was not found in piles without the labor of digging, and no one thought it strange.

" You will tell His Highness [continued Quevedo] that the *alcalde mayor* says that Vasco Núñez is free from the criminal accusations, or at least he is no more guilty than the rest of the people. Governor Pedrarias was of a mind to send the said Vasco Núñez to His Highness, but from fear of the things that his opponents said, he did not dare to send him. After His Highness wrote to Pedrarias recommending Balboa, and telling the governor to take his counsel and opinion and honor him; from that point and hour he never has regarded Balboa in a friendly manner.

" You will say to His Highness that when we came here the wealth of Vasco Núñez was valued at ten thousand *castellanos*, and now he does not have a loaf of bread to eat. Pedrarias took the house of Balboa and gave him for it little more than the yearly rental of the shops in it; they seized his land and gold; and he is left the poorest man in the land. The enemies as well as the friends of Balboa say that if he had been engaged in discovering the land, that now we would know and possess the news that we hope of the rich Dabaive.

" Furthermore, that I know, and so tell it to His Highness, for I swear it by the Holy Consecration which I received, that I believe that none of those who are here has more entire will for the service of His Highness than Vasco Núñez, nor would do all the good that is possible to do here with better art or dexterity."

Bishop Quevedo advised Ferdinand to get rid of the governor and officials, costing 5,600,000 *maravedís* annually; and to govern Castilla del Oro with a captain with five hundred men, on a salary list of only 150,000 *maravedís*. He concluded:

" And if His Highness or those of his council should wish to know if there is any person here to put in charge of the said *capitanía*, say in God and on your conscience what you feel and know about it."

The bishop's instructions were signed, " J. *Episcopos.—* S. M."

XVIII

PEDRARIAS SETS OUT TO PUNISH COMOGRE, POCOROSA AND TUBANAMÁ

"Alas! poor Knight! Alas! poor soul possest!
Yet would today, when Courtesy grows chill
And life's fine loyalties are turned to jest,
Some fire of thine might burn within us still."
—*Don Quixote*, AUSTIN DOBSON.

GOVERNOR PEDRARIAS would show his captains how to conduct a foray against the Indians and return safely to Antigua with slaves and treasure! The captains had brought back plenty of captives, gold and pearls; but they paid heavily in loss of life, and after a year and a half of effort had not been able to establish a single permanent post on either the Caribbean or South Sea.

On the day of St. Andrés, 30 November 1515, Pedrarias sailed from Antigua del Darien in three caravels and a brigantine, with a force of two hundred and fifty men and twelve horses, to go to the provinces of Careta, Comogre, and Pocorosa, and to the New Land. The governor announced that he was going to punish the caciques of Comogre, Pocorosa, and Tubanamá for killing the Christians at Santa Cruz. The wind was contrary for sailing westward, and the pilots were directed to change the course during the night and steer for Caribana, to learn the fate of Captains Francisco Becerra and Estéban Barrantes and one hundred and fifty Spaniards, who had gone to that province eight months previously to explore the land and look for the mines of Turufí.

Two hundred men under Captain Hurtado landed in a port called Aguada, near the town that Ojeda had settled, within the Gulf of Urabá. Here the people refreshed themselves for the matter of an hour, and drank water of the river, which was found to be good, and which the governor named Arias, his family name. After Pedrarias had rested ("*reposado*"), the men were put in order and they set out for the seashore, "all on foot and the water above the knee." The Spaniards saw an Indian town on a hill, which they mounted with difficulty. The royal banner was displayed and the trumpets blared; the Indians sounded their conch shells and shot arrows, wounding two Christians. The whites killed four Indians and took five alive, from whom they learned that Captain Becerra and his entire party had been wiped out by the natives. In some cooking pots the Spaniards saw the bones of men, lions, and *tigres*, from which they judged that these Indians were cannibals, and hurried back to the ships, first setting fire to the *buhíos*.

The flotilla resumed the voyage to the west, and on the fourth day the men debarked in a port of the province of Careta, twenty leagues from Antigua. From here the horses were able to go by land to the province of Acla, though the riders were compelled to dismount in some places, and the Spaniards arrived at the *estancia*, or seat of Cacique Careta. Pedrarias wrote to the king that he put the royal ensign in the hands of the chief, gave him plenty to eat, and much wine, "which is what they most like." The governor believed that they would be good, though he thought it would be a difficult matter to attract them to serve the Christians, "for they are vicious, idle people, and very avaricious and covetous, and they love gold more than the Spaniards."

His fever returned and Pedrarias remained in the port of Acla, which was one of the safest ports in those parts and free from the *broma*, with two rivers of very good water. It was a fit port for the northern terminus of a road to the South Sea, only twenty-two leagues away, and Pedrarias thought the king should give him license to go to Spain to kiss the royal hands and return to Darien with officials and materials necessary to make the road. Cacique Careta, friend of Balboa, had died, leaving two sons, aged seven and thirteen years, who were entrusted to the vicar of St. Francis to be instructed in the things of the faith. Pedrarias began to build a town and redoubt at Acla. He soon discovered that he was not the man he used to be when he won prizes in the jousts in Spain and Portugal many years before coming to the Indies. The governor continued to have fever, his liver pained him, and he developed an ulcer on the scrotum which never healed. He directed Espinosa, the *alcalde mayor*, to command his punitive expedition, left Lope de Olano to finish the work on the settlement, and went back to La Antigua.

In March of this year, 1515, Captain Gonzalo de Badajoz entered the land at Nombre de Dios and crossed to the South Sea, destroying the villages and robbing the caciques. He raided the country as far west as Panonomé and Natá. This was virgin territory for the Spanish method of mining, and yielded a rich harvest of gold. In this region was a great cacique named Parizao Pariba, abbreviated by the Christians to París. Hoping to forfend a visit by the ruthless white invaders, París sent Badajoz four basketfuls of golden jewelry, with the compliments of the ladies of his harem. This rich present, amounting to forty or fifty thousand pesos, did not appease the gold hunger of the Christians, and one night they fell upon the town of the cacique and took the rest of his gold. París felt that this was a shabby way to be treated after robbing his women of their ornaments to give to the white men. The cacique collected his neighboring chiefs, attacked the Spaniards when they were divided, killing about seventy of them, and recovered all his gold. Badajoz abandoned all his captive Indians and fled through the land of Chamé to the shore of Panama Bay. From here they sought refuge on Taboga, being the first Europeans to land on that island. After nursing their wounds and resting a few weeks on Taboga, the Spaniards returned to the mainland and went flying back to the North Sea. On the road, Alonso Pérez de la Rúa, enemy of Balboa, was killed by Cacique Chepó. Badajoz was very glad to meet Espinosa and his men coming from the new town of Acla. Only one member of the party, Alonso Martín de Don Benito, would turn back to act as guide for the *alcalde mayor*. Badajoz soon

Church in the present
town of Natá.

Airplane circling *El
Volcan de Chirqui*

returned to Spain and hurried to the court, where the only consolation he received was the opinion of Bishop Fonseca that he ought to have his head cut off for permitting Cacique París to recover all that gold.

When Pedrarias departed from Antigua to punish Pocorosa, Comogre, and Tubanamá, as he bravely announced, he directed Balboa not to leave the town during his absence. There is no evidence that the *adelantado* agreed to remain in La Antigua. On March 24, 1515, Balboa and the officers of his rule in Darien had turned over to Treasurer Puente gold to the amount of 1,565,568 *maravedís*, without counting the *guanin* and pearls, the balance of their accounts due the king's exchequer. This was a large sum and left them poor. Nevertheless, Balboa, not receiving any help from Pedrarias, as promised by King Ferdinand, was able to raise enough money among his friends to send Andrés Garabito to Española and Cuba to enlist men to aid him.

Instead of the long absence anticipated by Balboa, Pedrarias returned to Antigua del Darien on 29 January 1516, sick, irritable, and disappointed at his failure to carry out his boast to punish the caciques and continue on to the South Sea. Shortly thereafter, Garabito entered a port several leagues from Antigua with a shipload of sixty or seventy men to serve under the *adelantado*. Naturally, this caused great tumult among the people. Pedrarias was greatly alarmed, as most of his own followers were in Acla, or with Espinosa raiding the Indians. At this time, Balboa could have overthrown the governor, and resumed command in Darien. Instead, he permitted himself to be arrested by Pedrarias, who built a strong cage within his own house in which to confine him. Had the governor proceeded to do this, the adherents of the *adelantado* might have brought on a conflict between the rival parties in the town. Bishop Quevedo interceded for Balboa and he was not put in the jail. The bishop exerted himself to bring about a reconciliation between the opposing rulers, stressing the age and infirmities of Pedrarias and the valuable qualities of the younger man to promote the administration of the governor. Balboa was born an *hidalgo* and had earned the titles of *adelantado* and governor. What more reasonable and advantageous for both men than that Pedrarias should betroth one of his daughters to Balboa? Balboa was willing, and promised that he would not attempt to exercise the offices conceded to him by King Ferdinand. Doña Isabel, who always liked the polite attention of the *adelantado,* gave her consent. Pedrarias wrote that to calm and quiet the people, and that, with the advice and consent of the reverend Bishop, the better to pacify and appease the said *adelantado,* " I promised him one of my daughters in marriage, provided that Their Highnesses would be pleased with it." Doña María de Peñalosa, eldest daughter of the governor, so freely disposed of in the wilds of Darien, then was in a convent in Spain.

It is written that the marriage contract—" *el desposorio* "— was executed in the usual formal manner, though no papers concerning it have been found. The governor announced to the king that he had celebrated the marriage agreement for the reason that all might more directly serve God and Their Majesties. If we possessed the secret correspondence between the governor and Bishop Fonseca—" great friend of Pedrarias "— it would clarify many obscure points in our history of the life of Vasco Núñez de Balboa. Students of history naturally question the good faith of both contracting parties, especially of the governor. Knowing the character of Pedrarias Dávila as so far revealed, the reader will not place much reliance on the word or bond of the Governor. It appears that Balboa relinquished his position and rights as governor of the provinces of Panama and Coiba, but retained the title and authority of *adelantado.* While Balboa lacked foresight and sagacity in dealing with his own people, it is very certain that he would not give up his government of the New Land without assurance from Pedrarias that he would be engaged in some important enterprise. Whatever may have been the secret intent of Pedrarias at the time, he intended to at once make use of the energy of Balboa and his skill in managing the natives to found a town on both seas and open a road connecting them, and to build ships with which to explore the Sea of the South. The governor commenced to call

Balboa *hijo* (son) and they lived in apparent harmony for two and a half years.

The most needful project, as first recommended by Balboa, was to establish a permanent base on the Caribbean Sea, from which to improve the Indian trails, so as to be able to transport material and supplies to the south coast. In a letter dated 27 November 1515, the *adelantado* had informed Ferdinand that it would be fitting for the service of His Highness to rebuild Nombre de Dios, where Diego de Nicuesa had settled, " because it is a very good site and will be a rich port," gained and discovered by the Admiral [Columbus]. Balboa wrote the foregoing before he was placed in command at Acla, probably with the desire to direct Spanish activity away from the home of his beloved Caretita as much as because it gave more direct access to his provinces of Panama and Coiba.

Lope de Olano, left by Pedrarias to complete the post at Acla, failed miserably. The Indians of Careta remembered the evil committed by Hurtado in carrying off the porters loaned to him, and refused longer to suffer the adulteries and robberies, and killed Olano and twelve or fifteen Christians. Balboa was sent to build a new Acla on the ashes of the first attempt. He took with him the sixty men brought from the islands by Garabito and some of his close friends. This was about the middle of the year 1516. The *adelantado* kept faith with his accepted father-in-law and entered into the reconstruction of Acla with all his accustomed energy, glad to be engaged in some work that should wipe out all charges against him.

The few years of contact with the Christian civilization of Europe had not left many live Indians in the region about Acla. The Indians of Careta were so near to Antigua del Darien that they were the first and last to suffer from the marauding captains. Balboa put the Spaniards at work constructing houses, clearing the land and sowing seeds, setting an example with his own hands. Las Casas tells us that the *adelantado* was a man of much strength, then about forty years of age, and in all the work he led the advance, imitator of the old Roman captains. The water in the port was deep and the strong currents dangerous for boats entering and leaving the harbor. Balboa laid out the new town in regular order, similar to La Antigua, and named *alcaldes* and *regidores*. In March 1517, Espinosa came back from his prolonged *entrada* and quest for the gold of Cacique París. In his *carta-relación*, the *alcalde mayor* states that he returned by Careta, where he did not even expect to find water, after hearing of the disaster to Olano; but it pleased God that he should find the *adelantado* in the town of Acla and food to eat as good as they had in Sevilla. The *adelantado* not only fed them well, but he sent Espinosa to La Antigua in one of his brigantines, making the voyage in one night. Espinosa had picked up a lot of gold and pearls, and, says Las Casas, two thousand men, women and children, who were turned over to the slave merchants at Antigua to be sold on Española. From which, writes the judge, " it clearly will be seen that always they were carried and led by the hand of God."

News of the rich loot acquired by Espinosa soon reached Spain, followed by the report of Fray Francisco San Roman that forty thousand Indians had been killed by sword, spear, arquebuse, and dogs. Cardinal Ximenes, regent of the government, on 22 July 1517, wrote to Pedrarias that the *entrada* made by his chief judge seemed a very severe thing. The cardinal did not condemn making slaves of the natives, now the usual procedure, fully justified by that convenient *requerimiento*. What concerned the cardinal was carrying away so many Indians, " because it must have caused great unrest among the remainder." And then, as if to clear his conscience, the cardinal referred the matter to the reverend and devoted Padres Gerónimos on Española.

Balboa followed Espinosa to Antigua to secure men released by the judge to help him build ships for the South Sea. Herrera states that he got two hundred soldiers, returning to Acla in three small boats. Later, Balboa had three hundred white men, thirty negroes and hundreds of Indians engaged in the work.

XIX

BALBOA FORMS A COMPANY TO BUILD SHIPS AND EXPLORE ON THE SOUTH SEA

" Alma de esparto y corazon de encina."
— *Don Quijote,* CERVANTES.

W E now come to a wide hiatus in the story of Balboa and the history of Darien and Panama in general. In place of frequent letters, royal commands, and other papers on which to base statements, the student of history is compelled to rely largely on the general historians of that time. Many searchers have failed to fill in this gap. J. T. Medina, who spent many months in the *Archivo de Indias* in Sevilla, declares that from the beginning of January, 1516, to the middle of the year 1520, not a fragment is found of any correspondence between the officials in Darien and the monarch.

After the death of his grandfather Ferdinand, 23 January 1516, King Charles was a long time in reaching his kingdom of Spain, which, in the meantime, was governed by Cisneros and Adrian of Utrecht. The latter knew nothing about Spain, so Cardinal Cisneros ruled Spain, and Bishop Fonseca ruled the Indies. So many complaints against Pedrarias and other officials in the Indies reached Spain that the cardinal looked around for three honest men to send out to reform the government of her possessions in the New World, and selected three Jeronimite Friars, Fray Luis de Figueroa, Fray Alonso de Santo Domingo and Fray Bernardino de Manzanedo. They tried hard to better conditions in the Indies, especially for the natives, but the poor fellows were like fish out of water, and begged to be sent back to their convents.

Charles came down from Flanders and landed, 17 September 1517, at Villaviciosa, an obscure port on the Cantabrian Sea, northeast of Oviedo. Young Carlos had his Flemish counsellors and thought that he had no need for advice from Cisneros, who felt the slight keenly. The old cardinal was in the dying zone —being over fourscore years of age—and the indifference of the boy king finished him.

During these few years of transition and change in the government of Spain occurred another crisis in the life of Vasco Núñez de Balboa, at which time he received no consideration or protection from the crown, and was left altogether at the mercy of Governor Pedrarias and his officials. The governor and his staff of officers were a clever lot of politicians, and were in fear of losing their jobs with the coming of the new king and a new set of courtiers. There was talk, already, of a new governor to supersede Pedrarias.

It seems that Balboa entered into a formal contract and agreement with Pedrarias to construct certain vessels (at different times called ships, brigantines, and *justas*) for exploration on the South Sea. The ships must be completed in one year and a half, according to Andogoya, and the agreement would expire on St. John's Day, 24 June 1518. This indicates that the contract was made about 1 January 1517, before Espinosa returned from his raid. No reason has been shown why the task had to be finished by a certain date, unless it was to give the governor an excuse to take possession of all supplies if the ships were not completed. It proves that he had very little fatherly feeling, as he claimed, for his accepted son-in-law.

This extension and promotion of Spanish discovery and conquest was not financed by funds from the king's treasury, but by private contributions. Balboa associated with himself a number of adherents, who had so much confidence in the *adelantado* that they put all their gold in the undertaking. This partnership became known as the Company—*Compañía*—and like subsequent South Sea companies, not very profitable to the speculators. Balboa was joined by old friends and new: Andrés de Valderrábano and Hernan Muñoz, who had been with him when he took possession of the new sea; Diego de la Tobilla, who came to Darien in the armada, and who wrote of the barbarities of Pedrarias; Pedro de Arbolancha, Ferdinand's commissioner to report on Balboa, in 1513; Rodrigo Pérez, archdeacon of the church in La Antigua, who entrusted Balboa with 210 *castellanos* with no writing, " on account of the friendship between them," and Hernando de Argüello, who remained in Antigua as agent of the Company.

For the timbers of his vessels, Balboa selected certain trees in the neighborhood of Acla, the wood of which Careta and his Indians had assured the *adelantado* was impenetrable to seaworms. This freedom from *broma* was due to the extreme bitterness of the wood. All the sails, rigging, pitch, oakum, anchors, and other irons had to come from Spain or Santo Domingo. While the work was going forward at Acla, Balboa sent Captain Campañón across the isthmus to select a site on the Rio de la Balsa at which to assemble the hewn timbers and build the vessels. Campañón was a nephew of Diego Albítez, one of the rivals of Balboa for discovery on the South Sea. Hundreds of Indians were rounded up laboriously to carry the timbers and material over the mountains to the *astillero,* or location on the Balsa where the shipwrights assembled the parts. Much of the work was done during the rainy season when the rivers were raging torrents. At one time a flood in the Balsa carried away many of the timbers hewed on the north coast and transported with so much difficulty over the sierras. A party of workers isolated by a flood was supplied with food, by Campañón, whose Indians constructed a bridge of vines (*bejucos*) to swing across the river. The *adelantado* divided his force into three divisions: one to cut and hew the timber, another to transport material and supplies, and a third party to bring in food and natives.

The American Indians could endure much fatigue and bear great burdens for long distances in their own manner, but they could not do the work imposed upon them by their European masters, who made them labor in the white man's way of doing things. Much to the discredit of the Christians, Negro slaves were placed as taskmasters over the Indians to extract more work from them. This was done for years on the islands of the

Caribbean and on Tierra Firme. As already stated, a few Negroes were carried to La Antigua by the first settlers, and probably some more were secured on Española by Balboa for extra heavy work.

We read that the *adelantado* dispatched Captain Campañón with thirty blacks to construct a large house on the top of the mountains, twelve leagues from Acla, to serve as a rest house and storehouse for materials. That interesting character, Alonso Martín de Don Benito, later testified that he was one of three men who carried the first anchors from the North to the South Sea. Readers can be sure that Alonso Martín bossed a gang of Indians, who did the work.

Driven to their tasks by both Spaniards and Africans, the Indians fast succumbed to the unaccustomed labor. Oviedo declares that five hundred natives perished, a statement substantiated by Bishop Quevedo when he appeared before the young Emperor Charles V, in Barcelona, 1519. The bishop's secretary said that the number was even greater, and Las Casas, with his usual exaggeration, seized upon this to make the number two thousand Indians. Not a Spaniard or Negro died, though they, too, endured great hardship. It seems incredible that the Indians, working in their natural habitat and eating their usual food, should suffer so greatly, and clearly shows how harshly they were driven to their tasks, bearing the heavy planks and other materials over the mountains and streams to the *astillero* on the Balsa River. This stream emptied into the Gulf of San Miguel, and probably was the Rio Sabana of today. It is hard to excuse the *adelantado* for permitting this severity. He saw the time slipping by because the project was being delayed by floods and want of supplies. He was working under compulsion to complete the vessels by 24 June 1518, and this was his last chance to rehabilitate himself and his dream of sailing away on the southern sea, and finding out the truth about that rich country of Birú, or Perú, far to the south. Balboa's friends and supporters, who had put their gold in the venture, kept urging him to desperate efforts to meet the requirement of the governor. As the Indians died off, a party of Spaniards

In the Río Chucunaque, 20 miles above Yavisa, is El Salto. Left to right, Major Malsbury, Lieut. Townsend, Mr. Charles Charlton.

River raft 16–18 ft., made of two tiers of balsa logs, with hard wood skids for hauling over shallows.

would raid the country east of the gulf of San Miguel and bring in more Indians, any surplus being disposed of in the slave market in Antigua. The raiders brought back food as well as Indians, and usually collected some gold by the way, which was sent to Antigua and expended for supplies for the Company. On 25 October 1518, Andrés de Valderrábano, " in the name of Balboa and of the people with him in the expedition of the new land of the South Sea," deposited in the smelter golden jewelry to the value of 2331 pesos.

Balboa was woefully deceived in believing that the timbers so laboriously transported from the north coast were worm-proof. When carpenters had assembled two ships on the Balsa, it was found that the planks of the vessels were so riddled by the borers that they were like honeycombs. By the time the boats entered the gulf of San Miguel they were water-logged, and when the *adelantado* and party succeeded in reaching the Pearl Islands the two vessels sank.

The loss of his ships by the *broma*, which he went to so much time, labor, and expense to avoid, was a great blow to Balboa. Nevertheless, he at once began to build larger and better vessels at the Pearl Islands, where good wood for that purpose was found. Much of the tackle and equipment of the foundered boats had to be replaced, which required more time and additional expense. The *adelantado* sent Bartolomé Hurtado to Governor Pedrarias to obtain more men and supplies. Hurtado returned with sixty men and a few necessary articles. Medina calls attention to an item on the books of treasurer Puente, which shows that 45,000 *maravedís* had been loaned from the royal exchequer to Hernando de Argüello in the name of the *adelantado* Vasco Núñez when he was building the ships on the South Sea.

When it was plain that the new ships could not be finished on time, Balboa directed Argüello, agent of the *Compañía* in Antigua, to petition the governor and officials for prorogation of the limit (*el plazo*) fixed for completion of the work and an exploratory voyage.

On 13 January 1518, the governor, the bishop, Puente and

Márquez (Tavira having been drowned) met and considered the petition. After much discussion, they determined and agreed to extend the time four months first following the original termination, within which period the *adelantado* should furnish and execute the said voyage and what he was ordered to do—"*dentro del qual dicho termino le mandaban que acabase de hazer e complir el dicho vyaje e lo que le fue mandado, so las penas en los dichos mandamientos proveidas.*" The preceding lines found in Altolaguirre follow a copy made in the city of Santa Maria de la Antigua del Darien on 5 March 1520, in the presence of Captain Pedro de Gamez and Alonso de Verdejo, and certified by Martín Estete, *escribano*.

This prorogation proves the existence of a document full of instructions and orders to Balboa, in which he obligated himself, cheerfully no doubt, to build ships and explore the coasts of the South Sea, with penalty for nonfulfillment. The time limit, or *plazo*, seems to have been emphasized by Pedrarias as a check on his accepted son-in-law and ground for annulment of the agreement in case of failure. Diego Albítez and others were eager to make the first exploration along that southern sea. It was about this time, according to Herrara, that Don Diego de Deza, archbishop of Sevilla, wrote a letter to Balboa assuring him that if he followed the land to the west he would find Indians in armor and bearing lances, while by sailing toward the east he would run against people with great wealth and herds of cattle. Medina's copy of the prorogation is not signed by Bishop Quevedo, to which he calls attention; the version given by Altolaguirre is signed by the bishop. Shortly after signing this document, Bishop Quevedo left Antigua for Spain, stopping with the governor of Cuba on the way. The departure of the bishop left Balboa without a single friend among the officials at La Antigua.

If the original agreement terminated 24 June 1518, four months grace would extend the time for completion of the vessels to 24 October 1518. By the latter date, the *adelantado*, despite his setbacks, had two ships fit for sea, in which he sailed, with one hundred men, from the islands to the mainland.

Crossing the Gulf of San Miguel to its eastern shore, Balboa landed his men in a province called Pequeo, where they spent two months. This appears to have been the territory of Cacique Chucamá, whose people had killed the Spaniards under Gaspar de Morales. Re-embarking his men, the *adelantado* sailed out of the gulf he had named, passed Punta Garachiné into the Gulf of Panama, and went down the coast a distance of twenty-five leagues as far as the port of Piñas. Off Punta Piñas they ran into a school of whales, so numerous that the mariners feared to go near them. The next morning the wind was contrary, and Balboa turned back to the islands. While on this voyage, the *adelantado* learned more of Peru from the Indians, which was the third notice, says Herrera, of the riches of that country. No doubt these two vessels built by Balboa were the bark *San Cristóbal* and the *justa Santa María de Buena Esperanza*, in which, after the death of Balboa, the chief judge sailed from the " city and port " of Panama on 21 July 1519, with 115 men, to go to the provinces of París, Natá, and Cherú. Included in the party were Andrés Garabito, Francisco Pizarro, Pascual de Andagoya, Hernando de Soto, Alonso Martín de Don Benito, Blas de Atienza, and Rogel de Loria.

Balboa sailed back to the Pearl Islands to finish the construction of two more vessels. Some weeks later, when a prisoner in Acla, the *adelantado* declared that he had four ships on the South Sea.

The fortunes of Balboa continued to be determined in the court of Spain rather than in Darien and Panama. With the death of King Ferdinand, the power of Fonseca waned, and the Gran Chanciller of young Charles gave some heed to reports of atrocities and wrongs committed upon the Indians by Spanish officials in the Indies. Bartolomé de las Casas, Fernández de Oviedo, Fray Francisco de San Roman, and other friars received a hearing. Even Bishop Fonseca was willing to admit that it would be well to remove Pedrarias from office. King Charles, by *cédula* 2 September 1518, informed Lope de Sosa, governor of the Canaries, that he had been selected to succeed Pedrarias Dávila as governor of Castilla del Oro. By private letters, mariners, and traders, the news of a change in governors soon reached Antigua del Darien, and was carried across the isthmus to the *adelantado* and his command on the South Sea.

One of the conditions of the contract between Balboa and Pedrarias was that the former should make frequent reports of the progress of the work on his ships. Andagoya informs us that the *adelantado* paid little respect to the royal officials at Antigua, and did not give them a share of the gold and slaves secured in his *cabalgadas,* as did the other captains. The irascible old governor became much exasperated with his accepted *yerno* because he did not tell him all that he was doing over on the other coast. Puente took advantage of the strained relations between them to suggest to the governor that Balboa, on completion of his vessels, would sail away to unknown parts and perhaps find that fabulously rich territory called Biru, or Peru, where he would set himself up as lord of the land, independent of the goverment of Pedrarias. The vicious *Bachiller* Corral also hastened to inflame the suspicions of the old governor.

" *C'est toujours la genitale.*" At this time Pedrarias received a letter from Andrés Garabito, who was in the confidence of members of the *Compañia* on the South Sea, warning him that the *adelantado* was preparing to break away from all allegiance to the governor of Castilla del Oro. Las Casas states that this letter was written for revenge upon Balboa. It appears that Garabito had made amorous advances to Caretita, the favorite of the *adelantado,* " a thing which displeases and greatly angers honorable men." Careta's daughter repulsed Garabito and told her lord about the incident. Balboa, master of the sword, spoke some plain words to Garabito, but the matter was patched up, and Garabito was retained among the associates of the *adelantado.* It is said that Garabito assured Pedrarias that Balboa loved his Indian wife and never intended to marry the governor's daughter, a statement not calculated to soothe the rising choler of Pedrarias.

When it became known in Antigua that Balboa had four ships

about ready for sea, there may have been some careless observations, possibly by his own friends, that this was a good
time to sail away from the tyrannous rule of the governor to
some country where they could live as they did before the
coming of Pedrarias.

Hernando de Argüello, partner in the Company and representative of Balboa in La Antigua, was quick to realize what
might happen to their South Sea enterprise should a new governor with a horde of new officials come sailing into port. He
hastened to write to the *adelantado* that Pedrarias would not
extend the time for finishing the ships (apparently the last two
were not quite completed) and that there was great probability
of the arrival, almost any day, of another ruler for Castilla del
Oro, in which event the vessels constructed with so much labor
and expense might be put in the hands of a favorite of the new
governor. Argüello added in his letter that since the Padres
Gerónimos at Santo Domingo had authorized Balboa to make
the voyage on the South Sea, the *adelantado* should not risk
waiting for the coming of Lope de Sosa.

The few records available relative to the life of Vasco Núñez
de Balboa during this period seem to show that Pedrarias, the
royal officials, and other enemies of the *adelantado*, had been
patiently waiting to close in on him and get possession of his
ships as soon as completed. This letter of Argüello was inter-
cepted and delivered to the governor.

Balboa's ships, now four in number, still needed more iron,
pitch, and other things, which could be obtained only in Acla.
In the meantime, notice of the naming of Lope de Sosa had
been carried over to Balboa, and one night he conferred with
his friends, Andrés de Valderrábano, Luis Botello, Fernán
Muñoz, the archdeacon Rodrigo Pérez, and Andrés Garabito,
on what best to do. The *adelantado* said to them

" that it was possible that Lope de Sosa might have arrived, and if he
is come, Pedrarias my lord now is no longer governor, and we are left
defrauded of our desires and all the labors we have put in this undertaking are lost. It appears to me that in order to get notice of what

concerns us so much, the Captain Andrés Garabito go to the town of Acla for the iron and pitch that we need, and find out if the new governor has arrived. If there is a new governor, the party will come back and we will finish these ships as best we can and pursue our discovery, trusting in his good will for us, because we can aid and serve him. But if Pedrarias my lord still holds the government, tell him of the state in which we find ourselves and he will provide us with what we ask, and we will set out on our voyage, from which, I trust in God, will come to pass what we so much desire."

It is said that when Balboa consulted with his friends, it began to rain, and the sentinel posted near headquarters sheltered himself under the eaves of the *buhío* in which the officers were sitting. The sentinel heard part of the discussion within the building and understood that the *adelantado* and his companions were planning to sail away from any allegiance to Pedrarias Dávila. Conceiving in his dull mind that this was treason to the governor, and hoping for reward, the sentinel managed to send the information over the isthmus to Acla.

Balboa despatched Andrés de Valderrábano, Luis Botello, Fernán Muñoz, Garabito, and other Spaniards to the number of forty, with the usual native attendants, to secure the iron, pitch, and other supplies, with particular orders to learn news of the new governor. When near Acla, the party must halt, and by night send a messenger into the town, who would go to the house of the *adelantado* to learn whether Pedrarias had been recalled. If Lope de Sosa had arrived at Antigua, the messenger should return to his party, who would be waiting at a place called Chepabar, crying, " *Albricias! Albricias!* The *Adelantado* Vasco Núñez is governor of Tierra Firme," at the same time handing over certain papers purporting to be official confirmation of the announcement. If Pedrarias still was governor, the messenger should report that all was well, and that he would concede everything that Balboa had requested. Pedrarias declares in his rambling accusations against Balboa that the priest, Rodrigo Pérez, who was a member of the party, carried a command from the *adelantado* that all should return immediately to his camp on the South Sea, " under penalty of death " for

Marsh Darien Expedition.

Modern Acla, reputed site of the Acla built by Balboa.

Marsh Darien Expedition.

"White Indian" children. Note gold ring in nose of the women.

refusal. If this scheme of Balboa and his friends is true, and there is good evidence to support it, the plan appears to be as silly, involved and unnecessary as the oath taken in the church at Darien to refuse to receive Diego de Nicuesa.

The governor had given orders to arrest anyone coming from Balboa. When the messenger, who was Luis Botello, entered Acla at night and acted suspiciously, he was seized by the notary and imprisoned. This official was that Francisco Benítez who had been given one hundred lashes several years before by command of Vasco Núñez. Valderrábano and the other friends of Balboa not hearing from their messenger, foolishly went into the town, when they, too, were arrested and carefully guarded. Benítez and the justice at Acla immediately hurried a messenger to La Antigua to notify the governor of these important arrests.

It is probable that Pedrarias believed at this time, before leaving Antigua, that he had enough evidence on which to convict Balboa and had determined on his trial and death at Acla. To win the good will of the populace, the avaricious old governor directed Juan de Villanueva to buy wine, flour, oil, vinegar, and sides of bacon from Spain, and transport them to Acla, and there sell them to the people at cost, and even on trust if they had no money. All this at the expense of Pedrarias.

The governor, with the royal officials and soldiers, then hurried to Acla. Pedrarias, Espinosa, and lawyer Corral questioned the false Garabito and other prisoners. Apparently, the sentinel who overheard part of the discussion of Balboa and his friends was able to send his report to Alonso de la Puente, for Herrera states that Puente, " enemy of Basco Núñez," referred to Pedrarias what the soldier understood that Balboa said to Valderrábano. The officials urged the governor to arrest the *adelantado* at once. The clever old courtier knew a better and safer way to secure Balboa. In order to get him away from his command, Pedrarias wrote a very affectionate letter, like a father—" *muy sabrosamente, como padre* "—to his reputed son-in-law, asking him to come to Acla to confer about his contemplated voyage. Friends of Vasco Núñez in Acla, ignorant of what was going on, did not warn him of the arrest of his messengers.

Balboa, in the meantime, was waiting patiently on the little island of Tortugas in Panama Bay, and wondering what delayed his friends sent over to Acla. He had four ships, not fully equipped perhaps, yet capable of a long voyage, three hundred men at his command, the broad sea before him, and the pathway open to the treasures of Peru. Never in his life, observes Quintana, was his situation so brilliant and promising. One night, on looking up into the heavens brightly studded with stars, the *adelantado* noted the particular star which Micer Codro, the Venetian astrologer, had assured him ruled his destiny. Turning to his companions, Balboa said, " A nice man I would be to believe in diviners, especially in Micer Codro. Behold I see my star in that place in the heavens which he declared portends great danger to my life, when I find myself with three hundred men and four ships just about to set out on the Sea of the South."

Suddenly, the sky became overcast and it began to rain. The *adelantado* turned and entered his house, where he found waiting for him a messenger from Acla, who handed him the letter from Pedrarias. Balboa suspected no deception, and leaving Captain Francisco Campañón in command of his men, he immediately started north for Acla. To accompany him, the *adelantado* selected only a few men, among whom was Pascual de Andagoya, who certified to the fact in the year 1527. The party from Acla warned Balboa that the presence of Pedrarias and all the officials in Acla, and their suspicious behavior, meant danger to him; but, like an obedient son—" *como hijo obediente,*" says the historian, he continued on his way, thinking that he still was in the good graces of the governor. While yet on the Pacific slope of the mountains, between the Rio de la Balsa and the wooden *buhío* on top of the sierras, the *adelantado* ran into a party of soldiers under Francisco Pizarro, sent out by Pedrarias to arrest him. " What means this, Francisco Pizarro? " said Balboa, surprised. " You are not accustomed to come out to receive me in this manner! " Pizarro made no reply. The *adelantado* offered no resistance and was conducted a prisoner to Acla, and was confined in the house of Juan de Castañeda, said to have been the strongest house in the town, with sentinels to guard it.

Bartolomé Hurtado was despatched to the South Sea to take over the command of the ships from Captain Campañón, and to discourage any attempt at revolt by the followers of Balboa. With the hope of finding out something that might criminate the *adelantado,* the tricky old governor visited the prisoner, calling him *hijo* (son), telling him to make himself easy and have no concern for the charges brought against him, for he had ordered the trial only to satisfy Treasurer Puente and clear Balboa's fidelity from any suspicion of guilt. Pedrarias, at the same time, ordered Gaspar de Espinosa to prosecute Balboa and his associates with all the rigor of law. The governor also commanded that the old *residencia,* begun nearly five years before, be reopened and proclaimed against Balboa. The treasurer, Alonso de la Puente, the *contador,* Diego Márquez, and *Bachiller* Diego del Corral, took delight in concerting and devising a long criminal accusation against the *adelantado;* which all signed. *Bachiller* Corral presented the charges, and the *alcalde mayor* very willingly proceeded with the trial.

Andrés Garabito had been arrested with the others, but he was advised to tell what he knew of the treason, " which they imputed to the *adelantado* and his consorts." Garabito swore to his declaration, and he was set free. Apparently in reward for his action, Garabito later was taken over to Panama by the governor; he went with Espinosa in the ships constructed by Balboa, and then was appointed lieutenant of Pedrarias in Acla, the town built by the *adelantado.*

If there was a conspiracy, Archdeacon Rodrigo Pérez, intimate of Balboa, was involved as much as the rest of the accused. Pedrarias and Espinosa were afraid to kill a priest and prevailed on the dean of the church in Darien, Juan Pérez Salduendo, to send him a prisoner to Spain. At this time, Bishop Quevedo was in Spain and may have testified in the trial of his archdeacon. He was absolved of any guilt by the

Council, and in 1522 returned to La Antigua with Salaya, the new *alcalde mayor*. By command of the emperor, his property was restored to him, and he became dean of the church. " See, reader," observes the historian, " what could have been the guilt and treason of the unhappy *adelantado,* since this arch-deacon was one of the principal participants in it, and returned to the land freed from guilt! "

With the testimony of Garabito, the governor felt assured that he could, at last, with the help of the willing Espinosa, get rid of Balboa by process of law. Pedrarias again visited the *adelantado* in his jail, this time not addressing him as son; but, instead, with wrathful countenance, charging him with being dis-loyal to the king and to himself, telling Balboa that henceforth he would treat him as a rebel and deal with him as an enemy. To this, according to Las Casas, " Balboa replied that it was a falsehood which they had raised up against him, and never did he have such a thought; for if he should have such intention, he had no need to come at the call of the governor, since he had three hundred men who loved him and four ships with which he could have sailed away and settled elsewhere. Instead of which, he came quickly and without fear, innocent of such designs, only to find himself a prisoner and branded as unfaithful to the royal crown of Castile."

Completion of the ships was a crucial moment in the life of Vasco Núñez de Balboa, and the struggle for their possession was the chief factor in his trial. Probably Balboa's death was assured when it became known that he had four ships on the South Sea, two in which he had made a short voyage, and two more at the Pearl Islands needing only some iron, pitch and tackle to complete them. As early as November, 1515, Pedra-rias and his officials had written to Ferdinand recommending Diego Albítez, with whom they had made an *asiento* to settle in the lands given to Balboa and discover on the South Sea. This was confirmed by Doña Juana and Don Carlos in a royal *cédula* dated 23 March 1518; and Captain Albítez was author-ized to enlist men on Española, provided they first settled with their creditors, and carry them to the Isthmus.

No sooner was Balboa securely jailed than Puente and Espinosa laid plans to get possession of his ships. Puente started Andrés de Cereceda, an intimate friend, on a journey to the court of Spain to endeavor to secure the vessels for himself and the pilot Andrés Niño. Espinosa, always more adroit than the other officials and not restrained by the ethics of his profession, took a quicker and more certain method to get command of the ships. The chief judge, before trying Balboa or rendering a decision in his case, called on the Spaniards who had risked their money in Balboa's *compañía*, to petition the governor to shorten the usual period of proclaiming the *residencia* of the *adelantado* in order that the case against him be decided sooner, and the ships not held back from the projected voyage of discovery. Furthermore, the deputies, or shareholders, wanted Gaspar de Espinosa and no other to take charge of the ships, for none could do so well as he. All this was done, writes Oviedo, as Espinosa himself ordered—" *segund quel mesmo las ordenó.*"

It is said that the *adelantado* indorsed the petition of his associates, perhaps at the solicitation of Espinosa, trusting that the judge would be more lenient in his sentence, and protect him from the fury of Pedrarias. Or, believing himself doomed, Balboa may have signed the paper simply to preserve the financial interest of his friends.

The trial of Balboa and his consorts was conducted very hurriedly and with much secrecy, as if the officials feared that the devoted followers of the *adelantado* would rise up and free their leader. The veteran fighters under Balboa were able to overthrow any force that the governor could have mustered. Gaspar de Espinosa was the prosecutor as well as the judge, and, asserts Oviedo, ordered the entire proceedings.

The disappearance of many documents during this period of the rule of Pedrarias is rather suggestive. The *proceso*, or record of the charges and trial of Balboa, was preserved for a short time after his execution and then disappeared while in charge of Pedrarias and Espinosa. When Oviedo returned to La Antigua on 24 June 1520, as *receptor*, or receiver, of the property of Balboa and the others condemned with him, he asked the

escribano, Cristóbal Muñoz, for the *proceso* in order to check
the effects and estimate the notarial fees due Lope Conchillos,
at the court of Spain, who held the lucrative office of notary-
general of the Indies. The historian writes that he had the
document in his possession for some days, reading all of it,
during which he numbered the leaves and signed each with his
rúbrica, so that no leaf could be removed without its absence
being detected. Oviedo adds that the *proceso* was carried over
to the new town of Panama, where were Pedrarias and Espinosa,
and when they saw the marks and signs made by Oviedo they
suspected that he had noted the faults and merits of the trial
in damage of them. The chronicler was in much trouble at
this time or surely his historic sense would have prompted him
to copy this important document. When Oviedo came back to
Darien, he expected to find Lope de Sosa installed as governor
of Castilla del Oro, but the latter had died suddenly, without
putting foot on land, as his ship anchored in the port of Antigua.
Later on, in 1525, when the Council of the Indies called for the
proceso of the trial, on complaint of the brothers of Andrés de
Valderrábano, the paper was not produced. The death of Lope
de Sosa assured Pedrarias a long extension of his term of office,
and made him more independent and arrogant than ever.

The contract between Balboa and Pedrarias, and the *proceso*
of the trial of the *adelantado* have disappeared; but we do possess one document which throws much light on the trial of
Balboa and the denial of his appeal to the crown. This is a
long paper, dated 12 January 1519, purporting to be written
mainly by Pedrarias and addressed to Espinosa; but no student
of the events preceding the execution of Balboa can fail to see
in it an agreement and understanding between the governor and
his chief judge to make away with the *adelantado.* Knowing the
illegality and injustice of the deed they were about to commit,
the paper gives a rambling recapitulation in legal phraseology
of all the charges, civil and criminal, brought against Balboa
from the time that Pedrarias took over the government. It is
written in such a manner as to make it appear that Balboa was
guilty of a long series of crimes extending over a number of

years. Obviously, this was intended to befuddle and deceive the authorities in Spain when they received reports of the execution of Balboa. This would not beguile Fonseca, who was familiar with affairs in the Indies ever since 1493, when he quarreled with Columbus when outfitting the Admiral's fleet. But Bishop Fonseca, as we know, was a friend and protector of Pedrarias.

The governor made glaringly false charges that Balboa was " the principal in causing the death of Diego de Nicuesa, Alonso de Ojeda, Fernández de Enciso, and the other governors who have come to these lands." Most of these charges simply are a pack of lies. Espinosa, who probably dictated the document to notary Cuadrado, was the same judge who had declared four years previously that Balboa was no more guilty than the rest of the colonists in refusing to receive Nicuesa in Darien. The *residencia* of that trial was sent to Spain in 1515, where King Ferdinand must have wiped out the charges, otherwise he would not have praised Balboa so extravagantly and named him *adelantado* of the South Sea and governor of the provinces of Coiba and Panama. The reader is aware, already, that Alonso de Ojeda had departed from Tierra Firme before Balboa came to San Sebastián, and that he never returned to the mainland. When these charges were made, the *Bachiller* Fernández de Enciso was in Spain, very much alive and publishing his *Suma de Geografía* (Sevilla, 1519). Balboa performed a timely service for his country by ousting Enciso, who was unfitted for leadership, and holding together the colonists at Antigua del Darien. As for the other governors *(" los otros gobernadores ")* that Balboa caused to die *(" hazer morir ")*, that was the biggest lie of all—there were no other governors or commanders in Darien and Castilla del Oro during the lifetime of Vasco Núñez de Balboa.

The document of 12 January 1519 states that Espinosa informed the governor when the *proceso* against Balboa was concluded, and before definitely pronouncing sentence, he referred the case to Pedrarias. Espinosa, in the presence of notary Antonio Cuadrado, inquired of his lordship whether, in consideration of the quality, title, and dignity of the said *Adelantado* Basco Núñez, the *proceso* should be transmitted to Their Highnesses or the lords of the Council; or did Pedrarias command the said Señor Alcalde Mayor to determine the case according to justice, without remission to Spain; " or what it was that the governor ordered concerning the aforesaid."

Years later, the Count of Puñonrostro, grandson of Pedrarias Dávila, in his long controversy with the historian Herrera, claimed " that never was seen in these kingdoms a lieutenant asking his governor or his *corregidor* a command to sentence one to death, as the *Licenciado* Espinosa asked Pedrarias in this case."

Writers lightly accept the dictum of Las Casas, who never was in Darien, that Espinosa informed Pedrarias that Balboa deserved death, but he did not wish to pronounce the sentence because the *adelantado* merited a pardon on account of his rank of *adelantado* and the many services he had rendered the king in that land. The bishop of Chiapa then adds, and in this he is followed by Herrera, that the *alcalde mayor* protested that he would not sentence Balboa to death unless expressly commanded by the governor in writing to do it. This supports the assertion of Oviedo that Espinosa wrote and directed all the proceedings of the trial. The *alcalde mayor* dominated the governor, and after the departure of Bishop Quevedo he was supreme in Darien. The fact that the judge intrigued to secure command of Balboa's ships while prosecuting him, and before pronouncing sentence, is very good evidence that he intended to get rid of the *adelantado,* if not by death, then by sending him a prisoner to Spain. Pedrarias was clever, but Espinosa was more clever, and in the final showdown the cunning lawyer put the onus and responsibility for the death of Balboa on the old governor.

Pedrarias did not hesitate a moment in denying the appeal, and wrathfully replied, " that if Balboa deserved the penalty of death, it is not just to fail to execute it "—" *no es justo que si merece pena de muerte, se dexe de executar.*" The governor directed the judge to proceed with all brevity and without delay to sentence the accused persons with all the rigor of justice, and when sentenced, to put it in effect and execution against the persons and property of the said *Adelantado* Vasco Núñez de Balboa, Andrés de Valderrábano, and others. And from fear that he might weaken in his determination to have Balboa executed, Pedrarias delegated all his power and authority to Espinosa, with strict injunction to disregard any command of suspension or remission of sentence and execution issued by him or any other person in his name.

That legal document in which the *alcalde mayor* notified the governor, and the latter's reply, was read to both by the notary, Cuadrado, and Pedrarias signed it, writes Oviedo, just as arranged by Espinosa—" *todo lo ordenó al licenciado Espinosa.*"

XX

UNJUST TRIAL AND EXECUTION OF BALBOA AND COMPANIONS AT ACLA

" Para todo hay remedio, sino es para la muerte."
—Don Quijote, CERVANTES.

HAVING secured from Pedrarias the written assurance of a denial of any appeal by the *adelantado,* with strict injunction to pronounce sentence and put it in execution with all brevity—*" con toda brevedad "*—the chief judge, Gaspar de Espinosa, condemned to death Vasco Núñez de Balboa, Andrés de Valderrábano, Luis Botello, Fernán Muñoz, and Hernández de Argüello. We are told that Balboa appealed from the decision to the king and to the Council of the Indies, as no doubt did all the other condemned men, which was refused, as their fate already had been determined. It is very doubtful that Pedrarias had authority to permit the execution of an officer who appealed to Spain, as his commission limited his jurisdiction, civil and criminal, to causes less than six hundred pesos. Herrera declares that the governor was not empowered to put to death the *adelantado.* Perhaps the felony of treason was excepted, as that was the charge on which these men were condemned.

The protest and appeal of Balboa did not delay the execution. The writer knows of no record of the dates on which Balboa and his consorts were condemned, or of the day on which they were executed. For several centuries historians accepted the statement of Antonio de Herrera that Balboa suffered death in the year 1517. In recent years attention has been called to the document of 12 January 1519, already considered, and another paper recording an act of possession of the South Sea made by

Pedrarias on 27 January 1519. Allowing seven days for the governor to travel from Acla to the Gulf of San Miguel, it can be affirmed that the *adelantado* was executed between 12 and 20 January, if not on the first date mentioned. There are still other data to be considered: The execution took place when daylight was fading, and Pedrarias viewed the proceedings. Weighing in mind the speed with which the trial was conducted, the command of Pedrarias to Espinosa to hurry the execution, and the well-attested fact that darkness came on before all the heads were chopped off, we have reason for believing that the tragedy may have occurred on 12 January 1519. The crime of Acla was hastened, as if the governor and *alcalde mayor* feared that the friends of Balboa would rise up and free him.

We are told that the *adelantado* confessed to the *padre*, partook of the sacrament and put his soul in order. He made a will, naming Pedro de Arbolancha and at least one of his brothers, Gonzalo Núñez de Balboa, says Medina.

Late in the afternoon of that fateful day in Acla, the condemned men, heavily ironed, were brought forth from their prison, and the melancholy procession wended its way toward the scaffold erected in the plaza. In front walked the town crier proclaiming in a loud voice: " This is the justice which our lord the King, and Pedrarias his lieutenant in his name, command be done to this man as a traitor and usurper of lands subject to the Royal Crown." Hearing which and raising his eyes to heaven, the *adelantado*, with firm voice, replied: " It is a lie and falsehood which is stirred up against me! Never did I entertain such a thought! Rather it was always my mind to serve the king, and my desire to excel in this as a faithful and loyal vassal, and enlarge his dominions with all my power and strength."

In death as in life, Balboa marched at the head of his comrades. With firm step, he mounted the platform and calmly extended his head upon the block, which was covered with an old *repostero*. The headsman did his bloody work, and the *adelantado* of the South Sea was no more. The next victim was Andrés de Valderrábano, who was followed by Luis Botello, and after him came Fernán Muñoz. Like sheep, one after the other, they went to their death, says Oviedo.

It now was the turn of Hernando de Argüello to mount the scaffold.

The trial of these men had been conducted so hurriedly and with such secrecy that the people did not realize the gravity of the situation. We doubt that any of the citizens, however unfriendly to Balboa and the original settlers, believed that Pedrarias and Espinosa would go so far as to take the life of the *adelantado*. Being sent in chains to Spain was the usual procedure. But that was what the governor had been avoiding ever since he arrived with the armada. If young Charles and his Flemings heard the story of the conquest of the Isthmus and discovery of the South Sea from the lips of the *adelantado*, it was very probable that he soon would return to Darien as governor of Castilla del Oro.

When the people beheld Balboa and three of his companions beheaded—all pioneers in discovery and conquest on Tierra Firme—they were filled with terror and horror at the gory spectacle. Darkness was fast coming on, and it appeared to them that God wished to stop the execution. The weeping populace fell upon their knees before the governor, who was seen peeping between the canes forming the wall of a near-by house, and begged him to spare the life of Argüello. " No," said the inflexible old man, " if he sinned, let him die for it (*si pecó, muera por ello*). I would rather die myself than spare one of them."

In the dusk of the tropical evening the spurting blood of Argüello soon mingled with that of his friends.

Pedrarias carried his hatred of the *adelantado* beyond the grave. He ordered the head of Balboa to be stuck on a pole in the plaza, where it remained many days. It is probable that Balboa was in his forty-fifth year when he was executed. Of those beheaded with him, Valderrábano and Muñoz had been with their leader when he first viewed the Pacific Ocean from the Sierra of Quarequá.

We find mention of three brothers of the *adelantado* surviving him, Gonzalo, Alvar, and Joan Núñez de Balboa, all described as *gentiles-hombres*, or noblemen.

Pedrarias very promptly reported the arrest of Balboa, but was slow in announcing the execution. The governor declared to the king that Balboa had left a large amount of gold, the implication being that the *adelantado* had defrauded the crown of much wealth. When Oviedo, receiver of his property, came back to Darien, very little of value could be found. The Dominican friar, already quoted, declares that when Pedrarias killed Vasco Núñez, he gave the best of his *naborías* to his wife and servants, by which the king lost more than two thousand *castellanos* in dues.

On 20 May 1519, more than four months after the crime of Acla, the king had not heard of the execution of Balboa. On this date he wrote to Pedrarias to turn over to Charles Puper, Lord of Laxao, member of his Council, without delay, three-quarters of the king's fifth of gold, pearls, *guanines*, slaves, cotton cloth, and other things secured by the *Adelantado* Vasco Núñez de Balboa in his *entrada* of the South Sea. By 18 June 1519, the king had learned of the imprisonment of Balboa, and ordered Pedrarias to deliver to Gil González and Andrés Niño all the ships and *fustas* of the armada of the *adelantado*.

At Burgos, on 11 April 1521, the king issued a *cédula* in which he acknowledged the services of the *Adelantado* Vasco Núñez de Balboa in the discovery and settlement of Castilla del Oro, and commanded Pedrarias Dávila to deliver to Gonzalo Núñez, brother and heir of the deceased, all the household Indians (*"naborías de casa"*) belonging to the *adelantado*, and who had been distributed among other persons.

More than two years later, 4 July 1523, at Valladolid, the king repeated his appreciation of the services of the *adelantado* and reiterated the order to Pedrarias to put Gonzalo Núñez de Balboa in possession of the Indians left by his brother, without fail. It is safe to wager that the tricky old governor and his wife retained possession of the Indians.

Gonzalo complained to the king that the *adelantado* had committed no offense, and declared that Pedrarias beheaded him

(*" hizo degollar "*) unjustly, from envy to conceal Balboa's services, made at his own cost in Castilla del Oro and in the discovery of the South Sea. This charge was considered in the Council of the Indies, and on the foregoing date, 4 July 1523, the king ordered Pedrarias to quickly call and hear the parties involved, and do and administer entire justice in such a manner as to find out the persons, and none receive injury from which he would have reason to complain.

This is a sample of scores of commands from the kings of Spain purporting to do what they were pleased to call justice, always a verbose pretense of doing right to salve their conscience, and rarely administering true justice and equity. I can imagine no greater travesty on justice than the prelates and jurists of the royal Council commanding Pedrarias Dávila to investigate the parties who beheaded Balboa, and speedily administer justice. If the crafty old governor had any pigeonholes about his office, I feel sure that he stuck this order into one of them.

This Gonzalo Núñez resembled the *adelantado* in restless energy, and was becoming troublesome about the court. Apparently to get rid of all the brothers of Balboa, Emperor Charles decided to ship them to the other side of the earth. An order, dated 22 September 1525, at Toledo, directed the captain-general and deputies of the armada preparing to go to the discovery of " the Islands of Tarsis and Ofir and Cipango and the Catayo Oriental " to take along the three brothers of the *adelantado,* and to aid and favor them in conformity to the quality of their persons. Gonzalo was made treasurer of the third ship of the armada, and on 17 December 1525, a *carta* from the Council of the Indies ordered the captain-general to befriend Alvar and Juan and carry them in the number of the twelve *gentiles hombres* of the armada, having respect to their persons as brothers of the *Adelantado* Vasco Núñez de Balboa and what he had done for His Majesty. This letter is signed by the bishop of Orma, Doctor Beltran, and the bishop of Ciudad Rodrigo.

From the foregoing excerpts concerning the brothers of the

adelantado, it is quite evident that Balboa was not adjudged to be a traitor or malefactor by the king or the Council of the Indies.

Was Balboa guilty of any crime or act deserving death? We believe not, especially of the charge of treason for which he was executed. Treason is the offense of betraying the state to which the offender belongs, and surely Balboa could not be accused of betraying Darien and Panama to any foreign power. Rebellion is open resistance to constituted authority, and we know that the *adelantado* unsuspectingly responded to the letter of Pedrarias by hurrying to Acla with only a few attendants. Had he been guilty of treason or rebellion, and cared to find out what the old governor was up to, Balboa would have traversed the isthmus with one hundred or more of his devoted followers. Or, what is more likely, he would have ignored the call to come to Acla and set out in quest of Peru.

Balboa was a man of more courage and daring than of prudence and caution in his personal affairs; but, if engaged in any wrong-doing, would he have risked the fortunes of his friends by placing himself in the power of the governor? Not if he possessed a particle of the *maña* his enemies accused him of having. There is clear and positive evidence that Pedrarias authorized the *adelantado* to rebuild Acla, to construct ships, and to discover on the South Sea. The historians tell us that the Jerónimite Fathers, who then governed the Indies, had written to Balboa that he should make the voyage on the South Sea, since it so much promoted the service of God and of the king—" *que hiciesse el viage, pues tanto convenía al servicio de Dios é del Rey.*" Fernández de Oviedo, who knew Balboa, and was an official in Darien before and after the death of the *adelantado,* declares that he was not executed for what the *pregonero* announced to the public, " because what they called treason, no one took it for such "—" *porque la que llamaban traycion, ninguno la tuvo por tal.*"

But what availed Balboa's innocence when the governor and

his chief judge, aided by Puente, Corral, and others confederated their desires, plans, and energies to put the *adelantado* out of the way after he had built up Acla, improved the trail to the South Sea, and constructed an armada? From the scant records of affairs in Darien and Panama during the years 1516, '17 and '18, it looks as if these officials, who often opposed each other, worked as a unit to discredit and overthrow Balboa. Pedrarias was not acting in good faith when he promised Balboa his daughter in marriage, and subsequent events show that he never intended to permit the *adelantado* to reap the reward of his labors. On some pretext or trumped-up charge, Balboa would be deprived of his command and his ships turned over to Diego Albítez.

Pedrarias reckoned without his *alcalde mayor!* Twenty-odd years ago we wrote that Gaspar de Espinosa was one of the ablest men to come to the Indies during the first years of the Hispanic conquest, and further study of this period confirms our first impression of him. When Espinosa decided that he wanted Balboa's ships for himself, and that he would be an admiral on the sea as he had been a general on the land, he outwitted Pedrarias, put the blame for the death of the *adelantado* on the governor, and a few months later he sailed away in command of the vessels. Not long after the first voyage he made a second venture on the sea, each time sailing west and north, rather than south in the direction of Peru. The illiterate soldiers, Pizarro and Almagro, had more faith in the reports of the Indians, steered their ships to the south, and came upon the land of the Incas. When assured of the wealth of Peru, Espinosa, through Padre Luque ("Padre Loco"), invested considerable money in the enterprise, from which he greatly profited. The land which gave him gold also bestowed death. Gaspar de Espinosa died in Cuzco, 1537.

Immediately after the execution of Balboa and his associates, Pedrarias, Espinosa, and attendants departed from Acla for the south coast. The old governor could hardly make the transit of the isthmus in less than a week, doubtless following the road made by the *adelantado* and his Spaniards, Indians, and Africans in transporting timbers and supplies for his ships. Horses and canoes were available to Pedrarias, and he could be carried in a *hámaca* like the great chiefs.

To further discredit and efface the acts of Balboa, the governor, on 27 January 1519, took another possession of " all the coast of the New Land and of the Sea of the South." The site was the mouth of an inlet which was the end of the province of Paque. The Captains Andrés Garavito, Francisco Pizarro, Pascual de Andagoya, the *Canónigo* Francisco de Arroyo, and others were present, all the proceeding being attested by the notaries.

The party embarked in a brigantine left by the *adelantado* and sailed out to the Pearl Islands. Although the governor just had taken possession of the South Sea with " all its islands, ports, passages, coves and creeks," he took a special possession of these islands on 29 January, witnessed and attested as before. Ever since Pedrarias had acquired the rich pearl *La Peregrina*, the Pearl Islands possessed a peculiar charm for the avaricious governor, and it was not long before he took for himself the islands richest in pearls, Isla Rica (*Tarareque*) and Isla de Otoque.

There was no mention of Balboa in either of these two acts of possession.

Did King Charles, now emperor, or his Council do anything to punish Governor Pedrarias and his *alcalde mayor?* Quite the contrary. When Espinosa went back to Spain in 1522, with much gold, says Oviedo, he was made a *licenciado* in law, and the king gave him a coat-of-arms. In this escutcheon were depicted two caravels and above them a star. The two caravels undoubtedly represented the vessels built by Balboa, the *San Cristóbal* and the *Santa María de Buena Esperanza*. Did the star in the heavens refer to that one of Micer Codro, so fateful to the *adelantado?*

Lope de Sosa, the new governor, finally arrived in the port of La Antigua on 20 May 1520. While preparing to go ashore, Sosa suddenly died. Pedrarias was there at the time, and, with much manifestation of grief, interred the corpse with great pomp before the altar of the church. The governor at once informed his wife, then in Spain, of the death of Lope de Sosa. Doña Isabel hurried to the court early in September 1520, when the governors of the kingdom were occupied with the uprising of the Comunidades. Rebellion at home left no time to investigate an official in the remote Tierra Firme of the Indies. It is said that Doña Isabel was diligent about the court in working with Francisco de Lizaur, solicitor and *procurador* of her husband, to have Pedrarias continued in office as governor of Castilla del Oro.

On 17 September 1520, a laudatory letter, in the name of the king, was sent to Pedrarias thanking him for the great interest and care he exhibited in burying his intended successor. Seeing his great experience in Darien and the good way things were going there, and what Queen Juana had written on this matter, Pedrarias was directed to use the provisions and instructions carried by Lope de Sosa and remain in office, " for we hold for certain that it will be for the service of our Lord and the welfare of that land."

Pedrarias withdrew from La Antigua, leaving Oviedo there as his lieutenant, and made the new town of Panama on the south coast the capital of Castilla del Oro. The city of Santa Maria de la Antigua del Darien, to give the place its full name for the last time, was governed honestly by Oviedo, but the citizens fast abandoned the town for the more inviting prospect on the Pacific coast. At last, only Diego Ribero remained, and in September 1524, he and his family were killed by Indians, the buildings reduced to ashes, and the site returned to the jungle.

The chroniclers have not recorded anything fine or admirable of Pedrarias Dávila, all his acts being " horrid transactions," as Peter Martyr wrote. In Panama he quarreled with Salaya, who followed Espinosa as *alcalde mayor;* and with Bishop Pedraza, successor to Quevedo; and both men departed this life suddenly under suspicion of being poisoned. Finally deposed as governor of Castilla del Oro when replaced by Pedro de los Rios, Pedrarias, with his usual good luck, was made governor of Nicaragua, recently overrun by the Spaniards. There he cut off

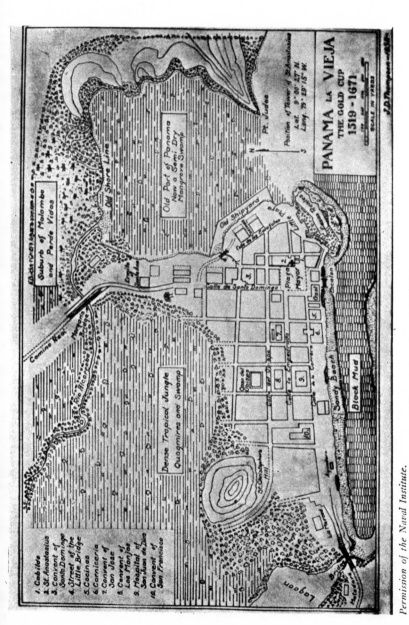

Plan of the city of Old Panama.

another head, that of Francisco Hernández de Córdoba. The old reprobate lived to be nearly ninety years of age. Spain honored her worst governor to the last. Pedrarias died in the odor of sanctity on 6 March 1531, in the new city of Leon, Nicaragua.

As for the Indians of Darien and Panama, most of them had been killed or sold into slavery. They could not survive the first impact of the Christian civilization of Europe. The few survivors fled to the high mountains or other parts not yet invaded by the Spaniards. The country was depopulated between Antigua, Acla and Nombre de Dios on the Caribbean shore, and the Gulf of San Miguel and the new towns of Panama and Natá on the Pacific coast. Natives of other parts of the Isthmus were saved from early extermination, like the Indians of Española, by the tide of conquest passing over the Isthmus and seeking other regions, always following the lure of gold. After the discovery of the rich empire of the Incas, Spanish adventurers landed at Nombre de Dios and followed a beeline overland to Panama (Panama la Vieja). In time this trail became the old Camino Real. From the city of Old Panama the Spaniards explored up the Pacific coast to Nicaragua, or hurried southward to share in the wealth of Peru.

In certain soils human skeletons persist for centuries. Did the town the *adelantado* built become his tomb? Do fragments of his bones still lie hidden beneath the ruins and vegetation of the old town of Acla? Does not the blood of Vasco Núñez de Balboa, though highly attenuated, still flow in the veins of the natives of Darien and Panama?

> " The Knight's bones are dust,
>   And his good sword rust;
>   His soul is with the saints, I trust."

EPILOGUE

DIRECTLY after the execution of Balboa, the governor, with Espinosa and others, crossed over the Isthmus to the South Sea. On 15 August 1519, Pedrarias formally founded the city of Panama Vieja at about the worst site for a settlement on the south coast.

When it came time to make his *residencia*, Pedrarias sent a notary to Acla to proclaim to the people that if they had any complaints to make against him they must pass over to the new town of Panama to present their charges. After it was cried throughout the streets of Acla, the *pregón*, or proclamation, was fixed on a post in the plaza, a few yards from where the head of Vasco Núñez de Balboa had been exposed on a stake.

Andrés Garabito, the false friend of Balboa, had been appointed lieutenant of the governor in Acla, the town built by the *adelantado* in the land of Cacique Careta. One Sunday, as the people came from mass in the church on the plaza, several persons accompanied Captain Garabito as far as the door of his dwelling, also situated on the plaza, where he tarried to converse with them until the hour of dinner.

While waiting thus there entered, from another side of the square, fifteen or twenty horses, which began to graze on the grass which grows so abundantly in the streets of towns in this humid land. One of the animals, which had been the favorite mare of Vasco Núñez, issued from the herd with head erect and measured pace, and without stopping to eat, advanced across the plaza to the post whereon was fixed the notice, or edict, of the *residencia* of Pedrarias. With her teeth, the mare seized the paper several times and tore it into pieces, after which the animal turned and marched, step by step, without stopping or looking to the right or left, to where the other horses were grazing, and began to pasture.

Garabito and many other persons observed the strange action of Balboa's mare and held it to be a mystery, murmuring among themselves of the *residencia* of Pedrarias, saying that since Balboa's mare protested it, what ought men to do? From that moment it was inferred that one must wait on God, for the true *residencia* of Pedrarias Dávila would have to come from heaven.

The mysterious conduct of Balboa's mare was held to be a marvel by many persons, not only in the town of Acla, but wherever it became known, and afterward, writes Oviedo, men offered to testify to the fact before the lords of the Council of the Indies in Spain.

" Let down the curtain; the farce is done."

INDEX